Therapeutic and Prophetic Narratives in Worship

STUDIEN ZUR INTERKULTURELLEN GESCHICHTE DES CHRISTENTUMS
ETUDES D'HISTOIRE INTERCULTURELLE DU CHRISTIANISME
STUDIES IN THE INTERCULTURAL HISTORY OF CHRISTIANITY

begründet von / fondé par / founded by
Hans Jochen Margull †, Hamburg

herausgegeben von / édité par / edited by

Richard Friedli
Université de Fribourg

Walter J. Hollenweger
University of Birmingham

Theo Sundermeier
Universität Heidelberg

Jan A. B. Jongeneel
Rijksuniversiteit Utrecht

Band 54

Verlag Peter Lang
Frankfurt am Main · Bern · New York · Paris

Jean-Daniel Plüss

THERAPEUTIC AND PROPHETIC NARRATIVES IN WORSHIP

A Hermeneutic Study of Testimonies and Visions

Their Potential Significance for Christian Worship and Secular Society

Verlag Peter Lang

Frankfurt am Main · Bern · New York · Paris

Library of Congress Cataloging-in-Publication Data

Plüss, Jean-Daniel:

Therapeutic and Prophetic Narratives in Worship : A
Hermeneutic Study of Testimonies and Visions ; Their Potential
Significance for Christian Worship and Secular Society / Jean-
Daniel Plüss. - Frankfurt am Main ; Bern ; New York ; Paris :
Lang, 1988
    (Studien zur interkulturellen Geschichte des Christentums ;
    Bd. 54)
    Zugl.: Leuven, Univ., Diss., 1987
    ISBN 3- 8204-1199-2

NE: GT

ISSN 0170-9240
ISBN 3-8204-1199-2

© Verlag Peter Lang GmbH, Frankfurt am Main 1988
All rights reserved.

Printed in Germany

ACKNOWLEDGMENTS

This dissertation is the result of a chain of felicitous circumstances. I would like to express my gratitude to all who have been part of this learning experience.

... to my promotors, the Right Reverend Professor Dr. J. LESCRAUWAET for his openness to the project and assistence, and to Professor Dr. G. DE SCHRIJVER, who has the gift of asking the right kinds of questions in season.

... to the Katholieke Universiteit Leuven, which welcomed me with a spirit of ecumenism.

... to Continental Bible College, which provided me with a truly intercultural exposure.

... to my pentecostal friends and teachers, who shared God's love with me in story and personal commitment.

... to my teachers and friends in the historic churches who opened my eyes to God's presence in the world.

And thanks to my parents, who not only were a constant source of encouragement, but who also introduced me to bilingualism. Finally, thanks to Susan, who keeps challenging me not only to speak, but also to understand more than one tongue.

II Cor. 9:15

TABLE OF CONTENTS

Contents IX

PREFACE

A Language between Experience and Faith

by Dr. Walter J. Hollenweger

At the beginning of our century, Vladimir PROPP analysed the Russian Folktales,[1] Antti AARNE, a Finnish scholar, published his Verzeichnis der Märchentypen (1910) and Hermann GUNKEL, who was acquainted with AARNE's research, founded the form critical school in Old Testament research. The simultaneous emergence of these trends in scholarship is no accident. It marked the beginning of painstaking and fruitful research into the oral and pre-literary forms of communication and tradition.

Later, Rudolf BULTMANN used GUNKEL's insight for analysing the pre-literary stages of New Testament texts. PROPP, AARNE, GUNKEL and BULTMANN thought they were describing a purely historical phenomenon. Little did they know that they described what was and still is the very essence of Christian communication and worship.

This is of course a controversial statement which needs some qualification. Using the tools of a theologian and a linguist, Dr. Jean-Daniel PLUESS shows that the structure of early pentecostal testimonies and visions can profitably be understood in terms of PROPP's and AARNE's research.

The choice of oral forms of Pentecostalism as a field of application for his research is an obvious choice for Jean-Daniel PLUESS. Being himself a Swiss Pentecostal, he discovered that at the very time when PROPP, AARNE and GUNKEL published their works, a type of Christian religion was emerging which could only be described - at least in its formative stages and in its Third World forms - as narrative and oral. PLUESS received his theological and philosophical training at the Catholic University of Leuven. His interest in the

---

[1] Vladimir PROPP, Morfolgia skaski, English translation: Morphology of the Folktale, Austin, 1968 (2nd ed.).

oral forms of communication of Pentecostalism, its "language of experience", its "religion in the making", its "pre-reflective forms of communication" stems from his own lived spirituality. Leuven provided him with the competence to analyse these forms of language in a sociological and philosophical context. For PLUESS, reflection and narrative are not in competition. Narrative is the elementary and primary mode of language, reflection has to feed on it.

What makes PLUESS's work even more attractive is his ability to show (with many examples) that oral language is by no means a thing of the past, not even in Europe. An example of this is T.B. BARRATT's testimony, which PLUESS analyses with PROPP's tools. It is the language of those who do not feel at home in the conceptual edifices of our theologies, both catholic and protestant, and look for a language in which they have a say; in other words, it is an attempt at a theology of the laity. "The issue of narrative in theology is more one of **Sprachform** and function than of 'narrative theology' as such. What is at stake is not a new theology, but rather a way of doing theology that is familiar with the relationship between faith and experience" (PLUESS, p. XXVII). It is a theology which takes BARTH's dictum "theology is a function **of the church**"[2] seriously and looks for ways and means by which theology becomes that discipline in which the experts of the texts of the past (the so-called theologians) and the experts of the faith-experiences of today (the so-called lay people) start a meaningful dialogue whose result hopefully may be more than a polite co-existence and may lead to some helpful theological insights.

This in turn produces a number of difficulties. First, a language of experience is by definition a plural language, since no two persons describe their lives in the same terms unless they have been forced into a unified language. This process can easily be observed in third generation pentecostal churches as well as in our catholic and protestant churches. In the case of the Pentecostals, everybody has

---

[2] See on this the first sentences in Karl BARTH, Church Dogmatics Vol. I, 1; and David FORD, Barth and God's Story. Biblical Narrative and the Theological Method of Karl Barth in the "Church Dogmatics" (in this series, vol. 27, Frankfurt, Peter Lang, 1981, 1985 (2nd ed.).

"the same testimony"; in the case of the historical churches, priest and ministers are the only ones who have a say, so that everybody else is reduced to silence.

The second difficulty which PLUESS faces is the relationship between written traditional and oral testimony. In order to tackle this difficulty PLUESS uses the critical tools of his university education in such a way as to make oral language transparent and accessible to critical analysis. The aim is to find a bridge between the two worlds, the world of oral and the world of conceptual language.

Whether Dr. PLUESS has built that bridge or not is another question. Surprisingly he presents in a doctoral dissertation a conclusion which has the form of a story. So this story is the conclusion, the **Zusammenfassung** of his thinking - that in itself is an interesting and daring move. It is the story of a Nigerian church in Birmingham. His story could perhaps best be called a narrative of a higher order. It transcends the elmentary order of primal narrative language. By doing this he can bring into focus many of the philosophical, social and political strands which appear throughout his dissertation (see for instance his report on visions during the Third Reich in Germany) without destroying the fellowship with the oral people whose story he tells.

Such a way of doing theology becomes more and more imporant for a global theology which wants to enter into dialogue not just with the "experience of lived faith", the lay people in Europe, but also with the theologians from the Third World. If European theologians want to contribute what they have to contribute in a global context and if they want to learn what can be learned from other cultures, they should take a leaf out of Jean-Daniel PLUESS's exercise in bi-lingual theology. In this respect this work is - just because it is such a thorough European work - an example of a European theologian who digs deep into his tradition in order to transcend it.

Dr. Walter J. HOLLENWEGER
Professor of Missions
University of Birmingham

INTRODUCTION

> God who "wills that all men be saved and come to
> the knowledge of the truth"...,"who in many times
> and various ways spoke of old to the fathers
> through the prophets"..., when the fullness of
> time had come sent his Son, the Word made flesh,
> anointed by the Holy Spirit to preach the Gospel
> to the poor, to heal the contrite of heart, to be
> a bodily and spiritual medicine: the Mediator
> between God and man.

This introductory sentence to the first chapter of the Constitution on the Sacred Liturgy[1] is filled with metaphorical connotations
and narrative suggestions which evoke in the reader a religious vision
of a grand salvific plan. God in his grace, it is said, reaches out to
mankind in his Son Jesus, the Christ, and through the power of the
Holy Spirit calls mankind to fellowship with him; in spite of, or
because of the many contingencies of human life.

Christians throughout history have made use of such language to
express their faith, their commitment and hope; but also their doubts,
hesitations and fears. It is a language of experience.[2] Religious
language has however only recently received philosophical and
theological attention through the writings of linguistic analysts,
exegetes, and death-of-God theologians to mention just a few.
Comparatively late, namely in 1973, two articles by Harald WEINRICH
and Johann Baptist METZ,[3] introduced "narrative theology" as a new

---

[1] Austin FLANNERY (ed.), Vatican Council II. The Conciliar and Post
Conciliar Documents, Dublin, 1975, p. 3.

[2] Such a claim needs substantiation. It will be an issue raised in the
discussion about the role of testimony (Cf. 4.2.3.1. and 4.3.). The
assumption that religious language is a language of experience is for
instance found in Dorothee SOELLE, Die Hinreise. Zur religiösen
Erfahrung Texte und Ueberlegungen, Stuttgart, 1976, pp. 39-50
especially.
[3] Harald WEINRICH, Narrative Theology, in Concilium 9 (1973), pp.

program to the continent of Europe.

In the same year Hans KUENG prepared his book On Being A
Christian. But he was rather sceptical about the ideas that were being
developed. He saw them against the background of a contemporary trend
of nostalgia which called for narrative, biography, autobiography and
stories in general.[4] KUENG's criticism should not be cast off lightly.
The question whether the current interest in narrative is only due to
a fashionable impulse or not must be answered.

As a matter of fact, a number of questions relating to this way
of doing theology arose in the mid-seventies. Bernd WACKER has noticed
that almost all theological disciplines have in one way or another
integrated a narrative option into their models of thought. But this
has not automatically clarified the meaning, function and structure of
narrative.[5] Is narrative a literary genre or a language game with a
wider field of application? Is it related to stories or to history? Is
it fictional or real? Does it relate to a written text or does it
belong to the act of speaking? Is it a tool for exegetes or
liturgists, for missiologists or moral theologians, for the university
or for the church? In other words, is it possible to locate a **Sitz im
Leben** for religious narrative in contemporary Christianity?

The catalogue of questions could easily be continued. But it has
already become clear that any work with the concept of (religious)
narrative will call for clarifications.

Status Quaestionis: Oral Narratives in Pentecostal Worship

The topic, as described in the title, seems vast. The intention
is not to write a comprehensive dissertation covering and critiquing
all aspects that can be envisaged with regard to therapeutic and

---

46-56. Johann Baptist METZ, A Short Apology of Narrative, in Concilium
9 (1973), pp. 84-96.

[4] Hans KUENG, On Being a Christian, New York, 1976, p. 52.

[5] Bernd WACKER, Narrative Theologie?, München, 1977, p. 7. Confer also
Guido VAN STEENDAM, De nacht van duizend-en-één verhalen. Orientatie
bij de narratieve theologie, in Tijdschrift voor Theologie, 19 (1979),
pp. 3-27.

prophetic narratives. Rather the aim is to use a number of testimonies and visions originating from a pentecostal liturgical context as a vehicle to a general christian concern, namely the question whether the use of narratives could deepen a religious awareness and a sense of christian mission in today's secular society. The following paragraphs intend to indicate why a hermeneutical study of oral narratives in pentecostal worship lend themselves as a catalytic agent for this concern. An outline of this enterprise will also allow for a delimitation of the presuppositions and the methodology involved.

For the sake of convenience, the scope of the study will be presented first. Secondly, the methodological procedure chosen will be indicated and, at the same time, an outline of the thesis given.

The scope of this study will become evident as the title with its implications are explained. First of all, a hermeneutic approach to testimonies and visions concerns itself with **oral** narratives. In this study it is not texts in the common sense of the term that avail themselves for interpretation, but narratives which are born of pre-reflective impressions, expressed within the flux of language use, and brought to a public audience. From a philosophical point of view a hermeneutical theory that attempts to interpret such narratives must come to terms with new expressions of meaning emerging from metaphors, that is, with religious language in the making. These narratives, therefore, need to be studied in terms of their linguistic situation with regard to synchronic / diachronic and paradigmatic / syntagmatic fields of tension[6] to see if they are relevant as a social expression of being. Consequently, contemporary linguistic theories will be studied in view of their feasibility as hermeneutic tools for narratives that are open to plural interpretation since they are not primarily text-bound (read by individuals) but word-bound (heard by a community of interpretation). From a sociological point of view, oral narratives need to be situated within their cultural traditions. That means that the social usure of meaning will have to be analysed. Can

---

[6] In other words, the challenge is to investigate to what extent religious and secular language have converging and conflicting linguistic systems.

language games, merely because they are still used by certain groups, retain their meaning in a particular society as a whole; or even on an inter-cultural level?

Another hermeneutical implication of orality relates to the contextual nature of these narratives. It is not liturgical rubrics (which had their evolution in an age when the religious world was the only focus of reality) that are going to be examined, but religious stories that emerge from everyday life; in other words, narratives which stand, so to speak, with one leg in the domain of religious, and with the other in the sphere of secular experience. Furthermore, oral narratives are contextual because they have to stand a trial of reception or rejection in the community of interpretation with its **wirkungsgeschichtliches** heritage.

The thesis is limited in scope insofar as it concentrates on two kinds of narratives. The focus on **testimonies and visions** (or communicated dreams) is due to the fact that they are universal paradigms of human experience whether they are specifically religious or not. Furthermore, it is typical for these narratives to relate to the awareness of temporality as an existential dimension in human life. On the religious level they relate to a sense of the past when they refer to a treasury of traditions and paradigmatic examples; they relate to an acute sense of the present in the formulation of personal experiences; and they relate to an awareness of the future by providing eschatological mosaics, but most of all through moral imperatives that require present action. Because of this relationship between time and being it will be indispensable to reflect also on the role of myths as dynamic activators and harmonizers of the three temporal dimensions in which men experience values and meaning. At the same time one needs to keep in mind that narratives provide also a sense of temporality in a purely secular context; they provide a sense of **Dasein** as Martin HEIDEGGER would call it.

The reasons why this study concentrates on oral narratives in **pentecostal** churches are manifold. Firstly, such narratives have traditionally received much attention in the pentecostal celebration of faith. It is an unwritten law in these religious circles that a true believer is able to tell stories of faith. By choosing the examples from a movement which has made testimonies and visions an integral part of their worship one has the benefit of studying a tradition, that is a phenomenon which has a tested praxis and allows for some coherence. A second reason for studying liturgical narratives of Pentecostals is due to the historical origin of this movement. It has its roots partly in North American slave religion and to a large extent in the personal and edificational emphasis of catholic spirituality and the nineteenth century holiness tradition which popularized in protestant circles the theological convictions of the WESLEY brothers.[7] These roots reflect a milieu of the formerly illiterate and working classes in which songs, testimonies, parables and biblical stories represented the oral library of Gospel-knowledge. Thirdly, in view of the phenomenal growth of pentecostal communities in the West in general and in the Third World in particular, it is reasonable to assume that a hermeneutic key to such religious narratives will provide a significant tool for dialogue with the emerging theologies in those parts of the world where Basic Christian Communities and Independent Non-White Churches demonstrate a comprehension of faith which is proper to their mostly oral culture. An understanding of the structure, receptive function and intentionality of oral narratives in pentecostal liturgy is, therefore, of ecumenical significance.

Finally, the scope of this thesis is set in the parameters of **worship** because of three reasons. First, it is assumed that worship is the pivotal context in which religious men, women, and children seek to: a) reaffirm "the faith of the their fathers", b) formulate their concerns of daily existence, and c) express their hope for a meaningful future. It will be argued that testimonies and visions have

---

[7] This is a greatly simplified statement. For more information on the socio-religious history of the Pentecostal movement see the essay in Appendix I, which owes much to Walter J. HOLLENWEGER, The Pentecostals, London, 1972; and his more recent After Twenty Years' Research on Pentecostalism, in Theology 87 (Nov. 1984), pp. 403-412; and to Robert Mapes ANDERSON's, Vision of the Disinherited. The Making of American Pentecostalism, New York, 1979, pp. 28-46. Numerous other histories of the Pentecostal movement have been written, but few consider the socio-cultural factors which are important in undergirding a hermeneutic theory of an oral tradition.

their **Sitz im Leben** in praise, prayer and religious commitment. Second, it should be clarified whether the practice of worship can figure as a meeting ground for religious as well as purely secular concerns. In other words, is worship an activity of missiological importance in which the secular and unreligious person can be introduced to the core of the christian faith? Is on the other hand christian worship open to the needs and demands of a secularized society?

The methodological procedure falls into two parts. The first part is theoretical in nature and locates a hermeneutic of narratives in the tensional field between theology, philosophy and sociology. This context is admittedly large, but is called for by the nature of linguisticality, which, after all, builds the foundation of any hermeneutic attempt. The second part will analyse various testimonies and visions, and suggest a basic interpretation in terms of their literary function, theological significance and social potential. The various findings will be gathered and reapplied in a reflection of liturgical pertinence.

Part 1 chapter 1 is thus **theological** in emphasis. It will first focus on the question whether the biblical literature justifies a narrative approach in religious communication. Special consideration will be given to the formulation of human experience and the function of myths. In other words, how does man narratively integrate events that touch him personally, and the events which he spiritually perceives to be God's prophetic word.

Part 1 chapter 2 will tackle **philosophical** problems since literary criticism has traditionally been a subdivision of speculative thought. As a whole the challenge will be to examine the basic problems concerning narrative, namely its language and feasibility for interpretation. The presupposition will be to apply phenomenological hermeneutics to the narratives in question on the grounds that an analytic approach, which restricts itself to the construction of linguistic signs, will not do justice to the logic of religious language. Then, the thesis which holds that emplotment serves as fabric for the formulation of temporality regardless whether the context is religious or not will be developed. The challenge arises:

should narratives be considered as expanded metaphors? The outcome of this question is vital to a critique of the common differentiation between truth and fiction, and, by implication, between religious and scientific language. Furthermore, questions will be asked concerning the role of narratives in relation to man's view of himself, and whether narratives lend themselves to self-transcending speech.

Chapter 3 of part 1 turns its attention to the problem of secularization. Here, the often neglected **sociological** implications of religious language will be addressed. Since it can be argued that language is the social institution **par excellence**, it is important to study the loss of meaning of formerly common language games. To what extent has religious jargon been rendered meaningless through the secularization of everyday vocabulary and modern thought? On the other hand, is there a challenge for religious language to be a tool for identity formation and social integration? Can narratives be meaningful to a secular western society and still be truthful to the claims of Christianity?

The principal aim of the first part will be to evaluate the feasibility of oral religious narratives as a means of communication in the christian congregation, in society, and by implication in inter-cultural dialogue. The authors with whom the dialogue is carried out could be said to agree at least on one point: that it is not meaningless to talk about experiences that are not strictly verifiable.

The second part will shed light on the two major genres of oral narratives which appear in the context of pentecostal worship.[8] Chapter 4 will attempt to elucidate the logic of personal **testimonies,** and their contribution to an explanation of the present moment of faith. In how far can religious testimonies be deceptive and trivial? How do they perceive the "will of God" and reflect the problem of theodicy? Some clarification will be brought by studying their morphology, semantic function and liturgical role.

---

[8] Homiletical narratives as an illustrative technique are excluded in this study, since they relate primarily to the reflective presentation of a sermon prepared by an individual for a mostly passive consumption by the audience, and are generally not part of the hermeneutic activity of the community as a whole.

Chapter 5 will study the structure of pentecostal **visions**. If they refer to an eschatological moment of faith, how can they be received by the community? Is it possible that the general function of these narratives is not eschatological at all? Some of these questions may not find an answer, but valid clarifications should be possible.

Finally, chapter 6 will collect the elaborated data under a new point of view and address theological, anthropological, catechetical and doxological implications of testimonial and visionary narratives in the context of **liturgy**. Can it be maintained that oral narratives have a privileged position in liturgy as a bridge between orthodoxy and orthopraxis, and between the secular and religious world?

The Basic Presuppositions and Preliminary Definitions

Why, by choosing a phenomenological approach, have we in fact claimed that a purely deductive or a rigorously reductive approach would not do justice to the narratives in question? Basically because the pursuit of meaning will be partly ontological and not just literary. This is especially true for religious narratives when they reveal metaphorical potential. Furthermore, a deductive way is not fully suitable, because narratives often leave things unsaid. Likewise, a reductive approach is not satisfying when it is used as the only measure for meaning, because, for example, the redundant may be significant. Two reasons may already be put forward in favour of a phenomenological approach although they shall be substantiated below. First, the narrative mode, by virtue of its self-transcending nature always points beyond itself.[9] Its self-transcending function makes it suitable for religious use. Secondly, as Karl RAHNER has pointed out, God's self-communication through the word is never merely given. Rather, it is a dialogual word of God in the church and in man. It is an event in human temporality with all the consequences it can entail.[10] An approach which would make allowance for such a dialogual

---

[9] Robert A. KRIEG, Narrative as a Linguistic Rule. Fyodor Dostoyevski and Karl Barth, in International Journal for Philosophy of Religion, 8 (1977), pp. 190-205. See also the discussion on Ian T. RAMSEY (2.1.) and Stephen CRITES (2.3.2.) below.

word could be inductive. However, the inductive possibility inevitably conjures suspicions of subjectivism, psychologism or anti-intellectualism. But, consciousness of the self can also be due to reflection, a weighing of one's life in the light of insight. Or, to speak with the words of Peter BERGER, "A truly inductive approach will take cognizance of both the human reality and the metahuman intentionality of the religious phenomenon."[11] In any case, a hermeneutic approach to religious language can never solely consider the flatly descriptive, and in the end it will remain open ended.

At the same time, recent writings on **narrative in theology** seem to come to an agreement that a competitive juxtaposition between reflective theology and expressive narrative is a false dilemma.[12] What should be stated is that the issue of narrative in theology is more one of **Sprachform** and function than of "narrative theology" as such. What is at stake is not a new theology, but rather a way of doing theology that is familiar with the relationship between faith and experience.[13] Consequently, it seems suitable to place narrative

---

[10] "Es (das Wort Gottes in der Kirche) kann sein eigenes Wesen nur in einem geschichtlichen Prozess vollziehen, ... es wächst auf es **wird**, was es ist und werden soll, es kann seine defizienten, vorläufigen, vorbereitenden Phasen und Momente haben...
Da es sich wesentlich um ein dialogisches Wort zwischen Gott-Christus in der Kirche einerseits und dem hörenden Menschen andererseits handelt, sind an diesen Momenten sowohl die eine wie die andere Seite beteiligt..."
Karl RAHNER, Wort und Eucharistie, in Schriften zur Theologie, Bd. 4, Einsiedeln, 1960, pp. 327f. (emphasis his).

[11] Peter L. BERGER, The Heretical Imperative. Contemporary Possibilities of Religious Affirmation, London, 1980, p. 142.

[12] Bernd WACKER, Narrative Theologie?, p. 100; Joseph MEYER VON SCHLOCHTERN, Erzählung als Paradigma einer alternativen Denkform, in Theologische Berichte, 8 (1979), 35-70, p. 70; Paul RICOEUR, De moeilijke weg naar en narratieve theologie. Noodzaak, bronnen, problemen, in Meedenken met Edward Schillebeeckx (Festschrift), Herman HAERING - Ted SCHOOF - Ad WILLEMS (ed.), Baarn, 1983, pp. 80-92; Hans KUENG, Being, pp. 416-419.

[13] Joseph MEYER VON SCHLOCHTERN in his article Erzählung als Paradigma (p. 39) sets a healthy accent when he says, "Die Gestalt einer solchen Theologie ist noch unklar: die narrativen Sprachformen werden jedoch in der Erwartung eingefordert, Glaube und Erfahrung in einer Form in Beziehung setzen zu können ohne darum Vernunft, Einsicht und Ver-

in a liturgical context, a context where Christians learn to explain
and express their faith, so that they may put it into practice. And
finally, it is in worship that the dialogual word of God has its most
telling **raison d'être**. Provisionally, <u>two definitions</u> shall be a
guide through the first two chapters of this study.

Religious Narrative

A narrative, in a religious context, is a pre-reflective
impression of an experience of God's presence and/or absence in man's
life world and his resulting response in the same.[14]

Worship

Christian worship is the twofold movement between God and mankind
sustained by faith and born in the human context of life.

As the turning of God to mankind it is an invitation to a
salutary encounter in Christ, through the Holy Spirit. It calls upon
human life to be worthy and meaningful.

As man's response to God it is a thankful celebration of salvific
memories, a praise of the divine presence in the circumstances of
life, and a responsible commitment to a common future.[12]

---

antwortung suspendieren zu müssen."

[14] It may be noticed that this definition is practically identical
with a working definition of grace. This is quite intentional.

[12] Thess definitions are not free from a certain amount of "God-talk."
Later on, non-religious explanations will be included. However, it can
be argued that a christian reflection on narrative in worship implies
by necessity a partisan standpoint.

1. THEOLOGICAL RELEVANCE OF NARRATIVE

FROM NARRATIVE TO MYTH IN THEOLOGY

"The Gospel is a story and a praxis."
E. SCHILLEBEECK

The rediscovery of narrative in theological thinking had its silent beginnings long before it emerged as a programmatic notion in the late 1960s in the United States of America and in the early 1970s in Europe. It happened as a parallel movement in the field of biblical studies on the one hand, and the domain of dogmatic theology on the other. It is, therefore, appropriate to highlight the key-ideas of each discipline separately before presenting more contemporary issues.

1.1. Biblical Studies

It is appropriate to begin with the Scriptures, not only because there one is faced with the origins of western religion, but also because the biblical pericopes read in the liturgies do provide an important link between narrated experiences, professed faith, and pledged commitment.

1.1.1. Old Testament

German Protestant theology in the late eighteenth and nineteenth
century lived through a period of great scholarly achievements.
According to Hans FREI, this period of intense theological activity
was also marked by a truncated understanding of biblical narrative.[1]
Interestingly enough, all of the parties involved (pre-critical,
moderate and progressive) commited, albeit for different reasons, the
same error of separating the meaning of a narrative from its natural
social, and therefore realistic, reference. There was a preoccupation
with history, but not with narrative as "history-like."[2]

It was not until the arrival of form criticism that a more wholesome approach to biblical narrative could begin again. It first
emerged in the field of Old Testament studies.

In the Anglo-Saxon world the rediscovery of narrative was
pioneered by H. Richard NIEBUHR and George Ernest WRIGHT. NIEBUHR in
his The Meaning of Revelation made the distinction between "internal
history" and "external history;" a reference to personal and
impersonal stories. In other words, he read the biblical narratives
constantly asking himself the question of revelation and personal
commitment.[3]

WRIGHT, being indebted to NIEBUHR, proposed in the early fifties
a "theology of recital." For him biblical theology was primarily
confessional: men and women of the Bible confessed their faith by
reciting the formative events of their history as the redemptive
handiwork of God.[4] Unfortunately, WRIGHT was not ready to apply his

---

[1] Hans FREI, The Eclipse of Biblical Narrative. A Study in Eighteenth
and Nineteenth Century Hermeneutics, New Haven, 1974.

[2] Hans FREI, Eclipse, pp. 8-13; for a definition of the term see
footnote 10.

[3] H. Richard NIEBUHR, The Meaning of Revelation, New York, 1946,
especially pp. 32-66. It is worth mentioning that H.R. NIEBUHR
attempted an approach (due to his methodist background?) that would
not only allow a syntactic reading, as it is now called, but also a
semantic and pragmatic understanding of the Bible.
See also Michael GOLDBERG, Theology and Narrative. A Critical Introduction, Nashville, 1982, pp. 146-150.

"recital theology" outside the immediate context of history. Furthermore, he failed to notice that narrative is more than recital. James BARR is accurate in his criticism of G.E. WRIGHT,

> Although this approach laid enormous emphasis upon events, which emphasis was grounded upon characteristics of the narrative form of the Old Testament story, it thereafter gave comparatively little attention to the actual narrative form of Old Testament literature...[5]

WRIGHT did recognize narrative as an event, but he was not aware of its structure. He listened to the word, but he did not pay attention to language.

On the European continent Old Testament theology was advanced, as far as narrative is concerned, by Gerhard VON RAD. He discovered the confessional summaries of the saving history of Israel, the best known being the passage of Deuteronomy 26:5-9.[6] According to VON RAD the subject of Old Testament theology consists of a word made up of testimonies of God's saving action; past as well as eschatological.[7] He considered the rise of narrative theology in Israel as a unique achievement, especially because it integrated not just the sacral but the secular as well. Every department of life was embraced by Jahweh's action.[8] The inclusion of secular reality, for indeed Hebrew religiosity was a secularized faith in comparison to the neighboring religions, was an important contribution to the understanding of biblical narrative. VON RAD had also a keen perception of narrative in the context of worship.

---

[4] George Ernest WIRGHT, God who Acts. Biblical Theology as Recital, London, 1952, p. 32. It is noteworthy to mention that WRIGHT senses the connection between narrative and liturgy. In his words, both are "unpretentious," p. 110.

[5] James BARR, Explorations in Theology 7, London, 1980, p. 10.

[6] Gerhard VON RAD, Theologie des Alten Testaments. Bd. 1. Die Theologie der Geschichtlichen Ueberlieferung Israels, (= T.A.T.1) Munich, 1957, pp. 127 ff.

[7] Gerhard VON RAD, T.A.T.1, p.117. According to the author, the "Zeugniswelt" has precedence to the "Glaubenswelt" in early Old Testament theology. This phenomenon is also present in Pentecostalism and many religious communities in the Third World.

[8] Gerhard VON RAD, T.A.T.1, p. 61.

But it was above all in worship that Israel extolled Jahweh's
acts in history... the poems did not confine themselves solely
to enumerating and glorifying the acts of Jahweh; they also made
Israel and her attitude, yes, and her failures as well, the
objects of their meditation.[9]

This relationship between faith, narrative, the secular life world and
worship is important indeed. It will reappear in different formulations below.

In spite of the many merits that are inherent to VON RAD's work,
there is, nevertheless, a problem as James BARR points out. VON RAD
still links narrative to history without differentiation,

Narratives are not necessarily written because of a primary
interest in the past. They can be written for a quite different
reason: they can be written to provide pictures of the promises
of God which will come to pass in the future... to present
paradigms for thinking about the present... The narrative
materials of the Old Testament (and of the New) should be
classed not as history, but at the most as "history-like" (Hans
Frei's expression).[10]

To summarize it can be stated that, first, narrative is
theologically significant. It has already played an important role in
the Old Testament, as a correlary of faith and daily existence.[11]

---

[9] Gerhard VON RAD, T.A.T.1, p. 354; English edition, London, 1975, p.
357. The notion of narrative as a plot is in an embryonic way already
present in VON RAD's thinking. It will have to be treated in greater
detail below (2.3.6.2.).

[10] James BARR, Explorations, pp. 36f. Hans FREI states the thesis of
history-likeness of narrative as follows: "... a realistic or
history-like (though not necessary historical) element is a feature,
as obvious as it is important, of many of the biblical narratives that
went into the making of Christian belief." Hans FREI, Eclipse, p. 10.
For a critique of FREI's point of view, especially his definition of
myth, see: John E. ZUCK, Tales of Wonder: Biblical Narrative, Myth,
and Fairy Tale, in The Journal of the American Academy of Religion,
44,2 (1976), pp. 299-308.

[11] This correlation has later found a typical expression in Judaism,
namely in the distinction between the written Torah (the Hebrew
Bible), the oral Torah (the Mishnah and the Gemara in the Talmud) and
more specifically the narrative material called Haggada (a most
illustrative example is the seder narration of the Passover liturgy).
For more information one may consult Schalom BEN-CHORIN, Narrative
Theologie des Judentums anhand der Pessach-Haggada, Tübingen, 1985;
and Jacob NEUSNER, Invitation to the Talmud, New York, 1973. A similar
correlation has developed in midrashic exegesis and hassidic
tradition.

Secondly, narrative is more than recital, for it also calls for action on the part of its hearers. To be involved in salvation history brings along a moral responsibility. Lastly, narrative, although history-like must not necessarily be historical (in the common use of the term), it may be purely fictional, or even, it may be fictional and yet true.

1.1.2. New Testament

A few words should be said about narrative in the New Testament, and about its role in early Christian worship.

Most theologians writing on narrative theology refer at one point or another to the character of the New Testament stories, parables and metaphors, or to the narrative kerygma of the early Church. Their common arguments emphasize that Jesus of Nazareth is said to have spent most of his ministry telling or retelling stories,[12] and that the early Church was primordially an oral community, whose faith came by hearing.[13]

Beyond that, an important contribution has been made by Gerhard LOHFINK who argues that the whole of the New Testament depends primarily on narrative structures. By this he does not deny that large segments of the epistles as well as the gospels are non-narrative in genre. But he claims that even the non-narrative material, for instance the Letter to the Romans, depends on central narrative phrases which build the nucleus of the christian message.[14] This

---

[12] Harald WEINRICH, Narrative Theology , pp. 47f. ; George W. STROUP III, A Bibliographical Critique, in Theology Today 32 (1975), pp.137f; Paul RICOEUR, Poetische Fiktion und religiöse Rede, in Christlicher Glaube in moderner Gesellschaft, Bd. 2, (ed.) Franz BOECKLE and others, Freiburg, 1981, p. 99; Eberhard JUENGEL, Gott als Geheimnis der Welt. Zur Begründung der Theologie des Gekreuzigten im Streit zwischen Theismus und Atheismus, Tübingen, 1977, p.418.

[13] Gerhard LOHFINK, Erzählung als Theologie. Zur sprachlichen Grundstruktur der Evangelien, in Stimmen der Zeit 192 (1974), 521-532, pp. 528-531; Harald WEINRICH, Narrative Theology, p. 49.

[14] Gerhard LOHFINK, Erzählung, pp. 523-528; such narrative texts in Romans are especially frequent in the first eleven chapters, e.g. 1:3-4; 3:21; 3:25; 4:25; 5:5-6; 5:8; 5:11; etc.

inevitably shifts the attention back to the role of narrative among
the early Christians. Both LOHFINK and WEINRICH emphasize that "the
Story" was the central issue among the first believers.

> Christianity is a community of storytellers. No doubt that is
> not an exhaustive definition; it is equally true to say that it
> is a community at table together. But after all the two are not
> so very different: in both cases everyone sits round, with the
> master of ceremonies in the middle, as in Leonardo's **Last
> Supper**.[15]

It is worthwhile to pursue this apparent overlap between word and
sacrament. For Oscar CULLMANN this convergence is demonstrated in the
Gospel of John, as well as in the Easter appearance narratives which
build the background to the rejoicing at the eucharistic meals in
Acts.[16] It can also be described as a fruitful tension between fixed
and open liturgy, or in Eduard SCHWEIZER's words, there is a dialectic
between order and charisma, between the awareness of historicity, the
celebration of a meaning-giving event in the past, and a sense of
newness, the miraculous presence of the Holy Spirit in the light of
Jesus.[17] The common element between these two poles is a narrative
communication of God's grace. On the one hand there is freedom of
spiritual expression, the edification of the Body of Christ by means
of doxological testimonies, hymns, visions and prophecies. On the
other hand there is the central focus on the Paschal Mystery, the
telling of the Christ-Event, the story of the Word made flesh. "It is
precisely in this harmonious combination of freedom and restriction
that there lies the greatness and uniqueness of early Christian
worship."[18]

---

[15] Harald WEINRICH, Narrative Theology, pp. 48f.

[16] Oscar CULLMANN, Early Christian Worship, London, 1953, pp. 15f.

[17] Eduard SCHWEIZER, Gemeinde und Gemeindeordnung im Neuen Testament,
Zürich, 1959, pp. 151f.

[18] Oscar CULLMANN, Early, p. 33. These elements of narrative communication just mentioned have found a revival in pentecostal, charismatic
and many third world christian communities. Their predominantly oral
form poses a fundamental challenge for the study of narrative in
worship.

The narrative element in the early Church does not exclusively center around the idea that actual stories are told.[19] Rather, stories are inherent in the communication of God's presence to and among the faithful, because proclamations of God's grace are by necessity contextual and evocative. They cannot merely be discursive, for they relate to a life world. This is one of the reasons why, as we shall see, Ian T. RAMSEY calls religious language "odd."[20]

1.1.3. Form Critical Studies and Oral Traditions

An important contribution to the understanding of biblical texts was made by the introduction of form critical studies. The central idea in that branch of criticism focuses on the realization that pronouncements, historical accounts, poems, etc., have been transmitted orally for some time before they were codified in a written text. It is argued that in order to have survived as oral traditions, the various materials existed in certain forms or oral laws, which related to their socio-religious use, but also facilitated memorization. In other words, there has been a period of oral tradition previous to the establishment of the Massoretic Text of the Hebrew Bible, just as there has been a gap of something less than a generation between the end of Jesus' ministry in Galilee and the beginnings of gospel writing. The heritage of faith, it is commonly argued, was maintained orally in specific socio-religious contexts in order to keep the transmission meaningful. Many of these forms can be classified within the genre of narrative.[21] It is, thus, the oral

---

[19] The Christ-Hymn in the Letter to the Philippians 2:5-11 is primarily a solemn confession of Christ's lordship, possibly situated liturgically in a baptisimal context. The language of the hymn is narratively evocative although the actual plot is assumed to be known. Cf. Ralph P. MARTIN, Carmen Christi. Philippians 2:5-11 in Recent Interpretation and in the Setting of Early Christian Worship, Grand Rapids, 1983, pp. 289-299.

[20] Ian T. RAMSEY, Religious Language. An Empirical Placing of Theological Phrases, London, 1957, pp.19-28. See also section 2.1. below.

[21] Rudolf PESCH mentions, for example, prophetic narratives in the first and third person, paradigms, controversies, miracle stories,

traditions and practices that relate to the narrative character of
much of the biblical material.

The point of bringing up the discussion on form criticism in this
study is that form critical reflection is not only useful in searching
for the pre-literary origins of the Judeo-Christian faith and relating
them to the context of Scriptures, but also in providing insight for a
correlation between the traditional faith narratives and any given
(religious) situation in the present. In other words, a form critical
approach should not only be applied to past texts, but equally so to
the contemporary problem of relating one's convictions of faith (or
the lack thereof) with the challenges of daily life, because it can be
argued that an immediate response to basic existential questions would
be pre-reflective and oral (even in a highly literate society).[22]
Furthermore, if one has a genuine interest in inter-cultural theological dialogue, one should learn to understand oral digests of faith
as they are largely practiced in the Third World, and not insist in a
westernization of thought models (e.g. requesting a written abstract
prior to discussing the issue, thus distilling it out of context). An
introduction to inter-cultural dialoge between mainly literate and
basically non-literate societies, for which work is already being
done,[23] would be a second benefit of studying oral narratives in

---

historical and composite narratives, the Passion narrative in the
Gospels, autobiographical sketches in the Epistles, or even the
liturgical context in the recitation of Psalms. Rudolf PESCH, Form
Criticism, in Encyclopedia of Theology. A Concise Saramentum Mundi.
Karl RAHNER (ed.), London, 1975, pp. 525-528.

[22] See the discussion below (2.2.6.3.) on the first stage of a threefold mimetic appropriation of truth.

[23] Walter HOLLENWEGER wonders, for example, why exegetes of the First
Letter to the Corinthians have so far failed to interpret the
religious conflicts between charismatic enthusiasm and rational faith
in the Corinthian church as directly relating to the inter-cultural
tensions between a socially high-ranking group of literates and a
socially low-ranking, predominantly oral group. It is worthwhile to
quote him at length:
"Le conflit à Corinthe est généralement présenté comme un conflit
religieux entre les enthousiastes, les illuminés helléniques et Paul
qui faisait appel à la raison, à l'argumentation de l'exégèse des
Ecritures, surtout de l'Ancien Testament. Or, ce conflit est aussi -
et en premier lieu - un conflit entre deux cultures. Comment les

worship. For these reasons, the theme of orality will be resumed below.

1.2. Dogmatic Theology

To argue that Christianity lost its "narrative innocence," when it began to dialogue with Hellenism, and that it was only rediscovered in this generation[24] has proven to be an untenable claim. It can be added that, firstly, the polarity between **mythos** and **logos**, between an oriental-christian and a hellenistic-western frame of mind should not be exaggerated; and secondly, one finds hints of narrative approaches to theology throughout Church history.[25] Previous theological epochs used the terms testimony, tradition, word, history, etc., to denote a theological approach similar to the contemporary narrative one.[26] According to Richard LISCHER, Martin LUTHER used a narrative technique in many of his sermons in order to relate the biblical teaching to the present age and circumstances of the hearers.[27] In more recent time, Eduard THURNEYSEN wrote that divine

---

esclaves qui ne savaient pas lire, qui ne savaient peut-être pas le grec suffisamment pour suivre un argument théologique, comment ces gens pouvait-ils exprimer leur identité, leur dignité humaine vis-à-vis de ceux qui 'lisaient' les Ecritures et notamment les lettres de Paul? Ils faisaient appel au Saint-Esprit, aux visions, aux inspirations, aux 'parler en language', à l'interprétation immédiate de leur réalité de tous les jours. Et les autres, les lecteurs, se défendaient, parce que c'était un monde étrange, dangereux et innaccessible pour eux, en s'appuyant sur les Ecritures et les textes de Paul." Walter J. HOLLENWEGER, Le livre oral. Portées sociale, politique et théologique des religions orales, in G. POUJOL and R. LABOURIE (ed.) Les cultures populaires. Permanence et émergences des cultures minoritaires locales, ethniques, sociales et religieuses (INEP, Sciences de l'homme), Toulouse, 1979, p. 126.

[24] Harald WEINRICH, Narrative Theology, p. 50; for an opposing point of view: Bernd WACKER, Narrative Theologie?, p, 97-99.

[25] Catchwords like: hagiography, medieval mystery plays and iconography shall suffice as a reminder.

[26] Bernd WACKER, Narrative Theologie?, p. 74 note.

[27] "Er schildert etwa die Geburt von Marias Standpunkt aus und die

revelation in the Bible is contingent on the play of events recounted
in the Scriptures.[28] Karl BARTH has also been called a pre-narrative
theologian by various authors.[29] No less important is the mention of
Karl RAHNER's Priester und Dichter.[30] There he makes a useful
distinction between primordial words (**Urworte**) pointing to transcendence, and ordinary usage words (**Nutzworte**). RAHNER calls the
whole Church to become bearers of the kerygma of these primordial
words by means of their existence.[31] Borrowing thoughts of Martin
HEIDEGGER, he states that the priest calls upon the poet (Holy
Spirit?) so that his words may become the effective word of God in
man.[32]

Epiphanias-Perikope aus der Sicht der erschreckten Eltern, weil in
seiner Gemeinde Frauen sind, die wissen, was es heisst, in einem
kalten Haus zu gebären, und Eltern die sich schuldig fühlen wegen der
Vernachlässigung ihrer Kinder. Zu all diesen Menschen, die analoge
Gedanken und Erfahrungen durch die Zeiten hindurch kennen, spricht
Luther." Richard LISCHER, "Story" in Luthers Predigten, in Evangelische Theologie 43,6 (1983), p. 533.

[28] "Seine (Gottes) **Offenbarung** ist aber von der **Zufälligkeit des
Gewandes** bestimmt in dem die sich offenbarende Wahrheit auftritt...
Dieses Gewand ist das in den Texten der Bibel **geschilderte** Geschehen."
Eduard THURNEYSEN, Schrift und Offenbarung, (Marburg: 20. 2. 1924), in
Theologische Bücherei 44, München, 1971, p. 48, emphasis added.

[29] Bernd WACKER, Narrative Theologie?, pp. 73-77; Robert A. KRIEG,
Linguistic Rule, pp. 191-202; John ZUCK, Tales of Wonder, pp. 299-308.

[30] Karl Rahner, Priester und Dichter, in Schriften zur Theologie, Bd.
3, Einsiedeln, 1956, pp. 349-375; English edition: Theological
Investigations, vol. 3, pp. 294-317.

[31] Karl Rahner, Priester und Dichter, pp. 353-359.

[32] "Wo das Wort Gottes das Höchste sagt und es am tiefsten in das Herz
des Menschen versenkt, da ist es auch ein menschlich dichterisches
Wort. Und der Priester ruft den Dichter, damit **seine** Urworte die
konsekrierten Gefässe des göttlichen Wortes werden, in denen der
Priester das Wort Gottes wirksam verkündet." Karl RAHNER, Priester und
Dichter, p. 374 (emphasis his).
It is likely that RAHNER toys with the German word for poet (**Dichter**),
which in its root carries also the meaning of density. The most
elevated Word of God, as it were, is boiled down to the concreteness
of human existence by the creative power of the poetical, or for that
matter, narrative word.

These brief examples of a narrative option in the past were given in order to relativize the image of newness which accompanied the advent of narrative theology ten years ago. Now that the first fervor has passed, it might be appropriate to have another look at the feasibility of narrative in the context of dogmatic theology. For this purpose the contributions of Johann Baptist METZ and Edward SCHILLE-BEECKX shall be considered.

1.2.1. J.B. METZ: Religious Narratives as Social Criticism

Johann Baptist METZ has become popular through his political theology. He defines the role of narrative in terms of social criticism. The Christians have "dangerous" and "subversive" stories to tell. These stories become the medium of salvation and history. But such a narrative memory of salvation cannot be purely argumentative theology, because this would conceal its origins, and it would not make this memory present again and again in the history of human suffering.[33] It is for this reason that, "Theology is above all concerned with direct experiences expressed in narrative language."[34]

However, what is of primary interest in this essay is not his justification for narrative, nor its practical use as a moral reminder and a social critique of society, to be practiced by all Christians in daily life. Rather, METZ's ideas concerning the relationship between narrative and sacramental action deserve special attention. He refers to Martin BUBER's Hassidic stories and quotes him extensively,

> The story is itself an event and has the quality of sacred action... It is more than a reflection - the sacred essence to which it bears witness continues to live in it. The wonder that is narrated becomes powerful once more... A rabbi, whose grandfather had been a pupil of Baal Shem Tov, was once asked to tell a story. "A story ought to be told," he said, "so that it is itself a help," and his story was this. My grandfather was paralyzed. Once he was asked to tell a story about his teacher and he told how the holy Baal Shem Tov used to jump and dance

---

[33] Johann B. METZ, Short Apology, pp.89-93. As far as political theology and its narrative implications are concerned see also James H. CONE, The Story Context of Black Theology, in Theology Today 32 (1975), pp. 144-150.

[34] Johann B. METZ, Short Apology, p. 85.

when he was praying. My grandfather stood up while he was
telling the story and the story carried him away so much that he
had to jump and dance to show how the master had done it. From
that moment, he was healed. This is how stories ought to be
told."[35]

In this story the linguistic action merges the effective word and the
effective sacrament into one. METZ mentions as christian examples of
this merger the institution narrative of the eucharistic prayer and
the narrative confession in the sacrament of reconciliation.
Furthermore, he advocates that "...it should also be possible to
relate the sacramental action more closely to stories of life and
suffering and to reveal it as a saving narrative."[36]

In the light of this strong emphasis on life-stories METZ is
aware of two possible misunderstandings. First, one must not think
that there is no longer room for arguments and reasoning. "There is a
time for story-telling and a time for argument." Second, one has to be
careful with regard to the secular tendency towards subjectivism, the
withdrawal "into the purely private sphere or the aesthetic sphere of
good taste."[37]

Another aspect of METZ's narrative theology shall be mentioned.
Considering the existing schism between theological systems and
religious experience, between orthodoxy and biography, between dogma
and mysticism, he suggests a "theology as biography." Biography would
include a subjective approach, but that does not imply the mere
projection of a mirror image, which could be deceptive. A theological

---

[35] Johann B. METZ, Short Apology, pp. 86f., quoting Martin BUBER,
Werke, Bd. 3, München, 1963, p. 71. Not just the Hassidic, but the
entire Talmudic tradition is full of narratives born of a tradition
that is eminently biblical and that could be called upon to strengthen
the argument in favour of a narrative approach in the teaching and
worship of the faithful. For a instructive selection of Midrash
Halacha (narrative interpretations to the law) and Midrash Aggada
(narrative interpretations to prayers) see: Aaron SINGER, Introduction
to Talmudic Thought and Teaching, 126/71, Jerusalem, The Hebrew
University of Jerusalem.

[36] Johann B. METZ, Short Apology, p. 87, In this context see also
Johann B. METZ, Glaube in Geschichte und Gesellschaft, Mainz, 1977, p.
176. METZ asks himself why eschatological memory has been confined to
sacramental theology.

[37] Johann B. METZ, Short Apology, pp. 88f.

approach would integrate religious experience into a public doxography of faith. According to METZ it would be a condensed narrative of life before God.[38] "Biography as theology" would function as a reconciliatory catalyst between theory and praxis. It would be a reflection on the life of faith with its everyday trials, a mystagogy for all.

METZ sees a paradigmatic example of these ideas in the life and theological work of Karl RAHNER. The multiplicity of topics that this priest and theologian has addressed becomes a testimony of contemporary Christianity. A testimony, because they have not been selected according to a system-oriented canon, rather they were imposed by the canon of life.[39] Indeed, a theological understanding of narrative should face the contingencies of life.

The salvific, sacramental and biographical accents of J. B. METZ have made the concept of narrative more accessible. But many questions relating to linguistic and theological criteria of narrative faith-talk still remain open. Edward SCHILLEBEECKX, although he would not call himself a narrative theologian, has attempted to establish a basic framework in this respect. It is to him that we now turn.

1.2.2. E. SCHILLEBEECKX: The Twofold Reception of Religious Narratives

There is common agreement that the meaning of language is determined by the particular language game in use. If, however, a language game, for instance religious language in the church, is no longer understandable by the majority of its hearers (and users), then it has begun to become meaningless, especially in reference to the lived experience in the world.

---

[38] "Biographisch soll eine Theologie heissen, weil die mystische Biographie der religiösen Erfahrung, der Lebensgeschichte vor dem verhüllten Antlitz Gottes, in die Doxographie des Glaubens eingeschrieben wird. Biographisch ist sie auch insofern sie... eine begrifflich abgekürzte und **verdichtete** Erzählung der Lebensgeschichte vor Gott (ist)." Johann B. METZ, Glaube und Geschichte, p. 196 (emphasis added). See also footnote 32.

[39] Johann B. METZ, Glaube und Geschichte, pp. 199-203.

The crisis in the church's use of language, in her creeds,
liturgy, catechesis and theology, therefore points to the fact
that this language can no longer be experienced by many
believers as a reflection of their contemporary association with
reality. Words such as "redemption," "justification," "resurrection" and "reconciliation" have for instance lost their
meaning for many people in the church because they are unable to
see any relationship between these key concepts and their lived
experience, which is now expressed in other concepts drawn from
the familiar sphere of modern socio-political life and
interhuman relationships.[40]

In view of this problem, SCHILLEBEECKX suggests a hermeneutics of
experience with a double function of meaningfulness. First, the
experience of everyday existence is to give meaning to theological
talk. Second, "all theological interpretation must, as a reflection
about religious talk, have a meaning that can be understood in and by
the world."[41] And just as the good news of the Gospel is doxological
in character, so must also a theological interpretation in a secular
age prove itself relevant and reliable by virtue of its doxological
value and truthfulness. Such a hermeneutic, which wants to pay full
respect to the demands of reason, is also a gift of God, a believing
creativity being faithful to the Son's message through the charism of
the Holy Spirit.[42] It would be a theological interpretation where
meaning and event would again meet each another.

Theologically this would imply that narrative could function as a
bridge between orthodoxy and orthopraxis. In a more and more pluralistic world, narrative as a linguistic representation of the humanum,
could mediate between the presuppositions of the christian faith
(orthodoxy, tradition) and the present situation (the christian
self-understanding in orthopraxis). It would be a substantial element
in the "hermeneutic circle" that SCHILLEBEECKX is calling for,[43] and

---

[40] Edward SCHILLEBEECKX, The Understanding of Faith. Interpretation
and Criticism, London, 1974, p. 15.

[41] Edward SCHILLEBEECKX, Understanding, p. 17.

[42] Edward SCHILLEBEECKX, Understanding, p. 19.

[43] Edward SCHILLEBEECKX, Understanding, pp. 45-77. There he produces
the theological criteria in the light of pluralism, orthodoxy and
reception (which he calls acceptance). But SCHILLEBEECKX does not
explicitly discuss the role of narrative in this context.

it could find a **raison d'être** as an expression of the reception of faith by the community of the faithful in worship. It would be an important element providing veracity to orthodoxy. "Because this orthodoxy is... the theoretical aspect of christian praxis, the 'acclamation' or 'amen' forms an essential part of the structure of christian liturgy in which orthodoxy is above all to be found: **Lex orandi, Lex credendi.**"[44]

Nevertheless, if theological narrative does not want to be unintelligible gibberish it must draw from a pre-understanding in order to convey a new understanding, and in doing so must follow linguistic criteria. These shall be picked up in chapter 2, but previous to that there is another issue which needs clarification, namely the theological relationship between religious narratives and the notion of myth.

1.3. The Myth of God Incarnate all over Again

In spite of the attempt of Rudolf BULTMANN and his disciples to demythologize the message of the New Testament for the benefit of a contemporary existential understanding of faith, and even after the recent campaign under the banner of John HICK, which has successfully convinced many that Christianity has generously incorporated Judaic and Hellenistic mythological material, it remains to be asked if man, religious or not, is at all able to live meaningfully without a mythological frame of reference. A thesis on the relationship between religious narratives and worship can certainly not afford to sidestep the function of myths, which have a cultic **Sitz im Leben** and a narrative formulation.

---

[44] Edward SCHILLEBEECKX, Understanding, p. 72.

1.3.1. Common Qualifications of Myth

The root problem causing so many divergent views on the issue, lies in the various approaches and connotations associated with myths. Consequently, it is necessary to qualify the reasons for whatever angle of approach one choses, and in so doing at least make mention of possible alternatives. Hence, the following explanations.

1.3.1.1. The Myths of the Gods?

When speaking about myths one often thinks in literary categories: of ancient polytheistic myths where magic and the fantastic form a great and terrible picture of man's fate in the light of the supernatural. Apart from the fact that there are classical myths which do not refer to the gods as protagonists,[45] it is, for the present study, not expedient to launch into a discussion whether such a literary genre has been adopted in the biblical corpus and therefore in the christian faith. More relevant is the question concerning the content and function of mythological narratives and their potential for liturgical representation. In this last sentence four important criteria for a definition of myth are given. They are suggested by the well known Finnish folklorist Lauri HONKO,[46] and could be set forth as follows:

1. In terms of its form a myth is a narrative.

2. In terms of their content myths are cosmogonic descriptions. This is understood in a large sense covering the start of any new era (i.e. not just the creation of the world, but also a conversion testimony, or the speeches of MAO Tse-tung for that matter).[47]

---

[45] Cf. Carlo Wing Chung KWAN, The Dimension of Time in Mythology, Vol. 1, University of Leuven, p. 6.

[46] Lauri HONKO, The Problem of Defining Myth, in Sacred Narrative. Readings in the Theory of Myth, Alan Dundes (ed.), Berkeley, 1984, pp. 41-52, especially pp. 49-51.

3. Myths function as models. They offer a cognitive basis or a pattern for behaviour. One can say that the function of myths is ontological.

4. Myths are normally contextualised in rituals. Their ideological content makes a celebration extra-ordinary. The ordinary is re-valued.

That problems arise if the notion of myth is only considered as a literary text can also be seen in the following problem.

1.3.1.2. Myth as "Falsehood"

The etymological development of the Greek term explains why **mythos** quickly gained a pejorative meaning; not only in western society but already in the texts of the New Testament and in the Greek language by the seventh century before the common era.[48] G. STAEHLIN believes the root meaning to be "thought," from where it developped into "expressed thought" to "account," "story," and eventually to "saga," "rumour," and with Aristotle it came to mean the "plot" of a drama. Three points can be retained. First, the original meaning of "thought", provided STAEHLIN is right, is a neutral one. Nothing has yet been said about whether it is an expressed or unexpressed thought, whether it is true or false. Second, STAEHLIN notices the intricate connection between myth, poetry and worship.

> Myth and poetry are both found on the soil of the cultus. They belong together during the whole of the ancient period. Even when it lost its religious power over souls, myth maintained its heroic greatness. It still had power to evoke fear and pity.[49]

The power of myth to affect human emotions is upheld throughout its etymological history. Third, the aristotelian definition of myth as "plot" is useful, because it can be appreciated in a secular context, regardless of religious connotations.

Thus, if someone uses the term "myth" to designate a "false story" or a "lie," he is basing himself on a common, but rather narrow literary understanding of the word originating from a Hellenistic

---

[48] G. STAEHLIN, **mythos**, in Theological Dictionary of the New Testament, Vol. IV, pp. 762-795.

[49] G. STAEHLIN, **mythos**, pp. 772f.

bias. Furthermore, if one attempts, as Heinrich FRIES has done,[50] to
clarify the significance of myths and mythology for christian theology
in literary terms alone, one must not be surprised if the mythic
question "What can Christ mean to us today?" remains unanswered. In
essence, the mythic material in the Bible makes demands on the
believer; the appeal is more than literary.

1.3.1.3. Myth as Phenomenon of Past Cultures

As already mentioned, the literary approach to "myth" is not the
only option; one can also consider its sociological context. Then one
inevitably meets another negative attitude towards myths, for it is
often argued that the western society of the twentieth century no
longer believes in myths, that the Enlightenment and, last but not
least, the theological debate over demythologization, have made a
mythological reference superfluous to the scientific mind. This at
least is the popular understanding of Rudolf BULTMANN's enterprise,
although, especially in his later years, he had a much more nuanced
approach to the interpretation of myths.[51] The crux of the matter is
not the question whether or not one can explain or translate the
out-of-the-ordinary. Rather, one should ask whether human beings can
make sense of their lives, individually and as community, without
mythological references, without the element of wonderment, and
especially without an existential (i.e. utmost personal) placement in
the here and now. The unshakeable confidence in technological
progress, the revolution through global communism, or the revitalizing

_____
[50] Heinrich FRIES, _Mythos, Mythologie_. in _Sacramentum Mundi_. Vol. 3,
Freiburg, 1969, pp. 661-670. Although socio-religious interpretations
are mentioned, the final evaluation of the theological significance of
myths is done without them (pp. 666-668).

[51] The hermeneutic problem obviously remains, whether one demytho-
logizes a myth or not. This is well illustrated in the dialogue
between Karl JASPERS and Rudolf BULTMANN entitled _Die Frage der Ent-
mythologisierung_, München, 1954. For concise presentations of Ruldolf
BULTMANN's intricate understanding of myth one may consult: J.W.
ROGERSON, _Slippery Words: Myth_, in _Sacred Narrative_, pp. 69-71; and
E.J. TINSLEY (ed.), _Rudolf Bultmann_, _Modern Theology_, Vol. 2, London,
1973, a selection of excerpts from BULTMANN's writings; see especially
pp. 64-78.

goodness of nature are just a few labels to mythical attitudes of the twentieth century, which indicate a basic need to situate oneself in a larger order of existence.

It may certainly be that some myths (e.g. polytheistic myths that are no longer "self-saying discourses"[52]) may loose their significance as primordial stories, but it is quite a different thing to claim that myths conveying meaning for living are a phenomenon of the past.

1.3.2. A Socio-Dynamic Understanding of Myth

How then can myths in general be understood? If one considers the socio-religious function of myths, a step in the right direction is taken.[53] Myths are then seen as narratives which help man to situate himself temporally in view of the Sacred and in society, because they relate to fundamental questions of existence. Such an approach takes into account the transcendent nature of the mythological narrative as well as the ritual dimension that can only be expressed if a myth is not individualized. This ascertainment is more important than a formal definition of myth, because any definition will be truncated[54] whereas

---

[52] On the possible degeneration of myths, which thus require demythologization, cf. Antoine VERGOTE, Interprétation du language religieux, Paris, 1974, pp. 73-93, specifically the section entitled "Le mythe déchu en croyance aliénée".

[53] This path is for instance suggested in Frans VANSINA, Philosophy of Religion. Ancient Symbols and Modern Myths, Leuven, 1974, and in the various writings of Mircea ELIADE, Paul RICOEUR or Robert BELLAH, to mention just a few.

[54] Walter HOLLENWEGER, for instance, refuses in his inter-cultural theology to give a definition of myth. He argues that definitions are Spalt-Worte, words which abstract and fragment notions, whereas myths, and narratives in general, are Zusammenhang-Worte, that is words which are only meaningful if contextually retained. Walter J. HOLLENWEGER, Erfahrungen der Leibhaftigkeit. Interkulturelle Theologie 1, München, 1979, p. 181. In a similar vein Karl JASPERS, "Man fragt, was Mythus sei, was mythisch heisse. Es ist das Sprechen in Bildern, Anschaulich-keiten, Vorstellungen, in Gestalten und Ereignissen, die übersinnliche Bedeutung haben. Dieses Uebersinnliche aber ist allein in diesen Bildern selber gegenwärtig, nicht so, dass die Bilder interpretiert werden könnten durch Aufzeigung ihrer Bedeutung. Eine Uebersetzung in blosse Gedanken lässt die eigentliche Bedeutung des Mythus ver-schwinden." Karl JASPERS, Entmythologisierung, p. 89.

a description, as it has been given above by Lauri HONKO, can help us
to come to terms with myths wherever they may be met. However, such a
description needs to be applied. How this can be done theologically
shall be exemplified through the contribution of Walter J. HOLLEN-
WEGER, missiologist and professor of intercultural theology in
Birmingham.

1.3.3. How Myths can be Brought to Bear

In his second book of intercultural theology, entitled Umgang mit
Mythen[55] HOLLENWEGER shows how contemporary myths function in western
society, and how as a Christian he establishes criteria for theologically responsible myths. For, myths need to be brought to bear,
and it is by their "fruit," not just by their ideological content,
that they can be appraised. How, concretely, does he go about it?

1.3.3.1. Examples of Contemporary Myths

First of all, HOLLENWEGER is careful to show that myths are alive
and doing well all around the globe. In the third world, they form an
essential part of everyday language and action. In the second world
one finds the all permeating myth of dialectical materialism with all
the elements of the christian sacred story such as the creation (the
natural order), the fall (the rise of capitalism), the people of
promise (the proletariat), the eschatological prophet (Lenin), his
death and resurrection (physically embalmed and spiritually kept alive
in speeches, monuments and ever-present pictures), the interim period
(in which the Party has control over the affairs of the proletariat),
the promise of a new earth (which also seems to take longer than
initially expected), and a fullfledged institution (the nomenclatura)
that keeps the convictions and programs alive.[56] The situation in the
first world is not any different; economic myths are celebrated with

---

[55] Walter J. HOLLENWEGER, Umgang mit Mythen. Interkulturelle Theologie
2, München, 1982.

[56] Walter J. HOLLENWEGER, Umgang, pp. 64f.

equal fervour,   and anonymous institutions like banks and insurance
companies try hard to give their customers an emotional, almost
sanctimonious, impression of participation in the supreme when they
enter the air-conditioned rooms with indirect lighting, immaculate
wall-to-wall carpeting, bronze knobs and low-key voices.[57] The point
is, people respond when the archetypal strings of their subconscious
begin to vibrate, when they can situate themselves existentially
within what is going on. What then can happen if the mythological
potential of Christianity is incarnated and re-enacted in a secular
world?

1.3.3.2. Criteria for a Theologically Responsible Myth

HOLLENWEGER draws three criteria for the recognition of true
myths from the mythological material contained in the Bible.[58] The
Christ-Hymn in the Letter to the Colossians 1:15-20 serves as an
example.

First, he notices that the mythological material in the Bible
relates to the historical, cultural and social context, that is, to a
specific situation. In the case of the Christ-Hymn, which may well
have a pagan origin, for the idea of the cosmic body was already known
to Plato, a popular theme is applied to the all-embracing presence of
Christ.[59] Historical and literary sources of the time show that the

---

[57] Other mythological functions are: the doctor's visit in the
hospital room, with his entourage of "acolytes" and "sisters", special
instruments, Latin formulas and spotless vestments. The number of
national mythologies is legion: William Tell for Switzerland, Joan of
Arc for the French, the victorian "We are on the Lord's side" for the
British, and the myth of the "new frontier" for the United State of
America. A more recent example are the mythological celebrations of
reconciliation (i.e musical charity concerts) in sports stadiums
around the world in fraternal support for the famines in Africa. For
additional examples see Frans VANSINA, Ancient Symbols and Modern
Myths. Philosophy of Religion, Vol. 1, Leuven, 1974, pp. 74-96; and
Mircea ELIADE, The Sacred and the Profane. The Nature of Religion, New
York, pp. 204-209.
[58] Walter J. HOLLENWEGER, Umgang, pp. 158-165. In this section I
follow closely HOLLENWEGER's comments without giving repetitive
credit.

world economic situation, although it was relatively peaceful, was not
pleasant for the average person. The cosmic body was torn apart and at
war with itself. But the Colossians sing "in him all things hold
together." The hymn is thus a statement of hope in spite of hardship.
HOLLENWEGER is convinced that this hymn was part of the local liturgy
at Colossae and gained mythological power because it helped to situate
man existentially through its temporal applicability.

It is interesting to note that the apostle reminds the Colossians
that they are reconciled through Christ "in his body of flesh by his
death." This is the second criterion for a true christian myth, namely
the historical reference to the cross event, the central myth of
Christianity. This is the paradox of a responsible christian myth says
HOLLENWEGER, that on the one hand it is open to temporal and cultural
adaptation, and at the same time will pivot on the central message of
the Gospel.[60] The kerygmatic value of such a myth is apparent, and
much other mythical talk, even when it presents itself in the guise of
Christianity, will crash on the cliffs of this test.

The third criterion, relates again to temporality,[61] but this
time not to that of a particular society. Rather, it points to the
surplus value that a true myth generates. The promise that the
Christ-Hymn contains is also a promise for today's believers. The same
could be said about the re-enactment of the Passover in the Jewish
communities, where the "dangerous memories" (to use J.B. METZ'

---

[59]HOLLENWEGER argues, following Eduard SCHWEIZER, that the text did
originally indicate that the Colossians conceived Christ to be the
cosmic body. The author of the Epistle seems to have added the phrase
"which is the church."

[60] "Der Mythos wird so relativiert und historisiert. Lässt er sich
diese Relativierung und Historisierung gefallen, so wird er zu einem
für die Botschaft der Versöhnung potentiell transparenten Mythos.
Lässt er sie sich nicht gefallen, so scheidet er als Medium der
Verkündigung aus." Walter J. HOLLENWEGER, Umgang, p. 162.

[61] For the intricate relationship between historical time and
mythical time see Carlo KWAN, Time, especially pp. 143-145, 164,
379ff., 397ff; and the discussion on Paul RICOEUR's Temps et récit in
chapter two.

terminology) have not ceased to be a warning against the threatened **humanum**. The surplus of meaning makes a mythological narrative not only worthy to listen to, but also worthy to live by.

These criteria are such that they allow for the origination of new myths without deviating from the fundamental christian option. Repentance might well lead to a paradigm shift. This is one important aspect in favour of studying the role of prophetic narratives in chapter five, where the question will have to be asked, is the change from one mythological model to the other a noncommitted escape into secularisation, or can it lead to a re-orientation toward the essence of being Christian?

1.3.3.3. Where are Myths Brought to Bear?

No clear distinction has been made between mythical ritual and mythological narrative, because in terms of their function they relate to each other. However, the following can be said.

As far as mythological narratives are concerned the above-mentioned criteria of HONKO and HOLLENWEGER seem to be a useful tool in evaluating the mythological potential of testimonies and visions in the context of worship. Concretely, christian testimonies can function as interpretative elements for the underlying Christ-myth. It is a heuristic interpretation of a mythological tradition that secular man can no longer understand and believe as such, because he no longer perceives the basic answers to human existence in the narrative of the myth.[62] Or, to put it the way Edward SCHILLEBEECKX[63] does, a conversion experience (or conversion vision) is the fruitful melting together of the Easter event (myth, disclosure of the past) and a testimony (disclosure in the here and now). His analysis of the Easter experience will again be picked up in chapter 4.

---

[62] Andrew M. GREELEY, Unsecular Man. The Persistence of Religion, New York, 1972, p. 250.

[63] Edward SCHILLEBEECKX, Jesus. An Experiment in Christology, London, 1974, pp. 379-397.

Although such narratives can be told everywhere, their full
potential is freed only in a communal event or celebration.[64]
Especially the Sacred can only be encountered with, or in relation to,
others, the reason being that myths do not leave any room for
solipsistic wholeness. In combination with sacramental action, where
the participants can experience the surplus of meaning according to
their personal and communal needs, griefs or expectations, myths help
to restructure experiences. The liturgical and sacramental aspects,
understood in a broad sense, are vitally important in this respect,[65]
so important that they cannot be limited to the activities within the
church building - although it is there that christian myths have
traditionally been brought to bear.

1.4. Summary

The aim of this chapter has been to situate a theological context
for the planned research in the field of religious narratives,
specifically their structure and function in the realm of communal
worship. The following theses can be suggested:
1. The faith expressed in the Old Testament and in Jewish history
reflects in its form a double narrative function. On the one hand,
religious narratives helped the Hebrews to relate their growing under-

---

[64] **"Myths,** in fact, often make such a profound impression that they
almost require some kind of acted response, a dance, a ritual, some
action to express the emotions which have been generated and
released." Morton T. KELSEY, Myth, History and Faith. The Remythologizing of Christianity, New York, 1974, p. 100 (emphasis added).

[65] "The true milieu of myth is to be found in religious rites and
ceremonial. The ritual acting out of myths implies the defence of the
world order... The reenactment of a creative event... is the common
aim of myth and ritual. In this way the event is transferred to the
present and its result... can be achieved once more here and now."
Lauri HONKO, Defining Myths, p. 49.
HONKO's statement has to be read carefully, the "defence of the
world order" in his text relates to the prevention of chaos and not
the maintenance of the **status quo.** Although some myths do aim at the
maintenance of a given social order, a responsible christian myth
would, if not spiritually and socially prophetic, at least be open
ended due to the eschatological reservation in view of man's
finiteness.

standing of God to concrete events in their personal history. On the other hand, their faith, which could be related narratively, found the potential for an active expression in everyday life .

2. Christianity, especially in its origins, has been a community of story tellers. The narrative practice was of vital importance in a liturgical context, in the proclamation of faith, and consequently in the formation of the New Testament.

3. Theologically, narratives can operate as a catalyst between fundamental convictions (orthodoxy) and experiences (orthopraxis). They may also be initiators of action (e.g. moral) and thought (e.g. reception into orthodoxy). Furthermore, narratives can serve as translators of religious meaning into a secular frame of reference and vice versa.

4. A socio-religious understanding of myth underlines the vital role of narratives: a) in sustaining faith through ritual celebration, b) in helping to restructure experiences, and c) in bringing into focus the commission of all Christians to ideological conviction and practice.

2. PHILOSOPHICAL CLARIFICATIONS:

RELIGIOUS MEANING DISCLOSED IN NARRATIVE LANGUAGE AND COMMON TIME

"Sein, das verstanden werden kann ist Sprache."

H.G. GADAMER

Although religious language has suffered a setback through the challenge of neo-positivist thought, it has at the same time received a positive re-evaluation under the influence of logical linguistic analysis, structuralism and phenomenology. Any attempt to establish the meaning and function of religious narrative cannot bypass the questions and contributions of these philosophical disciplines. Three domains shall receive special attention; one is the area of syntactic logic, which will be elucidated by the disclosure theory of Ian T. RAMSEY. Another field of interest will point to specific problems with regard to the interpretation of personal narratives. The phenomenology of Paul RICOEUR, in dialogue with contributions of other writers, will attempt to shed light on the semantic level of poetic language. A short excursion relating to Hans-Georg GADAMER's thoughts on the ontological nature of understanding will bridge these two endeavours. His notion of a fusion of interpretative horizons and questions relating to the pragmatic value of (hi)storical knowledge will be addressed in particular.

2.1. Language

Ian T. RAMSEY developed his disclosure theory in order to show
how religious language is rooted in experience, and how this kind of
language can still be placed empirically. His major thesis can be
described as follows.

2.1.1. Ian RAMSEY's Disclosure Theory

Religious language is rooted in and intends to evoke disclosures, which by means of odd situations reveal meaning in man's
life and call him to commitment. A disclosure is evoked by appealing
to an empirical fact, a familiar situation which operates as a model.
Then a qualifier is introduced, which provokes an unexpected turn in
the model, and an insight is given on another level. As a result a
logical gap between model and disclosure is bridged, and another
inner logic, as it were, waiting to be unveiled, is disclosed.[1] An
example may clarify the matter:

> There is a surgeon in a medium sized hospital. It is Tuesday,
> that means that minor operations are on schedule, such as
> appendectomies and the like. It is eleven o'clock in the
> morning and four patients have already been treated. The
> surgeon is looking forward to the coffee break. He suggests
> that the attending nurse go ahead and pour some coffee, since
> he can manage to "stitch up" the patient in no time. Just as he
> is done, the alarm goes of and calls him to the emergency
> operating room. He curses and wonders why in the world the
> emergency had to come now and not ten minutes later. His coffee
> will be cold by the time he is done. On the way to the other
> room he learns that a woman has been brought in who was
> involved in a serious car accident. As he enters and looks at
> the victim he notices with terror that it is his wife who is
> laying on the table. He immediately gathers his energies and
> operates on his wife with the utmost care. The trivial idea of
> drinking a cup of coffee has vanished from his mind.

The model can be described as the secular context (e.g. the surgeon
performing routine operations in a hospital), and the qualifier as
the religious dimension (e.g. realizing that it is his wife who has
been brought in for emergency treatment) which appears as "odd

---

[1] Wim DE PATER, Sense and Nonsense in Talking about God, in Saint
Louis Quarterly 6 (1968), pp. 15-19.

language" in the disclosure (e.g. shift of attitude from routine to utmost care). It is odd not only because it provides a new inner logic, but also because it points beyond itself, namely to transcendence.[2] This is why Paul RICOEUR calls religious language "limit language" (**Grenzsprache**) in correspondence with Karl JASPERS' definition of borderline situations in human existence.[3] A disclosure situation, by virtue of the fact that it points to the observable **and more,** is an experience of subjective transcendence as an answer to objective transcendence. Fundamental to such a disclosure is an attitude of openness to existence, not the vision of reality as a whole.[4]

Here narrative finds its **locus theologicus.**[5] Its creative role can be called eschatological, charismatic, sacramental, prophetic or therapeutic; it is salvific in all cases. The thesis can be put in popular language:

> A story... must reach me on some level to which I can respond, but it must also "stretch" me, pull me beyond where I now am, open up some new door of my mind or heart, so that wanting to explore further, I become an increasingly willing listener. This must happen whether I am reading a Tolkien story, or an Aeschylus story, or "The Story." Indeed, one of the most telling aspects of "The Story" may be this unexpectedness intruding upon the familiar. We know about kings, for example, but we do not know about kings who come as servants.[6]

---

[2] For practical purposes it might be helpful to think of transcendence as a philosophical notion also, rather than as an exclusively religious concept. The possibility of the "other than I" is important.

[3] Paul RICOEUR, Poetische Fiktion, p. 101. In the German translation the word points not only to a limit, but also implicitly beyond it, as it were to "the grass beyond the fence." This suggests transcendence, and not the end of things in themselves. Correspondingly, religious language is not to be misunderstood as what Dietrich BONHOEFFER calls a **Deus ex machina** appeal.

[4] "Religiöser Sprache geht es nicht so sehr um eine Vervollständigung unseres Bildes oder Modells von Wirklichkeit und Erfahrung, als viel mehr um deren Offenhalten durch eine Neuorientierung unserer Existenz..." Paul RICOEUR, Poetische Fiktion, p. 102.

[5] This has already been implied in: Wim DE PATER, Sense and Nonsense, p. 19, years before the **début** of narrative theology.

[6] Robert McAfee BROWN, My Story and "The Story," in Theology Today 32 (1975), p. 167.

It is the evocative nature of disclosure narratives that makes them
suitable in the context of liturgy. But to jump to a conclusion at
this point would circumvent serious questions that still need to be
asked. Concretely, how reliable is religious discourse and how can
Ian T. RAMSEY claim an empirical setting for such theological
discourse? RAMSEY answers this query by the method of "empirical
fit."

2.1.2. The Method of "Empirical Fit"

It will be evident that this model is not purely deductive, and
in so far as it evokes discoveries it relies on intuition. But to
argue that this subjective appeal escapes verification is to dismiss
the case before the last witness has appeared.[7] The empirical fit
method does essentially provide criteria for the reliability of
theological disclosures. Firstly, the question must be asked whether
the disclosed theory makes more sense with God than without him.
Secondly, the criterion of coherence needs to be applied. This is
done by weighing as many models as are available. For instance, if
God is disclosed in terms of fatherhood, then coherence is ascer-
tained if models are added that represent him as friend, judge, rock,
shepherd and so forth.[8] What is called for is actually a multi-model
discourse. Here, the model, or for that matter the narrative,
functions as a form of explanation. "... by drawing a number of small
or sub-stories into yet larger stories: we find our place in the
world, as it were, by having our individual stories 'placed' within a
larger story..."[9] The multi-model discourse will be discussed in
greater detail below in relation to Paul RICOEUR's hermeneutics of

---

[7] This impression is to some extent given in Anton GRABNER - HAIDER,
Semiotik und Theologie. Religiöse Rede zwischen analytischer und
hermeneutischer Philosophie, München, 1973, p. 174. It must be remembered that it is a coherent inner logic which is at stake, and not
an empirical verification in the sense that pragmatic sciences would
like to use it.

[8] Wim DE PATER, Sense and Nonsense, pp. 35f.

[9] Hugh JONES, The Concept of Story and Theological Discourse, in
Scottish Journal of Theology 29 (1976), p. 423.

testimony. The third criterion for the empirical fit is the consist-
ence within a larger context. That is, the multi-model disclosure is
tested against the whole world situation.[10] It is on this level that
the battle is fought between the "pro-factors" of an initial belief,
and the "contra-factors" that might oppose it. The possibility of de-
bunking a belief seems essential to RAMSEY. On the one hand, it
allows him to speak empirically of religious language ("...we must be
prepared to reject the Resurrection if too many contra-factors
appear..."). On the other hand, it shows that in the last analysis
religious language finds its veracity in the confirmation of human
commitment.[11]

In summary one can say that Ian T. RAMSEY's theory of religious
language accounts for the following: first, the empirical fit theory
is syntactic in its function. It allows a disclosure or narrative to
have a form, coherent and understandable as a whole. Second, the
evocative element in the disclosure corresponds to the semantic role
of language. In it narrative is the carrier of meaning, not only on
the informational level, but specifically in the symbolic dimension
of religious communication. Third, the evoked commitment that follows
reflects the pragmatic nature of religious language.[12] Religious
language, in other words, has a strongly performative aspect. "Such
language is less intent on proving than on showing, it is less
concerned with presenting 'blueprints of God' than with pointing to a
mystery and **inducing to worship** and to the 'works of faith.'"[13] In

---

[10] Wim DE PATER, Sense and Nonsense, pp. 36.

[12] Wim DE PATER, Sense and Nonsense, pp. 43-48; Edward SCHILLEBEECKX,
Understanding, pp. 20-44, who has also structured the chapter on
linguistic criteria along Charles W. MORRIS' division; Jean LADRIERE,
Language of Worship. The Performativity of Liturgical Language, in
Concilium 9 (1973), p. 52. A valid syntax is the precondition for
meaningful language. Semantics and pragmatics seem to overlap to a
certain extent, especially when narrative is also performative.

[13] Wim DE PATER, Sense and Nonsense, p. 48 (emphasis added).

sum, Ian T. RAMSEY has shown that religious language cannot be flatly descriptive. A disclosure always points to the observable and more.

2.2. From Language to Action: H.G. GADAMER and J. HABERMAS

Before launching into the hermeneutic implications for religious narratives, some fundamental questions should be asked concerning the task of a theory of interpretation. For this purpose Hans-Georg GADAMER's hermeneutical ideas will briefly be presented, and an objection by Jürgen HABERMAS will be examined.

2.2.1. Some Essentials of GADAMER's Theory

Hans-Georg GADAMER's seminal work Wahrheit und Methode[14] is an attempt to situate hermeneutics between philosophy and science. The high ambition, to situate language ontologically, explains itself in the historical development of the theory of interpretation. Whereas in the nineteenth century hermeneutics was focusing on the object of interpretation, that is, the aim was to uncover the author's original idea and history was considered an objective discipline, the twentieth century brought with HEIDEGGER a shift to the subject, the primordial question was now how does one understand a text (of the past) through one's (present) existentially shaped pre-understanding?[15] GADAMER brought to this thesis and antithesis a synthesis by postulating that any hermeneutical theory should not be grounded in the object (historicism) nor in the subject (sub-jectivism) of interpretation, but rather in the ontological status of language itself.

_____

[14] Hans-Georg GADAMER, Wahrheit und Methode. Grundzüge einer philosophischen Hermeneutik, Tübingen, 1962, 1963, 1972.

[15] Cf. Michael ERMARTH, The Transformation of Hermeneutics. 19th Century Ancients and 20th Century Moderns, in The Monist 64 (April 1981), pp. 175-194.

GADAMER argues for an ontological placing of language because he is convinced that man's way of understanding and of being is fundamentally related to a belonging to language.[16] Since language is presented as having a claim on us, it follows that (the language of) tradition has equally a claim to be heard. Now what HEIDEGGER had said about presuppositions coloring subjective understanding, GADAMER has radicalized in his notion of prejudice. In a etymologically neutral sense, GADAMER considers prejudice as an essential prerequisite to understanding at all, for it is through projections of ideas that one begins to understand and to experience.[17] But how is one able to discern between legitimate and illegitimate prejudices? It is here that the help of tradition is needed, which through its linguistic pre-existence has, in addressing the present, a certain weight of authority. This pertinence of the past in the present is ideally an authentic historical consciousness at work.[18]

Understanding a text, thus implies a mediation of two worlds, the context of that which is to be interpreted and the context of the interpreter himself. GADAMER introduces at this point the useful concept of the fusion of horizons. The image of the horizon incorporates some of GADAMER's basic convictions. First, no horizon is

---

[16] The following quotations from Hans-Georg GADAMER's Wahrheit und Methode, concisely outline language as horizon for a hermeneutical ontology.

"Die Sprache ist nicht nur eine der Ausstattungen, die dem Menschen, der in der Welt ist, zukommt, sondern auf ihr beruht, und in ihr stellt sich dar, dass die Menschen überhaupt Welt haben." (p. 419, emphasis his)

"Alle Formen menschlicher Lebensgemeinschaft sind Formen von Sprachgemeinschaft, ja mehr noch: sie bilden Sprache. Denn die Sprache ist ihrem Wesen nach die Sprache des Gesprächs. Sie bilded selber durch den Vollzug der Verständigung erst ihre Wirklichkeit. Deshalb ist sie kein blosses Mittel zur Verständigung." (p. 422, cf. also p. 426)

[17] "Der Fokus der Subjektivität ist ein Zerrspiegel. Die Selbstbesinnung des Individuums ist nur ein Flackern im geschlossenen Stromkreis des geschichtlichen Lebens. **Darum sind die Vorurteile des einzelnen weit mehr als seine Urteile die geschichtliche Wirklichkeit seines Seins.**" Hans-Georg GADAMER, Wahrheit, p. 261 (emphasis his).

[18] On GADAMER's notion of **wirkungsgeschichtliches Bewusstsein** see Wahrheit, pp. 284-290.

closed. That means that there is no dogmatic closure; that which from
afar seems foreign might eventually be recognized for what it stands
for. Second, if one looks at a horizon one must not focus on that
which is in the immediate vicinity; a hermeneutical horizon should
lend itself to far-sighted and all-embracing aspects of truth.[19] A
third significant aspect in the analogy with the horizon is that when
one moves into a horizon the horizon moves along with the viewer.[20]
One could say that from GADAMER's point of view, a hermeneutic
approach should be generous. Now since the contextualized horizon of
the past and the horizon of understanding of the interpreter are
historically not identical, it follows that meaning can only emerge
if the two horizons are fused into one.[21] Another consequence is that
all understanding is productive. Constantly new thoughts are brought
to understanding. In other words, one cannot understand the original
intention of the author, for "if one understands at all one understands differently."[22] Truth, then is dialogically, historically and
linguistically conditioned.

---

[19] Hans-Georg GADAMER, Wahrheit, p. 286.

[20] Hans-Georg GADAMER, Wahrheit, p. 288.

[21] "In Wahrheit ist der Horizont der Gegenwart in steter Bildung
begriffen, sofern wir alle unsere Vorurteile ständig erproben müssen.
Zu solcher Erprobung gehört nicht zuletzt die Begegnung mit der
Vergangenheit und das Verstehen der Ueberlieferung, aus der wir
kommen. Der Horizont der Gegenwart bildet sich also gar nicht ohne die
Vergangenheit. Es gibt sowenig einen Gegenwartshorizont für sich, wie
es historische Horizonte gibt, die man zu gewinnen hätte. Vielmehr ist
Verstehen immer der Vorgang der Verschmelzung solcher vermeintlich für
sich seiender Horizonte." Hans-Georg GADAMER, Wahrheit, p. 289.

[22] "Der wirkliche Sinn eines Textes, wie er den Interpreten anspricht,
hängt eben nicht von dem Okkasionellen ab, das der Verfasser und sein
ursprüngliches Publikum darstellen. Er geht zum mindesten nicht darin
auf. Denn er ist immer auch durch die geschichtliche Situation des
Interpreten mitbestimmt und damit durch das Ganze des objektiven
Geschichtsganges... Nicht nur gelegentlich, sondern immer übertrifft
der Sinn eines Textes seinen Autor. Daher ist Verstehen kein nur
reproduktives, sondern stets auch ein produktives Verhalten... Es
genügt zu sagen, dass man **anders** versteht, **wenn man überhaupt
versteht.**" Hans-Georg GADAMER, Wahrheit, p. 280 (emphasis his).

From the argumentation that GADAMER has followed it is possible for him to compare understanding and the search for truth with an aesthetic experience in art. He illustrates this comparison with an analogy of the nature of a game.[23] What determines the character of a game is not, according to GADAMER, any rapturous feeling that it might produce, but the rules by which it is played. A person who plays a game well is totally wrapped up in it. By analogy a serious hermeneutic has to be completely involved in the rules of linguisticality.[24]

Since the nature of language and understanding is in constant development, GADAMER refuses to admit any objective criteria for truth. Furthermore, his hermeneutic preoccupation is one that mediates essentially between the past and the present. So the question arises, does not the temporal nature of human existence also call for an occupation with an anticipated future?

2.2.2. HABERMAS' Critical Comment

To incorporate an anticipated future into the framework of interpretation would have the advantage of allowing for a prophetic element in the search for understanding. Jürgen HABERMAS, prolific member of the Neo-marxist Frankfurt school of interpretation, has made a valid critique of GADAMER's work in this respect. However, it should be mentioned first that HABERMAS has incorporated much of GADAMER's ideas in his critical theory of communicative action. For the hermeneutic fusion of temporal horizons is a dialectic way of linguistically uniting pluralistic expression in the present with values of tradition. It is in fact an integral aspect of socialization.[25]

---

[23] Hans-Georg GADAMER, Wahrheit, p. 97-105.
[24] Incidently one has here another reason for relating an interpretation of religious narratives to their mythopoetic function, for the truth conveyed in myth takes the form of a play which involves the audience actively.

[25] Jürgen HABERMAS, Zur Logik der Sozialwissenschaften, 5th ed., Frankfurt, 1982, pp. 279 + 284.

More specifically, HABERMAS praises GADAMER for having shown
that hermeneutic understanding relates transcendentally to the
articulation of action-oriented self-understanding.[26] That means,
understanding resulting from the fusion of horizons does not only
produce insight for knowledge, but also insight for consensus and
communicative action as a result of the application of knowledge.[27]
Furthermore, it maintains communicative links with one's own tradition as well as that of others, since the fusion of horizons relati-
vizes, and at the same time relates one standpoint to another.

So far so good; however, HABERMAS criticises GADAMER for his
indiscriminating appraisal of the authority of tradition. Is not the
power of reflection which originates in the understanding of
tradition in turn able to question the same?[28] This element of
suspicion warns against an understanding of tradition that maintains
the **status quo** and is pleased to think in predefined circles. It is a
suspicion favouring emancipatory reflection that moves from the
claims of the past, in view of the claims of the present, to
anticipatory claims of the future. Finally, it is a suspicion that

---

[26] "Ich sehe Gadamers eigentliche Leistung in dem Nachweis, dass
hermeneutisches Verstehen transzendental notwendig auf die Artiku-
lierung eines handlungsorientierenden Selbstverständnisses bezogen
ist." Jürgen HABERMAS, Logik, p. 295.

[27] "Das hermeneutische Verstehen ist seiner Struktur nach darauf
angelegt, aus Tradition ein mögliches handlungsorientierendes Selbst-
verständnis sozialer Gruppen zu klären. Es ermöglicht eine Form des
Konsensus, von dem kommunikatives Handeln abhängt. Es bannt die
Gefahren des Kommunikationsabbruchs in beiden Richtungen: in der
Vertikalen der eigenen Ueberlieferung und in der Horizontalen der
Vermittlung zwischen Ueberlieferungen verschiedener Kulturen und
Gruppen." Jürgen HABERMAS, Logik, p. 298.

[28] "Gadamer verkennt die Kraft der Reflexion, die sich im Verstehen
entfaltet. Sie ist hier nicht länger vom Schein einer Absolutheit, die
durch Selbstbegründung eingelöst werden müsste, geblendet und macht
sich nicht vom Boden des Kontingenten, auf dem sie sich vorfindet,
los. Aber in dem sie die Genesis der Ueberlieferung, aus der die
Reflexion hervorgeht und auf die sie sich zurückbeugt, durchschaut,
wird die Dogmatik der Lebenspraxis erschüttert." Jürgen HABERMAS,
Logik, p. 303, cf also pp. 304 ff.

can be expressed in a moral imperative, that is, in action. It is this kind of practical reason that HABERMAS misses in GADAMER's theory.

Since a hermeneutic system cannot criticize itself, Jürgen HABERMAS' warning must be taken seriously.[29] It also appears to be a valid criticism that GADAMER is preoccupied with the past, and that linguisticality, if it governs our being in the world, calls mankind to commitment. But, GADAMER should, for the sake of fairness, have the last word. First, he has never said that he considers tradition to be a closed entity.[30] It is just the system that lends itself to considering it as such. Second, in placing his hermeneutic approach ontologically, GADAMER points to the universal canon of beauty which he sees closely related to the ethical domain.[31] That logically implies that the hermeneutic fusion of horizons is open to change, because it is possible to express linguistically (and hence prophetically[32]) that which appears to be true, good and beautiful.

In an answer to the criticism of HABERMAS, entitled On the Scope and Function of Hermeneutical Reflection,[33] GADAMER admits, however,

---

[29] For a theological appraisal of the new critical theory see E. SCHILLEBEECKX, Understanding, pp. 102-155.

[30] GADAMER's essay on the speculative structure of language (Wahrheit, pp. 432-449) poses a warning against all kinds of dogmaticisms. He also notices that the conscientious fusion of horizons makes tensions appear, and it does not gloss them over (p. 290).

[31] Cf. Hans-Georg GADAMER, Wahrheit, pp. 452-465.

[32] In view of chapter five it might be worth while to point out that GADAMER considers prophetic speech to be metaphorical.
"Auch wo der Dichter wie ein Seher geehrt wird, meint man damit nicht in seinem Gedicht eine wirkliche Prophetie zu erkennen, etwa in Hölderlins Singen von der Heimkehr der Götter. Vielmehr ist der Dichter ein Seher, weil er selbst darstellt, was ist, war und sein wird, und damit das, wovon er kündet, selber bezeugt. Es ist wahr, dass die dichterische Aussage etwas Zweideutiges an sich hat, genau wie die des Orakels. Aber eben darin liegt ihre hermeneutische Wahrheit. Wer darin eine ästhetische Unverbindlichkeit sieht, der existenzielle Ernst fehle, verkennt offenbar, wie fundamental für die hermeneutische Welterfahrung die Endlichkeit des Menschen ist. Es ist nicht die Schwäche, sondern die Stärke des Orakels, dass es zweideutig ist." Hans-Georg GADAMER, Wahrheit, pp. 462f.

[33] To be found in: Hans Georg GADAMER, Philosophical Hermeneutics,

that from a rhetorical point of view understanding comes to consciousness in a temporally uncritical way:

> ... the orator carries his listeners away with him; the con-
> vincing power of his arguments overwhelms the listener. While
> under the persuasive spell of speech, the listener for the
> moment cannot and ought not to indulge in critical exami-
> nation.[34]

But he maintains that understanding on a second level is reflective.
In view of the social sciences GADAMER then underlines the universal
nature of hermeneutics.

> Just as in rhetoric and hermeneutics so also in **sociological
> reflection** an emancipatory interest is at work that undertakes
> to free us of outer and inner social forces and compulsions
> simply by making us aware of them... I maintain that the
> hermeneutical problem is universal and basic for all interhuman
> experience, both of history and of the present moment,
> precisely because meaning can be experienced even where it is
> not actually intended.[35]

This means that for GADAMER the universal nature of hermeneutical
reflection does not only in negative terms uncover the tensions and
disruptions of society, but positively, it brings the social
community back to the bargaining table, back to a common area of
social understanding through which it exists.[36]

2.2.3. GADAMER's Specific Contribution for this Study

GADAMER's theory can contribute to the interpretation of religious testimonies and prophetic visions for the following reasons.
First, his hermeneutic approach begs for dialogue between the
religious and the secular horizon.[37] It challenges us to investigate

---

translated and edited by David E. LINGE, Berkeley, 1976, pp. 18-43.

[34] Hans-Georg GADAMER, Philosophical Hermeneutics, p. 23.

[35] Hans-Georg GADAMER, Philosophical Hermeneutics, p. 30.

[36] Hans-Georg GADAMER, Philosophical Hermeneutics, p. 42.

[37] For GADAMER a fusion of horizons relates to the attempt to overcome
an historical horizon with its prejudices for the benefit of a new
comprehension; it is historical consciousness at work from a diachronic point of view. My specific application of that notion focuses
on a creative act of bringing two linguistic worlds (the religious and

whether a fusion of these horizons is possible in spite of the different language games used. Second, in worship a fusion of horizons would have to be twofold. For the religious person and/or community it could lead to a disclosure of grace in the context of human finitude, and therefore to practical commitment in view of this tension. For the secular person it could also lead to an experience of grace if the secular concerns are re-valued in the light of the transcendent. As regards worship, one could therefore re-examine what can be said about the hermeneutic role of the Holy Spirit in the community of faith, and the feasibility of poetic language to express existential concern.

2.3. Toward a Hermeneutics of Narrative

There seems to be a general consensus about the value of narrative in a religious context. Theologians are aware of the central role it has played in Judaism and Christianity. There is also agreement that theological discourse must at one point or another relate to the events (past, present and future) in the community of faith if it does not want to withdraw into an unsocial existential expression of God-talk.[38] Linguists on the other hand have pointed out that religious langugage (narrative and liturgical in particular) displays a variety of different linguistic operations. This implies that the communication of faith cannot simply be practiced in a chain of constative statements or propositional speech acts.[39] Rather, as the exposition of RAMSEY's disclosure theory has shown, religious language including theological propositions are at one point or

---

the secular), with the concerns they express, into productive dialogue; the fusion aims for a moral consciousness at work and is more synchronic in character.

[38] See Paul RICOEUR, De moeilijke weg, p. 80; and the remarks of Edward SCHILLEBEECKX, in chapter one (1.2.2.).

[39] For a short survey of the contributions by John L. AUSTIN, Charles W. MORRIS and John R. SEARLE, see Jean LADRIERE, Performativity, pp. 50-62.

another evocative. The state of affairs does, however, render a hermeneutical approach to narrative more difficult. This section shall therefore attempt to clarifiy some problems, and indicate a viable approach for the interpretation of narrative speech.

2.3.1. Structure, Word, Event

If one speaks about narrative, the association with structuralism, the science of synchronically investigated language models, is quickly made. No doubt, a structural analysis of a given text is important for exegesis. In order to be successful such an exegesis must recognize that,

> The fundamental postulate of structuralism is that the matter discussed and the subjects speaking are bracketed off from one another. There is therefore a sharp distinction between language as an institution ('language,' **la langue, die Sprache**) and language as a linguistic and verbal event ('speech,' 'talk' or 'discourse'; **la parole, le discours; die Rede**).[40]

This distinction is very important for the interpretation of narratives; in his article Structure, Word, Event,[41] Paul RICOEUR gives reasons why.

First, RICOEUR draws attention to the presuppositions of structuralism that have been germinated by Ferdinand DE SAUSSURE.[42] In the

---

[40] Edward SCHILLEBEECKX, Understanding, p. 23.

[41] Paul RICOEUR, Structure, Word, Event, in The Conflict of Interpretations. Essays in Hermeneutics, Don IHDE (ed.), Evanston, 1974, pp. 79-96. French edition: La structure, le mot, l'événement, in Le conflit des interprétations. Essais d' herméneutique, Paris, 1969, pp. 80-97.

[42] Although F. DE SAUSSURE did not use the term "structure," the five presuppositions can be presented in terms of opposites where structuralism represents the "fixed" pole, and the word as event is typified by the "open" pole. This was first done by Louis HJELMSLEV in his Prolegomena to a Theory of Language, Madison, 1961. (Originally published in 1943)

fixed	open
language (**langue**)	speech (**parole**)
synchronic	diachronic
form	substance
closed entity of	polysemic, open to change
internal dependencies	
signifying expression	signified content

end the analysis boils down to the fact that the structural point of view, confined to its systems, is globally opposed to the genetic point of view which is characteristic for the act of speaking. As far as narrative is concerned one can, therefore, distinguish between closed narratives, e.g. a miracle story fixed by the text in the New Testament, and open narratives, e.g. a liturgically celebrated narrative (discourse) exposed to the contingencies of life in the worshipping community.

According to RICOEUR these two opposites stand in a dialectical relationship to each other. Recent post-structuralist studies have revealed that the gap between the two poles can be bridged. With the help of Noam CHOMSKY and G. GUILLAUME, RICOEUR suggests that the nature of the word functions as a bridge builder, "a trader between the system and the act, between the structure and the event."[43] For the word is both more and less than the sentence. This is due to the polysemic character of the word. On the one hand, a word may have more than one meaning in a given sentence or in a given moment, but the actuality of meaning will still be subject to the sentence. On the other hand, there is also a history of usage which brings new meanings to a word. In this sense the word goes beyond the limits of the sentence and participates in temporality. The word, therefore, ties together structure and event, the synchronic and diachronic aspect, into what is called the panchronic order.[44] But when does this panchronic order manifest itself? RICOEUR says it happens when language is liberated to realize multiple meanings at the same time. Such a liberating function is easily recognized in symbolic and poetic language. In other words, whenever language or speech is evocative it is also in celebration (en fête).[45] This ontological

---

Cf. Paul RICOEUR, Structure, pp. 81-83, relying on HJELMSLEV.

[43] Paul RICOEUR, Structure, p. 92. French edition, p. 93.

[44] Paul RICOEUR, Structure, p. 94. French edition, p. 94.

[45] "More than one interpretation is then justified by a structure of a discourse which permits multiple dimensions of meaning to be realized at the same time...
Thus the exchanges between structure and event, between system and act, do not cease to be complicated and renewed. It is clear that

aspect of language, which has been constantly refined since its
initial formulation by Martin HEIDEGGER, deserves careful attention
in the discussion of the meaning and function of religious language
in the context of worship, because it points to the production of
insight.

By means of a summary it may be said that first, language as
structure and language as event must be distinguished. Second, there
is a mutually reinforcing dialectic between these aspects in the
nature of the word. And lastly, this dynamic is set free when
language transcends a given meaning in order to describe a new
reality.[46] This setting free of language happens in an exemplary way
on the level of discourse, that is, of saying. Saying is the
"opening-out" (**aperture**) of language, and finds its strongest expression in the "language in celebration,"[47] examples of which could
be poems, dreams, testimonies and myths. But this poses its own
problematic, namely that of orality.

2.3.2. Orality and Experience

In general, discussions, articles and books on the theme of narrative in theology have omitted to distinguish between the spoken and
the written word. This is understandable in view of the "devo-
calization of the world," which already became evident in the
eighteenth century, the age of the encyclopedias.[48] At present,
however, a re-evaluation of orality is taking place in such diverse

---

the installation of one or several isotopies is the work of sequences
much longer than the sentence and that it would be necessary, to
pursue this analysis, to change once more the level of reference, to
consider the **linking of a text**: dream, poem, or myth. It is at this
level that I would again encounter my problem of hermeneutics. But it
is in the complex unit of the word, it seems to me, that everything is
played out." Paul RICOEUR, Structure, pp. 94f. (emphasis his); French
edition, p. 95.

[46] Paul RICOEUR, Poetische Fiktion, pp. 98f.

[48] Walter J. ONG, The Presence of the Word. Some Prolegomena for
Cultural and Religious History, New Haven, 1967, pp. 65f., 69f. etc.

fields as biblical form criticism, cultural anthropology and mass
media communication. Not surprisingly the motivating reasons are
manifold. Only a few shall be mentioned here.

First of all, there are the psychodynamics of orality. In Old
Testament studies, for instance, much has been written about the
sounded word (**dabar**) as power and action. It is also being argued
that the structure of memory and consciousness are different in an
oral as opposed to a written context.[49] In addition, it is claimed
that sound is received psychologically in a different way than
vision.[50]

Ideologically oriented arguments point out that written language
fosters an illusion of the permanence of words.[51] Such an illusion
results in a fundamentalism of a highly literate society. A narrative
is no longer understood as a set of relationships (between speaker
and hearer, past and present, actors and participants, etc.) that
find a resonance, but as a text that presents a surface.

> Those cultures which retain strong ties to their oral sources
> recognize that, despite the advantages of writing for record
> keeping, written language is particularly lifeless when com-
> pared to its spoken counterpart. Writing lacks **pneuma**, the
> breath, the spirit of speech.[52]

---

[49] Walter J. ONG, Orality and Literacy. The Technologizing of the
Word, London, 1982, pp. 31-115.

[50] Walter J. ONG provides several criteria of which only the most
relevant will be mentioned in terms of oral narrative in the language
of worship.
  1) Sound is more real or existential than other sense objects
despite the fact that it is also more evanescent.
  2) Sound is a special sensory key to interiority.
  3) Sound unites groups of living beings as nothing else does.
  4) Sound situates man in the middle of actuality and simul-
taneity, whereas vision situates man in front of things and in
sequentiality. Walter J. ONG, Presence, pp. 111-138.

[51] Michael E. WILLIAMS, Story as Oral Experience, in Explor 5 (1979),
p. 5.

[52] Michael E. WILLIAMS, Oral Experience, p. 4. An example of the
spirit of speech is the rabbinic myth of the Oral Torah in Judaism,
which says that Moses, when he had his disclosure of God on Mount
Sinai, received a double revelation. One which is the Torah in
writing, the other which is the law handed orally from master to
disciple. It is argued by Jacob NEUSNER that it is this oral element

Orality means to "tell a story," not to speak **about** it. This is also
Gerhard LOHFINK's opinion. He says in a somewhat paranetic voice,
that the reason for the use of narrative is not the assumption that
simple people are incapable of thinking in abstract ways, but the
fact that narrative "presentifies." The lack of presentification is,
for example, evident in the liturgical **reading** of salvation history.
It is no longer the subject of the community's own experience.[53]

A triadic relationship between orality, experience and narrative
has already surfaced several times. Gerhard VON RAD, Eduard SCHWEIZER
and Edward SCHILLEBEECKX have in their own way pointed to this
relationship. This is also the claim of Walter J. ONG:

> **Narrative** is everywhere a major genre of **verbal** art, occuring
> all the way from primary oral cultures into high literacy and
> electronic information processing... Behind proverbs and apho-
> risms and philosophical speculation and religious ritual lies
> the memory of human **experience** strung out in time and subject
> to narrative treatment.[54]

An article on the narrative quality of experience was written by
Stephen CRITES[55] and found wide recognition. He argues from a
phenomenological point of view that the formal quality of experience,
consciousness and recollection is inherently narrative. And furthermore, he asserts that a sense of personal identity within temporality
is bound to be narrative.[56] That is why someone who experiences a
conversion has a "dramatically" new story to tell. This radical
aspect emerges out of the tension existing between the past re-

---

which kept the Talmudic tradition alive and relevant to the present
day. Jacob NEUSNER, Invitation to the Talmud, New York, 1973, p. 7.

[53] "Indem erzählt wird, was Jesus damals tat, wird das Vergangene
Gegenwart, wird das Wort Sakrament... Wenn wir ehrlich sind, müssen
wir allerdings zugeben, dass das Erzählen im Gottesdienst eigentlich
schon verstummt ist. Die Heilsgeschichte wird nicht mehr erzählt
sondern **verlesen.** Unsere eigenen Erfahrungen werden nicht mehr in die
Erzählung eingebracht." Gerhard LOHFINK, Erzählung, p. 531 (emphasis
his).

[54] Walter J. ONG, Orality, pp. 139f. (emphasis added).

[55] Stephen CRITES, The Narrative Quality of Experience, in Journal of
the American Academy of Religion 39 (1971), pp. 291-311.

[56] Stephen CRITES, Quality of Experience, pp. 302f.

membered and the future anticipated.[57] There is the present **and more**
as Ian T. RAMSEY would argue. But is this moment of subjective
transcendence not too vague to be meaningful to the interpreting
community as a whole?

Eberhard JUENGEL provides a qualifier to that thought-model
which leads to a surprising realization, namely that the "humanity"
(**Menschlichkeit**) of God, that is the objective transcendence, reaches
man in the very same way as does its subjective counterpart. If the
incarnation of God is to be a reality, then the word of God must be
born in temporality as well. Such primordial language is genuinely
narrative.[58] The tension between past remembered and future anticipated which is wrapped in narrative language has now revealed
itself to be at the very center of the christian faith, since God's
"humanity" in Jesus, in order to correspond to human language, must
constantly be re-told. Due to the power of the Holy Spirit the story
of Christ is an event that remains open to the future and is not
confined to the past.[59] According to JUENGEL it is this dialectic,
which by implication is fundamentally oral, that brings reality to
language. Narrative emerges from "**geschehene Geschichte**" and makes
headway as "**geschehende Geschichte**."[60] But how is this **Geschichte** to

---

[57] Stepheh CRITES, Quality of Experience, p. 303.
    A similar conclusion is also suggested by Sam D. GILL in view of
the function of oral traditions:
    "...we may see the processes of oral traditions more clearly as
reapplication and renewal of the forms whose historical roots may be
ancient. In the recitation of the stories, the experiences of concrete
time, of history, are digested so that the sanctioning description of
reality in the oral traditions corresponds with and interprets the
lived experience of reality." Sam D. GILL, Beyond "The Primitive." The
Religions of Nonliterate People, Englewood Cliffs, 1982, p. 62.

[58] "Die der Menschlichkeit Gottes entsprechende Sprache muss also in
ihrer **sprachlichen** Struktur zuhöchst **temporal** orientiert sein. Dies
ist aber der Fall im sprachlichen Modus des **Erzählens**, der... wegen
seiner Sprachlichkeit und Zeitlichkeit genuin vereinenden inneren
Ordnung, neben Interjektion und Evokation am ehesten als "ursprüng-
liche Sprache" verstanden werden kann." Eberhard JUENGEL, Entsprechungen, p. 413 (emphasis his).

[59] Eberhard JUENGEL, Entsprechungen, p. 415.

[60] Eberhard JUENGEL, Entsprechungen, p. 418.

be understood, as fictional story or as realistic history? It is with
this question that Paul RICOEUR's hermeneutics of narrative are again
resumed.

2.3.3. The Narrative Function

RICOEUR's aim is to sketch a general theory of narrative
discourse in which the "form of life" peculiar to narrative is exposed.[61] He proceeds in a twofold way. First, he evaluates narrative
on the level of sense; that is, he investigates whether history and
fiction have a common structure. Second, he asks whether history and
fiction, on the level of reference, relate to the same reality. Both
aspects call for explanation.

The structural unity of historical and fictional narratives is
derived from the recognition that both genres contain the concept of
plot.[62] Each event, no matter if it is in a story or an historical
account is inevitably more than a singular occurence. It contributes
to the development of a scenario. In a story situations change and
give rise to a new predicament, which in turn evoke a response or a
reaction. The conclusion of a story is usually not predictable
because of the many contingencies involved. But a narrative conclusion aims at being acceptable in spite of the contingencies.
Similarly, "history is a species of the genus story... history is
about some major achievement or failure of men living and working
together...," says RICOEUR quoting W.B. GALLIE.[63] Historical explanations are a means to promote the plot, not by pretending to be
conclusive, but by providing an acceptable point of view to help the
reader follow along. Relying on Louis O. MINK, RICOEUR states that,

---

[61] Paul RICOEUR, The Narrative Function, in Hermeneutics and the Human
Sciences, J. B. THOMPSON (ed.), Cambridge, 1981, pp. 274-296. First
published in French as: La fonction narrative, in Etudes théologiques
et religieuses 54 (1979), pp.209-230.

[62] Paul RICOEUR, Narrative Function, pp. 277-280; also Walter J. ONG,
Orality, pp. 141-151.

[63] Paul RICOEUR, Narrative Function, p. 277, quoting W.B. GALLIE,
Philosophy and Historical Understanding, New York, 1964, p. 66.

"To narrate and to follow a story is already to 'reflect upon' events with the aim of encompassing them in successive totalities."[64] In other words, the narrator as well as the "histor" are bound to have a narrative point of view. Although it might be different in the respective cases, this point of view is their common structural denominator.

The referential unity between narrative and history is already suggested by linguistic data; is it a coincidence that the term history reveals an ambiguity in most European languages (**Geschichte, histoire, storia, historia** etc.)? RICOEUR concludes,

> Our languages most probably preserve... a certain mutual belonging between the act of narrating (or writing) history and the fact of being in history, between **doing** history and **being** historical. In other words, **the form of life to which narrative discourse belongs is our historical condition itself.**[65]

As a result the formerly radically distinct types of discourse, the true and the fictional narrative, begin to fall together in what can be called the language of historicity, that is, "We belong to history before telling stories or writing history."[66] Another linguistic paradox underlining the proximity between historical and narrative production appears in the French phrase **inventer des documents.** The phrase points with its double meaning to the historical task of taking an inventory of documents, and at the same time it can be understood as a narrative invention. For the science of history this implies that there is more "fiction" in history than the positivist would like to admit. History in its own way is also a literary "artefact." The phrase of L. RANKE **"wie es eigentlich geschehen ist"** with its emphasis on "as" and "actually" does point a creative act, without denying that at the same time it intends to be a representation of reality.[67] For narrative fiction the consequence is

---

[64] Paul RICOEUR, Narrative Function, p. 279, drawing from Louis O. MINK, History and Fiction as Modes of Comprehension, in New Directions in Literary History, R. COHEN (ed.), Baltimore, 1974, p. 117.

[65] Paul RICOEUR, Narrative Function, p. 288 (emphasis his).

[66] Paul RICOEUR, Narrative Function, p. 294.

[67] Paul RICOEUR, Narrative Function, pp. 289-291. RICOEUR substantiates his argument by discussing "imaginative reconstruction"

that it is largely mimetic, an imitation of human action, a vision of
the world, a metaphor of reality. "... by its mimetic intention, **the
world of fiction leads us to the heart of real world action.**"[68] The
phenomenologically relevant conclusion can be subsumed as follows,

> It is only insofar as each narrative mode shares in some way
> the intentionality of the other that their references can
> cross upon historicity; and it is in the exchange between
> history and fiction, between their opposed referential modes,
> that **our historicity is brought to language.**[69]

A theological conclusion would emphasize that this "cross-fertili-

zation" of these two modes of narrative has been with Judeo-Christian

culture from the very beginning, as is clearly evident form the com-

pilation of the Old Testament. Furthermore, the place where these

cross references manifest themselves is certainly, although not

exclusively, the christian community at worship.[70]

One misunderstanding should, however, be avoided. Notwith-

standing the fact that historicity can rightly be regarded as the

common denominator of narratives, it does not follow that all nar-

---

and "explanation by emplotment." Paul RICOEUR's Temps et récit, Paris,
Vol. I-III, 1983-1985, is to a large extent dedicated to the relationship between historical and fictional truth. See especially Vol. III,
pp. 264-278, where he discusses a phenomenological commensurability
in the production and reception of "invented narratives." There
RICOEUR also discusses RANKE's statement (p.270). ONG makes the
valuable observation that oral cultures tell history with the aid of
oral memory and the "story line." The distinction between truth and
fiction is insignificant for those cultures. He also points out that
the narrative plot they employ is quite different from the one western
cultures take for granted, since the appearance of stereotyped
detective stories in the nineteenth century. Walter J. ONG, Orality,
pp. 141-151.

[68] Paul RICOEUR, Narrative Function, p. 296 (emphasis his).

[69] Paul RICOEUR, Narrative Function, p. 294 (emphasis his).

[70] This is also Joachim TRACK's emphasis in the conclusion of his
Sprachkritische Untersuchungen zum christlichen Reden von Gott,
Göttingen, 1977, pp. 321-328, although he does not treat a dialectic
between history and story, but follows Eberhard JUENGEL and the
distinction between **mythos** and **logos**.

ratives are equal. One could, of course, distinguish between story, epic, drama, history, novel and so forth, but Stephen CRITES has suggested a more far-reaching distinction, namely between sacred and mundane stories.[71] Such a distinction is theologically meaningful for the following reason. The sacred stories, it is argued, reach deeper than that which can be expressed by simply telling them. They are re-enacted, celebrated and symbolically expressed. They are called sacred "because man's sense of self and world is created through them."[72] The mundane stories, on the other hand, are told, that is they can clearly be articulated and have a mundane setting. One could say that they do not necessitate a fusion with a transcendent horizon, but the word mundane here is not used in a derogatory sense. RICOEUR sheds light on this distinction. The sacred stories are not sacred because of their language, but because of their **function**. These stories build a tradition, they have authority and evoke a cultic situation. In other words, they are mythical. The mundane stories have no institutional authority. Being bound to a certain **mundus,** they can be considered to be closed stories.[73] Their function is to articulate the sense of the world from which they were drawn, but their ability to reflect this world is always limited to an immanent horizon.

As it has been indicated in relation to history and story, so it can also be affirmed that the tracks of sacred and mundane stories may very well cross. This is possible according to CRITES, because of

---

[71] Stephen CRITES, Quality of Experience, pp. 294-297.

[72] Stephen CRITES, Quality of Experience, p. 295.

[73] Paul RICOEUR, De moeielijke weg, p. 87.

the mediating form of the experiencing consciousness.[74] Such a
partial overlapping may cause hermeneutical difficulties, but it
safeguards religious language from becoming meaningless, and everyday
language from utter profanity.

2.3.4. Narrative and the Idea of Revelation

In the preceding pages the religious notion of narrative has
constantly been widened. Religious narrative is more than a story, it
reaches beyond the categories of the factual and the fictitious. It
is not confined to predetermined functions.[75] In its appeal to the
intellectus and experience it speaks to man and his world, but it
also transcends the same. This widening of narrative needs to be
pursued even further. That is, if this kind of narrative has its
raison d'être in worship it has also to be placed in relation to the
idea of revelation. Paul RICOEUR sees in a hermeneutic of revelation
a twofold movement: first, the expression of revelation, second, the
response to it. The topic shall be discussed in this order.

2.3.4.1. The Expression of Revelation

When RICOEUR talks about revelation he understands it in its
most original way. It is revelation on the level of the discourse or
confession of faith, where the **lex credendi** is not separated from the

---

[74] Stephen CRITES, Quality of Experience, p. 297.

[75] Although the aim of narrative is to evoke, the effects of
evocations are not predictable.

lex orandi.[76] The consequences of such an approach are at hand. First, revelation on the level of the discourse of faith is revelation as it is encountered by the common believer. It is not the result of the speculative discourse of a philosopher. Therefore the study of revelation in our context concentrates on a variety of expressions of faith. This makes a second consequence discernible. Revelation on the level of the discourse of faith will inevitably be pluralistic. Revelation is not monolithic. It is not mechanically deductive from a "paper pope", nor is it simply produced behind a "bastion of a magisterium."[77] A pluralistic understanding of revelation does on the other hand not imply that it is without criteria and inner coherence. A third consequence implied in revelation is its polysemic character. That means, "A hermeneutic of revelation must give priority to those modalities of discourse that are most originary within the language of a community of faithful..."[78] These modalities of discourse, the different linguistic genres, are as diverse as narration, prophecy, prescriptive discourse, wisdom sayings and hymnic discourse.

The exposition of each of these modalities belongs to another place. What can be said here is that these forms are not to be perceived as abstract literary genres, but as genres that mutually

---

[76] Paul RICOEUR, Toward a Hermeneutic of the Idea of Revelation, in Lewis S. MUDGE (ed.), Essays on Biblical Interpretation, Philadelphia, 1980, pp. 73-118; first published in Harvard Theological Review 70 (1977).

[77] This is not intended to be polemic, but the reverie of fixed revelation should be avoided. Otherwise revelation is static. It would manifest the same limitations as a fixed narrative mentioned in section 2.3.1.

[78] Paul RICOEUR, Revelation, p. 90.

penetrate each other. The understanding of history can, for example, be prophetic on one occasion and narrative (in a strict sense) on another, or both simultaneously. The legislative texts of the Old Testament manifest their concrete meaning within the narrative framework of the sojourn at Sinai under the symbol of the covenant. Wisdom sayings, as a poetic description of the dramatic tensions of human existence under the presence of God, rejoin the prophetic spirit. The hymnic discourse elevates the story in celebration and turns it into invocation.[79]

Although these genres are of theological interest in their distinctiveness, there seems to be an overarching function which makes a hermeneutic of revelation more approachable. RICOEUR first points to the nonviolent appeal of biblical revelation. It is not dominated by knowledge. Its intention is not to verify truth, but it wants to show, to manifest it. He therefore calls the overarching function Poetics.[80] This function cannot be called narrative in the strict sense, but in light of RICOEUR's further specifications, and considering the clarifications on narrative above, it can be argued that this revelatory function can be called narrative in a large sense (i.e. not limited to a literary genre). Poetics according to RICOEUR is the conjunction and redescription, of **mythos** and **mimesis**.[81] This conjunction is analogical to his description of the narrative function, namely the conjunction between emplotment and metaphorical

---

[79] Paul RICOEUR, Revelation, p. 75-91.

[80] Paul RICOEUR, Revelation, pp. 93, 95, 99, 102. He capitalizes Poetics, since he relates it to Aristotle's work with the same name.

[81] Paul RICOEUR, Revelation, p. 102f.; cf. also 2.3.6. below.

reality.[82] The overlap between poetics and narrative directs attention to the second part of RICOEUR's work on revelation. What has emerged is the exposition of the response to revelation.

2.3.4.2. The Response to Revelation

The response to revelation takes place in the context of worship. It is to a large extent the celebration of sacred stories.[83] Revelation in worship, then, can be described as a dialectic between incarnated narration and manifestation, between the word of God and the world that the Bible portrays as the new creation, the new covenant, the kingdom of God. The mediator in this dialectic, between

---

[82] For some people the phrase "metaphorical reality" might appear to be infelicitous, since a metaphor seems to imply an unrealistic **nexus**. It is true that a metaphor like, "Mother Theresa is a dove" does not make sense as a phrase taken literally, but on the other hand it **does** make a claim as a direct comparison within a given context. Therefore, it does also deserve a positive reading in terms of what is said to be. In this a metaphor is different from a simile (and in its extended form in allegory) such as, "The Glory of the Lord was like a devouring fire" where the reference is limited to an expressed analogy. More problematic is a possible confusion between metaphor and metonymy. A metonymy like, "Jerusalem is mourning" is a statement functioning as a substitute, i.e. the population of Jerusalem is mourning. The metaphor represents a paradoxical category mistake (in religious language usually between the transcendent and the immanent), and "shows" a relation by resemblance. The metonymy, on the other hand, is a substitution within the same category; it points to a relation of correspondence. Cf. Paul RICOEUR, Rule, pp. 55-59. Obviously a hermeneutic difficulty would arise if a secular person would say "God is love" and understand this statement not as a transposition of category, but as a metonymy, i.e. "The inclination for the good in mankind is love."

[83] "... het opnieuw opvoeren van die verhalen in de eredienst, en het opnieuw vertellen ervan in lof-, klaag- en boetpsalemen voegt een laatste element toe aan het ingewikkelde weefsel van verhalende en niet verhalende taalspelen. Die hele reeks stijl- en taalvormen is dus te beschouwen als complex geheel, dat zich bevindt tussen de twee polen van verhalen vertellen en lofprijzing." Paul RICOEUR, De moeilijke weg, p. 89.

the already and the not yet, between revelation and historical contingency, is testimony. It provides a horizon for a specifically
religious and biblical experience of revelation.[84] Without being
pretentious or domineering it presents revelation as a nonviolent
appeal.

2.3.5. Hermeneutics of Testimony

The notion of testimony or witness has played an important role
in Judeo-Christian tradition. As examples one could cite the period
of the Macabbees and, of course, primitive Christianity as it is
reflected in the writings of John and Luke. Sometimes a theology of
testimony was incorporated in autobiographical works, for instance in
the Confessions of St.Augustine. Contemporary theologians usually
place the value of testimony in the context of the community of
interpretation. Not many have, however, attempted to elaborate a
hermeneutics of testimony. A fruitful approach has been suggested by
Paul RICOEUR under the inspiration of Jean NABERT.

2.3.5.1. Semantics of Testimony

The problem consists of the question whether a hermeneutic of
the absolute can be correlated with the hermeneutics of testimony,
whether an experience of the absolute can be joined to the idea of

---

[84] Paul RICOEUR, Revelation, p. 117.

the absolute. A definition of testimony shall be given at the beginning of the treatment of this topic in order to facilitate its
development.

> The term testimony should be applied to works, words, actions,
> and to lives which attest to an intention, an inspiration, an
> idea at the heart of experience and history which nontheless
> transcends experience and history.[85]

Testimony, for RICOEUR, is understood as a discourse in which event
and meaning are fused by means of a symbolic tradition. This symbolic
tradition mediates a relation between meaning and event, and thus
manifests an interpretation. Lewis MUDGE is emphatic that this
triadic formation is important in any hermeneutics of testimony and
especially in biblical and christian discourse.[86] The reason for this
will be clear when the semantic and biblical aspects of testimony
have been elucidated.

The semantics of the word "testimony" can be recognized by
classifying the meaningful contexts in which the expression is
employed. First, there is a quasi-empirical meaning attached to it.
The one who testifies reports an event; he gives a narration. Those
who hear the witness must decide whether or not they can believe in
the reality of the facts told. For the witness it is not enough to
state what he has "seen," he must also give account of its truthfulness.[87] As such, testimony is therefore always at the service of
judgment.

2.3.5.2. The Trial of Testimony

The idea of accountability leads to the second contextual
meaning. The circumstances in which a testimony is given or listened
to evoke the situation of trial. This trial is characterized by a

---

[85] Paul RICOEUR, The Hermeneutics of Testimony, in Essays on Biblical
Interpretations, 119-154, pp. 112f.

[86] Lewis S. MUDGE, Paul Ricoeur on Biblical Interpretation, in Essays,
pp. 18f.

[87] Paul RICOEUR, Testimony, pp. 123f.

party dispute; the pleading for one opinion against another is a
phenomenon of most human situations. "We cannot claim to have
certainty but only probability," writes RICOEUR, "and the probable is
only pursued through a struggle of opinion."[88] The trial does not
necessarily debunk the testimony. It may also enhance its value by
acclamation.

Consequently, the trial is also characterized by a decision of
justice. At stake is the veracity of the testimony. The possibility
of invalidating or defeating it is, consequently, essential to a
hermeneutics of testimony. RICOEUR develops this idea with the help
of insights drawn from HART's concepts of ascription.

> With the term ascription, built on the model of **description**,
> Hart focuses on a remarkable character of juridical state-
> ments: they can be contested either by denying alleged facts
> or by invoking circumstances which can weaken, alternate, even[89]
> annul the claim of a right or the accusation of a crime.

The invocation of circumstances which can weaken, alternate or even
annul a claim appears significant in a religious context as well. In
effect, it has the same intentions as RAMSEY's multi-model discourse,
namely as part of the test of empirical fit.

The trial as a party dispute characterized by a decision of
justice naturally also makes use of persuasion to the probable. The
testimony receives an exterior dimension through the judgment of its
hearers. Similarly, Karl RAHNER considers this exterior dimension as
a dynamic tension in the collective finding of the truth.[90] Being

---

[88] Paul RICOEUR, Testimony, p. 125.

[89] Paul RICOEUR, Testimony, p. 126, quoting HART, The Ascription of
Responsibility and Rights, in Proceedings of the Aristotelian Society
49 (1948-49), emphasis his.

[90] Presupposed are a) a certain amount of shared convictions, and b)
that the collective finding of truth has its media in language.
"Sind die zwei ersten Ueberlegungen richtig, die eben angedeutet
wurden, dann kann die kollektive Wahrheitsfindung nur eigentlich und
im letzten Grunde darin bestehen, dass man sich in diesem Gespräch
bemüht, die Gemeinsamkeit, die man voraussetzt, so wie sie im anderen
gegeben ist, als die eigene zu erkennen und, so wie sie in einem

fundamentally open to the future, it functions as a sacrament of initiation to the unutterable mystery.[91] Although RAHNER does not speak explicitly about the function of testimony, he nevertheless calls upon the same convictions elaborated in RICOEUR's concept of testimony in trial; the notion of transcendence and the use of language to evoke disclosures. For RAHNER the collective finding of truth avoids both the pitfalls of lifeless and abstracted formulations and the danger of subjectivism.[92] The danger of subjectivism eventually leads to un-truth, a problem that RICOEUR treats under the notion of false testimony, which constitutes the thrid contextual meaning in the semantics of testimony.

2.3.5.3. True and False Testimony

False testimony does not refer to an error in the account of the things seen, it is a lie in the heart of the witness. On a superficial level false testimony can reveal itself in various ways. For instance, it exposes itself when the witness is deliberately shaping the narrative by his own perspective of things, resulting in a loss at the cost of credibility in the minds of the interpreting community.[93] False testimony may also be the desire to tell an

---

selbst gegeben ist und im Gespräch vor das eigene Bewusstsein und den anderen gebraucht wird, den anderen als die seine erkennen zu lassen. Das Gespräch setzt also Einheit voraus und sucht sie und lebt in echter Spannung zwischen beiden." Karl RAHNER, Kleines Fragment "Ueber die kollektive Findung der Wahrheit" in Schriften zur Theologie, Bd. 6, Einsiedeln, 1965, p. 106.

[91] Karl RAHNER, Kleines Fragment, p. 108.

[92] Karl RAHNER, Kleines Fragment, p. 110.

integrated story no matter what the cost, even if it implies the
manipulation of parts of the testimony relevant to one's own life or
vision.[94] A final example would be the parroting of someone else's
story.

On a more fundamental level false testimony meets the test of
conviction. If the witness is willing to pay the price of life then
his name changes into martyr. Testimony now receives an interior
aspect. It is identification with a (hopefully) just cause.

> This engagement, this risk assumed by the witness, reflects on
> testimony itself, which, in turn, signifies something other
> than simple narration of things seen. Testimony is also the
> engagement of a pure heart and an engagement to the death. It
> belongs to the tragic destiny of truth... Testimony is the
> action itself as it attests outside of himself, to the
> interior man, to his conviction, to his faith... It is this
> engagement that marks the difference between the false witness
> and the faithful and true witness.[95]

For the Christian it is evident who symbolizes this total commitment,
this faithful and true witness. It is in Jesus Christ that the symbolic tradition, which mediates between meaning and event in the
hermeneutics of testimony, finds its focus.

2.3.5.4. RICOEUR's Theory Biblically Placed

It is equally obvious that the discussion no longer evolves
around a merely semantic understanding of testimony. There is an
irruption of the prophetic and kerygmatic dimension that qualifies
the religious meaning of testimony. "What separates this new meaning
of testimony from all its uses in ordinary language is that the

---

[93] Michael GOLDBERG, Theology and Narrative, p. 99.

[94] Michael GOLDBERG, Theology and Narrative, p. 104; also Gerhard
SAUTER, Wie kann Theologie aus Erfahrung entstehen? in Theologie im
Entstehen. Theologische Bücherei 59, Lukas VISCHER (ed.), München,
1976, pp. 99, 118. The theme of self-deception will again be taken up
in sections 3.3.2.2. and 4.2.2.

[95] Paul RICOEUR, Testimony, p. 129f.

testimony does not belong to the witness. It proceeds from an absolute initiative as to its origin and content."[96] Analysing the prophetic meaning with a text of Isaiah[97] RICOEUR sees a fourfold
irruption. First, the witness is one who is sent in order to testify.
That implies that the testimony comes from somwhere else. Secondly,
the testimony is not about something peripheral; it refers to the
global meaning of experience. Thirdly, testimony is oriented toward
proclamation. And finally, the testimony is not only an act of
speech, but it implies action and the sacrifice of life.[98] In the
biblical sense testimony emerges from the union of a certain narrative kernel (event) with the confession of faith (meaning), and there
is again a situation of trial as has been described above. The
witness of the absolute is also a witness of historic signs, the
confessor of the absolute meaning is also a narrator of the acts of
deliverance.[99] This prophetic meaning of testimony introduces also
the New Testament meaning of the word.

In the writings of Luke the strong unity between the confessional pole and the narrative pole is still evident.

> Primitive Christianity never perceived any fundamental dif-
> ference between the eyewitness testimony of the life of Jesus
> and the encounter with the resurrection Lord... The profound

---

[96] Paul RICOEUR, Testimony, p. 131.

[97] Isaiah 43:8-13 (Revised Standard Version). Bring forth the people
who are blind, yet have eyes, who are deaf, yet have ears! Let the
nations gather together, and let all the peoples assemble. Who among
them can declare this, and show us the former things? Let them bring
their witnesses to justify them, and let them hear and say, It is
true. "You are my witnesses," says the LORD, "and my servant whom I
have chosen, that you may know and believe me and understand that I am
He. Before me no god was formed, nor shall there be any after me. I, I
am the LORD and besides me there is no saviour. I declared and saved
and proclaimed, when there was no strange god among you; and you are
my witnesses," says the LORD. "I am God, and also henceforth I am He;
there is none who can deliver from my hand; I work and who can hinder
it?" Cf. also Isaiah 44:6-8.

[98] Paul RICOEUR, Testimony, p. 131.

[99] Paul RICOEUR, Testimony, p. 134.

unity between testimony about facts and events, and the testimony about meaning and truth has survived for some time.[100]
A change in emphasis was, however, bound to come. Paul already speaks preferably about faith by hearing than witnessing to what was seen. John stresses the confessional aspect even more, and emphasizes testimony as internalized witness of the Holy Spirit. Nevertheless, "Luke and John, as different as they are, agree on this point. Testimony-confession cannot be separated from testimony-narration without the risk of turning toward gnosticism."[101] Besides it must be added that John, although he internalizes testimony, brings to the fore the juridical element of testimony. The paraclete is the counterpart of the accuser and defends the Christian "in the struggle which is waged between Christ and the world before the court of History."[102] In spite of the fact that there has been a certain dissociation between testimony of confession (meaning) and testimony of narration (event), it may well be that this juridical element retains a tie between the two moments.

A contemporary theology that is aware of the same dissociation between confession and narration, between orthodoxy and orthopraxis, could find in a hermeneutics of testimony a new symbolic force as well as a critical element,[103] in which religious experience is at the witness stand before the community of the faithful and before the world.

As a witness of God's grace in Jesus Christ and through the Holy Spirit testimony would constitute a nonviolent appeal that has divested itself from the pretentions of absolute knowledge.

---

[100] Paul RICOEUR, Testimony, p. 135f.

[102] Paul RICOEUR, Testimony, p. 141.

[103] An interpretation of testimony would be hermeneutical in a double sense. First, it would give to interpretation a content to be interpreted (i.e. the immediacy of the absolute). Furthermore, it would also call for an interpretation due to the dialectic between meaning and event which testimony traverses. See Paul RICOEUR, Testimony, pp. 142-153; and also Edward SCHILLEBEECKX's hermeneutics of experience mentioned above (1.2.2.).

2.3.6. RICOEUR's Understanding of Time and Narrative

The repeated remarks concerning a pluriform notion of temporality, for instance during the comments on myth in sections 1.3.3.2.
and 2.3.4.1., need some clarification if a hermeneutic of religious
narratives is to bear fruit in the here and now of the religious
and/or secular person. For this purpose a further excursion into Paul
RICOEUR's studies on the creation of meaning in language is
suggested.[104]

It is specifically part 1 of the first volume of Time and
Narrative that will be consulted. There, Paul RICOEUR reflects on the
hermeneutic circle existing between narrative and temporality, that
is the narrative representation of the temporal character of human
existence.[105] His starting point is twofold: as far as a phenomenological perception of time is concerned, he is engaged in a
discussion with St. AUGUSTINE's speculations; as far as narrative
theory is concerned he is in dialogue with ARISTOTLE, whose
definitions of poetry have, after all, shaped western thought in
terms of its cosmological perception of time (i.e. history and
narrative).

---

[104] The following books on this topic are interrelated and have,
according to RICOEUR, the same aim, namely the pursuit of truth beyond
the deliberate, but unfortunate, distinction between history and
fiction: The Rule of Metaphor. Multi-Disciplinary Studies of the
Creation of Meaning in Language, London, 1977. (I have chosen to quote
from the English translation because it is a slightly revised version
from the Frensh original, La Métaphore vive, Paris, 1975.) Temps et
récit, Tome I, Paris, 1983. Temps et récit, Tome II, La configuration
du temps dans le récit de fiction, Paris, 1984. Temps et récit, Tome
III, Le temps raconté, Paris, 1985.

[105] "Le monde déployé par tout oeuvre narrative est toujours un monde
temporel. Ou... le temps devient temps humain dans la mesure où il est
articulé de manière narrative; en retour le récit est significatif
dans la mesure où il dessine les traits de l'expérience temporelle."
Paul RICOEUR, Temps, Vol. I, p. 17.

2.3.6.1. The Experience of Time

AUGUSTINE, in the 11th book of his Confessions, vividly describes two conditions of the human soul in which time is conceived.[106] On the one side there is the **intentio animi**, understood as a sense of concordance in the present, on the other side there is the **distentio animi**, a "tornness" resulting from a recollection of the past and the anticipation of the future which always finds an expression in the present.[107] This dialectic is due to the fact that AUGUSTINE argues that time cannot be conceived of as spatial, but must be considered as being in transit. He illustrates his idea as follows,

> I am about to repeat a psalm that I know. Before I begin, my attention is extended to the whole; but when I have begun, as much of it as becomes past by my saying it is extended in my memory; and the life of this action of mine is divided between my memory, on account of what I have repeated, and my expectation, on account of what I am about to repeat; yet my consideration is present with me, through which that which was future may be carried over so that it may become past... And what takes place in the entire psalm, takes place also in each individual part of it... This holds in the longer action, of which that psalm is perchance a portion; the same holds in the whole life of man, of which all actions of man are parts...[108]

Then there is strictly speaking no past, present, and future, but only a present memory of the past, a present of the present, and the present anticipation of the future. Existentially, the human spirit is placed within this perception of time (similar to HEIDEGGER's notion of **Dasein**), but the resulting **distentio** does not only relate to the passivity of impressions, it is also an activity of the spirit manifested in the very tension of the present.[109] In other words, the

[106] St. AUGUSTINE's Confessions, Book 11, especially chapters 38 + 39.

[107] Speculation about the measure of time, which is at the base of AUGUSTINE's argument cannot be unravelled in this limited study. RICOEUR, however, dicusses it, Temps, Vol. I, pp. 30-34 and context.

[108] St. AUGUSTINE's Confessions, Book 11, chapter 38, in A Selected Library of the Nicene and Post-Nicene Fathers of the Christian Church, Vol. I, Grand Rapids, 1979, p. 174.

[109] AUGUSTINE contrasts the tornness of human temporality with the longing of stability (**intentio**) of eternity. See: Paul RICOEUR, Temps,

experience of human time generates action. Two typical examples of this enactment are the producion of novels[110] and the dynamics of worship.

This metaphor of time being in transit constitutes a parallel to ARISTOTLE's theory of emplotment as we will now see.

2.3.6.2. The Theory of Emplotment

RICOEUR builds his argument on the Aristotelian definitions of **mythos** and **mimesis**. **Mimesis**, in the context of poetics, is understood as a re-presentation of tragic action.[111] It belongs to the tragic, because for ARISTOTLE this was the only noble representation of reality, not because mimesis would not also be applicable to comedy or epos. Furthermore, mimetic reality is not to be misunderstood as a mere "copy" of the empirically real, just as little as myth has been defined in negative terms. A re-presentation of human action as such would be neutral. It is its interpretation that makes a value judgment on it. The tragic aspect of **mimesis** contains a tension between the perception of that which is and that which should be, thus it lends itself to a comparison with AUGUSTINE's **distentio**.

The central idea behind ARISTOTLE's use of **mythos** is, as already mentioned, emplotment. The intrigues of life are given shape and coherence in a plot. Part of the plot is often the use of a **peripeteia**, that is a reversal of fate or the **coup de théâtre** as the French would say.[112] The **peripeteia** is resolution of conflict where

---

Vol. I, pp. 41-53.

[110] Paul RICOEUR has made the literary configuration of time the theme of the second volume of Temps et récit. He interprets Virginia WOOLF's Mrs. Dalloway, Thomas MANN's Der Zauberberg, and Marcel PROUST's A la recherche du temps perdu (pp.150-234).

[111] Paul RICOEUR, Temps, Vol. I, p. 58.

[112] One can use the notion of **peripeteia** in the general sense of a "reversal," thus also including the aristotelian notions of **anagnôrisis** (recognition) and **pathos** (violent impact), which also bring about a fundamental change in the development of the plot. Cf. Paul RICOEUR, Temps, Vol. I, p. 72; and the discussion on Vladimir PROPP in chapter 4 (4.2.1.).

the real hero is after all recognized, the protagonist finds grace in spite of all predictions, and the saviour rises from the dead. RICOEUR therefore draws parallels between **mythos** and **intentio**, because through reversal myth not only reveals coherence but gains a harmony.[113] As can be expected, ARISTOTLE's conceptions of plot and representation overlap. The two are aspects of the same narrative production. The one cannot do without the other, just as the human perception of time cannot free itself from a dialectic tension and the desire to overcome it. It is in this way that Paul RICOEUR has related time and narrative. This correlation is for him of trans-cultural value.[114] The metaphorical transposition of lived experience in narrative is a movement from the ethical to the poetic domain. RICOEUR, sharing the intention of the classical authors, will make sure that there is again, in the end, a descent to the practical domain.[115] And indeed, in the third volume of Time and Narrative he introduces the concept of "narrative identity"[116] as a bridge between phenomenological time (AUGUSTINE) and cosmological time (ARISTOTLE). This notion will be picked up and explained in section 3.3.2.2.

2.3.6.3. The Threefold Mimesis

Now the hermeneutic task can begin, for the representation of human action happens in various moments. The interpretation of a text cannot simply be distilled, as the human sciences have been busy trying to prove during the 19th century. RICOEUR approaches the problem of interpretation by postulating three mimetic moments.

---

[113] Paul RICOEUR, Temps, Vol. I, pp. 55, 59.

[114] "... mon hypothèse de base, à savoir qu'il existe entre l'activité de raconter une historie et le charactère temporel de l'expérience humaine une corrélation qui n'est pas purement accidentelle, mais présente une forme de nécessité transculturelle." Paul RICOEUR, Temps, Vol. I, p. 85.

[115] "Nous discuterons, le moment venu, la question de savoir si une modalité de lecture est possible qui suspende entièrement tout évaluation de charactère éthique." Paul RICOEUR, Temps, Vol. I, p. 94.

[116] Paul RICOEUR, Temps, Vol. III, pp. 352-259.

The first mimetic moment is a pre-reflective representation of
ethos and praxis. Pre-reflective reactions are largely culturally
conditioned and reflect our common understanding of temporality.
Their stucture of intelligibility is drawn from the world of action.
The resources for the representation are the general treasury of
symbols, and its character is typically temporal.[117] To put it
simply, the first mimetic moment is the preunderstanding one brings
to any event due to one's being in the world and caring about it.[118]
It is the very disclosure of an experience. It has not yet been
explained (narrated) but it already makes sense.

The second moment of mimesis relates to the production of the
text (considered as oral or written composition). The temporal is not
just given, it is configurated. This aspect of mimesis includes
scientific historiography as well as narrative tradition in the
poetic sense. It is basically concerned with emplotment and is
therefore a symbolic representation of human activity on a secondary
level. It is a synthesis of elements pertaining to an event,
individual and/or collective, with heterogeneous factors that are
thought to shed light on the understanding of what was going on. It
is a reflective activity that brings concordance to the discordant or
fragmentary, and is thus congruent with the Aristotelian notion of
myth.[119] The second moment of mimesis makes it possible that a
thought, a theme, or an argument can be spelled out. This struc-
turating possibility also leads to the closure of the text.[120] It is

---

[117] Paul RICOEUR, Temps, Vol. I, pp. 87-100.

[118] RICOEUR intentionally introduces the Heideggerian notions of
Dasein and Sorge in order to establish a connection between the production of meaning and ethics at the very beginning of "poetic"
thought. Paul RICOEUR, Temps, Vol. I, pp. 96-100.

[119] Paul RICOEUR, Temps, Vol. I, pp. 101-109.

[120] "Nous pouvons maintenant ajouter que c'est dans l'acte de
re-raconter, plutôt que de dans celui de raconter, que cette fonction
structurelle de la clôture peut être discernée." Paul RICOEUR, Temps,
Vol. I, p. 105.
     This argument favours the point of view that oral narrative,
although belonging to the second moment of mimesis, is a degree
removed from the closure of the written text. In other words, it is a
degree closer to "intuitive understanding," or can one say "faith?"

a constituent element of tradition.

The third moment of mimesis is the refiguration of represented
human experience in the mind of the spectator, hearer or reader of
the narrative. It is basically a time of action, in which the
receptor makes the narrative his own, for instance when he is struck
by the **pathos** of a tragedy. Here the world of the "text" touches upon
the world of the "reader" and provokes him within his own temporality. It can be a time of pleasure, recognition or **catharsis**, that
is, it is essentially (in the words of Ian RAMSEY) a time of
disclosure that calls for commitment. If this happens, a mimetic
cycle has been established without being a vicious one. The receptor
of the story has entangled himself in the narrative in order to
ponder its meaning.[121]

In my opinion, the threefold mimetic approach is essential for
understanding religious narratives. Ideally the three levels of
representation should be found in the act of worship. There should be
room for the first moment of mimesis in which the participant
(believer or not) is invited to be open to the symbolic universe that
is already his own, and to share those experiences which up to now he
could not formulate. The second moment of mimesis in worship would be
realized if the proclamation of the Gospel, the mythical celebration
thereof, as well as the possibility for the formulation of utmost
concern is given. Finally, the third moment of mimesis would come to
bear if the receptors of the "word of life" are given an opportunity
to respond to it practically, and preferably in community (religious
and secular).

---

[121] RICOEUR refers to Wilhelm SCHAPP, In Geschichten verstrickt,
Wiesbaden, 1976, p. 85, where the analogy is made of a judge, who has
to penetrate into the intricate story of causes and circumstances,
arguments and counter-arguments, which have brought the accused before
court. One may also remember what has been said about Hans-Georg
GADAMER's thoughts on hermeneutic as being wrapped up in the play of
linguisticality.

2.3.6.4. The Analogical Character between Historical and Fictitious
Narrative

The argument can be made that RICOEUR's theory can only be
applied to traditional narratives, that especially the 20th century
anti-novel is not based on the presupposed narrative structure. For
example, many modern novels deliberately have no concordance-of-
discordance theme, or try to suspend the temporal. This criticism, if
valid, is important because it would make a correlation between
secular and religious narratives difficult. RICOEUR answers this
objection on the basis that the discordance of the so-called
anti-novels stands precisely in opposition to traditional narratives
because they explain themselves in terms of each other.[122] They are
simply the negative formulation of the tradition, a variation on the
theme.

2.3.6.5. Metaphorical Truth

Finally, since, according to RICOEUR, narrative configurations
of the human world are always to some degree metaphorical, and the
representations are never purely historical, nor merely fictitious,
it must be asked in what sense they are to be understood as true.
RICOEUR argues in The Rule of Metaphor that the relational tension
existing in the metaphor (a is b) also relates to its existential
function.[123] That means that the truth which a mimetic representation

---

[122] "..l'innovation reste une conduite gouvernée par les règles: le
travail de l'imagination ne naît pas de rien. Il se relie d'une
manière ou d'une autre aux paradigmes de la tradition." Paul RICOEUR,
Temps, Vol. I, p. 108.
    Frank KERMODE in his book The Sense of an Ending. Studies in the
Theory of Fiction, London, 1966, p. 174, comes to the same conclusion:
"Novels, however, no matter how much they shift time, put slices of it
layer on layer in search of intemporal concord, are always in some way
bound to what SARTRE calls its 'manifest irreversibility.' Their
beginnings, middles, and ends, however refined, however distorted from
the paradigm, will always join it somewhere."

[123] Paul RICOEUR, Rule, p. 248. The tension in the metaphor exists in
the copula "is" (e.g. King David is a lion), because at one and the
same time the "is" implies equivalence and also the difference of the

can convey is ontological and not literally deductive,[124] because it
cannot be identified as absolute it must be perceived in dialectical
relation to what it is and what it is not. What RICOEUR says here is
consistent with what he has said about two decades earlier,[125] "The
symbol gives rise to thought."

2.4. Narrative and Liturgy: Summary and Projections

    Halfway through the first part, the basic issues of this study
have begun to christallize. In order to keep focussing on what is
essential, a retrospection of where the path of argumentation has
led, and preview of the work that still needs to be done seems
appropriate.

"is not." The logical positivist would argue that one cannot say that
something is and at the same time that it is not. This would be a
category mistake according to Gibert RYLE. The point, however, is that
a category mistake can be intentional. And this point makes sense
because one can understand it from the context of human life. (Paul
RICOEUR, Rule, p. 252.)
    "The paradox consists in the fact there (sic) there is no other
way to do justice to the notion of metaphorical truth than to include
the critical incision of the (literal) 'is not' within the ontological
vehemence of the (metaphorical) 'is'." Paul RICOEUR, Rule, p. 255.

[124] Harrison HALL disagrees polemically with RICOEUR because he,
according to HALL, fails to distinguish between the syntactic meaning
of a metaphor and the semantic meaning that the speaker intends
(Harrison HALL, a book review on The Rule of Metaphor, in The
Philosophical Review 89 (1980), pp. 117-121). This argument, besides
making an incorrect assumption, for RICOEUR insists on the retension
of the dialectic between the syntactic sign and the semantic
significance, shows that the methodological presuppositions between
the two writers are so different that a reconciliation of the
respective views seems difficult. Either one has a positivist theory
of metaphor (I.T. RAMSEY's empirical fit would already fail the test!)
or one approaches language production phenomenologically.

[125] Paul RICOEUR, The Symbolism of Evil, Boston, 1967, p. 348.

2.4.1. Another Look at the Definition of Narrative

The definition (still provisional) shall be stated as a theological thesis with a description thereof following.

A narrative in a religious context, is originally a pre-reflective sharing of an experience of God's presence and/or absence in man's life world and his resulting response in the same.

2.4.1.1. Narrative

If narrative is only understood as a particular literary genre, then a corresponding narrative theology would face the problem of a dichotomy between a theological argumentation and conceptualization on the one side, and a confessional/pastoral proclamation on the other. This hermeneutical gap between theological narration and speaking about narrative theology in a deductive way has been especially evident in the early forms of narrative theology.[126] Another impasse is an existentialized reception of narrative in terms of privatized experience. We suggest, therefore, that narrative is telling a story **and more**. Story is understood in the sense of **Geschichte / histoire**, that is, there is no preconceived decision as to the historical or fictional intention of the narrative. Instead its truth value[127] would be discerned in terms of its metaphorical representation of temporality and the ethical consequences it implies. This means that narrative does not only refer to the past, but also finds its expression in the present, in the act of telling, as a sacramental re-enactment or as doxology. Furthermore, it also relates to the future, possibly as a hypothetical or prophetic narrative of eschatological hope, but more basically as an expression of concern that needs to be put into practice.

---

[126] Bernd WACKER, Narrative Theologie? pp. 83f.

[127] The question of truth value as a pragmatic judgment is, of course, not identical with propositional truth claims.

2.4.1.2. ... in a religious context:

CRITES' distinction between sacred and mundane stories, taken up
by RICOEUR, is important here. The distinction avoids a drift into
narrative nothingness, in which indiscriminate telling degenerates
into meaningless verbosity. It must be recalled that an interaction
between sacred and mundane stories is not denied. On the contrary, it
is essential for a comprehensive hermeneutics of testimony and
prophecy. Others have also refered to "secular liturgy" in order to
point to this cross reference.[128] One can place the hermeneutic
tension between the "is" and the "is not" of the metaphor parallel to
the relationship between the sacred and mundane. This tension is the
key to the hermeneutic circle established in the phenomenological
approach of identity narratives with the various mimetic levels. It
is a key because it can be expressed within and without the
linguistic system in the practice of justice and love.

2.4.1.3. ... originally a pre-reflective sharing

Here a slight modification has taken place. Narrative is a
pre-reflective sharing of an experience as long as it is a first
sharing of an evocative disclosure in oral form, and in so far as it
presents an expression of being.[129] Narrative **expression** (mimesis I)
is an activity of the **intellectus**, of direct knowledge, rather than
of the **ratio** as indirect knowledge.[130] Under this demarcation
narrative relates to the **lex orandi, lex credendi** principle.

---

[128] Walter J. HOLLENWEGER, Erfahrungen der Leibhaftigkeit. Interkulturelle Theologie, Vol. 1, München, 1979, pp. 135-155.

[129] It will be noticed that a repetition of a testimony is liable to
drift into the trivial for its temporal aspect has been closed. A
living testimony, on the other hand, remains in the flux of time.

[130] If one considers narrative **production** as a term indicating a conscious configuration (mimesis II), then there is room for **ratio**.

2.4.1.4. ... of an experience of God

The fundamental narrative quality of experience, consciousness and recollection has been mentioned. A religious narrative, however, is not bound to be anthropocentric because it is self-transcending in its intentionality.[131] It is an experience of God's presence, and as such it is called to acknowledge the primacy of Grace. Consequently, narrative as a testimony knows about its source and fulfillment. The experience of God's grace is possible, because God's self-communication in Jesus Christ took place in this world,[132] and cannot be understood apart from it.

2.4.1.5. ... God's presence and/or absence:

A theological presupposition comes to play; God's presence is a gift and cannot be arrogated. The tension between God's presence and/or absence expresses this gift and forms the basic narrative plot in the economy of salvation. The tragedy of **mimesis** (the configuration of suffering and injustice in this world) and the **peripeteia** of **mythos** (the reversal and surplus of meaning) are free to interact. In the celebration of God's presence the two poles of meaning and event, of confession and narrative, are tied together and form a metaphor of hope (the essence of a christian myth, and the impulse for practical commitment).

---

[131] In a certain sense a secular narrative of self-transcendence (e.g. a selfless dedication for the wholeness of others) could also be called religious. However, one would need to ask the question whether such a narrative would be open-ended (i.e. What is the surplus of meaning and how is it related?).

[132] "Indem Gott mit den Mitteln der Welt dadurch Raum gewinnt, dass er zur Sprache kommt, erweitert sich der Horizont der Welt so, dass die Wirklichkeit der Welt (in ihren Problemen, Konflikten, Werten) **schärfer** erfasst wird. Die Sprache des Glaubens schärft den Wirklichkeitssinn, in dem sie den Menschen auf mehr anspricht, als wirklich ist. Strukturell geschieht dies in metaphorischer Rede." Eberhard JUENGEL, Entsprechungen, pp. 156f. (emphasis his).

2.4.1.6. ... in man's life-world:

As with God's self-communication the **nexus** with the world is
important. Man cannot live meaningfully if he is detached from the
world. In his temporality man recognizes himself as related to others
(as God's creation) and is able to commit himself. The narrative
involvement brings this to light. Analogously, christian worship does
not make sense if it is practiced in an inaccessible enclave of the
world.[133]

2.4.1.7. ... and his resulting response in the same.

Thus, narrative is only an event if it can be communicated.
Being basic to Christianity, it underlines the necessity for a
community of interpretation. It is in the light of the church as a
whole that hermeneutics of experience and testimony are possible,[134]
and are received[135] in the **koinônia** of their Lord. This community of
interpretation fulfills different functions with regard to the
narrative and the teller's life-world. First, it enables an open and
non-dominating approach to persons. Hugh JONES, giving credit to
James WHARTON, remarks,

> I identify myself in communal interaction by means of selective
> recall of my story. Indeed, to tell my story or to listen
> openly to someone else's story is the most fitting and the most
> humane way of respecting our human personhood.[136]

Narrative, as it were, cultivates the **shalom** of the community. But
being in a life world implies that it is not enough to tell one's
story, unless one would be willing to pay the price of plain
subjectivism.

---

[133] The the verbs of the monastic slogan **ora et labora** did relate to
the same sphere of action. The secular religious person is, however,
tempted to separate the two. For some people, going to church
corresponds to taking a vacation on an exotic island.

[134] Gerhard SAUTER, Theologie aus Erfahrung, p. 106.

[135] Edward SCHILLEBEECKX, Understanding, pp. 70-77.

[136] Hugh JONES, Concept of Story, p. 426.

A second function consists in comparing different stories with one another, and ultimately with the normative story or the meta-story. One's life world is made up by experiences and the narratives received. At the same time it is constantly being reviewed and changed by the stories of temporality.

> Within this multitude of stories, I accord one story or several stories a higher authority than others, using it (or them) as normative. If things go well, my normative story is increasingly bolstered and authenticated... But things may not go well. My normative story may be rudely challenged by another story or several stories... I (R. Brown) choose, as far as I can, to make the Christian story my normative story, ... and all the rest of my stories subordinate to it, ... But I cannot tell my normative story in isolation from them, nor ... in isolation from stories that are not part of my original story but need to be increasingly interwoven with it...[137]

In the community of interpretation man's normative narrative is being refined; on the one hand by the claims of secular reality (plurality, political oppression, economic suffering, etc.), and on the other hand by the vision of truth. As we will see, the danger of self-deception will have to be avoided. The normative narrative is refined to the point where one's life-story (fundamental option) may be put to the ultimate trial of testimony.

A Christian may want to distinguish between his normative story and the meta-story as an overarching interpretation of reality, or in other words, God's own story. "He is someone to be 'greeted', a giver of stories, someone working out his purposes in Christ in real contact with human experience."[138] The meta-story, then, breaks the conceptual language games of mankind. Because it is now a myth, it can only be told as a sacrament, or in the "language in celebration."

The third narrative function in the community of interpretation is related to the evocative character of religious language. Narrative is proof of, and evokes anew, a response and a commitment. To tell a story always implies the making of an ethically relevant statement. But in order to find the right relationship between orthodoxy and orthopraxis the church as a whole needs to pray for,

---

[137] Robert McAfee BROWN, My Story, pp. 167f.

[138] Hugh JONES, Concept of Story, p. 428.

and practice, the charism of discernment.[139] For not only the story, but also the practice is a gift of God, which has its source and fulfillment in the Body of Christ worshipping God. But in between the telling and the doing is the long and winding road of secular reality.

2.4.2. Narrative in Liturgy

The preoccupation with religious narrative has brought several observations of historical interest to the surface. Three of these shall be delineated here in order to set accents for further research.

First of all, there has been repeated reference to the classical **lex orandi, lex credendi** principle. The oral nature of narrative and its pragmatic function reveal its **raison d'être** in the sphere of worship. Paul RICOEUR's hermeneutics of revelation and testimony have laid a foundation for the theological use of narrative. The tension between the divorced ways of "doing" theology, however, still remain unresolved. Historically, the notion **lex orandi, lex credendi** has been used in different ways to prove different points.[140] The ambiguity of this Latin phrase also allows a reading which emphasizes the primacy of the rule of faith. The fact that the two aspects can be traced individually in the history of theology may be helpful, but on the other hand they also evolved simultaneously before they were first united as a notion by PROSPER of AQUITAINE in the fifth century. It appears to be a false dilemma if one had to chose the one over the other. The early church, particularly in the East, considered worship as a **theologia prima**. That is to say, orthodoxy was still a matter of authentic praise.[141] But even there the expression

---

[139] Gerhard SAUTER, Theologie aus Erfahrung, p. 110.

[140] For a historical survey of the development of that notion see: Geofrey WAINRIGHT, Doxology. The Praise of God in Worship, Doctrine and Life, London, 1980, pp. 218-283.

[141] Josephus LESCRAUWAET, Confessing the Faith in the Liturgy, in Concilium 6 (1970), p. 128; Gerard LUKKEN, The Unique Expression of

implies that there was also a **theologia secunda,** a dogmatic exploration in terms of authentic doctrine.

Considering the issue as a fruitful dialectic, rather than as a unresolvable tension, the following question needs to be pursued. What role does narrative play as a mediator between the two poles. Or, is narrative an incentive for a third rule, **lex faciendi,** as George S. WORGUL suggests?[142]

A second observation of liturgical interest is the relationship of narrative to symbol and sacrament. As mentioned above, Johann B. METZ considers narrative to be a linguistic action uniting the effective word with the effective sacrament. Therefore, it is understandable that he pleads for the integration of life-stories into the sacramental realm. He calls for an acknowledgement of salvific action wherever it happens. This intention must be discussed. Is it just an escape into aesthetic feelings, or is it fundamental to the appreciation of man's symbolic horizon? The latter point of view also seems to be the conviction of Langdon GILKEY,

> I suspect, however, that the present weakness of both classical forms of Christian worship lies... in their common indifference to... the divine works in and **on** us as creatures too, and that awareness of this **our** role as "symbols"... lies at the heart of any experience of the holy that is to be relevant to and effective in us.[143]

Others argue more basically that the more narrative is incorporated in the symbolism of worship, the more the sacraments are true to their fundamental intention, since the primordial symbol of transcendence is man himself, or his language respectively.[144] Another reason for pursuing the role of narrative in a liturgical context has

---

Faith in the Liturgy, in Concilium 9 (1973), 11-21, pp. 19f.

[142] George S. WORGUL, From Magic to Metaphor. A Validation of Christian Sacraments, New York, 1980, p. 77.

[143] Langdon GILKEY, Addressing God in Faith, in Concilium 9 (1973), p. 69 (emphasis his).

[144] Walter KASPAR, Wort und Symbol im sakralen Leben. Eine anthropologische Begründung, in Bild, Wort, Symbol in der Theologie, Wilhelm HEINEN (ed.), Würzburg, 1969, 157-175; George S. WORGUL, Magic, pp. 129-140; Walter J. ONG, Orality, pp. 74f.; Eberhard JUENGEL, Entsprechungen, pp. 415-427.

been presented by Wim DE PATER. He suggests interpreting miracle
narratives not primarily as diclosure models, but as symbols of God's
presence in the events of mankind.[145] In any case, the sources just
quoted seem to agree that the church at worship is the narrative
institution **par excellence**, in which men and women of a highly fragmented and technological society can be called to wholeness again. As
RICOEUR would say, their narrated experiences can be restructured
symbolically. It is a pity if this happens only in the "confessional"
or at the "mourners bench."

A third and last observation of liturgical interest evolves
around the phenomenon of secularization. Because of the temporality
involved in narratives, secularization has eventually begun to transform the liturgical life of Christianity. Time and again it has been
asserted that liturgy, at least, ought to be kept undefiled by the
profane. It is certainly true that worship loses its meaning if it is
congruent, or indifferent to the profane. Nevertheless, it must
always be a priority of liturgy to let the **humanum** have access to the
Holy. Furthermore, there is again a growing conviction that the Holy
manifests itself particularly there where the **humanum** seems godfor-
saken and utterly at the mercy of the "Word made flesh."[146] The
attention that is being directed toward the profane is not a result
of syncretism. It is due to the increased importance given to the
temporal in this age, and the acknowledgement of God's acts of grace
in mankind.[147] If secularization is seen from this point of view,
then there is a glorious challenge for the role of liturgy in the
life of the church. Raymundo PANIKKAR argues that, "... only worship
can prevent secularization from becoming inhuman, and only secular-

---

[145] Wim DE PATER, Theologische Sprachlogik, München, 1971, p. 77.

[146] "Das Heilige vollzieht sich jetzt im Profanum, mitten in der Welt,
überall da, wo menschliche Situation ist. Deshalb hat Jesus ganz
bewusst die Grenze des Sakral-Kultischen durchstossen und Sünder,
kultisch Unreine, sozial Deklassierte in seine Nachfolge gerufen und
in seine Tischgemeinschaft einbezogen." Walter KASPAR, Wort und
Symbol, p. 169.

[147] This acknowledgement depends to a large extent on the willingness
to allow for stories of God's grace to be told.

ization can save worship from being meaningless."[148] The burden of
this double responsibility cannot be delegated to one or the other
aspect of liturgical activity, even less so to the **diakonia** of the
minister. It is a responsibility shared by all believers.[149] Their
life world is just as much the **locus** of God's grace as is their place
of worship. They are all called to be witnesses of Jesus Christ, the
sacrament of the world. Their testimony is a mediator between the
secular and the Sacred, between the meaning of life and the events
that shape it.

2.4.3. Looking Ahead

So far, theoretical aspects of narrative theology, or better, of
theological narratives, have been surveyed. How does this compare
with the praxis? The birthpains of a narrative approach in theology
have largely been due to the lack of a correlation between the
elaborated ideas and the execution of the same. Research relating to
theological narratives should also apply to the study of this
phenomenon in the concrete context of the Christian community.

What would be the aim of such an inquiry? First and foremost, to
study the structure, function, and intentionality of narrative in the
community of the faithful; as they address themselves to their God,
to one another and to the world. The structure of narrative would
reveal its typical form from a syntactic point of view. The intentionality of narrative would raise questions of meaning, whereas the
functional aspect would shed light on the pragmatic side of
narrative.

Where would such a praxis-oriented investigation take place? The
nature of narrative would suggest a predominantly oral community of
faith. There one would find open forms of worship which are important
in this respect. Furthermore, a community that lives with an oral
tradition is likeley to incorporate various forms of theology in the

----

[148] Raymundo PANIKKAR, Secularization and Worship, in Studia Liturgica
7 (1970), p. 28.

[149] In chapter six this challenge will be taken up in form of a
theology of laity (6.2.).

making, for instance, the sharing of one's faith to others and its
impact on daily experiences. This type of communication can be called
a market place theology,[150] reminiscent of Luke's presentation of
Paul's dialogual theology in <u>Acts</u> 17:17. Still, where are such
communities to be found today? Liberation theologians and
missiologists (Johann B. METZ and Walter J. HOLLENWEGER among others)
mention, for example, the Basic Christian Communities in Latin
America or the young African and Asian churches. Their common element
is that they have not yet been institutionalized (**verkirchlicht**),
they are churches in the making. Granted, not every new church or
community is automatically also an oral congregation and vice versa.
But the criterion of **Verkirchlichung** is useful if one searches for
oral communities in Europe, because the cultures in Europe are highly
literate, and genuine forms of orality are scarce. In many cases
Verkirchlichung and literacy go hand in hand.

Certain pentecostal churches would qualify for the type of
research envisaged, for they have not yet institutionalized to the
degree where oral forms of theology are considered impractical.
Furthermore, early (ca. 1910) and present forms of pentecostal narratives could be compared in view of progressive secularization.

Finally one would have to ask how such a praxis-oriented
analysis should be undertaken. The majority of narratives which I
have at my disposal have come to me indirectly and in written form.
Nevertheless, the orality of narrative ought to be considered. For
speech cannot be reduced to the written word without some loss of
meaning. This ascertainment has lead to an increased appreciation of
field studies.[151] A field study of narrative in worship would provide
valuable data for an evaluation of the theological implications
presented in this essay. The data would not consist of narratives in
terms of words alone; it would include the event of narration, that

---

[150] Walter J. HOLLENWEGER, <u>Erfahrungen</u>, p. 18; cf. also the larger
context, pp. 15-26.

[151] For a discussion on the incommensurability of language and
language games, and the need for field studies see Paul FEYERABEND,
<u>Against Method</u>, London, 1975+1978, pp. 271-285. Whether one has to
accept his provocative conclusions is, of course, another question.

is the evocation of its disclosure.[152] The evocation could range from praise to prophecy, from confession to commitment or from testimony to trial. In any case it would be a reflection on a christian community in dialogue with their God and their world.

---

[152] Whenever possible such data has been incorporated in this essay. But a solid field study of oral narratives in worship would demand the writing of a separate thesis.

3. ON THE PHENOMENON OF SECULARIZATION

THE RELATIONSHIP BETWEEN SECULAR BIOGRAPHY
AND RELIGIOUS TESTIMONY

"And now the end is near
and so I face the final curtain
my friend, I'll say it clear,
I'll state my case, of which I'm certain.
I've lived a life that's full,
I've travelled each and every highway
and more, much more than this.
I did it my way."

Frank A. SINATRA

3.1. Introduction

Just as religious narratives are subject to a theological critique because they claim to speak about the transcendent (chapter 1), and to a philosophical questioning because they claim to be meaningful (chapter 2), so must those narratives also be studied from a sociological point of view, for the language they employ is a social institution with its proper culturally contingent rules. In other words, language as a fundamental tool of all societies is not immune to the changes that history provokes. As will be shown, the issue of secularization arises when large segments of society no longer share the same basic convictions and linguistic codes by which they make themselves understood in the society as a whole. Thus the aim of this chapter is to establish a relational field between the narrator, the audience, and the social reality in which language "dwells."

3.1.1. A Working Hypothesis

The presuppositions for this exercise can be stated in the following working hypothesis.

> Human beings, whether secularized or religious, have to
> tackle the same fundamental questions of existence, and
> sense the need to communicate their experiences with
> others on a personal and/or societal level, in order to
> be able to digest insight and transform it into action.

Thus, an existential issue is at the basis of this hypothesis, situated between conviction and praxis. Furthermore, secularization and the affirmation of faith are not seen as antagonistic opposites, but as movements of thought standing in dialectic tension with each other.

Another preliminary clarification relates to the use of the terms "biography" and "testimony". The former is used as a sociological as well as literary notion. The context will reveal in what sense (a and/or b) biography is to be understood. Testimony, on the other hand, shall be used as a religious notion, although it will in a few instances stand as a juridical term. In short, biography and testimony are considered to have a textual as well as a contextual significance.

Finally, it is assumed, in the light of contemporary hermeneutic ideas (chapter 2), that any critical model of interpretation should have not only theoretical, but also practical consequences.

3.1.2. What Aims are to be Achieved?

The second section of this chapter will look in greater detail at the various views concerning secularization. The basic question will be in what sense can the phenomenon of secularization contribute to the understanding of contemporary religious narratives (in this case testimonies and prophetic visions in particular) as they may be told in public religious meetings and services, as well as in the context of practical commitment.

This assumption implies that the dynamics of secularization are a necessary element for the clarification of religious issues today, because the development of critical thought since the Enlightenment and the historical circumstances of the last two centuries have brought to light the fact that society in general and religious consciousness in particular are in an ongoing process of transformation.

The third and fourth sections of this chapter will try to discern whether or not it is viable to compare secular biography with religious testimony. Basically it will be argued that both modes of expression intend to strengthen personal identity and social integration in a pluralist society. Although different language games may be used, both genres still employ similar linguistic devices. Hence it will be emphasized that religious narratives are not utterly meaningless to the non-religious person, and that a partial fusion of hermeneutic horizons is possible.

The final section will then try to mark off such a field of reference in practical terms and from a theological point of view.[1] It is evident that language, and by implication narrated life experience, is a common denominator of the believer, whether traditional or secularized, and one who does not profess to believe. It is a bridge between man and his self, and between man and the other. Our hermeneutical approach to religious narratives in the context of worship will, therefore, take this double dialectic into account.

3.2. The Issue of Secularization

The term secularization is derived from the Latin **saeculum** and **saecularis**. The words refer to the temporal and at the same time to that which pertains to the world. In the Latin translations of the Greek New Testament it stands for **aion**, whose significance in the singular can generally be translated as "the time or duration of the world."[2] Theologically **saeculum** therefore acquired the meaning of the world of mankind in this day and age as contrasted with the age of God's reign to come. In the Middle Ages secularization was a juridical notion referring either to an acquisition of a religious object, for

---

[1] Although this thesis limits itself to the interpretation of a certain kind of liturgical narrative, it is understood that the practical consequences for theological hermeneutics will also relate to the secular context of life.

[2] Hermann SASSE, Aiôn, in Theological Dictionary of the New Testament, Vol. I (Gerhard KITTEL (ed.), English translation: Geoffrey BROMILEY) Grand Rapids, 1964, p. 203.

instance a piece of property, for use by the government, i.e. worldly
authorities, or, in canon law, it indicated the permission for a
member of a religious order to leave the monastic community
permanently.

The notion as it is used today by sociologists, literary critics,
philosophers, and theologians has only emerged since the nineteenth
century. G.J. HOLYOAKE, founder of the early "secular societies," is
considered to be the first freethinker to speak of secularization as a
socio-philosophical phenomenon. Then Max WEBER, Wilhelm DILTHEY and
Ernst TROELTSCH[3] began, at first sporadically, to speak of **secularization as the detachment of different spheres of life**. The term has
become common currency since the 1920s. So far, the scholars are in
agreement,[4] but their interpretation of what secularization does has
become quite varied. It will, therefore, be profitable to study the
different usages of the term (and its related derivatives) before the
impact of secularization on society and religious language can be
discussed.

3.2.1. Different Usages of the Term

For the purpose of clarity, the usage of the notion will be
divided into three spheres. A certain overlap between these semantic
fields admittedly occurs, which increases the already problematic use
of this polysemic concept.

---

[3] Ulrich RUH, Säkularisierung, in Christlicher Glaube in moderner
Gesellschaft, Bd. 18 (ed. Franz BOECKLE and others), Freiburg, 1982,
p. 66.

[4] See for instance: Ulrich RUH, Säkularisierung, pp. 66-68; Antoine
VERGOTE, La sécularisation. De l'héliocentrisme à la culture
d'ellipse, in Herméneutique de la sécularisation (ed. Enrico
CASTELLI), Paris, 1976, p. 346; Albert KELLER, Säkularisierung, in
Sacramentum Mundi, Bd. 4 (ed. Karl RAHNER and others), Freiburg, 1969,
pp. 360 + 361.

3.2.1.1. The Popular Religious Understanding

The first sphere of usage is the popular religious understanding of the idea. The word stands, as the etymological explanation of secularization in a christian context has shown, in contrast to religious claims. It describes a process in which various aspects of life and thought (philosophy, science, politics, sexuality, etc.) gain an independent, i.e. religion-less right to exist, and are no longer in need of religious sanction. In theory this development need not be antagonistic toward convictions of faith, as Albert KELLER has argued.[5] But it is understandable that large segments of the religious hierarchy perceived in secularization a threat to their institutions and faith. Especially after the second half of the nineteenth century it seemed that the tide of "liberal thought" would ultimately make an end to all religion. In conservative circles of all religious groups secularization came to be regarded as anti-traditional, anti-clerical and therefore also an **anti-religious** act of **hybris**. A point in case was the threat to roman catholic identity when the papal states were lost.

Among the religious working class, for instance in the protestant revival movements, secularization was not really thought of as a intellectual movement, but it was nonetheless experienced as a **worldly** trend that "denied God the glory" and "tempted man into sin." Take for example the abundance of religious pamphlets written attacking Darwinism, new forms of government, the emergence of mass media and space technology, to mention just a few. For the historic and many of the newer independent churches this apprehensive attitude did change when it became evident that one's faith, although considered transcendent, was not immune to the transformations that were going on in society and that these developments could not be reversed.

A third variant of popular reaction to secularization was, for instance, the **Kulturprotestantismus** of the Lutheran church of Germany. The separation between church and state was a convenient means to delegate secularization culturally as a **non-religious** movement that

[5] Albert KELLER, Säkularisierung, pp. 362-366.

was part of the internal affairs of the state. Or else, in theo-
logizing circles, secularization was considered as a **religious**
consequence of the **geistesgeschichtliche** development of the nation.
The popular notions of secularization,[6] whether branded as anti-
religious, worldly, non-religious, or even religious, are probably not
very helpful for the clarification of the issues involved. Provisionally, it seems best to bracket the loss of religiosity, which is
perhaps most commonly considered as the major negative factor, and to
define secularization as essentially an **a-religious**, that is neutral,
development in recent history (which is best explained in sociological
terms), otherwise a hermeneutic of oral narratives as it is envisaged
would contain a terminological prejudice which does not belong to its
structure, but to the narrator's convictions.

3.2.1.2. The Theological Use

The theological application of the term secularization is the
second sphere of usage. The treatment of secularization as a
theological theme has been one of the predominant preoccupations of
theologians in the twentieth century.[7] There are good reasons for this
as will be seen below. But first, it is necessary to look at the
termini technici used. In order to make dialogue on this topic
possible, a sizable number of theologians have adopted the classic
distinction between secularization, secularity and secularism
elaborated by Friedrich GOGARTEN in the years following World War II

---

[6] The newer works published on recent church history generally tend to
mention the growing influence of secularization, as of course, books
on western sociology of religion do. Perhaps the most telling source
for the study of popular opinion on secularization is, however, the
literary output of religious groups in the form of sermons, pamphlets,
apologetic gazettes, pastoral letters, or the visions and prophecies
in pneumatic or revivalist communities.

[7] To mention just a few: Thomas ALTIZER, Dietrich BONHOEFFER, Harvey
COX, John MacQUARRIE, J.B. COBB, William HAMILTON, Dorothee SOELLE,
Paul TILLICH, Gabriel VAHANIAN, W.H. VAN DE POL, Heinz ZAHRNT.
    W.H. Van DE POL, in his book The End of Conventional Chris-
tianity, New York, 1968, discusses the background, some aspects and
prospects of this development; especially in the chapter "Toward a
Responsible Belief in God" (pp. 283-297).

and clearly stated in his book Verhängnis und Hoffnung der Neuzeit.[8]
According to him one has to differentiate between those terms.
Säkularisierung, i.e. secularization, refers to a historical process
in which ideas, insights and experiences, formerly attributed directly
to christian revelation, gain autonomy under the auspices of universal
reason.[9] Consequently, secularization is understood as a progression
from the sacred to the secular context of explanation. This in itself
can be a quite neutral affair, since the movement of secularization
has not necessarily a competitive intentionality against religion. The
state of secularization, that is secularity, Säkularität, can
therefore be described as a secular order, tolerant of the sacred
especially in those domains where all-encompassing answers cannot be
given. But when the movement of secularization becomes a totalizing
phenomenon, if it considers it a must to give an ultimate answer to
all questions of life, then secularization has become an ideology that
is called Säkularismus, secularism. If on the other hand, the movement
of secularization considers it useless to acknowledge the value of
fundamental questions of life and wholeness, then secularism has moved
to nihilism.[10] In view of these distinctions it is understandable why,
for instance, the "God-is-dead" debate in the 1960s was so controversial. Based on Dietrich BONHOEFFER's reference to H. GROTIUS'
natural law "etsi deus non daretur"[11] some attempted to reformulate

---

[8] Friedrich GOGARTEN, Verhängnis und Hoffnung der Neuzeit. Die
Säkularisierung als theologisches Problem, München, 1958.

[9] "Geistige Erscheinungen, Ideen und Erkenntnisse, die bis dahin als
Offenbarungen und unmittelbare Wirkungen Gottes und darum als allein
dem Glauben zugänglich galten, werden durch ihre Säkularisierung zu
Erkenntnissen, die der Vernunft, ganz unabhängig vom Glauben, aus
deren eigener, säkulären Kraft zugänglich sind." Friedrich GOGARTEN,
Neuzeit, p. 7.

[10] Friedrich GOGARTEN, Neuzeit, p. 143.

[11] Dietrich BONHOEFFER, Widerstand und Ergebung, München, 1962, pp.
240f. BONHOEFFER's emphasis on Redlichkeit, a term denoting honesty
and personal integrity, brought him to the conclusion that man had to
admit his being-in-the-world without a fearful appeal to God as a
passe-partout to all of man's questions, or an escape to a medieval
universe in which ultimate responsibility could be pushed off into the
hands of the clerical hierarchy. "Und wir können nicht redlich sein,
ohne zu erkennen, dass wir in der Welt leben müssen - "etsi deus non

their faith (without as such denying it) in non-religious categories,[12] while others thought it impossible or blasphemous to do so,
and thus considered secularization as a deistic or even anti-religious
phenomenon. Arnold LOEN summarizes the tension as follows,

> If 'secularization' means the stripping off the divine from the
> world this can be taken in a good sense; for the world is not
> divine. If, however, it means the conception of the world as
> 'reality' in the sense of a self-contained totality of effects
> this must be viewed unfavourably; for the world is creation and
> the object of the saving activity of God in creation, recon-
> ciliation and redemption.[13]

Such a theological clarification is certainly fundamental, but it will
eventually be necessary to ask what Arnold LOEN, or for that matter
anyone else, means when he says, "world," "divine," "reality,"
"redemption" and so on.

3.2.1.3. The Sociological Use

Thirdly, one should understand the sociological use of the word
secularization before investigating its underlying issues.In the
sociological sense, secularization refers to an empirically available
process in modern western history "by which sectors of society and
culture are removed from the domination of religious institutions and
symbols."[14] The plausibility structures in which societies and

---

daretur". Und eben dies erkennen wir - vor Gott! Gott selbst zwingt
uns zu dieser Erkenntnis. So führt uns unser Mündigwerden zu einer
wahrhaftigen Erkenntnis unserer Lage vor Gott. Gott gibt uns zu
wissen, dass wir leben müssen als solche, die mit dem Leben ohne Gott
fertig werden. Der Gott, der mit uns ist, ist der Gott, der uns
verlässt (Markus 15,34)! Der Gott, der uns in der Welt leben lässt
ohne die Arbeitshypothese Gott, ist der Gott, vor dem wir dauernd
stehen." (p. 241)

[12] Perhaps the most radical attempts at non-religious reformulation,
under the influence of anglo-saxon positivism and empiricism, were
brought forth by Paul VAN BUREN, Thomas J.J. ALTIZER and William
HAMILTON. For a concise discussion of their premises see John
MacQUARRIE, New Directions in Theology Today. Vol. 3, God and Secularity, Philadelphia, 1967, pp. 21ff., 72ff.

[13] Arnold E. LOEN, Secularization. Science Without God?, London, 1967,
p. 117.

[14] Peter BERGER, The Social Reality of Religion, Harmondsworth, 1967,

cultures were traditionally held together by institutionalized religion are breaking apart. Especially science and technology in the process of universalizing rationality force mankind to rethink his existential and organizational presuppositions. The problem is thus one that society as a whole has to face.

More acutely, the process is a secularization of consciousness as well, and relates to the individual directly. For if there is a loss of plausibility in areas which traditionally were covered by the religious institutions, such as the justification of social order and human existence, then the modern individual[15] is faced with a loss of meaning and a possible crisis of identity unless he can adapt to new or reviewed norms. Along the same lines a problem is posed by the emerging difficulties of communication between individuals or groups with varying degrees of secularized identity and vocabulary. It is therefore important to distinguish at least a social, an individual, and a linguistic aspect in the sociological discussions on secularization. Finally one may want to recall that secularization is to be understood as a social process rather than a particular view of society in the light of secular changes.[16] With this in mind one is

---

p. 113. For an adverse view see Andrew M. GREELEY, Unsecular Man. The Persistence of Religion, New York, 1972. His polemic thesis is that the basic human religious needs and religious functions have not changed notably since the late Ice Age. But in the long run he agrees with most sociologists that the face of religion has changed through the process of secularization. The polemicizing is apparently based on a lack of distinction between religious need, ritual function, and intelligible content.

[15] The choice of vocabulary may be somewhat precarious, for the notion "modern individual" or "modern man" is rather vague. However, it is found in sociological studies on secularization and stands in contrast with the concept of "traditional man". This characterization points to the fact that in the past, say the Middle Ages, the structure of society provided man with an identity, whereas today the individual is personally responsible for the mapping of a world view.

[16] "Der gegenwärtige Stand der kritischen Diskussion des Begriffs Säkularisierung und seiner verwandten Vorstellungen ist dadurch gekennzeichnet, dass dabei nicht der mit diesem Begriff als vorgegeben anzusehende Prozess selbst erörtert wird, sondern die mit diesem Begriff erzeugte Sicht des Prozesses." Trutz RENDTORFF, Theorie des Christentums. Historisch-theologische Studien zu seiner neuzeitlichen Verfassung, Gütersloh, 1972, p. 123.

now able to approach the social and theological issues of secularization proper.

3.2.2. Secularization and the Social Reality of Religion

This section will uncover the basic aspects and notions of the
process of secularization from a sociological point of view. It is
assumed that such an approach is necessary, if a fruitful dialogue
between people representing religious and/or secular values is to take
place.

3.2.2.1. An Anthropological Definition of Religion

A sociologist of religion, no matter how sympathetic to someone's
faith, should, according to Thomas LUCKMANN, begin his work with an
anthropological or functional definition of religion.[17] For one thing,
theological definitions are metaphysical and difficult to assess
empirically. For another, functional definitions are likely to avoid
"ethnocentrism" and ideological bias. Following LUCKMANN, there are
general anthropological conditions of religion, which can be described
within a dialectic between individual and society, between subjective
experiences of the transcendent on the one hand, and social objectification and institutionalization on the other. This personal and
social objectification of the symbolic universe is based on three
conditions.[18] First, the historical priority of a world view is
postulated, providing the subject with an accessible logic and a means
of expression. Second, a subjective experience transcending the self,
or immediate experience, in view of a face-to-face confrontation with
the other(s) is necessary. This leads to a sense of detachment and
allows the individuation of consciousness and the construction of a
system of meaning. The third condition for the objectification of the
symbolic universe is the integration of recollections and projections
into a more or less coherent biography which is morally relevant.

---

[17] Thomas LUCKMANN, The Invisible Religion, London, 1967, pp. 41 ff.
[18] Thomas LUCKMANN, The Invisible Religion, pp. 47-49, 53.

These elementary conditions of religion (world view, self-transcending experience and moral integration) are all affected by the phenomenon of secularization. The traditional world views are changing, the rationality of modern society seems to stress the immanent values rather than the transcendent ones, and the coherent integration of experiences and values is made more difficult through the availability of a steadily increasing number of interpretative options. This has significant consequences for the individual appropriation and social integration of religious values.

3.2.2.2. The Subjective Appropriation of the World

As far as the individual appropriation of the world is concerned, Peter BERGER has pointed to the need of the human being to remain in conversation with others if he wants to maintain a subjective reality of the world that is both meaningful to him and to significant others; such as to parents, teachers and 'peers.'[19] For it is assumed that society has a nominizing function beyond the institutional plane.[20] For instance, if there is a disruption of order on the subjective level when a person or a group of people are faced with the inevitability of death (the most incisive marginal situation imaginable), then a sense of reality and identity is threatened that calls for a communicative solution.

Traditionally religion intervened on such occasions and provided a legitimation for the state of affairs or the changes taking place. Not only major marginal situations (e.g. the fall of an empire or the theodicy problem), but also everyday challenges to world-integration (e.g. nightmares or the raising of taxes) were explained and legitimated by religious counsel and practice. Following the tradition of Emile DURKHEIM,[21] Peter BERGER states, "The further back one goes

---

[19] Peter BERGER, The Social Reality of Religion, pp. 26-28.

[20] "Society is the guardian of order and meaning not only objectively in its institutional structures, but subjectively as well, in its structuring of individual consciousness." Peter BERGER, Social Reality, pp. 30 f.

[21] "Or c'est précisément ce que nous avons tenté de faire et nous

historically, the more does one find religious ideation (typically in mythological form) embedded in ritual activity - to use more modern terms, theology embedded in worship."[22] It is important to note what is being claimed, namely that the legitimating activity of religion has so far been a mixture of narrative explanation and the ritual re-enactment of events in a legitimized order. In view of the contemporary context some questions consequently arise. What happens if the reality-maintaining task of religion fails to be effective? Why does the secularized person apparently no longer understand the intention of religious celebrations? What happens to personal identity when recourse to a higher cognitive status (be it the realm of transcendence or institutionalized religion) is no longer plausible?

In order to understand the problem of plausibility, whether it relates to propositional truth claims, to rather sophisticated rituals of worship, or to attitudes of practice, one should remember that it is, sociologically seen, the "conversational" character which is necessary for reality-maintenance that is at stake. One is faced with a problem of language.

---

avons vu que cette réalité, que les mythologies se sont représentées sous tant de formes différentes, mais qui est la cause objective, universelle et éternelle de ces sensations **sui generis** dont est faite l'expérience religieuse, c'est la société... Car ce qui fait l'homme c'est cet ensemble de biens intellectuels qui constitue la civilisation, et la civilisation est l'oeuvre de la société. Et ainsi s'explique le rôle prépondérant du culte dans toutes les religions, quelles qu'elles soient... C'est par l'action commune qu'elle (la société) prend conscience de soi et se pose; elle est avant tout une cooperation active... C'est donc l'action qui domine la vie religieuse par cela seul que c'est la société qui en est la source." Emile DURKHEIM, Les formes élémentaires de la vie religieuse. Le système totémique en Australie, Paris, 1968, 5ème ed., p. 597f.

DURKHEIM's main idea centers on the general social functionality of religion. From this point of view it is a small step to consider religion to be the anthropological phenomenon **par excellence**, as Thomas LUCKMANN has done (see above). Cf. also Peter BERGER, Social Reality, p. 178f.

[22] Peter BERGER, Social Reality, p. 49. The value of relating the notion of myth to an interpretation of religious narratives has found not only a theological (1.3.), a philosophical (2.3.6.), but now also a sociological reason.

It is common nowadays to relate the individual's formation of his world view with the acquisition of his mother tongue. As one internalizes a language one takes over its common logic and semantic taxonomy. In addition, it is fairly clear that common linguistic logic is evolving. To provide an example: in medieval Europe, certain medical conditions where literally considered to be a problem of "bewitchment," whereas today the term "bewitchment" is almost exclusively used in a metaphorical sense. The problem between literal and metaphorical language is, however, not only a historical one. It also causes, according to Thomas LUCKMANN, a major problem in the objectification of a symbolic universe.

> The formulation of interpretative schemes and modes of conduct in everyday life depends, primarily, upon the straightforward referential function of language. The linguistic articulation of a sacred cosmos, however, rests upon what we may term the symbolic potential of language which appears in the personification of events, the formation of divine names, the construction of "different" realities by metaphorical transposition, and so forth.[23]

The problem of plausibility is, therefore, not only one of credibility (Can a supernatural understanding of the resurrection be maintained?), but also one of understanding (What do they mean when they say "Lamb of God?"), meaningfulness (Why should I be a church member?) and alienation (What do old-fashioned religious exercises have in common with my search for self-fulfillment?).

The process of secularization in the twentieth century has advanced these problems from the desks and lecture halls of a few intellectuals to the masses of entire societies through media and public protest. BERGER correctly states, "This (the loss of plausibility of religious legitimation for broad masses) opened up an acute crisis not only for the nomization of the large social institutions, but for that of **individual biographies.**"[24] This crisis has come about, because as religious legitimation is suffering a loss, a variety of "secularized soteriologies" eagerly fill the void. The individual, in a rapidly pluralizing society, is faced with a competitive "market

---

[23] Thomas LUCKMANN, Invisible Religion, pp. 59f.

[24] Peter BERGER, Social Reality, p. 130 (emphasis added).

situation" for meaning-supply. He "...will prefer religious products that can be made consonant with secularized consciousness over those that cannot."[25]

To put it differently, pluralization is multiplying the number of plausibility structures. This brings about several consequences from a religious point of view. For instance, this makes commonly shared plausibility more difficult. Faith becomes increasingly a privatized affair. To give an example, the majority of Americans still profess to believe in God, but their commitment to church attendance is quite low.[26] If an individual has strong religious convictions it is easier for him to find equals in small self-made communities than in the established parishes, as, for instance, the phenomenal growth of the recent House-church movement in Great Britain indicates.[27]

Another consequence of the pluralization of plausibility structures is that the traditional legitimations undergo a process of translation. Christianity, no longer part and parcel of an encompassing cosmology, is being psychologized. Faith is legitimated as psycho-therapy in which "inner healing" and harmony with the pace of life can be found.[28] Another process of translation is taking place

---

[25] Peter BERGER, Social Reality, pp. 148f. The choice of vocabulary reminds one of Max WEBER's theory on the protestant ethic and the spirit of capitalism.

[26] Andrew GREELEY, Unsecular Man, pp. 10-13; based on Guy A. SWANSON's study Modern Secularity, in Donald R. CUTLER (ed.) The Religious Situation: 1968, Boston, 1968. SWANSON's survey, made in 1965, indicated that the percentage of those who believed that there is a God was 99% for Catholics, about 98 % for Protestants and 77% for Jews, whereas the number of those who attended church weekly was 78% for Catholics, 21 % for Protestants and 1% for Jews!

[27] A mixture of personal faith and authoritarian leadership marks many of those communities. See for instance: William DAVIES, Rocking the Boat. The Challenge of the House Church, Basingstoke, 1986.
      Joyce V. THURMAN in her book, New Wineskins. A Study of the House Church Movement, relates the strong emphasis on anti-worldliness and discipline, the desire for a new religious experience, and fraction from the established churches as a direct consequence of secularization. (Studien zur interkulturellen Geschichte des Christentums, No. 30, Frankfurt a. M., 1982.)

[28] This claim is not absurd as chapters 4 and 5 will show. In fact there are indications that "healing" becomes in many cases a secular

with regard to the role of history. For many a Christian, the resurrection of Jesus is essentially neither **historisch** nor **geschicht-lich**, but subjectively experienced in community. History has become biography.[29] Personal stories, if they elicit a commonly shared concern can be understood by everyone willing to listen and become the new underlying universal principle of legitimation. Biographical narratives, whether religious or not, whether in print or televised, are in fashion again.

As a consequence of pluralization and the relativization of plausibility models, modern man is faced with unavoidable choices, many of them introduced by modernity. The increasing accentuation of the subjective side of human existence, the perplexing tension between liberation and alienation, and the necessity to make decisions in a time-conscious society forces the individual to what Peter BERGER, with a stroke of genius, has called "the heretical imperative."[30] Basing his religious word play on the etymological meaning of the Greek verb **herein**, to choose, he states that "For pre-modern man, heresy is a possibility..., for modern man, heresy typically becomes a necessity... picking and choosing becomes an imperative."[31]

"The heretical imperative" is, however, not a **carte blache** for personal bliss. For if individual religiosity is to be stable it has to demonstrate coherence on the social plane. In the past, tradition provided everyone with a socialized, objective system of meaning as soon as it could be communicated via language and customs. But if secularization does indeed relativize religious institutions (especially religious language, eccelsiastical practice and education) then it becomes increasingly difficult for a person to internalize

---

substitute for "salvation."

[29] Peter BERGER, Social Reality, p. 168.

[30] Peter BERGER, The Heretical Imperative. Contemporary Possibilities of Religious Affirmation, London, 1980, especially pp. 1-31.

[31] Peter BERGER, Heretical Imperative, p. 28. In the same vein one could say that all existential narratives are heretical narratives, because "Biography too is a sequence of choices..." (p. 20).

socialization; that is to say, to integrate his experiences into a coherent biography in which he can locate himself in relation to his fellow men, the social order, and the sacred universe.

3.2.2.3. The Social Integration of Religion

Consequently, the question arises, what influence did secularization have on the social integration of religion? There is, according to Thomas LUCKMANN, an apparently self-defeating dialectical movement taking place in the social forms of religion.[32] On the one hand, when certain religious convictions become socially objectified the sacred universe begins to be standardized. It becomes possible for the majority of society to "grasp" the religious legitimation of existence in view of daily contingencies. In turn this allows for institutional specialization (especially in a Judaeo-Christian context). An institutionalized priesthood of some kind takes over as authority with differentiated functional roles, a well-established doctrine and ritual practice.[33] An official model of religion is now available for generations to come.

---

[32] Thomas LUCKMANN, Invisible Religion, pp. 50-68.

[33] Edwin Oliver JAMES underlines the dominant social function of institutional priesthood in the introductory statements of his article.
"Throughout the history of religion, the official institution that mediates and maintains a state of equilibrium between the sacred and profane aspects of human society, and that exercies a stabilizing influence on the social structures and cultic organization, is the priesthood... The primary role of the priest is that of the ritual expert." Edwin Oliver JAMES, Priesthood, in Encyclopedia Britannica. Macropaedia, Vol. 14, p. 1007.
Maybe the most telling example of institutionalized priesthood can be found in the organization of early Hinduism. The social division was threefold. It consisted in a class of priests, of warriors and of farmers. The king was chosen from among the warrior caste and had to be submissive to the elect who held the universe in order. To quote E.O. JAMES again: "The Vedic India... when the priestly caste (Brahmin, or Brahmana) was vested in a particular tribe or special class, it occupied the primary place of importance in the segmentation of Hindu society." (p. 1011)

On the other hand, "Only if religion is localized in special social institutions does an antithesis between 'religion' and 'society' develop."[34] That means that the problem of secularization only emerges where religion has made herself socially at home. This dialectic, between the attempt of any faith to establish itself and the resulting threat by the very social forms it has acknowledged, has probably come about because the original move towards institutionalization took place within a specific historical background. But as time passes and subsequent generations develop a different sense of their temporality, a clash with traditional values seems inevitable. It can therefore be argued that the cradle of secularization is religion itself.[35] LUCKMANN has universalized Max WEBER's thesis on the relationship between Protestantism and secularization.

But why, specifically, does secularization tend to weaken the subjective plausibility of the official religious convictions? Subjective plausibility refers to the individual's choice of fundamental options, and the basic difficulty comes up when the normal **repertoire** no longer satisfies the basic questions of existence. There are three points, LUCKMANN claims, that have the potential to induce an alienation of basic values.[36]

Firstly, any official model of religion not only contains insights into the realm of the Sacred, but also interpretations of its own institutional role. Both are to a certain point accepted and internalized by the believer. The potential danger of alienation lies in the fact that obviously institutional convictions cannot pretend to have the same ultimate significance as self-transcending beliefs. The hierarchy, especially when it senses a threat, is keen to assure its own survival, **as if** its structure were of ultimate significance. Modern man has detected this vested interest.

---

[34] Thomas LUCKMANN, Invisible Religion, pp. 66f.

[35] This has also been argued from a theological point of view by Jacques ELLUL and others; see below (3.2.3.1.1.).

[36] Thomas LUCKMANN, Invisible Religion, pp. 74-76.

Secondly, a ready-made model of religion contributes to secularization when particular requirements of conduct (e.g. Easter Duty or the observance of the Sabbath) overshadow ultimate and global values. But the very pervasiveness of religion centers on the fact that the sacred universe has a general rather than social basis. Particular requirements, prescribed by the officials, though, seem to indicate the opposite.

The third element of religious alienation gains momentum when the full-time experts of religion become divorced from the typical events and crises of the lay person. The separation between professional and amateur takes place not only on the level of experience, but also in terms of the language used to express fundamental convictions.

As a consequence, it becomes increasingly difficult for a individual to integrate him- or herself biographically (in the sociological sense) into the traditional social forms of religion. At the same time an individual's biography (in the literal sense) tends to express itself in a new, non-alienated language that obviously no longer conforms fully to the traditional code of faith.

3.2.2.4. Consequences for Theology and Biography

With the above in mind it is understandable that sociologists of religion suggest that the secularization of the social reality of religion brings about new theological options in general, and consequences for personal biography in particular.

As far as the theological options are concerned one can distinguish between pertinent new theological themes on the one hand, and different theological systems on the other. Probably the most influential themes emerging in secular societies have their commonality in subjectivation. The increasing plurality of world views calls for a new consciousness of the subject as well as of community. This means that subjectivation does not only refer to the individual but also to an increasing number of highly specialized movements of political, economic, sexual, ecological and religious convictions, to mention just a few.[37] The coming and going of revivalist groups, non-conformist fraternities, etc. points to the transitory character of modern models of thought.

The impact of subjectivation, though, is more easily understood when studied from the point of view of the individual. The emphasis on human autonomy, says Thomas LUCKMANN, favours a variety of concerns that relate to one's "private biography" in the contextual sense of the word.[38] There is the constant stress on self-realization, self-expression, and the management of small units of meaning which are chosen deliberately. Benita LUCKMANN argues,

> A relatively recent dimension of the social structure and of human existence, it (the private sphere) is located between and within the institutionally defined 'spheres of interests' and represents a 'no man's land', unclaimed by the powers that be. Within its confines man is free to choose and decide on his own what to do with his time, his home, his body and his gods.[39]

Formerly theology and religious practice provided a well-defined answer for these spheres of interest. Concerned believers are aware that this "no man's land" is expanding. But they also realize that modern man lives in an impoverished symbolic universe, but that he would also like to rediscover self-transcending values (e.g. recent trends in sexuality, new attention given to one's family, the myth-making industries of film and novel, the political celebration of anniversaries and summit meetings). A theological challenge may, therefore, consist in the reformulation of holistic meaning in man's sheltered subjectivity and in the vast structures of society alike.

---

[37] It is quite possible, in view of the difficulties of retaining stability within a community, that an increasing number of individuals will make use of multiple conversions; that is, the repeated transfer into another "world." The danger that the never ceasing reality-maintaining task may end in a pathological fragmentation of the individual is possibly thwarted if the ongoing biography is able to integrate misfortunes and **peripeteia** of meaning. Cf. Peter BERGER, Social Reality, p. 26-28; and for the notion of **peripeteia** 2.3.6.2.

[38] Thomas LUCKMANN, Invisible Religion, pp. 109 ff.

[39] Benita LUCKMANN, The Small Life-Worlds of Modern Man, in Thomas LUCKMANN (ed.) Phenomenology and Sociology, Harmondsworth, 1978, p. 280.

What theological approach would be most suitable to achieve this goal from a sociological point of view? Peter BERGER distinguishes three possibilities in his book The Heretical Imperative. Firstly, there is what he calls the deductive possibility.[40] It is a **re-affirmation of tradition** with a "leap of faith" as it is exemplified in Barthian neo-orthodoxy.[41] Although this position is empirically not falsifiable and grounded in experience (a plus factor for modern man), it is problematical in so far as it is rooted in a particular historical and biographical situation. In other words, the deductive possibility can be criticized for its static presuppositions. It is either a denial or an expulsion of secularization into non-religious domains, and in many ways akin to religious fundamentalism.

The second theological option is the reductive possibility.[42] It is concerned with an existential **translation of tradition** suitable to modern consciousness and fully aware of the process of secularization. A point in case is the bultmannian school of demythologization. But here again, "intellectual leaps" are taken. First, it is assumed that modern consciousness is superior to that of tradition, and second, it is by no means certain that man can no longer believe in and through myths. But the most fundamental problem is, according to BERGER, the following.

> It is difficult to stop the secularization process and, after a certain point, it becomes self-liquidating... On the practical level... All the secular benefits that the tradition is now supposed to "really be about" can be had without the tradition.[43]

The reductive approach, although open to the future, has virtually dismissed the voice of the past. A conscientious discussion on the function of contemporary religious narratives will, however, have to

---

[40] Peter BERGER, The Heretical Imperative, pp. 66-94.

[41] This "leap of faith" was due to a resolute refusal to accept the possibility of a natural theology, and the postulation that because God was the "wholly other" his revelation had to be accepted as a whole by an act of faith, or else one could not claim to "stand under the Word of God".

[42] Peter BERGER, The Heretical Imperative, pp. 95-124.

[43] Peter BERGER, The Heretical Imperative, p. 116.

take history and the symbolic universe of the past seriously, as the
discussion of GADAMER's notion of prejudice has suggested. Or to
repeat the words of Walter KASPAR, man is still a symbolizer as well
as a symbol.

The last option suggested by BERGER,[44] is a sort of phenomenological movement **from tradition to experience**. He calls it the
inductive possibility. Basically it is the outgrowth of Friedrich
SCHLEIERMACHER's fusion between historism and the subject.[45] Any
inductive approach is, of course, highly vulnerable to criticism and
it cannot provide absolute religious certainty, but it can take faith
and anthropological reality seriously. It is an oscillation between
the meta-human intentionality of religious consciousness recorded in
tradition and the contingent human perception of reality.[46] Provided
that it does not degenerate into a totalitarian ideology or a
fantastic utopia, man may be able to span a coherent biographical view
of events past, present and future, and to act accordingly.

In any case, the question at stake is, How can one communicate
matters of ultimate significance meaningfully? It will be the object
of this study to investigate whether narratives could contribute
positively to the dilemma of pluralized and often fragmented
communication. So far one aspect of the problem has crystalized.
Modern man, whether secular, religious, or both, is faced with the

---

[44] Peter BERGER, The Heretical Imperative, pp. 125-156.

[45] In the introduction to Friedrich SCHLEIERMACHER's Ueber die
Religion, Hans-Joachim ROTHERT states that the relationship between
historism and personal feelings of dependence is caught up in the dialectic of thought and faith.
"Es handelt sich darum, der Anschauung und mehr noch dem Gefühl
aus ihrer Isoliertheit herauszuhelfen und ihre ontologische Begründung
zu finden und das Gefühl damit als Fundament alles dessen zu erkennen,
was hernach in Denken und Glauben ergriffen wird. Geschichtlich aber
hat beides zu sein. Und dieses vom Ursprunge an "Erlösung" und
"Vermittlung" sind die beiden Grundworte, welche im Sinne
SCHLEIERMACHER's die Geschichtlichkeit nennen, um damit - so weit sich
das auf diese Weise tun lässt - die von aussen gegebene Gewissheit des
im Gefühl Ergriffenen und durch das Gefühl Bestimmten zu erreichen und
zu gewährleisten." Friedrich SCHLEIERMACHER, Ueber die Religion. Reden
an die Gebildeten unter ihren Verächtern, Hamburg, 1958, p. viii.

[46] Peter BERGER, The Heretical Imperative, p. 142.

same challenge of integrating experiences personally and socially into a meaningful whole. Life story, **histoire vécue**, may well be a universal language game that deserves closer attention from the sociologist and the theologian alike.

3.2.3. Secularization as a Religious Theme

As indicated above[47] the confrontation between the phenomenon of secularization and religious/theological beliefs has been varied. This section will limit itself by focusing on theological attempts which take secularization seriously, based on the conviction that it may contain positive potential for the advent or renewal of faith. Furthermore, the sociological notion of biography will be carried over and applied to a theological context referred to as "testimony."

3.2.3.1. Interpretations of Secularization

Recent western reflections on the function of secularization in relationship with religion have emphasized the open nature of the phenomenon. Especially Reformed Judaism, Protestantism and Catholicism have entered into a committed dialogue with the world that has become conscious of its temporality in its power and impotence. Generally, one can distinguish at least two lines of argumentation for the justification of such an enterprise. The first emphasizes that secularization is legitimated as a movement inherent to religion. A second considers secularization as a necessary social dialectic in which faith must be placed if religion wants to remain a credible proposition.

3.2.3.1.1. The argument that the process of secularization cannot be disassociated from religion can be based on the observation that the phenomenon is as old as religion itself.[48] Jacques ELLUL,

---

[47] In sections 3.2.1.1. and 3.2.1.2.

[48] "Dass sich einzelne Menschen oder Gesellschaftsschichten oder selbst eine ganze Epoche bisweilen nicht an die vorgefundenen religiösen Bestimmungen halten, sondern sich von ihnen freizumachen

endorsing the same argument, even though he, like others, distinguishes between "sacred" and "political or profane" secularization,[49] claims that there are three elements qualifying secularization. Firstly, all secularization is relative to a specific Sacred and a given societal situation. Secondly, a process of secularization can only begin if factors of replacement are already present in the social body. Thirdly, secularization can only come about if it absorbs and re-uses elements basic to the anterior Sacred.[50] To give an example, the cause, the internal dynamics, and the relative success of the protestant reformation can be studied with respect to these three aspects. These common denominators between "sacred" and "profane" secularization actually show that such a distinction can only be of theoretical/speculative value, since the sociological and religious aspects belong to the same life-world.

Perhaps ELLUL's most significant contribution lies in his suggestion that modern man is not without beliefs and references to a Sacred, and that if he is no longer committed to traditional religious values it might be because he has embraced the historical reality of secularization as a new system of belief.[51] Two claims are being made. The first is that the secularized person still relates to a Sacred (e.g. technology, the state), to myths as images of beliefs and power (e.g. history, science), and to spontaneous or organized religion with their specific values, dogmas, designation of heretics, and "clergy" (cf. the examples of contemporary myth in section 1.3.3.1.). The second claim relates to an ideological attitude towards secularization

---

suchen, ist ein Tatbestand, so alt und so verbreitet wie die Religion selbst." Albert KELLER, Säkularisierung, in Sacramentum Mundi, Band IV, p. 362.

[49] "Sacred" secularization emerges as a religious motivation concerned with the integration of new human insights, or as an attempt at reformation, or else as a necessity due to new divine revelation. "Profane" secularization is a result of social developments and interests. Cf. Enrico CASTELLI, Le problème du témoignage, in Herméneutique de la Sécularisation, Paris, 1976, pp. 13-16, 17 etc.

[50] Jacques ELLUL, Essai sur l'herméneutique de la Sécularisation fictive, in Herméneutique de la Sécularisation, pp. 155ff.

[51] Jacques ELLUL, Essai sur l' herméneutique, pp.158-170.

much in the same vein as GOGARTEN's description of secularism.[52]
Jacques ELLUL sees this as a form of "profane" secularization
overshadowing the possibilities of "sacred" secularization as well as
aspects of a re-emerging religious consciousness.[53] In other words,
secularized forms of substitute religion exist and do well because
they rely on similar dynamics as those which have motivated religion
in the past.[54] If this assertion is correct then the hermeneutical
tension between secularized language and religious narrative is not a
fatal one, and possibly bears in itself a vitalizing dialectic for new
meaning.

The classical protestant argument for the interpretation of
secularization as an inherently christian movement has been provided
by Friedrich GOGARTEN. He sees the relationship between faith and the
world in view of the doctrine of redemption from the world (in the
light of sin) and the christian responsibility for the world (in the
light of a liberating sonship in Christ).[55] Salvation is for GOGARTEN

---

[52] Cf. section 3.2.1.2.

[53] Whether there is indeed a movement of de-secularization as ELLUL
claims (Essai sur l' herméneutique, p. 164) is not of primary
importance to the present study of religious narratives. However, the
suggested presence of secularized forms of the sacred, myth and
religion is worthy to be noted, because they build a common ground for
the use of metaphors.

As far as the ideological critique of secularization is
concerned, one may consider ELLUL's threefold word of caution. A)
According to the model of T.S. KUHN, ideological paradigms
automatically delineate a certain field of experience and are
consequently not comprehensive. B) Christianity, in an effort to adapt
to secularization for the sake of credibility, may lose its specific
christian character and power as a factor for "sacred" secularization,
because it might become uncritical and insensitive to new forms of
religiosity. C) In the light of FEUERBACH's hermeneutics of suspicion
one may see belief in secularization as a need-fulfiller
(psychologically speaking), as social legitimator (sociologically
speaking), or as a guarantee and protection for man's seizure of the
world (religiously speaking).

[54] It will be the task of a hermeneutics of prophetic narratives to
see whether they are able to unmask the God-less aspects of
secularized substitute religion.

[55] Roman catholic approaches tend to emphasize the notions of creation
and incarnation as starting points for the theological placing of
secularization. Cf. Ulrich RUH, Säkularisierung, p. 192; Johann

a transformation to wholeness, which must take place not only on a vertical (i.e. sacred) level, but also on the horizontal (i.e. mundane) plane. Following the Pauline distinction between Law and Gospel, the lutheran theologian stresses that the New Testament's call to care actively for the world becomes the central issue of lived faith and the argument for secularization as a typically christian phenomenon.[56] In view of a possible totalitarian misinterpretation of secularisation and human freedom GOGARTEN maintains, however, an eschatological questioning. Any ideological fixation of secularization, he says, amounts to a mythological enclosure due to man's sinfulness, resulting in a secularized utopia void of any historicity and future.[57]

Although one can disagree with GOGARTEN on his bultmannian treatment of **mythos** as in stark contrast to **kerygma** because confession and narration should not be separated, he nevertheless has pointed out that it is possible and necessary to relate a concern for secularization with that of christian convictions. Furthermore it is important to put this relation into praxis, not only to place it theoretically, as proponents of political theology rightly emphasize. If religious narratives could facilitate a partial fusion of secular and religious horizons, then they could be a legitimate means of communication between those who affirm to believe and those who maintain not to do so.

Baptist METZ, Glaube in Geschichte und Gesellschaft, pp. 23 f.

[56] "Ist die Unterscheidung zwischen der göttlichen Wirklichkeit des Heils und den Werken des Gesetzes, wie wir sagten, das eigentliche und höchste Geschäft des Glaubens, weil er nur so das Heil, wie es von Gott verwirklicht ist, zu bewahren vermag, dann hat die Säkularisierung ihren Ansatz im Glauben selbst. Denn in dem der Glaube in dieser Unterscheidung die Werke in ihrer irdisch-weltlichen Bedeutung hütet, lässt er sie eine der Vernunft des Menschen überantwortete Angelegenheit der Welt, des Säkulums sein." Friedrich GOGARTEN, Verhängnis und Hoffnung, p. 102.

[57] Friedrich GOGARTEN, Verhängnis und Hoffnung, pp. 49, 194, 224.

3.2.3.1.2. A different approach to a christian view of
secularization is upheld by Paul RICOEUR. He considers <u>secularization</u>
<u>as a social dialectic</u> that places faith between the poles of ideology
and utopia. His view is interesting in so far as it allows a
consideration of the linguistic problems which are involved in the
formulation of ultimate values.

For RICOEUR secularization can pose a hermeneutic question only
if it fulfills three criteria.[58] First of all, it must relate on the
level of symbolic systems. Secularization questions the semiotic forms
of cultural expression. Secondly, secularization becomes a hermeneutic
question only if it relates to global symbolic systems, if one is
faced with a problem of **Weltanschauung**. Thirdly, it follows, according
to RICOEUR, that the interpretational challenge relates to fundamental
existential questions which are collectively shared. It is therefore
understandable that he places the notion of faith totally within the
tension **between** ideology and utopia, and speaks of secularization if a
belief system has submitted to a preferential option for either
extreme.[59] Granted, RICOEUR's hypothesis is speculative, but it does
suggest that the phenomenon of secularization can be approached
dialectically.

He stresses that ideology and utopia must be understood as
polysemic notions, and not just as pejorative designations of
pathological thought-systems; that is, not as diametrically opposed
distortions, but as complementary functions of social imagination.
Only then do they contribute to an analysis of underlying symbolic
structures of social action.[60] They are functions of social imagination because ideology, on the one hand, allows for the integration

---

[58] Paul RICOEUR, L'herméneutique de la sécularisation. Foi, idéologie,
utopie, in Enrico CASTELLI (ed.), Herméneutique de la Sécularisation,
Paris, 1976. pp. 49f.

[59] "... **la foi d'une communauté entre dans le processus de la
sécularisation lorsqu'elle se laisse inscrire dans l'alternative de
l'idéologie et de l'utopie,** lorsqu'elle n'est plus pour les uns qu'une
idéologie et lorsqu'elle n'a plus d'autre resource, si elle veut
échapper à cette réduction, que de se réclamer de l'utopie?" Paul
RICOEUR, L'herméneutique, p. 50 (emphasis his).

[60] Paul RICOEUR, L'herméneutique, pp. 51f., 56f.

of coherent meaning of action in relation to history and a given world view (e.g. tradition); on the other hand, utopia has a subversive function in so far as the individual is encouraged to dissociate himself from a symbolic system and the institutions belonging to it (e.g. alternative medicine). Both aspects can, of course, be involved in a power play; ideology often with "conservative action" legitimating an idealized system, utopia repeatedly with "anarchistic" options of life.[61] It is essential for social imagination that the tension between the two poles remains an open one.[62] Only then is the possibility and power of discourse granted.

Paul RICOEUR then suggests that it is within this tension that the faith of any religious community must be played out, without giving in to a reduction of purpose by identification with one of the poles. If an ideological reduction takes place, faith answers polemically with an ideological self-criticism delineated by its own social system.[63] If a utopian reduction occurs, faith is communicated apologetically as a reaction against self-criticism.[64] It is obvious that a "situation" of faith can only take place between the two if the concepts of ideology and utopia are allowed to play with each other more freely than their pejorative use would indicate.

The christian faith, then, finds a double linguistic expression, or rather a symbolic system on two levels. On the one hand, religion has its identity in the ideological side of faith, in memory, its ritual roots, as part of a model that **affirms that which is.** On the other hand, religion has its eschatological dimension in the utopian side of faith, uprooted because of or in spite of the social circumstance and maintaining a vacuum for the kingdom of God,

---

[61] Paul RICOEUR, L'herméneutique, pp. 56, 58f.

[62] "L'image-reflet et l'image-fiction ne sont que les figures extrêmes issues de l'éclatement de la dialectique de l'imaginarie social.
C'est pourquoi la tension entre idéologie et utopie est indépassable... La dialectique... est ouverte et sans fin." Paul RICOEUR, L'herméneutique, pp. 59f.

[63] Paul RICOEUR, L'herméneutique, pp. 61f.

[64] Paul RICOEUR, L'herméneutique, pp. 62f.

expecting **that which is not yet.**[65] In other words, faith has its home
in at least two narrative genres, in stories that integrate the past
into a meaningful whole and in prophecy which is not lured into a
false security of the present.

In summary one could say that recent christian interpretations of
secularization admit that the phenomemon must be taken seriously, and
not in the least because it is quite likely that Christianity has
provided an essential impetus to the development of this social
phenomenon. Furthermore, it is generally recognized that the
discussion between Christianity and the secularized world must by
necessity remain open. Finally, religion and its institutions should
not be content to fulfill the tasks which are assigned to them by
modern society and circumstance.[66] The christian faith is more than
just an ethical and cultural presence, a harbor of classical values.
It is responsible for voicing a critique of the social **status quo.** The
language it employs to do this must be able to bridge the two spheres
of influence. To speak theologically, the church must exercise the
gift of discernment when in dialogue with the world, to which it has
been called to minister by word and deed.

3.2.4. Secularization of Hermeneutics

Much has been said as to how a christian self-understanding can
cope with the process of secularization. A few words should also be
spent reflecting on the influence of secularization on the very
practice of interpretation that spells this self-understanding.

---

[65] (L'ultime constitution de la foi) "... est le déni même de la
dichotomie. En tant que Remémoration de certains événements qui font
époque - l'Exode, la Résurrection - elle a quelque chose en commun
avec le concept positif d'idéologie. En tant qu'Attente du Royaume à
venir, elle est parente du concept constituant d'utopie. Au niveau
même des genres littéraires de la Bible, elle conjoint la narration
qui donne son sense au passé et la prophétie qui ébranle toute
sécurité fondée dans le passé. La racine de la foi est près du point
où l'Attente jaillit de la Mémoire." Paul RICOEUR, L'herméneutique, p.
66; cf. also pp. 67, 68.

[66] Ulrich RUH, Säkularisierung, pp. 96f.

The influence of secularization on christian hermeneutics cannot be denied for three reasons. Firstly, the autonomous development of the sciences has increasingly been acknowledged by the protestant churches since the beginning of this century. The Roman Catholic Church, likewise, has conceded autonomy to the developments of technology and science; for instance in the pastoral constitution of the Second Vatican Council on the relation between the church and the world.[67] Non-christian interpretations of life are taken seriously by professionals, and are attractivly communicated to a large segment of society.

Secondly, since the critical impact of Ludwig FEUERBACH, Friedrich NIETZSCHE, Karl MARX and Sigmund FREUD, theories of interpretation are no longer content with simply reading a given text in order to understand its meaning.[68] They also ask about the psychological, social, economic and/or political motivations of the author and his of her social milieu. To a large extent christian hermeneutical theories, have accepted the social reality of language and have, therefore, integrated certain aspects of these **Rückfragen** as a necessary criticism of possible power structures. A relevant example of such an approach is illustrated by the study of Hans BLUMENBERG on secularization[69] where he suggests that secularization has not brought a change in content, but one of function. Secularization is understood as a Hegelian sublimation of values through a metaphorical play with notions in order to legitimate the **status quo** in the light of past developments. As a result the myth of eschatological salvation is

---

[67] Gaudium et Spes, chapter two, no. 57.

[68] These authors have essentially changed the discipline of hermeneutics by claiming that one could not interpret matters at face value. This "suspicious" approach sees underlying tendencies of human interest such as the projection of order, the drive to maintain power, alienation, and the subconscious control of desire as fundamentally influencing the framework of any thought system. A critique of ideology as integral part of any hermeneutical approach is often considered to be a basic presupposition.

[69] Hans BLUMENBERG, Säkularisierung und Selbstbehauptung, Frankfurt a. M., 1974. See especially chapter 5 entitled "Geschichte machen zur Entlastung Gottes?" pp. 64-74.

historically translated into the western notion of progress, and as
such deprived of its critical element by making it present and
consequently irrelevant.[70]

Thirdly, modern man, whether religious or not, is intensely aware
of his own temporality.[71] Whereas it was still possible in the Middle
Ages to integrate experiences and ideas in a large, stable and eternal
network of meaning, the modern individual demands valid answers for
the here and now, quite independent of a consent by the majority.
Theodicy is often transformed into a socio-dicy, and for many a person
all that matters is what one could call an idio-dicy, a private, or
more positively, personal justification of life. Many contemporary
religious models of meaning reflect the same temporal and often
personal imperative. In a similar way Ewert COUSINS suggests that many
new hermeneutical approaches to religion make use of a "sacred prag-
matism"[72] which tries to integrate resurgences of the Sacred with a
radically temporalized and historicized existence.

The secularization of hermeneutics has furthermore a quite
positive but often neglected side effect. It is not only exposing
religious interests and de-sacralizing (dis-enchanting?) traditional

---

[70] Another example BLUMENBERG discusses is the theodicy of LEIBNIZ in
which evil is no longer qualified morally (content) but instrumentally
(function). Hans BLUMENBERG, Säkularisierung, p. 66f.

[71] A good example of this approach is provided by Raimundo PANNIKAR,
La sécularisation de l'herméneutique. Le cas du Christ: Fils de
l'homme et Fils de Dieu, in Enrico CASTELLI (ed.), Herméneutique de la
Sécularisation, p. 213 - 248.
    "... l'événement de la sécularisation nous a amenés jusqu'à la
sécularisation de l'herméneutique. Elle consiste dans l'introduction
du facteur temps à l'interieur du processus herméneutique; ce dernier
nous rélève alors le caractère le plus profond de la sécularisation
qui consiste dans la présence du saeculum, entendu comme temporalité
incarnée, au coeur même de l'être et donc de tout la réalité." (p.
214)
    PANNIKAR attempts to show how christological interpretations have
changed emphasis within the history of Christianity, and pleads, in
the light of secularizing developments, for a "democratic" and "transcendental critique" conscious of the relativity of truth.

[72] Ewert COUSINS, La métamorphose de la sécularisation. Une
perspective américaine, in Enrico CASTELLI (ed.), Herméneutique de la
Sécularisation, p. 449 - 461.

christian values,[73] it also promotes a new "currency of meaning" a
language that believers learn to use, and non-believers can understand. This claim, though, has to be examined from a linguistic point
of view.

3.2.5. The Problem and Challenge of Language on the Intersection
Between "Official Currency of Meaning" and "Personal Expression
of Ultimate Concern"

The problem with language in general, and religious language
specifically, is (as it has been pointed out before) that secularization is able to outdate it. Not just words, notions, and sayings
may loose their meaning for large segments of society, but basic
functions and ways of using language may be "pushed away" by more
current forms of expression.[74]
The challenge of language is that, no matter where it has its
home, it can be learned. It seems that many scholars too easily assume
that if a certain way of speaking loses credibility, it is doomed for
ever or must be "written off." Much of the theology of the 1960's made
such hasty claims relating to the death of traditional religious
language. Now one is bound to be more careful in view of the emergence
of new forms of religion and communication. The question arises
whether there are intersections between religious and secular language
games?
In order to ascertain this possibility some insights and likely
consequences to the ambiguous character of language as it displays
itself in the tension between modern official (bureaucratic) language

---

[73] In the long run, this might not even be certain, as the resusci-
tation of old, and the introduction of new forms of religiosity seem
to indicate. Andrew GREELEY, Unsecular Man, pp. 160 f.

[74] A point in case is the argument of Marshall McLUHAN, who asserts
that the invention of the printing press has fundamentally changed
western man's use of language. But beyond this, McLUHAN claims that
the "typographic man" of the modern age is living with a different
world view, than that of medieval or oral cultures, and that the
"electronic man" of the twentieth century is again beginning to
perceive reality differently. Marshall McLUHAN, The Gutenberg Galaxy,
Toronto, 1962.

and religious illocutionary speech can be sketched out. Special emphasis will be given to the **function and use** of language, because it is believed that the argument that the process of secularization brings about a translation problem for religious communication, is only meaningful if the two linguistic worlds share common syntactic and semantic denominators.[75]

3.2.5.1. Basic Presuppositions

Three fundamental presuppositional questions need to be answered if indeed a dialogue (and therefore also a tension) between secular and religious language is possible. First, what exactly is implied when one refers to the act of translation. Second, is there a relationship between the use of a certain language game and the institutional authority behind it? Third, what does linguistic ambiguity bring about?

3.2.5.1.1. As far as translation is concerned what is at stake? Is it a substitution of secular notions for religious? Does translation refer to a shift from metaphorical to literal language? Or is it a question of exchanging one language game for another? First of all, no language (except maybe mathematical/logical codes) is in itself neutral. If one follows contemporary schools of interpretation[76] one

---

[75] Otherwise it would be meaningless to utter the criticism in the first place. Even if one claims that only language which is grounded empirically is useful, and that this condition cannot be met for instance when speaking about God, one still assumes that the accusation is understood based on the logic common to both linguistic fields. To give an example: It is possible to say, "I don't understand the statement 'Jesus was born of a virgin'." It is, however, meaningless to say, "When you speak about the divine, you may not use metaphors," because metaphors are used in all language games.

[76] From a heideggerian point of view no act of translation can be disassociated from the historicity of the translator. As has been mentioned one can say with H.G. GADAMER that every act of translation is at the same time an act of understanding going beyond the interpreting self. Finally if one opts for a marxist hermeneutic one would assume that any act of translation is bound to a network of causalities and social power structures, and is therefore a critique of ideology. Accordingly translation also implies a transposition of

comes to the conclusion that an act of translation is never merely a substitution of terms but also an act of interpretation, a placing within a world view. A translation from religious to secular language is therefore not simply: for "God" read "universal reason," but: for "God" plus implied value read "universal reason" plus implied value. In other words, only the larger context of discourse can approximate what meaning the translatory notions contain, and in what measure they overlap.

From this it also follows, that translation cannot limit itself to the deliberate change from metaphorical to literal language. Firstly, because it is unlikely that literal language is a sufficient condition for communication. Secondly, because metaphorical speech can be found in all language games.[77] It is thus probable that the intersection between official secular language and religious speech can be partially located in the metaphorical residue of secular language. Indeed, Hans BLUMENBERG warns against a secular sublimation of religious metaphors in order to enrich the aesthetic potential of secular language; for example by speaking about God without any

presuppositions, values, and meaning. Cf. the article by Michael ERMARTH, Transformation, pp. 175-194.

[77] Examples from philosophy and scientific theory can be found in: Jacques DERRIDA, White mythology, in Margins of Philosophy, Chicago, 1982, pp. 207-271; and Paul FEYERABEND, Against Method, London, 1975, chapter 17, pp. 223-285.
  Jacques DERRIDA argues that western philosophy is inherently metaphorical because of its metaphysical presuppositions and because any concept of metaphor is by itself a philosopheme.
  Paul FEYERABEND follows B.L. WHORFF's argument "that languages and the reaction patterns they involve are not merely instruments for **describing** events (facts, states of affair), but that they are also **shapers** of events (facts, states of affair), that their 'grammar' contains a cosmology, a comprehensive view of the world, of society, of the situation of man which influences thought, behaviour, perception." (p. 223) FEYERABEND then applies this linguistic theory to the elaboration of scientific models and argues that new insight necessitates the building of new language, for the already existing categories of thought are usually incommensurable with newly aquired knowledge because perfect translation is never possible. The metaphoricity of common language is implied in typical statements like: "Now we know that almost every language contains within itself the means of restructuring large parts of its conceptual apparatus. Without this, popular science, science fiction. fairy-tales, tales of the supernatural, and science itself would be impossible." (p. 273)

transcendental substance.[78] But the very problem suggests also the
possibility of speaking meaningfully in metaphorical ways about God,
because religious connotations survive.

Furthermore, an act of translation is not complete if it is
limited to changing the language game. Precisely because it is a
language "game" it is bound to agreed-upon rules of communication.
Stated negatively, those rules pose the major problem for translation,
because it is so difficult to pin them down. Positively seen, the very
agreement to abide by rules (even if they are anti-rules as in modern
literature) is the common denominator of all language games. One can
say that this linguistic intentionality goes beyond the borders of any
single language game; and by affirming intentionality one no longer
speaks about a translation, but quite appropriately about an **act** of
translation.

3.2.5.1.2. As far as the relationship between language and institutional authority is concerned, one can say that each language game
has its own linguistic "home." General psycho-analysis, for instance,
emphasizes that each relatively healthy human being feels the need to
communicate, and that he or she is successful in doing so because
there is the strong tendency to speak coherently in "normal"
circumstances. There is a correlation between language and personal
integrity. The individual can communicate best where there is a
harmonious relationship between the self and the others. Consequently,
it is appropriate to formulate and study the problem of secularization
and religious language in terms of **loci** in which particular ways of
expression manifest the greatest amount of institutionalized
authority. Those **loci** in turn could indicate something about the
intentionality of particular modes of expression. It has been

---

[78] Hans BLUMENBERG, Säkularisierung, pp. 119-139.
" Die Rede von der 'Omnipotenz' des Gesetzgebers ist erkennbar auch
(sic?) ein staatstheoretischer Kraftakt, für den sich die Anspielung
auf den stärksten Selbstvergleich geradezu anbietet. Als Stilwille
sucht die Säkularisierung bewusst die Beziehung zum Sakralen als
Herausforderung. Es bedarf eines hohen Masses an Fortgeltung der
religiösen Ursprungssphäre, um eine solche Wirkung zu erzielen, so wie
'schwarze Theologie' ihre blasphemischen Schauder nur dort entfalten
kann, wo die sakrale Welt noch besteht." (p. 120).

suggested that the "home" of religious language is liturgy, and that
the "home" of secularized language can be found in highly specified
speech occasions such as the classroom, the judicial court, or the
business meeting.[79] The study of religious narratives in the context
of worship is thus an attempt to take their linguistic home seriously.
In addition, those narratives cannot be isolated from the temporality
they relate to. Once more the problem of the secularization of the
religious can therefore be defined in terms of the breakdown of a
formerly global linguistic system on the one hand, and the multipli-
cation of authoritative and integrative settings on the other.

3.2.5.1.3. Finally, there is the presupposition that linguistic
ambiguity has certain causes. That language is ambiguous has not only
been shown above by the practical difficulties met in the various
interpretations of the notion of secularization, but it can also be
observed when a speech act does not produce the desired effects.[80] In
view of the function of religious and secular narratives of the self
and/or ultimate meaning three particular causes of ambiguity need to
be considered.

Firstly, there is the effect of metaphors, producing an
intentional "category mistake" as explained in chapter two. As far as
"official language" is concerned, it attempts to eliminate as many
metaphorical statements as possible for the benefit of clarity and
preciseness. But biographical speech, whether religious or secular,

---

[79] Richard K. FENN, Secular Constraints on Religious Language, in The
Annual Review of the Social Sciences of Religion 4 (1980), pp. 61ff.
It is interesting to note that those "homes" of maximal language/
integrity correlation are quite literally edifices of authority, or
metaphorically speaking "temples" in which absolute statements are
easily made. For religious language it is the church or the chapel,
for secular education it is the school building or the university
campus, for the court it is the "classic halls of justice", for
politics it is the "White House" or the palace, for the business world
it is the office of the "boss" or the well-furnished conference room.

[80] E.g. when some authority issues a command that is not being
followed, either because of a misunderstanding (Common evangelistic
motto: "Jesus is the answer!" But what is the question?) or because of
its conscious violation (Popular slogan of the peace movement:
"Suppose they declare a war, and no one goes?"). In both cases there
may also be the loss of the illocutionary force.

consciously employs metaphorical expression in order to say more than
the immediate and tangible. It can be interpreted as a poetic move to
self-transcendence. Or in other words, affective emotions cannot be
contained in flatly descriptive language.

Secondly, Emile BENVENISTE has pointed to the significance of
what are now commonly referred to as "shifters."[81] Pronouns,
especially the word "I," give stability to a certain context. In spite
of polysemy and the danger of dissemination pronouns are effective
limiting concepts, because the hearer has a certain idea (if necessary
by heuristic fiction) to whom the pronoun refers. However, these very
pronouns are called shifters because the context changes when someone
else is telling the same story. That is, the "I" of the individual as
others see it may change the emphasis or even the basic meaning of
what is being said. Personal speech is, therefore, set on trial,
especially when absolute claims are made. It is paradoxical that
secularization has brought an increase in linguistic ambiguity by the
proliferation as well as relativation of absolutes, but at the same
time it has provided an element of linguisitc stability by the
increased importance it entrusts to the individual.

Thirdly, language can become ambiguous because of the conscious
disruption of communicative patterns, for instance through the
eruption of utmost personal and prophetic speech. A given religious
linguistic framework, e.g. a completely fixed liturgy, is disrupted
and possibly called into question when an unofficial but equally
craft-bound language is introduced, e.g. the **ad hoc** prayer of a lay
person. Or in a secular context, the procedures in court are
interrupted when a witness suddenly begins to advance his own
interpretation of the case. By agreement, courts consider such a
linguistic performance as illicit. But the question remains, can it be
that such disruptions do have a linguistic legitimation in spite of
the western tendencies to outlaw them?

---

[81] Emile BENVENISTE, Problèmes de linguistique générale, Paris, 1966,
pp. 251-257.
    Cf. also Leonard LAWLOR, Event and Repeatability: Ricoeur and
Derrida in Debate, in Pre/text 4, 3-4 (Fall Winter 1983), p. 331.

The use of metaphors, the function of shifters, and the disruption of communicative patterns seem to indicate that linguistic ambiuity has an important function in the establishment and questioning of world views. On the one hand, it allows for an expansion of the communicative horizon, on the other hand, it plays a critical role in relation to what is being uttered. In any case, the elimination of linguistic ambiguity seems to be counter-productive with regard to the study of the relationship between secular and religious language, because neither seems to be able to cope without it. The following section is a sociologist's attempt to correlate the two lingistic fields in view of the presuppositions enumerated above.

3.2.5.2. Richard FENN's Theory of the Secularization of Religious Language

Richard FENN, a North-American sociologist of religion, has a particular interest in the tension existing between religious and secular discourse. What power plays exist between the two and what consequences are thereby implied? In spite of the occasional lack of terminological clarity, his theory of secularization as it pertains to religious speech provides some useful insights. First, his theory will be explained with particular attention to notions that also occur in the writings of the other scholars consulted so far. Second, his contribution will be critiqued in order to situate it within the context of the present research.

3.2.5.2.1. FENN's basic argument is based on a differentiation and comparison of two ideal types: eventful religious language on the one side, and literal secular speech on the other. FENN claims that,

> The translation of religious into secular discourse... is facilitated by the development of secular authority in the context of the classroom, for instance, and the court. In these contexts the authority of a religious community or tradition is suspended as a guarantee of a speaker's seriousness. The reduction in authority is especially likely if religious discourse is not initially framed within a liturgical context. On the other hand, liturgical contexts minimize the effective-

ness of prophetic utterances, since the latter are effective to the extent that they disrupt discourse in everyday life or in secular institutional contexts.[82]

To put it concisely, FENN sees the problem as one related to the authority implied in any given use of language. Secularization brings about a **continuous** trial situation that is basically foreign to liturgical discourse, although the idea of a trial has definitely religious roots.

As a matter of fact, FENN assumes that **the situation of trial** is a typical element of western cultures. On the religious level there is a rich tradition of themes that situate mankind before a major test or trial; it might be called "Odyssey," "Covenant," "Last Judgment;" and on a semi-religious level "the eventual triumph of the proletariat," or "victory of human reason."[83] On the secular level trials are no less common.

> A lifetime on probation can fairly characterize social life in secular institutions. In the schools, colleges, and universities of Western societies the majority of youth are subjected to a process of continuous testing and evaluation. Positions in these institutions are initially probationary... "Management by objective"... guarantees that convenants between supervisors and employees will be carried out faithfully if the relationship is to continue... Political campaigns themselves resemble a primitive test of stamina... In the scientific community hypotheses enjoy a probationary status and require repeated testing...[84]

The western person is put on constant trial, because he is frequently compelled to "speak for the record." His words are constantly weighed. The trial has become a social arrangement for closing the gap between language and reality.[85]

Now FENN argues that in "the **liturgy**"[86] the trial is "finished,"

---

[82] Richard FENN, Secular Constraints, p. 61.

[83] Richard FENN, Liturgies and Trials. The Secularization of Religious Language, Oxford, 1982, pp. 45f.

[84] Richard FENN, Liturgies and Trials, p. 48.

[85] Richard FENN, Liturgies and Trials, p. 51.

[86] Here unfortunately he does not qualify what kind of liturgy he has in mind although he consistently uses the definite article. He admits using the notion ideally, but the concept in a secular society is too

the battle is fought, the deliberation is certain. A gap between language and reality is inadmissible. Secularization, according to him, sets in when worship in its turn is being placed before a trial, and when it can no longer afford to celebrate a mock-trial in which the verdict is always the same.[87] Whereas in the past a liturgical context guaranteed the seriousness of religious and symbolic language, today it is faced with a legitimation crisis that came about, according to FENN, because of a conflict between two divergent rules of discourse in the western world.

FENN follows the common **distinction** between a Hellenistic and a biblical type **of discourse.** The first is concerned with meaning and whether a word is true or false, the second is preoccupied with utterance and whether a word comes about or is empty. Secularization, he claims, works as paradox between the two.[88] On the one hand, it brings about a separation between religious language and the sacred "reality" which was its home. Language is suddenly on its own. On the other hand, the secularization of language, as it leads to this dis-enchantment and alienation, creates a "hunger for words that require a relationship and issue in solid deeds."[89] The paradox of western secularization is a dialectic between language, trial and the concern for ultimate meaning and truth.

The **consequence for secular language,** according to Richard FENN, is that it is increasingly losing eventful speech. For instance seminar talk is typical of uneventful speech. There secular speech acts constantly make use of qualifiers such as: "It seems to me that..," "I agree..., but," "I would like to suggest that..." If an individual does advance a personal directive idea it is often formulated implicitly. It is potentially dangerous to offend the teacher, and therefore safer to speak as neutrally as possible.

---

pluriform as to allow this. Furthermore, FENN's own deductions should lead him to a larger functional understanding of religious language; cf. below.

[87] Richard FENN, Liturgies and Trials, pp. 22, 27.

[88] Richard FENN, Liturgies and Trials, pp. 74-77.

[89] Richard FENN, Liturgies and Trials, p. 77.

In judicial language, to give another example, constant attempts are made to reduce the interpretative possibilities of speech acts. A testimony has to be as literal as possible if the account of the witness is to be credible, and the reliance on an unscientific or spiritual authority is being frowned upon.[90] An illustrative case in point was the trial in the matter of Karen Ann QUINLAN.[91] Although religious convictions where the basic motivating force in desiring passive euthanasia, the court ruled against the validity of religious testimony (the story of the spiritual struggle that led up to the decision to disconnect the girl from the life support system) and authority (of the priest that had repeatedly counseled her parents and advised them according to the teachings of the Church as he understood them).

Finally, secular language limits the relevance of possible speech acts. For instance the phrase, "The Prime Minister is gone," is usually considered to be a statement about a state of affairs. It could be understood as a suggestion (for a **coup d'état**) only in a a few instances. In contrast, religious speech, due to its kerygmatic nature, employs a variety of speech acts within a single utterance. The phrase "Jesus is Lord" may be understood as a telling, an announcement, a directive command or even a warning. To put it concisely, FENN claims that the modern person must resort to other than secularized language games if he wants to speak eventfully.

The **consequence** of secularization **for religious language** is a tendency to become less eventful. Whereas religious words used to make things happen, (e.g. "I pronounce you man and wife" or "Your sins are forgiven") they now tend to conform to the language of everyday life. They conform to the descriptive criteria found in dictionaries. Furthermore, religious speech loses the power it formerly had of allowing for an identification between speaker and meaning, because the secular trend towards plurality and private convictions undermines corporate beliefs and values.

---

[90] Richard FENN, Liturgies and Trials, pp. 189 + 193.

[91] Richard FENN, Liturgies and Trials, chapter 6.

Positively seen, this development makes inter-subjective discourse, at least on a superficial level, between different interest
groups easier. But the negative aspect is that religious language
loses its evocative aspect. There is consequently the tendency to
separate theological from liturgical language. The one is flatly
descriptive and explanatory, the other is mythological and ritual-
izing. FENN illustrates this process of secularization by means of the
following table.[92]

Corporate beliefs and values	Mythical framework	
	Present	Absent
Present	(1) Prophecy	(3) Metaphor
Absent	(2) Allegory	(4) Literalism

He claims that the ideal religious speech situation is prophetic,
evoking a mythological atmosphere in all its openness, ambiguity and
suggestiveness. Prophetic speech has the complete freedom to speak the
mind of the religious community. But the sociologist claims that such
an ideal state does not last for long. Adopting arguments from Norman
PERRIN,[93] FENN reasons that a partial secularization of the Gospel
already took place in the early church.[94] In the course of history
prophetic signs became standard symbols, parables were no longer
applied but interpreted as allegories, and eventually myths of the
kingdom were reduced to mere metaphors. Today religious language is
tempted to yield to the plain advantages of literal language as the
powerful secular institutions seem to suggest. Secularization is thus

---

[92] Richard FENN, Liturgies and Trials, p. 175.

[93] Norman PERRIN discusses the hermeneutical transformation of
biblical symbols as he claims to notice them, for example, in Luke
17:20-37, arguing "that Jesus' reference to the coming of the Kingdom
of God is being interpreted as a reference to the coming of the Son of
Man." Norman PERRIN, Jesus and the Language of the Kingdom. Symbol and
Metaphor in New Testament Interpretation, Philadelphia, 1976, p. 58.

[94] Richard FENN, Liturgies and Trials, pp. 171ff.

the movement away from the "home" of religious language where corporate beliefs and a mythical framework are present to an area where these components are increasingly absent.

Many religious communities today try to rescue eventful language by ritualization, but their success is limited to the degree that the liturgical rubrics have ousted disruptive prophetic speech. Modern man, FENN claims, accepts well defined and explicit symbols more easily than open-ended and suggestive signs. When prophecy does appear it is likely to be misunderstood as allegory or "bad metaphor."[95]

It is important to note that Richard FENN made a conscious choice as to how he was going to use literary notions such as "sign," "symbol," "metaphor," and "prophecy." The fact that his usage of these terms is the reverse of Paul RICOEUR's is acknowledged[96] and thus not as problematic as could be assumed. The linguistic dynamics discussed are the same for both authors. These dynamics are active in signs and prophetic speech, and they are alive in symbols, living metaphors, as well as prophetic and some other literary genres. Further common elements between the two scholars of the social sciences is the importance they attribute to testimony and trial. Both are also interested by the resurgence of religious language in spite of the **moratorium** feared or announced by people as different as Max WEBER, Karl MARX,[97] and some post-religious theologians.

3.2.5.2.2. A critique of Richard FENN's theory allows a summary of his major contributions as well as an evaluation. An important aspect is certainly the situation of trial for modern man. It is a socio-linguistic experience that has established itself in all strata

---

[95] Richard FENN, Liturgies and Trials, pp. 95ff.

[96] Richard FENN, Liturgies and Trials, p. 168.

[97] Max WEBER feared a moratorium on Christianity because he considered the capitalistic spirit able to assert itself without the backup of a religious morality, since it could provide its own reasons for social togetherness. On the otherhand, Karl MARX and Friedrich ENGELS were certain that the influence of the French revolution and the English Enlightenment would give a fatal blow to all forms of religiosity. Bärbel WALLISCH-PRINZ, Religionssoziologie. Eine Einführung, Stuttgart, 1977, pp. 38, 56.

of life, and functions as a common denominator of religious and
non-religious issues alike. Trial is more than a common problem, it is
the matrix of life.[98]

Another positive element in FENN's theory is the role attributed
to language. Irrespective of the individual's or community's
situation, language is the privileged means for the search and
expression of meaning. Its paradoxical nature (literal preciseness and
poetic ambiguity) makes the quest for meaning an unending one. The
secularization of religious language shows that the community of faith
is not exempted from this process, and that it has fundamental
implications for the language of worship. However, it must also be
kept in mind that the literary emphasis of secular language creates a
vacuum relating to the expression of existential and/or spiritual
values. A substitution of secular language for religious is therefore
no solution to problems of communication. Rather the linguistic state
of affairs can be described as a tension between the liturgical spirit
and the literalism of the law. Richard FENN has correctly pointed out
that any serious attempt at communication between the two aspects of
modern life will have to take place at the threshold of the two
linguistic fields, because neither is without some element of the
other.

FENN's analysis has also to be examined negatively. As indicated
above his use of literary and religious vocabulary, although
consistent, will not satisfy many a linguist, psychologist of
religion, or liturgist. Notions like metaphor, symbol, prophecy, myth,
vision and even testimony have to be discussed in their own right.
From a theological point of view it is necessary to consider the
common usage of terms, but this is not sufficient.

A second problem arises when FENN speaks about the liturgy. He
consistently uses the definite article and treats liturgy as if it
were a well-defined, self-contained system of rubrics. But liturgy
under the influence of secularization is no longer a closed system (as
it was for instance in the eighteenth century). Furthermore, the

---

[98] The ubiquity of trial constitutes a fundamental reason for the
practice of prophetic speech in the religious community. Besides, it
encourages responsibility towards the secular sphere of life.

history of prophetic, reform and revivalist movements shows that
liturgy has not been immune to trial in the past. In view of the
contemporary pluriformity of religious expression and celebration it
is safer to speak in terms of the broader notion of worship, if for no
other reason then to assess more clearly the function of disruptive
religious speech, and to dispel the presumption that liturgy does not
exist unless the order of worship has been textualized.

3.2.6. Consequences For Religious Narratives in View of Their Secularization

This section intends to situate the insights on secularization in
relation to the literary genres that are going to be taken up in the
remaining chapters of this study on therapeutic and prophetic
narratives in the context of worship.

3.2.6.1. Primary Considerations

In general it must **first** be taken into account that religiously
significant narratives are most likely to remain a mixture of
secularized (mostly literal) and sacred/poetic (mostly metaphorical)
language. A translation in terms of a substitution of secularized
vocabulary for religious, although at times fruitful, cannot be
considered as the primary resolution of the plausibility problem in
religious speech.

To illustrate this point one may look to the writings of Dietrich
BONHOEFFER, the early partisan of religious secularization. On the one
hand BONHOEFFER emphasizes that religious notions are problematic in
our age, and that they should be translated into a "religion-less"
language (in the Barthian sense of the word) if they are not to lose
their biblical significance and meaning.[99] To provide an example, a

---

[99] "Noch ein paar Worte zu den Gedanken über die 'Religions-
losigkeit'... Nicht nur 'mythologische' Begriffe wie Wunder, Himmel-
fahrt etc. (die sich ja doch nicht prinzipiell von den Begriffen Gott,
Glauben etc. trennen lassen!), sondern 'religiöse' Begriffe schlecht-
hin sind problematisch. Man kann nicht Gott und Wunder von einander

word like "sanctification" may in many contemporary contexts have to
be translated as a progression towards "integrity." On the other hand
BONHOEFFER is a poet and consciously theologizes by making full use of
biblical metaphors - as the following examples show:

> God is teaching us that we must live as men who can get along
> very well without him. The God who is with us is the God who
> forsakes us (Mark 15.34). The God who makes us live in this
> world without using him as a working hypothesis is the God
> before whom we are ever standing... God allows himself to be
> edged out of the world and on to the cross. God is weak and
> powerless in the world, and that is exactly the way, the only
> way, in which he can be with us and help us.

And elsewhere,

> Who am I? This or the other?
> Am I one person to-day and to-morrow another?
> Am I both at once? A hypocrite before others,
> And before myself a contemptibly woebegone weakling?
> Or is something within me still like a beaten army,
> Fleeing in disorder from victory already achieved?

> Who am I? They mock me, these lonely questions of mine. Whoever
> I am, Thou knowest, O God, I am thine![100]

The point to be made is that the secularization of religious language
relates to the content of communication rather than to its form. This
basic fact has often been overlooked by analysts of religious language
and narrative theologians alike.

A **second** basic consideration relating to the credibility of
religious narratives in view of their secularization concerns their
context. Not just what is being said is relevant for interpretation
but also how and where it is said. In other words, the problem of the
communication of faith to another world of discourse should also be

---

trennen (wie Bultmann meint), aber man muss **beide** 'nicht-religiös'
interpretieren und verkündigen können." (emphasis his) "Ich denke
augenblicklich darüber nach, wie die Begriffe Busse, Glaube, Rechtfertigung, Wiedergeburt, Heilung 'weltlich' - im alttestamentlichen
Sinne und im Sinne von Joh. 1, 14 - umzuinterpretieren sind." Dietrich
BONHOEFFER, Widerstand und Ergebung, München, 1962, pp. 183, 185.

[100] Dietrich BONHOEFFER, Letters and Papers from Prison, London, 1953,
pp. 122, 173. In the first example one finds an abundance of
existential paradoxes along with theological oxymorons. In the second
example the same dialectic is at work, but now reinforced with
metaphorical imagery and a parallelism that allows an identification
with Jesus' dilemma on the cross.

seen from the **Sitz im Leben** of non-religious plausibility systems. For
this reason it will be appropriate to study the function of secular
biography in its narrow sense (cf. 3.3.) and to compare it with religious testimony (3.4.). Afterwards it will be possible to suggest the
hermeneutical and theological implications relevant to this study.

However, in order to facilitate a comparison between religious
(possibly secularized **and more**) and non-religious (certainly secularized and self-sufficient) narratives, a preliminary sketch of oral
religious narratives and their basic aspects will be given.

3.2.6.2. The Symbolic Level

Regarding secularization, one can describe the importance of
symbols for religious narrative in at least two ways, provided its
Ricoeurian definition is valid. First, parallel to the ambivalent
nature of language, one can understand the function of symbol as
integrating the individual and the religious community into society.
Symbols then do not only serve to illustrate a transcendent universe,
but they can also express an intentionality of the here and now, and a
horizon common to two world views. Precisely because a symbol is
ambiguous (i.e. referring to different "realities" at once) neither of
its referents can afford a closure. This is, for example, the opinion
of Antoine VERGOTE.[101] Such a view does, of course, presuppose that
there is no total division or antagonism between the world of faith
and the world of faith-less praxis. In other words, the process of
secularization is acknowledged. On the other end of the same spectrum
one finds Raimundo PANNIKAR's insistence that the secularized world
taken in its own right is not a world without symbol. A non-religious
person, especially if he is part of western society, may not consider
Jesus Christ to be Lord and Saviour; nevertheless Jesus of Nazareth
may still be a real symbol to him.[102]

---

[101] "Dans l'existence personelle et dans la société, une unité s'opere
à partir des differences maintenues." Antoine VERGOTE, La Sécularisation. De l'héliocentrisme à la culture d'ellipse, in Enrico CASTELLI
(ed.), Herméneutique de la Sécularisation, Paris, 1976, p. 364.

[102] Raimundo PANNIKAR, La sécularisation de l'herméneutique, pp.

The second significance of symbols in narratives (whether
secularized or not) is that their meaning finds fulfillment in praxis.
It is no coincidence that symbols relate to rituals and the re-
enactment of myths. A criticism of narratives contributing to a
coherent world view does, therefore, not lie in their use of "mere"
symbols, but in the question whether these symbols encourage a closure
of a thought model, or whether they invite the community of interpretation to action, symbolic and otherwise, somewhere between
ideology and utopia.[103]

3.2.6.3. Testimony

Religious testimony, especially in protestant circles, is often
put in the context of an experience of conversion. This is convenient
in so far as secularized branches of knowledge (e.g. sociology and
psychology) do relate to the same phenomenon. Testimony as an account
of the formation or change of convictions has a footing in both worlds
of discourse. Trutz RENDTORFF even sees in representational con-
sciencization a basic justification of religion in society, for he
claims that any theory formation must pass through the assimilation of
personal experiences.[104]
     Wayne E. OATES has studied the transformatory aspects of secular
as well as religious conversion, and suggests that it is important to
acknowledge the common ground between the two for the following
reasons.[105] Firstly, religious testimonies, if they are told in

---

246-248.

[103] For an excellent introduction to the linguistic, inter-subjective
and religious dynamics of symbols see Louis-Marie CHAUVET, Du
symbolique au symbolism, Paris, 1979, especially pp. 13-79.

[104] "Der genetische Ort für die Theoriebildung liegt in der sich
ständig erneuernden Präsenz des individuellen Bewusstseins und seiner
Erfahrungswirklichkeit... Wirklichkeit im ganzen kann im Spiegel
individueller Erfahrung durchsichtig gemacht werden." Trutz RENDTORFF,
Gesellschaft ohne Religion?, München, 1975, p. 81.

[105] Wayne E. OATES, Conversion. Sacred and Secular, in Walter E. CONN
(ed.) Conversion. Perspectives on Personal and Social Transformation,
New York, 1978, pp. 149-168.

"official currency," are not meaningless to secularized individuals, for they also want to make sense of experiences relevant to the formation of personal identity. Secondly, it is important to notice that secular conversions find, like their religious counterparts, expression in "poetic, mythical and rhapsodic" language.[106] Thirdly, these peak- or plateau-experiences, as Abraham MASLOW calls them, are now more than ever before acknowledged in their own right in the secular realm.[107] This is significant, for the question must be asked in how far then religious testimonies are different from secular ones? In brief, secular biography and religious testimony cannot be completely separated from each other. Their commonality and difference lies to a large extent in their ambiguous use of language in order to express human experience.

3.2.6.4. Prophecies and Visions

Richard FENN has strongly emphasized the disruption of institutionalized speech patterns as a problem in the secularization of religious language. In the secular domain the sudden incursion of prophetic speech, as he calls it, cannot be completely avoided. In the religious domain there is a strong tendency to diffuse the critical

---

Both may be: 1) an acceleration of growth, 2) a unification of a divided self, 3) a change of direction, 4) an act of surrender, or 5) a programmed conversion to another social reality.

[106] Wayne E. OATES, Conversion, p. 166.

[107] Since Abraham H. MASLOW wrote Religions, Values, and Peak-Experiences, New York, 1964, he has qualified his notion of "peak-experience", in a more recent preface, by adding the more secular concept of a "plateau-experience" to his psychoanalytic model.
"...I would now add to the peak-experience material a greater consideration... of the 'plateau-experience.' This is a serene and calm, rather than poignantly emotional, climactic, autonomic response to the miraculous, the awesome, the sacralized, the Unitive, the B(eing)-values.... Peak- and plateau-experience differ also in their relations to death. The peak-experience itself can often meaningfully be called a 'little death,' and a rebirth in various senses. The less intense plateau-experience is more often experienced as pure enjoyment and happiness..." (pp. xiv, xv)

power of prophetic speech by delegating it to a limited realm of
legitimacy. In either case, the power of disruptive speech patterns is
kept at a minimum.

Another aspect in FENN's research consists in the accentuation of
the fact that established speech patterns tend to be secularized no
matter whether they belong to the sacred or the "worldly" realm.
Prophecy, although formerly an exclusively religious affair, now has
its home in both domains. Its role is to indicate that the dialectic
between human identity and social integrity goes beyond the letter of
the law. Prophetic narratives in worship can function as an eschatological reservation, as a warning against hidden interests (ideology)
and utopian escapes provided they are situated in a self-critical
praxis of faith, as Paul RICOEUR and others have pointed out.[108]

Negatively, it must be observed that FENN's notion of the
phenomenon of prophetic speech is so vague that it is difficult to
study it concretely. For this purpose it will be helpful to
investigate disruptive narratives as concrete literary genres, namely
in the form of prophetic visions. The aim of chapter five will be to
establish their function and intentionality in the religious realm.

3.2.6.5. Myth

As mentioned above,[109] Jacques ELLUL has stated that the process
of secularization can only come about if it partially absorbs and
re-uses elements basic to an anterior Sacred. If this argument is
valid, it follows that modern man is just as much in need of
integrating images of belief and power as the religious person of the
past. Myths, in such a context, are considered to be providers of
meaning and explainers of global/ existential circumstances, but as
BLUMENBERG has pointed out, myths must not be sheltered from an

---

[108] Paul RICOEUR, L'herméneutique de la sécularisation, pp. 64-68
especially; Concilium General Secretariat / Nijmegen, Toward a
Renewal of Religious Language, in Concilium 42 (1969), pp. 178-180,
which speaks about the necessity for religious language to be set free
a) from out-dated socio-linguistic forms, and b) to the self-examining
power of faith.

[109] Cf. 3.2.3.1.1.

ideology critique. In addition Andrew GREELEY stresses that the
changes in the world challenge the believers to a new hermeneutic act,
which basically consists in a reinterpretation of their mythological
traditions.[110] One way of keeping the meaning of myths open to the
challenges of the present is by maintaining a prophetic presence. In
considering the mythologizing power of certain liturgical narratives,
it will be important to welcome their affinity to secular "models" of
universal explanation (cf. 1.3.3.1.), to study their function in the
community of faith, and to assess their suitability as currency of
communication, praise, and as blueprint for committed action.

3.2.6.6. Liturgy

Finally, the process of secularization also has its impact in the
very act of worship and the constitution of the liturgy. On the one
hand encrusted liturgical celebrations may run the danger of no longer
being relevant or meaningful to secular man. On the other hand the
"privatized" secular individual longs for some form of social
integration.[111] It will be the task of the remaining chapters to
investigate whether narratives of identity formation and of visionary
discernment can contribute to an appropriate act of worship which is
relevant in both the self-transcending and the immanent aspects of
life.

---

[110] Andrew GREELEY, Unsecular Man, pp. 246-264. This new hermeneutic
act is made difficult because: a) the meaning of myths is no longer
self-evident, b) the supermarket of secular meaning systems provides
the individual with options, and c) the pluralism within the religious
community suggests a more conscious appropriation of "myths" or
"models".

[111] Cf. the discussion below (3.5.1.1.) on Robert N. BELLAH's study
Habits of the Heart on individualization and public commitment in
American society.

3.3. The Structural Function of Autobiography

In the preceding section it has been shown in what ways the current process of secularization is influencing religious and non-religious thought alike. This section will throw light on the nature of autobiography as it is understood in literary terms. As a result, it will be possible to make a comparison between the intentionality of secular biography and of religious testimony.

3.3.1. Preliminary Clarifications

A certain confusion in the use of the terms biography, auto-biography, and testimony could impose itself. This is partially due to the sociological notion of **biography**, which refers to a general inclination of humankind to make sense of personal experiences in a mostly social context. As such it has little to do with the homologous literary notion in which the author is not identical with the protagonist of the biography. It would be therefore wise to keep in mind that the sociological concept actually refers to an **autobiographical** activity in the sense that the individual is opening himself communicatively (i.e. he makes a personal but non-private statement about himself) when he, for instance, joins a particular interest group and gets involved.

Terminological confusion can also arise in the religious context where it is very important to distinguish between the written biography with a frequent hagiographic tendency nurtured by another party, the autobiography which is equally text-bound and often has doxological aspects, and the typically oral nature of **testimony** which has its raison d'être in the gatherings of the religious community and the proclamation of religious convictions.

Furthermore, it is useful to distinguish between autobiography and **self-portrait**. For clarity's sake it can be said that the self-portrait is static in nature, because the author presents himself, as it were in a picture, as he sees himself at a given point in time.[112] But the autobiography emphasizes by necessity dynamic elements, since the author speaks about himself in the light of his relationship to society and as a human being coming to terms with temporality here and now.

Finally, autobiography is easily referred to as a **literary genre**. Although it is certainly true that typical classifications can be made, the notions of genre or style tend to cover up two essential aspects of autobiographical activity. First, in the process of speaking or writing the author engages in a heuristic activity related to his self-understanding. Second, the oral form of autobiography contains a self-critical element that the written counterpart does not necessarily share, because the audience's reception or rejection of the content is immediate in the former.

The objective in the following pages will be to substantiate these qualificatory remarks.

3.3.2. The Debate on Philippe LEJEUNE's Autobiographical Pact

In the 1970's Philippe LEJEUNE came to the forefront of the literary forum due to several publications on the nature of autobiography. His most incisive article, "Le pacte autobiographique,"[113] has been vigorously discussed. Although some criticism is justified, it is impossible to bypass his contribution in this field.

3.3.2.1. LEJEUNE's Theory

As Philippe LEJEUNE initiates his thesis with a general definition of autobiography, as perceived from a contemporary reader's point of view,[114] he is aware of two qualifying aspects. Firstly, he choses the reader's point of view because textuality seems to relate

---

[112] Problems arising from the self-portrait (or the self-centered testimony) are discussed below in section 3.3.2.2..

[113] Philippe LEJEUNE, Le pacte autobiographique, in Poétique 6, 14 (1973), 137-162.

[114] Philippe LEJEUNE, Le pacte, p. 137.

to a triangular relationship between the author, the text itself and the reader. Secondly, he notices that every definition has its historical context, and therefore limits himself to a contemporary understanding of autobiography. His definition states that an auto-biography is:

> a retrospective prose-narrative of a real person, made of his/her own experience, accentuating his/her individual life, especially the history of his/her personal chararacter.[115]

This definition is elaborated upon on four levels. First, the linguistic form is said to be a **prose-narrative**. Of course, it could be conceivable that someone would write an autobiography in verse, but this would be rather exceptional. However, the fact that autobiographies are generally in prose makes them relevant in oral communication.[116] In most instances, personal experiences are told long before some of them are written down. At the same time LEJEUNE stresses the narrative nature of autobiography. Personal experiences only make sense if they characterize themselves within the emplotment of life.[117]

The second remark centers on the subject. Philippe LEJEUNE describes autobiography as a **history of personal character**. The emphasis is not placed on the society in which one lives, nor on the family, group or community with which one identifies. The story communicated is basically about experiences of the self, personal opinions and insight gained in dialogue with, but also in isolation from others. This emphasis on the search of the self can be seen as a

---

[115] "Récit rétrospectif en prose qu'une personne réelle fait de sa propre existence, lorsqu'elle met l'accent sur sa vie individuelle, en particulier sur l'histiore de sa personnalité." Philippe LEJEUNE, Le pacte, p. 138.

[116] That does not mean that, for instance, Greek poetry did not also have oral origins, as the works of Marshall McLUHAN and Walter J. ONG indicate. But in western thought the lyric style is bound to paper at least in the origins of composition.

[117] Critical questions will therefore have to be asked as to the life world of secular as well as religious accounts of identity formation. Is there a relationship between the narrated self and the world depicted? Is the life world open or ideologically closed? Is it stereotype, trivial, static or showing aspects of ambivalence, paradox and change?

direct result of the western process of secularization with its
emphasis on self-realization. The popularity of this (auto)biograph-
ical element has been much nurtured in literature and the mass
media.[118]

In autobiography the self comes into focus because there is an
identity between author (whose name figures on the cover), narrator
(generally the signs of the "I"[119]) and protagonist (typically the
hero). The anonymous autobiography constitutes an exception, in which
case the reader automatically tends to complete the picture of
identity. But the anonymous work only points again to the pertinence
of oral autobiography, for the speaker is public and his identity is
to a certain degree exposed. There is a critical element in oral
testimony that the written counterpart does not have.

The third aspect LEJEUNE considers in the light of the definition
is the specific **identity between the author and the narrator.**
Generally this identity is expressed in the use of the pronoun in the
first person singular. But even if the narrator (i.e. the voice) of
the "text" speaks in the third person singular, as it was common in
religious monographs in the 17th and 18th century in order to
emphasize submission to God and humility, the link between author and
narrator can easily be established.[120] The same is true when the self
of the author is boosted into the third person singular or the first
person plural for historico-political reasons (e.g. "We, the German
Emperor and I" refering to the same person). In other words,
autobiographic deviations from the first person singular are
linguistic and symbolic devices in order to accentuate the events that
surround the person.

---

[118] One notices, for instance, the popularity of talk shows on radio
and television, the autobiographical coloring of novels, the non-
abating marketing value of trivial literature, and the flood of person
centered scenarios in the film industry.

[119] Cf. Gerald PRINCE, Narratology. The Form and Functioning of
Narrative, Berlin, 1982, pp. 7-16.

[120] Jean STAROBINSKI, Le style de l'autobiographie, in Poétique 3
(1970), p. 260.

But even if the autobiographic account is placed in the first person singular, attention must be paid to the function of the "I." For as Emile BENVENISTE has pointed out, the concept of the "I" is open. Its reference is easily determined syntactically by the context, but its locutionary impact varies due to the discourse situation.[121] That means that the reality suggested by the identity between author and narrator cannot rest objectively in the use of a certain pronoun, but is found in the unrepeatable and subjective situation of enunciation.[122] What needs to be retained for the present study is twofold. First, the autobiographical identity between author and narrator throws light upon the problem of anonymity in the current process of secularization. Second, the elusive character of the subject in autobiographic speech calls for a critical element in the interpretation of such narratives in general and religious testimonies in particular.

The fourth comment of LEJEUNE relating to his definition of autobiography centers on the **position of the narrator**. His activity is typically a retrospective one.[123] It stands in contrast to the peri-spective position of a self-portrait.[124] In other words, the autobiographical narrative makes a statement of the historical circumstances of the individual and his relation to society. It has, therefore, potential for programmatic communication and is relevant for secular, religious and profane contexts alike, provided the retrospective view also allows for a prospective horizon.

---

[121] "... que les pronoms ne constituent pas une classe unitaire, mais des espèces différentes selon le mode de langage dont ils sont signes. Les uns appartiennent à la syntaxe de la langue, les autres sont caractéristiques de ce que nous appelerons les 'instances de discours', c'est-à-dire les actes discrets et chaque fois uniques par lesquelles la langue est actualisée en parole par un locuteur." Emile BENVENISTE, Problèmes, tome I, p. 251.

[122] Emile BENVENISTE, Problèmes, p. 254.

[123] Cf. chapter two above on AUGUSTINE's notion of the distention of the soul and the narrative consequences elaborated by Paul RICOEUR.

[124] On the solipsist nature of the self-portrait see: Michel BEAUJOUR, Autobiographie et autoportrait, in Poétique 32 (1977), p. 448, as well as the discussion in the next section with Stanley HAUERWAS on the problems with a peri-spective position.

Furthermore, the position of the narrator indicates an identity between him and the protagonist. LEJEUNE is emphatic about the difference existing between biography and autobiography in this respect. In the former the relationship between narrator and protagonist is one of resemblance, in the latter it is one of identity.[125] That means that any communication, whether oral or written, points to an extra-"textual" reality. For one thing, because it relates to an audience or the reader, for another, because the protagonist cannot be fully re-presented linguisticallly, neither in the act of communicating nor in the minds of the others. The biography, then, is aware of its limits; it can only describe a subject. The autobiography or the testimony has, however, the advantage of claiming an identity between the protagonist and the producer of the narrative.[126]

The differentiation between resemblance and identity in relation to the extra-textual reality provides a key to the interpretation of secular and/or (non)religious narratives of the self, as well as to testimonial statements about God in general and his "will" in particular.[127] The narrator guarantees the extra-textual reality of his testimony in autobiographical accounts with serious intent.

It is understandable now that LEJEUNE speaks about an auto-biographical pact.[128] The identity between author, narrator and protagonist is clearly stated in classical autobiographies. It is a social contract, between author and "reader," that should guarantee a serious intentionality, the reliability of information and the production of meaning. Or, as Richard FENN has pointed out, liturgies

---

[125] Philippe LEJEUNE, Le pacte, pp. 154 ff.

[126] "On aperçoit déjà ici ce qui va opposer fondamentalement la biographie, c'est la hiérarchisation des rapports de ressemblance et d'indentité; dans la biographie, c'est la ressemblance qui doit fonder l'identité, dans l'autobiographie, c'est l'identité qui fonde la ressemblance. L'identité est le point de départ réel de l'auto-biographie; la ressemblance, l'impossible horizon de la biographie." Philippe LEJEUNE, Le pacte, pp. 156f. (emphasis ommited).

[127] Cf. chapter four below.

[128] Philippe LEJEUNE, Le pact, pp. 160ff.

and secular trials alike (albeit in their own way) demand an authentic
account of the self, but it remains a question in how far the
testifying person can or does measure up to this demand of authenti-
city. For both scholars, therefore, the community of interpretation is
called to be involved in communicative action (and ideology critique)
due to the extra-textual reality that has been referred to.

3.3.2.2. Critique of LEJEUNE's Model

First of all it must be admitted that LEJEUNE's definition of
autobiography is rather arbitrary. For instance, it can be argued that
the emphasis on the personal history over against the societal one is
exaggerated. Neither has it been established to what extent the
narrative character of the autobiography allows for the inclusion of
flatly descriptive language. Nevertheless, the definition is an appropriate working hypothesis provided one is aware of its limits.
Criticism of LEJEUNE's idea has been mainly on two levels. First,
he uncritically adopts **the common distinction between truth and
fiction**. In chapter two it has already been pointed out that these two
categories, from a mimetic point of view, cannot be separated
completely.[129] Paul RICOEUR, whose notion of "narrative identity" is
in many ways similar to the autobiographical pact, prefers to locate
autobiography on the middle ground between truth and fiction, because
the narrative identity reflected is unstable. On the one hand it has
the tendency for verification analogous to the historical approach. On
the other hand, is constantly challenged by imaginative production.
That implies negatively, that autobiography is susceptible to
self-deception and needs verification, positively it is a motor for an
ethical response, for the reception of such a narrative always
involves a world view which is not ethically neutral; a dynamic is set
free in which the "reader" is compelled to take a stand.[130]

---

[129] Cf. 2.3.6.4.

[130] The problem of self-deception will be discussed shortly. As far as
the narrative identity is concerned, RICOEUR says, "... l'identité
narrative n'épuise pas la question de l'ipséité du sujet, que celui-ci
soit un individu particulier ou une communauté d'individus... le récit

Furthermore, it is not so easy to distinguish between the truth
factor of an autobiography and the fictional character of an autobiographical novel as LEJEUNE suggests.[131] Antonio GOMEZ-MORIANA, for instance, has studied autobiographical fiction which at first sight
seems to be autobiographical literature in the strict sense because it
fulfills the criteria for LEJEUNE's pact.[132] In a similar vein, Robert
ELBAZ has argued from a semantic point of view that LEJEUNE's concept
of truth cannot be assumed to be transparent and homogeneous.

> For language is functional to the ideological position of the
> speaking subject, and "reality" is the creation of this same
> subject. One does not report, duplicate or verify the truth: one
> makes it.[133]

One need not embrace ELBAZ' epistemological presupposition in order to
appreciate his point, namely that much of what is considered fictional
or true is a matter of inter-subjective agreement and is not a magical
property of the text. Finally, one can also argue from a literary
perspective as Roy PASCAL has done. He compared the intentionality of
the autobiographical novel with that of the autobiography, and states
that each autobiographer is also a bit of a novelist to the degree
that "...out of the manifold data of his life he has to construct a

---

exerce l'imagination plus que la volonté, bien qu'il demeure une cate-
gorie de l'action... Or, la lecture... comporte aussi un moment d'
envoi: c'est alors que la lecture devient une provocation à être et à
agir autrement. Il reste que l'envoi ne se transforme en action que
par une décision qui fait dire a chacun: ici, je me tiens! Dès lors
l'identité narrative n'équivaut à une ipséité véritable qu'en vertu de
ce moment décisoire, qui fait de la responsabilité éthique le facteur
suprême de l'ipséité... La théorie de la lecture nous en a averti: la
stratégie de persuasion fomentée par le narrateur vise à imposer au
lecteur une vision du monde qui n'est jamais éthiquement neutre, mais
qui plutôt induit implicitement ou explicitement une nouvelle
évaluation du monde et du lecteur lui-même: en ce sens, le récit
appartient déjà au champ éthique en vertu de la prétention, insé-
parable de la narration, à la justesse éthique. Paul RICOEUR, Temps,
Vol. III, pp. 358f. (emphasis his).

[131] Philippe LEJEUNE, Le pacte, p. 138.

[132] Antonio GOMEZ-MORIANA, Autobiographie et discours rituel. La
confession autobiographique au tribunal de l'Inquisition, in Poëtique
56 (1983), p. 445.

[133] Robert ELBAZ, Autobiography, Ideology, and Genre Theory, in Orbis
Litterarum 38 (1983), p.193.

coherent story and a coherent character, and for this purpose he has
to select and arrange from the standpoint at which he writes."[134] From
a psychological point of view he even argues that an autobiographical
novel may be able to convey a general truth that an autobiography does
not reveal.[135]

The problem of the "ideological position" needs to be treated in
greater detail, because it allows for deception in the sense that Paul
RICOEUR, Michael GOLDBERG, and Gerhard SAUTER have already touched
upon,[136] and more importantly because it allows for self-deception as
a study of Stanley HAUERWAS on Albert SPEER's autobiography Inside the
Third Reich shows.[137] HAUERWAS mentions various reasons for consciously or unconsciously allowing self-deception in an autobiographical narrative. To give a few examples the following desires are
cited: to stay morally ignorant about a certain state of affairs, not
to spell out certain activities, to cherish an illusion, to fit a
social role. To illustrate the possible extent of self-deception
HAUERWAS points to SPEER's deliberate avoidance of the Jewish issue by
clinging to the narrative thread that presented him as HITLER's
apolitical architect.[138] HAUERWAS focuses on the major problem of
self-deceptive narratives when he says,

---

[134] Roy PASCAL, The Autobiographical Novel and The Autobiography, in
Essays in Criticism 9 (1959), p 134.

[135] Roy PASCAL, The Autobiographical Novel, pp. 146-150. As a literary
critic it is not surprising that he mentions the symbolic power of
fictional accounts to convey an embracing truth (e.g. "deeper elements
of a personality"), which may easily be undermined by the (auto)-
biographer's preoccupation with particular events.

[136] Cf. 2.3.5.3.

[137] Stanley HAUERWAS, Richard BONDI and David B. BURRELL, Truthfulness
and Tragedy. Further Investigations in Christian Ethics, Notre Dame,
1977, pp. 82-98.

[138] SPEER used his role as architect to gloss over his responsibilites
as Minister of Armaments. "...my new political interests played a
subsidiary part in my thinking. I was above all an architect." (SPEER,
Inside the Third Reich, p. 51, quoted by HAUERWAS, Truthfulness, p.
91.) In other words, SPEER put aesthetics over ethics and correlated
his identity picture to that decision.

The extent of our self-deception correlates with the type of
story we hold about who and what we are. If it is to counter our
propensity to self-deception, the story that sustains our life
must give us the ability to spell out in advance the limits of
the various roles we will undertake in our lives. The story must
enable us to discriminate within those roles the behaviour that
can easily entrap and blind us. The more noble and caring the
role, the more discriminating the story must be.[139]

In other words, LEJEUNE's emphasis on the desire to tell the truth is
not a sufficient criterion for establishing the identity of the
autobiographer. The story itself must allow for a discernment of
role-limits. HAUERWAS does not fail to mention that for the Christian,
the ability to discover self-deception depends on his master-image,
the dominant story of the Gospel which he aims at embodying in his
character.[140] One should add that in both secular and religious
contexts, the vigilance called for realizes itself primarily when a
community of interpretation is at hand which can judge the narrator's
presentation of the humanum.

The second criticism leveled at LEJEUNE's theory focuses on the
autobiographical pact itself. The identity between author, narrator
and protagonist, although structurally verifiable, may easily be a
false identity, just as there may be false testimony. The problem is
increased when autobiographies center around a formative experience, a
conversion that allows the author to differentiate between "the old
man" and "the new man."[141] Changes in personality must certainly be
taken critically into account, but it does not necessarily seem
appropriate to speak of a rupture of the threefold identity as Antonio
GOMEZ claims.[142] Nevertheless, he is right in so far as one cannot
take the autobiographical identity for granted simply because the
scheme allows it. This is especially true if one considers, as
BENVENISTE has pointed out, that personal narratives are intended to
influence the audience and that one can therefore differentiate

---

[139] Stanley HAUERWAS, Truthfulness, p. 88.

[140] Stanley HAUERWAS, Truthfulness, p. 95.

[141] Antonio GOMEZ-MORIANA, Autobiographie, pp. 454f.; Jean
STAROBINSKI, Le style, p. 261.

[142] Antonio GOMEZ-MORIANA, Autobiographie, p. 456.

between a personal identity and a functional identity.[143] The "I" is
then not only subject but also object, and the autobiographical act is
an exercise in self-interpretation,[144] for the communicator and the
audience alike.

In view of the above criticism Philippe LEJEUNE's model has been
relativized, rather than proven to be false. In modified form,
especially with the inclusion of ethical **Rückfragen**, it will serve to
clarify claims advanced by autobiographical activity in secular
society and those made in the context of specifically religious testimonies. For the autobiographical pact is located in the tensional
field of public integrational identity formation, and the act of
coming to terms with what in one's own life calls for a liberation
from anonymous privacy.

3.3.3. Differences and Similarities between Written Autobiography and Oral Testimony

In light of: a) the linguistic clarifications presented in
chapter two, b) the study of the impact of secularization on the
legitimation of personal experiences, and c) the contractual nature of
autobiographical activity, one can establish general aspects of
similarity and difference between the characteristic types of written
autobiography and oral testimony. It should, however, not be forgotten
that this distinction is instrumental and therefore limited in
scope.[145]

---

[143] Emile BENVENISTE, Problèmes, p. 241.

[144] Jean STAROBINSKI, Le style, pp. 258, 261.

[145] Of course there are combinations and varieties of these types such
as oral biography and written testimony, but a basic classification
can be maintained between open and closed narratives of the self. The
hermeneutic intentionality of open narratives is different in so far
as the narrative fulfills its function only if it is simultaneoulsy
"digested" by the audience. The synchronic nature of closed narratives
allows an interpretation at demand.

3.3.3.1. Similarities

The first common denominator is, sociologically seen, the tendency of narratives of the self **to integrate meaning** on a personal and a societal level. Shared life situations and social conventions make this possible.[146] It is significant that this activity is of necessity a communal one in spite of the privatizing tendencies of secularization.[147]

The second aspect the two types share is that they are involved in the **justification of existence** in spite and because of adverse contingencies of life. As STAROBINSKI and others[148] have pointed out, such experiences provoke changes and conversions that call for an interpretation. But the process of secularization has shifted the emphasis from a theodicy to a sociodicy, and possibly to a justification of existence in purely individual terms. As the account of A. SPEER has indicated one must remain attentive to deceptive moves which could take the form of a sham-justification and/or conversion from or to a lifestyle which is morally questionable.

Another point of similarity is that experiences of personality formation have a **typical linguistic expression.** It may be called symbolic or metaphorical language (RICOEUR), evocative disclosure (RAMSEY) or craft-bound discourse as James ROSS prefers to call it.[149] It seems important to remember that such a use of language is not the exclusive right of the religious community of interpretation, but

---

[146] Although it remains to be asked whether this commonality is also granted when life situations differ strongly, for example between the economically affluent North and the deprived South. Furthermore, in the context of inter-cultural communication one would have to study the variety of social conventions for the integration of meaning.

[147] But religious communal activity as such does not yet guarantee an openness to secular sociality, and by implication, it only constitutes one step towards bridging the communicative gap between traditional and secular values. Cf. section 3.5.1.

[148] Jean STAROBINSKI , Le style, p. 261; C.W.E. BIGSBY, The Public Self: The Black Autobiography, in Zeitschrift für Literaturwissenschaft und Linguistik 9,35 (1979), p. 28; Peter BERGER, Social Reality, pp. 58f.

[149] Lecture at the Philsophical Institute Leuven, Dec. 1984.

rather that the dynamic linguistic representation of truth (whether different from, relative to, or congruent with heuristic fiction) may vary among the different groups of interest.

Finally, the basic similarity among the narratives of the self can be seen as an **invitation to share** in human problems, insight and values. The making public of an autobiographical account is always also a challenge to inter-subjective dialogue in which the account must stand the test not only of semantic meaning, but also in terms of ethical truthfulness.

In a nutshell, the similarities between the two types allow a common hermeneutic approach. On one hand, the similarities center on the nature of human experiences (whether strictly speaking religious, generally secular, or void of any sense of the Sacred). On the other hand, they are based on linguistic grounds allowing for critical **Rückfragen**.

3.3.3.2. Differences

It is also important to recognize major differences between these stereotypes, which must be kept in mind if any common hermeneutic effort is to yield fruit.

It has repeatedly been mentioned that there is a fundamental distinction between oral and written narratives due to the different circumstances of their production and reception. In the light of this differentiation the following can be noticed.

Firstly, **from an existential point of view,** the oral narrative tends to focus on the present implication of past events,[150] whereas the written account of a person's life is free to limit itself to any period of the past. It appears that the difference in accentuation leads to the predominance of an aesthetic form in written material, especially when it has been cast in a secularized and/or market-oriented mold. Oral testimony, especially in religious and (quasi)-

---

[150] This emphasis is not to be identified with the present-ing aspect of the self-portrait mentioned above. Rather, the testimony is a recital of past events, which only make sense in the light of the present.

legal contexts, does retain a predominant ethical imperative. Secularization has brought this differentiation sharply into focus.[151] Consequently, in an oral situation the verdict of the testimony is only suggested, the court of interpretation is adjourned, but in written (auto)biographies the verdict is already integrated and the trial concluded through the synchronic closure of the text. It needs to be added, however, that many religious life stories tend to be hagiographic, thus adding an additional narrowing of the space of judgment, whereas secularized biographies tend to mention, to a larger degree, also the less-glorifying aspects of human life and consequently allow for a more critical reading.

This last remark has shifted attention to **the literary differentiation** between testimonial and biographical types. Burkhart MECKING has studied christian biographies[152] and noticed a tendency toward trivializing personal events, root experiences as well as happenings in daily life, and the descriptions thereof. In speaking about trivial biographical literature, it should be remembered that the bulk of it is non-religious in nature and that trivialization relates basically to the taste of the masses. In other words, the idea of the trivial should not in itself contain a value judgment if the notion is to be used critically.[153] But considering the element of the trivial, two aspects gain pertinence for this study of oral narratives in the context of worship. First, there is a real danger that religious testimonies drift into a trivial representation of life due to excessive simplification, the relatively small oral vocabulary, and the specialized language games of the community. In groups where "God-talk" is common, metaphorical expressions may in deed cover up

---

[151] This seems to me to be the fundamental contribution of Richard FENN even though he does not dwell on it.

[152] Burkhart MECKING, Christliche Biographie. Beobachtungen zur Trivialisierung in der Erbauungsliteratur, Frankfurt, 1983.

[153] "Für den Begriff trivial werden beide beschriebenen Seiten wichtig. Einmal muss mann sich davor hüten, sich über das, was gemeinhin als trivial bezeichnet wird, erhaben zu wissen. Das Problem der Einfachheit ist komplexer, als man meistens denkt. Zum anderen ist dem Umschlag von Vereinfachung in Verfälschung nachzugehen." Burkhart MECKING, Christliche Biographien, p. 29; cf. also pp. 38ff.

that which is truly personal, and therefore also of value for the non-religious audience. Second, secular biographies with a non-trivial interest (e.g., texts for a selected audience with educational investment) are from a historical point of view more critical. It will be necessary to study in what ways the critical element of socio-historical consciousness is (or could be) present in religious narratives of the oral kind.

A second remark on the literary differentiation between the two types centers on the role of the self in religious narratives. The following hypothesis can be suggested.

Oral testimony implies a public self, and as a consequence the autobiographical pact is taken seriously unless proven deceptive. Although a testimony may show a preference for a particular community of interpretation, it theoretically desires to be understood by all. The written (auto)biography, on the other hand, tends to be received in privacy and factually cares little by whom it is read.[154]

As far as oral testimony is concerned, this could indicate that it is less likely to drift into a trivial representation of life than its written counterpart.[155] But it must remain conscious of the universal nature of its hermeneutic intentionality. As to written (auto)bio-graphy, one wonders whether the suspension of the autobiographical pact (the distance created between the author, the self and the public) leads to an interchangable and expendable use of personages and events. If that is the case, then the human community as a whole has been trivialized, and the individual made anonymous will have to search for an identity in fractional groups of that society.

A final remark relates to the use of heuristic fiction by the two types. In other words, the question here is not which of the two modes of narrative is more susceptible to the danger of presenting falsehood

---

[154] Although a book may be written for the public interest and is sold publicly, it is still being read individually, and only in the rarest cases is the author available for dialogue with the reader.

[155] MECKING notices the lack of **individuelle Konturen** in stereotyped biographies. Burkhart MECKING, Christliche Biographien, p. 123.
    Elsewhere he writes on the advantages of autobiography in comparison to biography, "Sie zeigen Denk- und Handlungsweisen in ihrer Motivation und gewähren dem Leser Einblick in die Zusammenhänge, die ihm ohne das persönliche Zeugnis verschlossen wären." (p. 89)

in form of fantasy, but rather how do they employ imagination in an attempt to convey more clearly an actual experience, genuine convictions and truth claims. In favour of the written (auto)biography and the autobiographical novel, Roy PASCAL has given three examples of how symbolic fiction can provide insight which the author would otherwise feel unable to communicate.[156] The accent lies on the utmost personal search for meaning that is, in the end, symbolically communicated to the readers. In favour of personal narratives with an oral origin, C.W.E. BIGSBY, who studied contemporary black-American autobiographies, has argued that the telling of personal experience "had apparently only been processed once; it had been filtered through the sensibility but not yet through the imagination."[157] Here the accent would lie on the appropriation of meaning by a social group which shares the same hermeneutic currency. The problem with these two statements is that they can be understood to contradict the above hypothesis on the hermeneutic intentionality. The symbolic language that heuristic fiction employs is paradoxical to the extent that it can be democratic and undemocratic at the same time if various levels of interpretation are possible. It is democratic in so far as symbolic interpretation is open to re-interpretation. It is undemocratic because the "meaning" of a symbol is often held as a copyright by the interest group that uses it. Whether this paradox can be upheld and stated meaningfully will have to be seen.

    More basically I would argue that the authors of both types are engaged in a metaphorical activity that allows them to make sense of loose ends of life. To interpret religious narratives would necessitate an introduction to the symbolic function of their language. At the same time, secular narratives cannot be assumed to be flatly descriptive either. Speaking positively, the differences indicated between the deliberate opposition of these two types show a variable priority of interests, a different context of meaning, rather

---

[156] Roy PASCAL discusses the following autobiographical novels: Villette, by Charlotte BRONTE, Sons and Lovers, by D.H. LAWRENCE, and James JOYCE'S A Portrait of the Artist as a Young Man. In Roy PASCAL, The Autobiographical Novel, pp. 137-150.

[157] C.W.E. BIGSBY, The Public Self, p. 27.

than a difference in method. For the religious witness it may be the sense of community and the experience of religious and consequently ethical self-transcendence; for the secular writer it may be the attainment of personal truth and a new formulation of beauty.

3.4. The Hermeneutic Theory of E. SCHILLEBEECKX as an Attempt to Correlate Christian and Non-Christian Communication

If it is true that the difference between strictly religious, generally secular, or strictly non-religious identity formation relates to the formulation of meaning rather than to the methodology employed then it seems sensible to pursue, from a theological point of view, a correlation between the human question and the christian answer as Edward SCHILLEBEECKX puts it.[158]

SCHILLEBEECKX sees the necessity of this correlation because of the historically conditioned situation. Before the current process of secularization set in, the question about God in the western world was immediately answered by the christian understanding of the Gospel. But today neither the question about God nor the christian answer is taken for granted. It sounds like a "category mistake" when human questions are met in terms of a transcendent reference, that is, when an (apparently) non-religious question is answered religiously. Edward SCHILLEBEECKX, therefore suggests: **"The christian answer** to the question of what the christian religion means by 'God' can only be **made intelligible** if it is related to the radical and necessary question which man is himself."[159]

The significance of this statement is underlined in the following thesis: the question of meaning precedes the question of truth. This does not mean that a christian truth claim can be false, rather that such a claim may be meaningless to many people because they cannot relate it to their personal concerns and experiences. What should be

---

[158] Edward SCHILLEBEECKX, The Understanding of Faith, chapter 5.

[159] Edward SCHILLEBEECKX, The Understanding, p. 83 (emphasis added).

avoided, therefore, is an unintelligible leap from one language game
(and the human experiences it describes) to another. SCHILLEBEECKX
states:

> The missionary task of christianity and the transition from
> non-christian to christian thus confront us with the need for **an
> explicitly non-religious context of experience within which it
> is possible to listen** meaningfully **to christian talk** about God
> in a secularized world.[160]

In one sense this radical statement points clearly to the necessity of
relating faith to an experience of meaning, and that this correlation
has to be so fundamental as to be accessible to all human questions
relating to the meaning of life. The narrative and everyday character
of testimonies seems suitable in this respect. On the other hand, the
non-religious context of experience necessary for a correlation needs
to be situated in common human experiences that allow a religious
interpretation. However, if the hypothesis holds true that religious
narratives of existence have their **Sitz im Leben** in the practice of
worship, would this not again preclude the possiblility of a
non-religious context? An evaluation of SCHILLEBEECKX' suggestion is
at this point premature, for he does develop the correlation further.

The correlation between the human question and the christian
answer would, according to SCHILLEBEECKX, necessitate the universal
validity of christian talk about God.[161] It can be affirmed indirectly
in two ways. First, from a negative point of view it can be affirmed
that in spite of plurality there is a common search to realize the
constantly threatened **humanum**. But unlike some other philosophies,
Christianity would refuse to postulate a secular or universal subject
of history.[162] From a christian point of view, the correlation would

---

[160] Edward SCHILLEBEECKX, The Understanding, p. 88 (emphasis added).

[161] Edward SCHILLEBEECKX, The Understanding, pp. 81, 91-101.

[162] "The **humanum** that is sought only becomes a universally recognized
value via a negative and indirect mediation, that is, via a resistance
to the inhumane... In a pluralist society such as ours, these negative
dialectics must be seen as a critical resistance to the threat to the
humanum, without being able to define this **humanum**, the form in which
a universal experience is mediated. If this is taken as the point of
departure, the christian message does not, in order to be understood,
need first to place itself at the mercy of one definite philosophy or
one definite image of man out of all the philosophies or views of man

have to include, negatively, a protest against the inhumane, an "eschatological reservation".

The second affirmation of the universal validity of christian talk about God can be stated positively, says SCHILLEBEECKX, namely in terms of salvation from meaninglessness.[163] Now, of course, it is acknowledged that also non-religious people try to improve the world. But the christian answer in word and deed provides specific "signs and glimpses of transcendence" which come into focus in faith in Jesus Christ.[164] How these "signs and glimpses of transcendence" are experienced and communicated is a question that leads back to a study of worship, the nature of religious language, and to the religious ramifications of the christian answer in general. I, therefore, believe that a dialogue between Christian and non-Christian in a secularized world will also have to take into account the symbolic universe, a sensitivity to the mythological representation of life providing a deepening of meaning and an incentive for action beyond self-interest. This theme will be addressed in chapter six.

In the meantime, the contribution of SCHILLEBEECKX needs our full attention. It centers on the meaningful communication of what Jesus Christ can mean to mankind today. Or in his own words,

---

that we know." (p.92) Edward SCHILLEBEECKX, The Understanding, pp. 91-93.

[163] "Because man experiences so much that is meaningless in his own life, in society and even in the churches, it is quite impossible for him to be reconciled with his fate, with his fellow-men and with society as a whole. It is only possible for him to be fully reconciled with the whole of reality, that is, to be in a state of justification, when meaningfulness and meaninglessness are no longer insanely inter-woven and when fully realized meaning is actively experienced. This situation can be described as 'salvation', being whole." Edward SCHILLEBEECKX, The Understanding, 95.

[164] "Christian talk about God will not be accessible to contemporary man if he does not experience, in his actual life, signs and glimpses of transcendence, and does not come to understand that an exclusively scientific and technological interpretation of reality leads to many forms of inhumanity." Edward SCHILLEBEECKX, The Understanding, p. 99.

"In the man Jesus, man's question about himself and the human
answer to this question are translated into a divine question
put to man and the divine answer to this question: Jesus is the
Son of God, expressed in terms of humanity. He **is** the question-
answer-correlation."[165]

The divine revelation of grace has not automatically been reduced to a
man-made system, and the basic human questions can receive a christian
answer that is humanly understandable **and more.**

From such a theological point of view a partial fusion of
horizons between christian and non-christian concerns is possible,
provided religious language with its metaphorical dimensions relates
to a praxis, and seriously tries to avoid obscuring daily existence
with insider-talk, just as the symbolic universe of a novelist or
poet, if it is meant to evoke a meaningful response in the reader,
ultimately refers back to an imaginable life world.

3.5. Some Theological Implications

Insights into the social reality of religion and the phenomenon
of secularization lead to a sharpened awareness of what religious
speech can do and where its limits lie. Major implications for a
theological interpretation can be sketched.

3.5.1. The Personalization of Faith

Maybe the most prominent factor in the discussion on secularization has been the increased attention which is being paid to the
individual. For the secularized person religious attitudes are no
longer related to social custom and cultural musts, rather they have
become an option, or even a luxury as far as the ethical domain is
concerned.

Whereas this trend toward subjectivity has alarmed many religious
leaders because they see a communal way of life threatened, it is also
possible to deduce from the secular state of affairs some affirming
ideas about man and his trust in God.

---
[165] Edward SCHILLEBEECKX, The Understanding, p. 100 (emphasis his).

3.5.1.1. In Terms of the Self

First, the personalization of faith has brought about a positive re-evaluation of the "self." In spite of scientific and technological trends toward objectification, there has been an increased awareness of man's **subjecitvité irréductible**. It is a refusal to ultimately define and claim the **humanum**. The other person, the neighbor, must as a consequence always be taken seriously, because he too has a story to tell, a story that can never be mine.[166] In a certain sense then, secularization has, because of its emphasis on plurality, restored dignity to the individual.

Nevertheless, it must be borne in mind that in the light of secularization, personalization also brings along privatization. The privatized "I" must not lose touch with the socio-historical reality of which he or she is a part.[167] An ideological or utopian escape of the individual is a real danger and foreign to the symbolic notion of the "body of Christ". What has just been said can also be stated differently. The contemporary process towards a privatization of faith has shed light on the fact that it is no longer enough to belong to a religious tradition, to be a nominal Christian. Either one consciously lives with a personal christian option, or else one has become a factual unbeliever. People who have consciously joined an active religious community as well as those who have deliberately left the church have put the "heretical imperative" into praxis.

---

[166] Incidently, one finds here another argument for the preference of oral testimony to written biography. For the autobiographical account is, ideally, only a beginning. Further action is bound to be envisaged. Moral decisions have to be taken, as the "self" is never a finished product. But the printed word gives the deceptive impression of a closure. The "self" is caught between the covers of the book, and has become property of the market; it has sold its soul.

[167] This problem will have to be studied in relation to the religious testimony and its tendency toward the trivial. Herein, lies also the narcissistic danger of the self-portrait, according to Michel BEAUJOUR. "Le péché originel de l'autoportrait est donc de pervertir l'échange et la communication, tout en dénonçant cette perversion. Son discours ne s'adresse à un éventuel lecteur qu'en tant que celui-ci est placé en position de tiers exclu." Michel BEAUJOUR, Autobiographie et autoportrait, p. 448.

The delicate balance between the affirmation of the utmost personal and the enclave of privacy has been studied by the Californian sociologist Robert BELLAH. He points out that it is typical of American society to promote an individualistic way of grounding the self. Common signs of this are the cultural emphasis on leaving one's parental home, loosening the ties with one's church, and finding a job where one can "make something of oneself."[168] By untying the bonds with traditional values as they used to be practiced in the local community, the family, or the church, the western person becomes increasingly dependent on his own feelings to evaluate his experiences of disassociation and reassociation to shape his world view.[169] But feelings are a poor guide to personal and social development. The privatization of the self fostered through subjective impressions leads easily to a lifestyle which makes interpersonal relations difficult and even meaningless. The difficulty arises if there is no common ground by which subjective experiences and values can be shared. These are meaningless if they cannot be reappropriated through approval or rejection by others.

Theologically, the problem could be expressed as follows: A religious testimony can be formulated correctly and still fail to reflect a christian intentionality if the witness lives in the church community as if it were a larger enclave of his private opinions; this

---

[168] Robert BELLAH, Habits of the Heart, pp. 56-65.
It is significant that the American individual is commonly portrayed as being on a journey to find him- or herself through various tests and experiences. For instance one may think of the typical hero in cowboy stories, who must leave society in order to realize some moral good, or of the hard-boiled detective who is at odds, not only with lawbreakers, but with the very society whom he serves. The development of identity formation is expressed narratively in much the same way in which the Russian formalist school has analysed fairy tales. Cf. chapter four and specifically the discussion on Vladimir PROPP.

[169] Robert BELLAH writes, "Finding oneself means, among other things, finding the story or narrative in terms of which one's life makes sense." (Habits, p. 81) But BELLAH also makes clear that finding a story equally implies finding the language in which to speak it, and finding someone not only willing but also able to listen to it. This is a consideration that not all enthusiasts of religious narrative have taken into account.

results in a self-deceptive sociability. Robert BELLAH points clearly
to the dilemma between internal and external religion, which he sees
as a linguistic problem in the broad sense of the word.

> The limitation for millions of Americans who remain stuck in
> this duality in one form or another is that they are deprived of
> a language genuinely able to mediate among self, society, the
> natural world, and ultimate reality.[170]

The language of modern individualism is so current in secular society
that the language which expresses most personal and yet commonly
shared convictions and values appears as a second language that many
people find hard to use. The first language of secular individualism
avoids speaking about long term commitments, social virtues, responsibility and solidarity and is wanting in corporate symbols (i.e.
symbols that carry full meaning only if used in a social context).
This leads to problems on both sides of the spectrum. The religious
person may fall into the trap of interpreting the experiences of the
Holy in terms of secular individualism. Such an outlook would come
close to mythical individualism in which the self has become the main
form of reality, and the question is whether such a view can be
sustained, or whether it is bound to give way to nihilism.[171] In any
case such a person is blind to the secularizing process because he is
completely caught up in it. For the secular person the problem could
be described as spiritual and subjective starvation. The want is
spiritual because the deepest personal experiences can only be
expressed in an individualist language game. Even the secular person's
subjectivity is under attack, because subjective meaning is no longer
relational if the language of commonly shared values has fallen out of
use.

A solution for this acquired lack of bi-lingualism is to be
sought in a correlation of the two language games, and in paying
attention to the communal aspects of communication. This conviction
happens to be congruent with Robert BELLAH's suggestions on how to
transform American culture,[172] but in fact it is the **cantus firmus** of

---

[170] Robert BELLAH, Habits, pp. 237 and also the following pages.

[171] Robert BELLAH, Habits, p. 143.

[172] Robert BELLAH, Habits, pp. 275-296. He points to the need to give

this chapter specifically and of this study in general.

3.5.1.2. In Terms of Community

The personalization of faith has a communal dimension in the church. It is not enough for the church to provide opportunity for individuals to give their testimony of conversion and identity formation. The Christian is, by virtue of the pneumatological activity of God, also invited to participate in the kerygmatic commission of the church. Especially the secularized Christian is no longer satisfied to leave the interpretative task up to the institutionalized and highly specialized clergy, for the plausibility of his personal faith also demands a personal legitimation. It is for this reason that a theology of the laity, and the individual's participation in the prophetic activity of the church must be taken seriously. The personalization of faith calls for a democratic awareness in communal life; in the name of Christ as well as in view of universal reason.

3.5.2. The Dual Role of Community

The emphasis on the personal does, however, by no means obliterate the fundamental necessity for the christian **koinonia**. Two reasons can be given for this.

First, because of the increased theological activity of the lay person, the community of believers becomes acutely aware that it is also a community of interpretation. As Jean Pierre JOSSUA sees it, the advantage that secularization brings is that the individual can come to a vital understanding of faith once he has struggled through a personal deliberation. But this personal identity, forged in cultural plurality, needs to be affirmed in a community that modern society no

---

coherence to a fragmentary culture by paying attention to what he terms "communities of memory." His vision for the restoration of the social world of the West includes the restoration of tradition and corporate symbols, especially in the ethical domain, the striving towards a political democracy with a conception of the common good, and increased attention to the transdisciplinary aspects of science.

longer provides automatically.[173] Oral religious narratives are a
suitable didactic means for this process of formation and affirmation
of faith, as well as for the ensuing moral commitment. At the same
time such narratives are subject to reception or rejection by the
community, provided the necessary tools for dialogue, praise and
criticism are available. Those tools, I believe, lie in the matrix of
worship and the subsequent practical commitment.[174]

Second, as a result of its kerygmatic and hermeneutic activity,
the christian community also has to function as a model community. It
is challenged to realize its vision practically as well as its
mythological potential liturgically.

In this respect an excursion into the work of James M. GUSTAFSON
is enlightening. His book Treasure in Earthen Vessels[175] portrays the
christian community in its full contextuality. By displaying the
human, political, linguistic, and hermeneutic aspects of the christian
community he prepares the ground for correlating belief and moral
action, a theme which he treats more fully in his work entitled The
Church as Moral Decision-Maker.[176] He sees the basic need for the
church to practice a social ethic because its members, being part of
more than one socially defined community, need to make judgments about
the relative worth of values in a pluralist society if they want to
influence shifts in the moral climate of the society they live in.[177]
GUSTAFSON exhorts the christian church, in a way similar to that of

---

[173] Jean Pierre JOSSUA, Un christianesimo senza christianità, in
Christianesimo nella storia 5, 1 (1984), p. 158f.

[174] Some of these tools are inter-subjective verification in discussion, praise and prayer; the autobiographical pact in the presence
of God; recognition of God as the **auctor** of visionary and prophetic
insight; the enactment of faith, hope and love in communal celebration
and common action.

[175] James M. GUSTAFSON, Treasure in Earthen Vessels. The Church as a
Human Community, New York, 1961.

[176] James M. GUSTAFSON, The Church as Moral Decision-Maker,
Philadelphia, 1970.

[177] James M. GUSTAFSON, Decision-Maker, pp. 34-38.

Robert BELLAH, to keep all aspects of community in view. Vital for
this task is not the highly specialized clergy, but the christian body
as such.

> It is in the common life of the church that both intentions and
> dispositions on the internal, subjective side, and purpose and
> patterns of life on the external, objective side are to be
> engendered, fashioned, critically scrutinized and arti-
> culated.[178]

If this task is truly to emerge from the common life, and if it is to
be truly practicable by all believers then it is essential that
testimonial and prophetic narratives have a place in christian worship
from which in turn morally responsible action can emerge, provided the
liturgical set-up allows for the formation of intentions and is
instrumental in generating spiritual/moral strength.

3.5.3. Worship as the **Locus Vivendi** of Religious Narrative

The argument that religious narratives and worship call upon each
other can be illustrated by a set of dialectical relationships.
Firstly, there is the relationship between the self and the community.
Then, there is the interdependence between the religious group and the
world. And thirdly, there is the dialectic of faith between the
believer(s) and God.

As far as the relationship between the self and the community is
concerned, C.W.E. BIGSBY has noted that there is not much difference
between contemporary (i.e. secular) black autobiographies and the
early American spiritual ones. In both cases, the identity formation
pivots on a conversion experience[179] and: "The individual makes sense
of his or her own condition by relating it to that of the group."[180]

---

[178] James M. GUSTAFSON, Decision-Maker, p. 79. He rightly stresses the
fact that the biblical message is not only therapeutic, i.e. speaking
the language of salvation, self-fulfillment, relief from guilt, and
anxiety; but that it also calls for obedience, responsibility, and
discernment between good and evil, right and wrong, better and worse
(p. 89).

[179] Conversion understood as a deeply personal disclosure (cf. chapter
2) solidified in a mythological matrix (cf. chapter 1).

[180] C.W.E. BIGSBY, The Public Self, pp. 31, 32.

This mutual affirmation, for one can say that the community also makes sense of its own condition by relating it to the individual, is certainly true in a general context. Two extremes, however, as it has been pointed out, must be avoided. There is the danger of pure monologue and a fixation of the self, and there is the problem of a denial of the self in the face of the community.[181] Furthermore, as the study of Antonio GOMEZ-MORIANA shows, autobiographical language may easily give way to a ritual language.[182] Dissecting the text psycho-analytically he argues, negatively, that the testimony is a culturally engineered passive suppression of drives, a submission to the state of affairs. But positively, GOMEZ is aware of the therapeutic function of testimony in worship where personal language can become sacramental, opening up new horizons. He agrees with Paul RICOEUR that in such a dialectical relationship language can be set free symbolically and can lead to celebration. The movement is one from the human subject to the divine Subject.[183] The gratuity of God's grace is acknowledged.

The relationship between the religious group and the world as a whole, and the dialectic between the believer(s) and God evolves around a double notion of witness. On the one hand, the community is confessing its self-transcending faith and facing up to its response-ability to the world in which they live and to their God in whom they have found the affirmation of life. The confession is a narrative of salvation from meaninglessness, and the response-ability is an answer to the Gospel narrative. On the other hand, God himself

---

[181] Cf. Jean STAROBINSKI, Le style, p. 260; and Michel BEAUJOUR, Autobiographie et autoportrait, pp. 148ff.

[182] Antonio GOMEZ-MORIANA, Autobiographie, pp. 458f.

[183] "Il n'y a donc pas de "discours de la vie" en tant qu' information sur la trajectoire d'un sujet individuel, mais en tant que "discours épidictique" où le sujet qui parle n'est rien d'autre qu'un sujet-vicaire du véritable Sujet. Comme dans 'ceci est mon corps' de la consécration transsubstantiatrice, le 'moi, pécheur, je me confesse...' est voix de l' 'Autre' inscrite en un 'je' de référentialité ambiguë." Antonio GOMEZ-MORIANA, Autobiographie, p. 459.

is understood to be **the** witness. He is known to be witness to the
veracity of what is being said, and he is witness in Jesus Christ to
the threatened **humanum** in this world.

Worship, therefore, can be said to be the **locus vivendi** of
religious narratives, because they point beyond themselves by inviting
to confession (both as self-critical element and as programmatic
action) and praise (both to God and as an experience of restored human
diginity).

3.5.4. The Necessity of "Double-Talk" and Religious Experience

A final word should be added in reference to the nature of
religious language. The impact of secularization has led many to
believe that the language of Christians in worship should not be
significantly different from their everyday communication. Whereas it
is certainly true that meaningful communication depends on the clarity
of terms used, and that many religious expressions now fail to convey
their meaning to an ever increasing segment of society, it still holds
true that the religious community cannot do without poetic language.
The church is not a financial or legal institution with an inter-
cultural code of communication. Rather, it is a segment of society
which points, by virtue of its metaphorical language to an affirmation
of life that transcends the common reference to life in its social
forms.

On the other hand, the religious community will, of course, not
cease to speak "plainly" on the human issues (especially the moral and
political ones) that call for attention. There is no doubt that the
secularized language of the church is being listened to.

Therefore, I would advocate a conscious practice of "double-talk"
in the christian churches. The complementary practice of poetic and
discursive speech could overcome the tension between truth and
heuristic fiction, on the condition that what metaphorical language
refers to is illustrated by a christian way of life. For this reason,
religious experiences belong in the public forum of interpretation and
in the congregation of praise. Their evocative origin, their didactic
quality when told, and the potential for surplus of meaning create a

dynamic that sets worship, human praxis and discourse in relation to each other. To speak metaphorically, the Word of God is incarnate in the Body of Christ and challenges to a truly ecumenical activity, inside and outside the Church, through the power of the Spirit.

4. TOWARDS A PRACTICAL HERMENEUTIC OF TESTIMONY

FROM MORPHOLOGY TO METAPHOR AND METAMORPHOSIS[1]

"Wir haben Angst davor, unsere eigenen Erfahrungen auszu-
sprechen, und vor allem haben wir Angst, die wichtigste Sprache
menschlicher Erfahrungen, die religiöse Sprache, zu gebrauchen.
Lieber verleugnen und verdrängen wir uns selber und verviel-
fachen die eigene Sprachlosigkeit, als dass wir uns ausgerechnet
von der Religion 'das Hemd ausziehen' liessen."[2]

4.1. Introduction

In general terms the notion of testimony has been touched upon
several times in the preceding chapters. In the beginning, biblical
narratives were mentioned which function as testimonies of divine
presence in human history. Then testimony was considered from a
quasi-juridical point of view; as a claim to truth that faces a
hermeneutical trial. Finally, social aspects of testimony have been
mentioned in terms of biography, the testimony of one's life in this
world.

At this point a more direct approach to a hermeneutic of
testimony will follow, albeit from a specific point of view, for the
semantic field of the word "testimony" is too large as to allow a
comprehensive approach. Even from a christian point of view there seem
to be various kinds of testimony.

---

[1] Some rudimentary aspects of this chapter have been read at the Third
Conference on Pentecostal and Charismatic Research in Birmingham, 1984
and published under Towards a Practical Hermeneutic of Testimony:
Morphology, Meaning, Metamorphosis, in Walter J. HOLLENWEGER (ed.)
Pentecostal Research in Europe. Problems, Promises and People, Studies
in the Intercultural History of Christianity, Frankfurt, 1987.

[2] Dorothee SOELLE, Die Hinreise. Zur religiösen Erfahrung: Texte und
Ueberlegungen, Stuttgart, 1976, p. 39.

First, there are what one could call testimonies of grace. They
are mostly personal accounts in which the divine presence is
experienced as a gift (from "above") and as a disclosure. It may be an
account of a conversion, that is, a paradigm shift, or it can be a
telling related to an experience of healing or the awareness of a
spiritual endowment. The language used in these narratives is deeply
personal, but it is not private. It concerns subjective impressions,
but they are shared publicly. From this point of view one can consider
the function of testimonies of grace as mainly therapeutic. They shed
light on how a person has found wholeness.

A second group of christian testimonies can be called testimonies
of justice and love. They concerns the social reality of human
existence. Christian convictions are expressed in action. They allow
the (secular) world to find access to the values of the christian
faith without being immediately entangled in the metaphoricity of the
christian language. Again, it is a testimony that expresses a gift
(from "below") which can lead to a disclosure. Its function is now
mainly pragmatic, for it has social wholeness in view.

A third type of testimony, could be called testimony of life. It
is a communal exercise which concerns the all-embracing gift of Jesus
Christ as a disclosure. Jesus Christ's life and love for the other is
a model to which one is narratively related, which is mythologically
represented and pragmatically resumed. The dynamics of this testimony
are integrated in a prophetic vision of wholeness and in concrete acts
of love to the Sacred, the self, and society. Therefore, the function
of this testimony can be described as mainly confessional, having
ultimate wholeness in view.

In this chapter therapeutic testimonies of grace will be
examined. But that does not mean that the other two aspects will be
completely neglected. In chapter five indirect reference will be made
to testimonies of justice and love will indirectly in the discussion
of the intentionality of visions. And in the final chapter the
liturgical testimony of life will be presented as the coordinating
agent for religious and secular experiences.

4.2. A Syntactic Analysis of Testimonies of Grace

The importance of folklore is attested in all cultural contexts. As a popular form of narrative the life story or personal testimony is in many ways akin to the fairy tale. The beginning of its systematic study took place at the turn of the last century as literary researchers started to explore the nature of folk tales. In the spirit of evolutionism they were eager to find the universal myth or narrative that provides the interpretative key for cultural folklore. In 1910 Antti AARNE published his famous _Verzeichnis der Märchentypen_, in which he classified folk tales according to types and content. This book proved to be a catalyst for literary and biblical studies. On the one hand Vladimir PROPP, the Russian folklorist, used it in his morphological study of fairy tales, on the other hand Hermann GUNKEL, the father of biblical form criticism, was acquainted with AARNE's contribution. PROPP's _Morfologjia skaski_ was first translated into English and French after World War II, consequently experiencing a vogue in structuralist circles. In religious circles, Vladimir PROPP is sometimes considered to have been the forerunner of narrative theology.

This chapter will also take PROPP's first work as a starting point. First, because the material studied by him in many cases proves similar to the kind of testimonies that are heard in pentecostal churches. More specifically, because Russian fairy tales evolved for many centuries without being subject to institutional literary influences.[3] Due to its origins in American slave religion and the working-class, the testimonial tradition in pentecostal circles has had equally non-literary beginnings. But it is just because of the oral nature of testimonies that a hermeneutical approach has to step beyond the narrow framework of formalist and even structuralist points of view. Therefore, an attempt is made to find a suitable approach to

---

[3] Vladimir PROPP, _Morphology of the Folktale_, Austin, 2d ed., 1968, p. xix.

the interpretation of religious testimonies by referring to a context large enough to consider the particular nature of spoken language and the setting in which such narratives find an audience.[4]

4.2.1. The Contribution of PROPP

As mentioned, V. PROPP was aquainted with AARNE's index for coding fairy tales. Furthermore, A.N. VESELOVSKIJ had compiled a thematic collection of Russian fairy tales. But PROPP clearly demonstrates that such collections, although they point to certain similarities among different tales, do not prove very helpful for literary analysis. A thematic approach is not precise enough, for it only considers surface similarities.[5] It is more productive to look for motifs instead. However, identical acts can have different meanings. The criteria for motifs, therefore, are rather arbitrary. PROPP suggests evaluating popular narratives according to their function. He gives the following definition:

Function is understood as an act of a character, defined from the point of view of its significance for the course of action.[6]

The functions, accordingly, are considered as the stable element in the tales, and their sequence is thought to be uniform. PROPP was convinced that a list of functions of the **dramatis personae** would provide the key for understanding every narrative. After analyzing about 100 Russian fairy tales, he concluded that there were 31 different functions.[7] Not all tales would necessarily contain all of them, but all would respect the same sequential order. Thus, the idea

---

[4] Such an interpretative approach is consciously called **practical**, for it aims at being operative in the very heart of the religious community of interpretation. It stands in contrast to a theoretical hermeneutic, whose scientific intentionality would focus more on logical deduction, and possibly on a strictly structural approach.

[5] Vladimir PROPP, Morphology, pp. 14ff.

[6] Vladimir PROPP, Morphology, p. 21.

[7] Vladimir PROPP, Morphology, pp. 25-65.

of an **Urmärchen,** a primeval tale that would be the source of all Russian fairy tales was at hand. He elaborates this fundamental deduction by arguing that

> this single source may come from everyday life... and it is very possible that there is a natural connection between everyday life and religion,[8] on the one hand, and between religion and the tale on the other.

This claim provides the reason why a morphological comparison between the structural functions of fairy tales and the elements of religious testimony seems useful. A syntactical analysis of their respective language could provide criteria for a hermeneutical approach for the latter.

The procedure for the following analysis has been as follows: firstly, the more important functions were selected and grouped according to PROPP's main headings. Such a selection is somewhat arbitrary due to the nature of the material, but PROPP's definition of a tale, as well as his appendixes have been used as a guide.[9] The second step was a more or less random choice of two early pentecostal testimonies, which, although they exist in written form, demonstrate the typical structure of oral testimonies as, in deed, they were originally communicated orally. These were compared with PROPP's functions, which did not need a significant chronological regrouping

---

[8] Vladimir PROPP, Morphology, p. 106.

[9] "Morphologically, a tale (**skazka**) may be termed any development proceeding from villainy or a lack, through intermediary functions to marriage, or to other functions employed as a dénouement. Terminal functions are at times a reward, a gain or in general the liquidation of misfortune, an escape from pursuits, etc. This type of development is termed by us a **move**. Each new act of villainy, each new lack creates a new move. One tale may have several moves..." Vladimir PROPP, Morphology, p, 92 (emphasis his).
    Appendix I in the Morphology provides material for a tabulation of the tale and appendix III in PROPP's study contains a table of individual schemes and commentary; cf. pp. 119-127 + 135-148. For the sake of tabulation the first move and a possible second move have been placed together in the following examples. Technically, the basic development of a story as a whole is considered to be a move.
    In Appendix II below example (A) is taken from PROPP's Morphology and illustrates his basic theory applied to a fairy tale consisting of a single move; example (B) is an application of that theory to the Joseph story (Gen. 37-47) where the first and second move have been renamed main plot and sub-plot.

in order to fit on the same table. The third step consisted in writing
an imaginary conversion story that contained all functions chosen
above. The text was then given to pentecostal and evangelical
Christians. They were asked whether they could identify themselves
with such a testimony.

A Proppian Analysis of Testimonies

Elements of the Fairy Tale	T.B. BARRATT's Testimony (Spirit-baptism)	Frank BARTLEMAN's Testimony (revival)
Initial Situation		
misfortune (struggle)		
lack (task)	"When praying I felt constantly the need of a still greater blessing over my own soul! ... there must be a still deeper work and a constant victory."	"I arrived... little Esther... passed away... Little Esther's death had broken my heart.... I could only live while in God's service."
		cf. misfortune
absentation from home		
future hero		
future false hero		
Preparation		
command	"They asked me only to tarry before the Lord in prayer..."	
interdiction		
violation of interdiction		
dispatch of seeker	"One day I spent twelve hours before the Lord..."	"He made a fresh covenant with me."
departure		"I then begged Him to open a door of service quickly..."

A Proppian Analysis of Testimonies

Complication

appearance of
the villain
villainy

"Over and over again, the enemy
tempted me with the thought, that
the manifestation of tongues was
not for me."

"The desire of self-justification is
the cause of all the distress of the
heart."

Donor

journey to
donor

testing of the
hero

"All the trials I had passed through
during the last year... brought me down
- deeper down, before the Lord, seeking,
praying, weeping in his presence."

"Beside that little coffin... I pledged
my life anew for God's service."

difficult task

"God dealt with me about giving all my
time to Him."

riddle

reaction of the
hero

"... we wrestled with Him for the outpouring of His Spirit upon the people."

provision

"The spirit of revival consumed me."

Helper / Magical Agent

receipt of magical
agent

"Whilst weeping Sunday afternoon,
a little before five p.m., the
fire came back to my breast."

"I had received a new commission and
anointing."

cf. branding

A Proppian Analysis of Testimonies

First Move

transference

"When I think of it now, it seems strange to me that the Lord should take me to such a place, of no reputation, to give me the greatest blessing..."

"I felt strongly impressed to go to the little Peniel Hall... to pray."

struggle

"...I had to wait more than a month before the Power was turned on again, as it were, in an ever increasing degree,

"We prayed... the burden became well nigh unbearable."

branding

until I burst forth in tongues and loudly magnifying God in the power of the Holy Spirit. This time nothing interfered with the workings of the Divine Spirit..."
cf. complication / villainy

"Then suddenly... the Lord Jesus himself revealed himself to us. A burning fire went through me... I was lost in the pure Spirit."

Second Move

(new villainy, unrecognized arrival, etc.)

pursuit

"I could scarcely take up human conversation again. Human spirits seemed so harsh, earthly fellowship a torment."

rescue

A Proppian Analysis of Testimonies

Continuation

defeat of villain

liquidation of initial lack / misfortune

"... immediately the power of God began to work in my body, as well as in my spirit."

"He had come to strengthen and assure us for his service."

transfiguration of the hero

"The very same moment, I was being filled with light and an indescribable power, and I began to speak in a foreign language..."

return

"Once a great concern came over me, not for myself, but for others..."

"I spent the following day in prayer... where I had a ministry in intercession."

exposure / punishment of villain

wedding

"Glory! Glory! Glory! Oh! That I, unworthy as I am should experience anything like this."

"Heavenly peace and joy filled my soul. Jesus was so real."

A Proppian Analysis of Testimonies

A Testimony for PROPP's Morphology

Initial Situation
misfortune
lack
absentation from home
future hero
future false hero

It was when my father died, I was still a teenager then, that I began to think about the meaning of life. I imagined that if you had a strong personality things would work out all right. Richard, a friend of mine, impressed me strongly, because he was a member of a socialist youth party. He knew a lot about politics and music. Once he told me that the most important thing in life was love. It didn't really matter how you loved as long as you knew what it was. It all seemed to make sense, so I resolved to imitate him.

Preparation

command
interdiction
violation of
    interdiction
dispatch of the seeker
departure

But not long after my resolution I met the pastor who used to teach us catechism. He knew me well and said, "Your mother needs you, now that your father has gone. Be careful and do not forget that loyalty is the key to a happy life." Sure, this was good advice, but I also wanted to live and enjoy my own life. I began to make many friends and met them frequently in the pubs. But in a matter of months I had turned into a habitual drinker, my character had become aggressive and negative. One day, I was just recovering from a hangover, I swore that I had better shape up, or else I would never make it in life. Thus, I began my search for real meaning in life. I yearned for a new beginning.

Complication

appearance of the
    villain
villainy

On that same day I happened to meet a group of young people singing and talking to people in the open air. They appeared happy, but I was wondering if they were not too enthusiastic. Nevertheless, one of the guys invited me to one of their meetings, and I was about to accept, had I not noticed Richard walking towards me. I was embarrassed that he had seen me in this situation and quickly turned away from the Christian. Richard laughed and sneered, "Watch out, or you catch their disease. It's called holy egotism!" For the rest of the day I felt terrible. Richard's accusation just wasn't fair. I was utterly disappointed in him. His behaviour didn't match the expectations I had of him.

A Proppian Analysis of Testimonies

Donor
Journey to the donor
testing of the hero
difficult task
reaction of the hero
provision

It dawned on me that I had to make up my own mind. Consequently I undertook to find the church in which the meeting was to be held and entered the building at the appointed time. Again they sang folk-style songs and told stories of their lives. Then, a pastor preached, a Bible in his hand, and I wondered whether all of this could be true. If Jesus really could give new life, would I still have a say in it? It was difficult for me to concede total sovereignty to God, but if he really was love, as the pastor explained, I had nothing to lose. As soon as this thought had crossed my mind I began to feel a deep peace in my heart.

Helper / Magical Agent
receipt of magical agent

In a matter of minutes my whole life appeared to me in new dimensions. As the pastor made an invitation, at the end of his sermon, for a private talk with him I felt strongly urged to accept.

First Move
transference
struggle
branding

At the back of the meeting hall was a little room where he and some other people went in. I followed. We were seated in a semi-circle and the pastor talked and prayed silently with each individually. As I was waiting for my turn doubts arose again, "wasn't this simply the manipulation of souls?" But when the pastor finally explained to me that a conversion to Christ was not "cosmetics" I understood that I had to ask God to renew my life. And as I had done so the pastor told me that I now was a child of God. Indeed, my doubts were gone!

Second Move
(new villainy)
pursuit / rescue

My mother was waiting for me as I returned home. I told her about my experiences, but she didn't seem thrilled at all. But I shall not go into detail as to what happened between us.

Continuation
defeat of the villain
liquidation of initial lack / misfortune
transfiguration of the hero
return
exposure/ punishment of the false hero
wedding

In the following weeks I noticed a change in me. I began to grow in faith. Doubts as to the rightness of my decision disappeared. I no longer was as irritable as before. Actually, I had never expected that a new beginning in life could be possible. God knew my heart's desire. My friends also noticed a change in me. They said that I was somehow different. - happier. Richard also has discerned a change, but he tries to keep his impressions to himself. I care for him and for my mother and pray for them. God in his love will certainly also touch their lives. For it says in the Bible, "I will build my church, and the powers of death will not prevail against it." And somewhere else "Come to me, all who labour and are burdened, I will give you rest."

The first table compares the testimonies of T.B. BARRATT and Frank BARTLEMAN,[10] both early preachers of the Pentecostal movement, with typical fairy tale functions. The initial situation in fairy tales is generally either an event that caused a misfortune (e.g. the loss of a family member) or the perception of a lack (e.g. desire for a priceless object).[11] Closely related to these is the orientation of the tale as a whole, namely if the problem will be resolved by means of a struggle, or if the main feature is a difficult task to be achieved.

These elements also introduce the two testimonies. They lead to what can be called the departure. Such a move is in a testimony often psychological. It seems important, however, that the subject needs to cross the prior parameters in order to gain a new experience. But just as the departure is a significant function of tale and testimony alike, so also is the eventual return. Fairy tales emphatically point to the necessity of the hero's return to ordinary life. Similarly, theologians have emphasized the danger of escaping into the world of religious narrative, without the subsequent, and hopefully trans-formed, return to the life world.[12] The testimonies compared clearly evidence such a return, expressed in terms of a commitment.

---

[10] T.B. BARRAT's testimony was taken from Nils BLOCH-HOELL, The Pentecostal Movement, Oslo, 1964, pp. 132-135.
    F. BARTELMAN's account is taken from his autobiography, Another Wave Rolls In (formerly: What Really Happened at "Azusa Street"), Monroeville, 1970, pp. 22-30.

[11] A conversion testimony might reflect either "lack" or "misfortune" as a catalyst for the religious discovery. The socio-economic situation of the communicator may play a role as to which factor becomes the original incentive. Testimonies of Spirit-Baptism are often presented in terms of an awareness of "lack." This is evident in theologies that speak of a "second work of grace."

[12] Dorothee SOELLE, for instance: "Das fünfte und letzte Stadium (des Märchens) ist der Weg zurück in die Welt. Wir charakterisieren ihn meist als das für alle Märchen typische Happy-End, aber diese formale Benennung verdunkelt eher das, worum es geht. Erlösung bedeutet im Märchen nicht ein Versetztwerden in die andere Welt... Diese Welt wird nicht durch eine andere ersetzt, sondern sie wird mit Hilfe der Erfahrungen der anderen Welt verändert. Versöhnung beider Welten ist das Ziel." Dorothee SOELLE, Die Hinreise, p. 74.
Cf. also the article by Amos N. WILDER, Story and the Story-World, in Interpretation 37 (1983), p. 364.

Other points of comparison are: a) the function of the donor. It may be assumed that in a religious context the donor is God, but some testimonies might well reveal a human dependence in this respect! b) In pentecostal testimonies of a baptism with the Holy Spirit the function of the helper and/or the magical agent would naturally be emphasized. c) If a dualistic world conception is essential, the function of villainy would play an important role. And lastly, the function of branding which in turn leads to a transfiguration of the hero seems to play an irreplaceable role in pentecostal circles.[13]

The second table is an attempt to construct a model testimony according to PROPP's criteria. If, as he claims, everyday life is indeed the nurturing ground for the birth of fairy tales, then it might be possible to apply the logic in reverse and argue that a model testimony, because of its life-relatedness, might be accepted as canonical, thus undergirding the presupposition that such life stories function as "map makers" of a life world. It is for this reason that a number of pentecostal and evangelical Christians, thus people acquainted with a testimonial tradition, were asked about their impression regarding this testimony, and if they could identify themselves to a certain degree with the contents of it.[14]

With respect to the first point, the general impression of the readers was that this testimony was realistic. Many remarked that this account was very typical in relation to what they had experienced themselves, or to what they were used to hearing in church services. Some had the impression that the testimony was too simple, not very dramatic, lacking dynamism, and not attributing enough emphasis on the divine activity. These remarks center around the role of emplotment, that is, the tension between the themes of "complication," the "donor"

---

[13] Along the same lines one can understand the insistent emphasis on the **shibboleth** of speaking in tongues as the "initial evidence" of Spirit-Baptism in many pentecostal institutions. However, other forms of "branding" are known. Furthermore, a general study of the phenomenon of branding in hagiographic literature could prove valuable (cf. stigmata, visions, etc.).

[14] The theological convictions that can be identified between the lines, and the religious lingo, have been included in the model to approximate the test-readers' use of liturgical language, for the aim was to discover structural (and not theological) identification.

and "villainy." But they could also point to the private form of this
imaginary testimony. It seems likely that a testimony which presents
itself as being detached from social realities is particularly
lifeless and lacks evocative power.

As to the question of identification, the answers fell into two
categories. On the one hand there was the great majority which could
identify itself with the story due to the similar circumstances of
their own conversion. On the other hand, those who said that they
could not, attributed this to the fact that they were reared in a
christian home.

The following tentative conclusions could be drawn: First, if the
structures of this testimony are paradigmatic, then more in relation
to conversions from a non-christian life world into a christian one.
Their formal similarity with fairy tales makes the "testimony of
grace" functionally understandable to people largely unacquainted with
religious language games. That means that the secular person can
understand the disclosure referred to, although this does not
guarantee a disclosure of wholeness in the mind of the listener.
Second, the first deduction seems to suggest that another paradigmatic
testimony could be written, which would reflect the situation of those
who have grown into a conscious form of Christianity ever since they
were children. It is likely that PROPP's functions would equally
apply. Instead of a "lack" or a "misfortune," the functions of
"interdiction" and "command" are likely to have a prominent role.
Third, the general impression of the readers was that it was certainly
possible to integrate this testimony into their personal set of
convictions. It represents a resolution of conflict, whether
inter-subjective or imaginary, which they had experienced in a similar
way. Its therapeutic nature was acknowledged.

The Proppian model of syntactical narrative analysis, as attractive as it appears at first sight, has some fundamental short-comings
as Claude BREMOND pointed out in his article Le message narratif.[15]
This French structuralist was interested in examining the possible
application of PROPP's analysis to every kind of narrative. In doing

---

[15] Claude BREMOND, Le message narratif, in Communications 4 (1964),
pp. 4-32. English translation in Semeia 10 (1978), pp. 5-55.

so he clearly established that PROPP's claim that the sequence of functions is always identical could not be verified. One function could not be said to lead necessarily to another. In applying PROPP's model to his own examples, BREMOND came to the conclusion that it was impossible for the Russian folklorist to conceive of functions being capable of opening up alternatives in the plot of the story.[16] BREMOND pointed out that one can find many dead-ends in the Russian folk tale, blind alleys whose narrative potential simply had not been used. Consequently he postulated the necessity of never presenting a function without presenting at the same time the possibility of a contradictory option.[17] What does this mean? First, every function contains per se the potential for bifurcation. For instance, an interdiction can either be violated or obeyed, a deception can either deceive or fail to deceive, a struggle must not always end in victory. This binary character of functions seems to be essential to an appropriate understanding of the temporality in which the personal testimonies of wholeness are set. It allows for an expression of "existential evil" and contingency in testimonies. The second aspect to be noted is that bifurcations provide a certain liquidity to the structure of the narrative. At the same time one needs to remember that although the functions must not necessarily follow a given sequence, they often do because of probability relationships and logical necessities. To give examples: on the one hand it follows by necessity that prior to the return of the hero there must have been a departure, on the other hand the branding of the hero must not necessarily follow a struggle with the villain or the donor; it might already have been given at the hero's birth. For structural purposes it would be useful to discover the aspects of bifurcation and probability. Or in theological terms one could ask: In how far are orthodoxy and orthopraxis bound to a given "path" of actions (e.g. a conversion experience) and reactions (e.g. a public testimony such as

---

[16] Claude BREMOND, The Narrative Message, p. 18.

[17] Claude BREMOND, The Narrative Message, p. 24.

baptism). Furthermore, the theodicy problem could find a more appropriate formulation in the light of contingency. There would be more room for **peripeteia**, the unexpected turn of events.

So far, only syntactic considerations have been voiced. Tentatively, one could draw the following conclusions. First, religious testimonies certainly follow a logical structure. The functions relate coherently to one another. Theologically they emphasize the otherness of God (the favour of the donor is an act of grace), the necessity of self-transcendence (journey), but also a disclosure of meaning in this-worldly terms, for the hearer of the tale has no context of experience but his own by which to interpret the content of the story. Second, as with fairy tales, these functions are akin to the existential nature of human decisions and actions.[18] Therefore, they reflect on a deeper level of meaning the trial of **Dasein** and ways of being answerable to it. Furthermore, the composition of structures and / or functions (e.g. a departure without return) could point to theological problems and difficulties with socialization.

4.2.2. The Problem of Falsehood and Self-Deception

Probably the easiest criteria for the discovery of self-deception in testimonial narratives is the question, "Who speaks?" The testimony as such speaks for itself. It is through "the irruption of something higher" that the witness feels compelled to testify. If the witness intends to speak through his testimony then he brings a foreign element into the narrative. As Raimundo PANIKKAR puts it,

> I do not bear witness to the truth of my faith if I proclaim it in order to be a witness... Of course falsehood is also possible here. As long as the audience believes the testimony of the witness, he bears true witness - **ex opere operantis** - but he ceases to do so when the audience discovers that he - rather than the testimony itself - intends to speak, to bear witness. In fact, the will to bear witness implies wanting to show... to convert him because I myself am convinced that the contents of

---

[18] It would certainly be rewarding to compare these functions with models of affective and cognitive phases of learning as they have been elaborated by Jean PIAGET (e.g. experience by trial and error), Lawrence KOHLBERG (development of moral standards), Erik H. ERIKSON (biographycal identity formation) and others.

my testimony are proper for him too... the purpose is no longer the passive blossoming of a grace that the audience freely discovers, but the active communication of a value...[19] Interpretative comments are therefore rare in spontaneous testimonies. If they are present, they indicate that the witness has already passed the pre-reflective stage, for instance by virtue of having testified to the same experience on several occasions or because the testimony has been written down. This, for instance, is evident in Miss SISSON's testimony.[20]

The question "Who speaks?" can shed more light on inauthentic testimonies of grace from another angle, namely in the way it relates to a third party, as the Latin roots **testis** and **tri-stans** already indicate. A testimony is not a dialectical activity between two parties, but is rather a witness to transcendence which may be simply institutional or religious, as the practice of oath taking exemplifies. Now if the witness does not admit the existence of a third party, then self-deception is well on its way. Alphonse De WAELHENS gives, from a psychoanalytic viewpoint, two examples where triple inter-subjectivity is thwarted.[21] The first case applies to the schizophrenic person, for whom there cannot be an address to a third person, due to the difficulties of speaking as a self.[22] The second example applies to the paranoiac. For him the third party is his very self, for he remains psychologically at the mirror-stage and reacts aggressively to any deviation of his perception of himself. If asked

---

[19] Raimundo PANIKKAR, Myth, Faith and Hermeneutics, New York, 1979, p. 249.

[20] See in the appendices: Testimony (D), lines 15f., 59ff., 326ff.

[21] Alphonse DE WAELHENS, Ambiguïté de la notion de témoignage, in Le témoignage, Paris, 1972, pp. 467-476.

[22] The case of schizophrenia should however not be confused with the double aspect of the self making a testimonial narrative possible. Paul BROCKELMAN distinguishes a self which is characterized in the temporal process brought to light in the testimony, and the self which causes any reflection about it. The abilitiy to keep one's distance from a temporal experiences also explains self-deception, namely the interplay between a deceiving self and a deceived self. At the same time it allows awareness of this process and a correction of self-deception. Paul BROCKELMAN, Time and Self. Phenomenological Explorations, Decatur, 1985, pp. 15-16, 82-83.

who speaks, he would answer "Me, who else!" For him that means that all truth is his truth. In testifying he actually makes apodictic statements in which any form of ambiguity is excluded.[23] But it is ambiguity that characterizes testimony and bestows unpretentious power on its speech. After all, to testify is to be involved in an act of faith. Signs of ambiguity, in the Proppian functions of testing and riddles, refer to the awareness of the third party. Phrases like "I asked myself," "I wondered," or "it dawned on me" are typical pointers to such inter-subjetivity.[24]

Similarly "bad faith" is evident when the faith expressed in the testimony refers, as a closed movement, back to the self,[25] instead of being a confidential gesture to the other. From the formalist point of view one could ask, Is the donor a hidden form of the hero? It is clear that the community of interpretation plays a vital role in discerning the veracity of a testimony of wholeness, and deliberating whether there is an event of grace, or if healing becomes the very need of the witness. The criteria that can be analyzed syntactically in fact exist in the common sense of faith of the community; at least among those who are acquainted with the practice of communicating experiences involving an act of faith.

Another problem arises, however. If ambiguity is essential to the testimony, and a testimony is generally understood as a pre-reflective narrative, then how can one make claims of truth in such a relative context? Can there be truth in relativism? Stanley HAUERWAS adopts an

---

[23] Alphone DE WAELHENS, Ambiguïté, pp. 470-473. By implication the objective to "tell the truth, the whole truth, and nothing but the truth" is in fact a paranoiac fallacy!

[24] Miss SISSON's testimony (D) serves again as example. The inner struggle with her illness is described as a dialogue between God's Spirit (Word) and her human reactions, which finally leads to a deliberation. Cf. lines 43, 197f., 241ff., and the larger context.

[25] "Il n'y a que' une mauvaise foi, celle qui s'épuise dans la foi elle-même, à savoir, en dernière analyse, la fidélité absolue à nous-mêmes." Enrico CASTELLI, Les significations du témoignage, in Le témoignage, p. 29 (emphasis his).

interesting answer from Bernard WILLIAMS. The argument runs that only
in real confrontation does one employ the vocabulary of contrast
(true/false, right/wrong, acceptable/unacceptable).

> That we often do not feel the need to employ such language
> reveals the truth of relativism since we find that many
> confrontations do not involve questions of a real option at all,
> and thus issues of appraisal simply do not arise - or they arise
> only notionally... this understanding of relativism, unlike most
> of the other alternatives, is coherent because it manages to
> cohere with two propositions, both of which are true: first,
> that we must have a form of thought not relativized to our own
> existing system of beliefs or thinking about other systems of
> beliefs which may be of concern to us, and to express those
> concerns; but, second, we can nevertheless recognize that there
> can be many systems of beliefs "which have insufficient relation
> to our concerns for our judgments to have any grip on them while
> admitting that other persons' judgments could get a grip on
> them, namely, those for whom they are a real option."[26]

It is generally assumed that testimonies emphatically claim only one
interpretation of truth. That this is not the case is illustrated by
the early pentecostal testimonies of healing in which the medical
profession stands in an ambivalent position. On the one hand, the real
physician is Jesus, on the other hand medical terminology is used to
describe the worsening of the initial situation and doctors are
invited to verify miraculous healings.[27] Indeed such testimonies are
not incoherent, but reflect the divided character of human existence
and the delicate enterprise of placing moral commitment between
strongly held beliefs and constantly emerging models with new
formulations of what is held to be true. It follows that the function
of testimony for the mapping of a life world fulfills a pivotal role
especially in a secular and pluralist society.

---

[26] Stanley HAUERWAS, The Church in a Divided World. The Interpretative
Power of the Chistian Story, in Journal of Religious Ethics 8,1
(spring 1980), p. 70, quoting from Bernard WILLIAMS, The Truth of
Relativism, in Aristotelian Society. Supplementary Volume 52, 1978, p.
226.

[27] See for instance testimonies (D) lines 126-132; (E) lines 17ff.,
26f., 77ff.; and (F) lines 28f., 33, 35ff. in the appendixes.

4.2.3. The Problem of Triviality

The striking similarity between therapeutic testimonies and fairy tales conjures up questions concerning their popular appeal. Does not the very structure of religious testimonies point to a trivial understanding of life? As already mentioned (3.3.3.2.) the fact that an account can be said to be trivial need as such not be a value judgment. After all, the trivial points primarily to a popular appeal. The trivial, though, becomes theologically problematic if experiences of grace are communicated in an oversimplified way, or if they give way to misrepresentations.

4.2.3.1. Everyday Language / Everyday Experience?

One aspect of the trivial that can easily be singled out is the everyday context in which these experiences take place. Everyday language is to a large extent pre-reflective in nature. It attributes causes, reasons, and results to handy interpretation-categories, because answers have to be made quickly. The same language brings disclosures to words. In this sense the testimonies studied all represent a simplification of what happened. Often the life previous to the experience of reversal is painted in the darkest colours, whereas the life following is illustrated in brightness. This is, as form critics pointed out,[28] also the case in the miracle stories of the New Testament. The contrast, because it is a movement from sin to grace, is understandable. But such a paradigm shift must also be seen in the social context in which it takes place. In other words, the

---

[28] Fundational work on the literary structure of exorcisms, nature and healing miracles was done by Martin DIBELIUS and Rudolf BULTMANN. Stephen H. TRAVIS in his article Form Criticism, in I. Howard MARSHALL (ed.), New Testament Interpretation, eloquently summarizes the structural nature of miracle stories in the gospels, "All the stories follow the same basic pattern: (1) a description of the disease or situation to be remedied; (2) a statement of the cure or solution achieved by Jesus; (3) a statement of the result of the miracle - either the effects on the person healed or the reaction of the onlookers. This is a natural pattern for any story of this kind, shared by Jewish and pagan miracle-stories, as well as by TV adverts for vitamin pills and medicated shampoos." (p. 156).

subject experiencing the irruption of the divine into the common
circumstances of life, in spite of the radical transvaluation which
has taken place, lives and relates to a surrounding that has not
changed. The contrast, although real, cannot be lifted out of the
hinges of common existence.[29] It can thus be said that it is **not**
absurd to discover the divine in the experiences of daily life (e.g.
disclosure of love, healing), but it would be absurd to interpret
signs of the Sacred with categories of trivial communication. In order
to differentiate between the two one needs a finer frame of reference
than the pigeonholes of fast categorization typical in daily life.[30]
Tradition can serve as a finer interpretative horizon. But in view of
the necessity of being understandable to the secular domain, one
should add the innovative and the critical, or simply put, the
prophetic.

Another common problem of trivialization in religious communities
can be detected in the use of the Bible in autobiographical accounts.
It is typical to read scriptural texts (often only verses) in an
existential way, thus appropriating, for instance, a promise to the
end of Israel's babylonian captivity as a promise of private physical
restoration.[31] It is clear that one may not do violence to the

---

[29] "Soziologen und Sozialpsychologen weisen angesichts von Umbrüchen
im Leben des Individuums und in gesellschaftlichen Entwicklungen auf
die notwendige Identität, die solchen Bruch erträglich machen kann.
Vorher und Nachher können nicht gänzlich auseinanderfallen." Burkhart
MECKING, Christliche Biographien, p. 93.

[30] "Um überhaupt handlungsfähig zu bleiben, müssen wir uns entlasten
und tiefergreifende Problematisierungen unseres Verhaltens geradezu
programmatisch ausschalten. Da wir uns aber ständig entscheiden
müssen, entscheiden wir uns auf der Grundlage von Wahrscheinlichkeits-
einschätzungen, vorläufigen Urteilen, die auf Ueberallgemeinerung
basieren und daher leicht zu Vorurteilen gerinnen, und Nachahmungen
von Handlungen, Verhaltensweisen, die zu Klischees erstarren können.
Dass die Alltagserfahrungen aufgrund von Wahrscheinlichkeit gemacht
werden, verweist schon auf die Oekonomie und den Pragmatismus des
Alltagslebens." Peter BIEHL, Erfahrung als hermeneutische, theologische und religionspädagogische Kategorie. Ueberlegungen zum
Verhältnis von Alltagserfahrungen und religiöser Sprache, in Günter
HEIMBROCK (ed.), Erfahrungen in religiösen Lernprozessen, Göttingen,
1983, p. 19.

[31] See Appendices: Testimony (D), other examples could be the alle-
gorical use of non-allegorical passages, the use of doxological

biblical text by interpreting it at random, but in judging this phenomenon one has to be careful. First, one may recall that the authors of the New Testament have also been rather generous in interpreting passages that seemed relevant for their purposes, and they apparently had better knowledge of the Scriptures (O.T.) as a literary whole than most average Christians today. Second, there is a metaphorical use of the Scriptures that is well aware of the different contexts, but which perceives phenomenologically a similarity and thus a parallel between two different sets of circumstances, bringing about new pertinence due to the simultaneous similarity and dis-similarity involved. Third, if one is aware of a certain gap between the text and one's understanding of it, then an interpretation is positively relativized.[32] The identification with the Bible cannot be so close, that an interpretation is made difficult because there is not enough distance between the reader and the text in order to allow a hermeneutic tension to play itself out. Once more the community of interpretation is called upon to participate in the testimonial event, by responding in an appropriate manner to the suggested relationship between personal experience and the religious interpretative context.[33]

4.2.3.2. Recourse to the Will of God?

If recourse to the will of God is made too frequently, the idea of perceiving it is trivialized.[34] It loses an impact that should not necessarily be absent from testimonial speech; after all not much is

---

statements as commands (cf. Mt.11:25), or the use of promises as a precondition (Ps. 113:7). Cf. Burkahrt MECKING, Christliche Biographien, p. 127.

[32] Burkahrt MECKING, Christliche Biographien, p. 130.

[33] In pentecostal circles this is done by chosing an appropriate hymn as a response to the testimony, or by allowing another person to speak up, or also in a prayer which focuses on that which can be endorsed. In a way one could call it a modern type of Bible class in which spiritual sensitivity is a necessary prerequisite of those leading the service.

[34] Burkhart MECKING, Christliche Biographien, pp. 106-115.

left to religious experience if the idea of joining the intentionality
of the Sacred is ruled out. According to Burkhart MECKING, there seem
to be be two major possibilities for formulations of God's will in
religious testimonies. Firstly, there is the doxological perception of
the divine as it pertains to the plan of salvation (e.g. the
disclosure of divine guidance after a period of spiritual darkness or
suffering). Secondly, there can be an ethical aspect in the idea of
God's will (e.g., the autobiographical question "What does God want me
to do with my life?" or, "How can I correct the wrongdoings of the
past?"). Whereas in the first case, the will of God can still be seen
in a larger salvific context, it is almost certainly personalized in
the second case. It seems to be a by-product of secularization and
growing individualism that God's will is increasingly sought for in
personal matters. This would not be a negative development as such, so
long as a larger historical context is maintained. It is precisely
here that a major problem arises. The will of God becomes too
ordinary. Only if it cannot be perceived, for example in case of a
theodicy problem, is the context enlarged to contain the greater
wisdom of God. Two testimonies and one set of visions in the
appendixes relate specifically to the perception of the will of God.[35]
One notices that "locating" the will of God is not that easy. The
reason may lie in the varied forms in which it appears, and in the
realization that one is standing in the presence of otherness.

The following symptoms can be diagnosed in the deliberation of
God's will. Firstly, there is frequently a hesitation to respond to
the perceived will of God, as if one did not quite know how to

---

[35] In testimony (D) the search for the will of God is expressed in the
following: An illness sets in when the protagonist is just about to do
the will of God (i.e. joining others on an evangelistic campaign,
lines 12f.), the delay in healing is not understood and room is made
for the theodicy problem (lines 38-45), the death wish (139-147 and
especially 170-178), the heroine gives herself up to the will of God
(lines 214ff.), the will of God is recognized as obedience (lines
251-257), and finally the whole experience is interpreted as an answer
to prayer in a general context (lines 326-339).
    Testimony (G) illustrates how the will of God was sought for
(lines 22ff., 29-37, 48-62), and again related to obedience.
    Appendix III, example (C) recounts three visions in relation to
physical restoration, providing the reason for the same.

approach the burning bush.[36] Secondly, sometimes a second party
initiates a perception of the will of God; this compares with the
function of the "helper" in Proppian terms.[37] Lastly, it is not only a
question of attributing an idea to the Sacred, for circumstantial
actions and feelings are also attributed to divine causation. The
"branding" is a typical phenomenon in which a physical sensation is
considered to be a sign of transcendent affirmation. It is so typical
in pentecostal testimonies and narratives of the methodist Holiness
movement that Walter HOLLENWEGER wonders if this is, for Europe and
America in any case, a form of learned behaviour.[38] Of course, learned
behaviour need not be **a priori** wrong. It is only remarkable how
tangibly the Holy is "experienced." The attribution of insight to the
divine cannot by its very nature be verified empirically, nevertheless
an analogous form of I.T. RAMSEY's empirical fit could be applied. Or
in Paul RICOEUR's words, such experience would benefit from a double
exegesis of poetics and ethics.[39] This means in more practical terms
that a statement concerning the will of God can only be shown to be
reliable if it is brought to bear in the life of the individual,
specifically in his ethical commitment. One could argue that this is
also the case for personalized claims of divine intervention, for
instance in the provision of spiritual gifts (**charismata**) or in the
experience of healing. There too the "hero" can be expected to be
answerable to the gift of grace in a way which reflects a
self-transcending concern.

---

[36] This can be seen in the testimony of Miss SISSON, as well as in
Louise GRANDJEAN's vision (Appendix III: Vision (D)).

[37] Cf. Testimonies (D) lines 88ff., 220-231, 260-271; (E) line 37f.;
(G) lines 25ff.

[38] "The longing for the supernatural and for the healing of sickness
by prayer is a constant feature of nineteenth-century works of
edification, as anyone who reads them can tell." Walter J.
HOLLENWEGER, The Pentecostals, London, 1972, p. 353. But see the
larger context pp. 353-376.

[39] Paul RICOEUR, Toward a Hermeneutic of the Idea of Revelation, in
Essays, p. 112.

4.2.3.3. The Theodicy Problem

Finally a trivial rendition of experience can also be noticed in
relation to the problem of justifying the unexplainable before God,
who, it should be remembered, is the third party in religious
testimonies. The great majority of public testimonies have a happy
end. There is no sense of the tragic, except in the case of prolonged
suffering, which then is interpreted as a period of **catharsis**, of
purification and self-examination.[40] Some people have wondered why
only victorious testimonies are told in religious assemblies. Why
indeed are there no testimonies of defeat, since their inclusion would
render a more truthful picture of human reality? Walter HOLLENWEGER
gives an account of a woman who was certain she had received a promise
of physical healing through a prophetic utterance of an evangelist
known for his gift of mediating healing. However, the healing failed
to take place. She wrote to HOLLENWEGER, who had on that occasion
translated for the evangelist and begged for help. He writes,

> Unfortunately, to avoid yet more disappointment, I had to
> decline. But I considered it would be right, since the journals
> of the Swiss and foreign Pentecostal movement had for years
> publicized the testimonies of those who had been healed, to
> publish at least once a testimony from one of the majority who
> had not been healed... This suggestion was turned down by the
> leaders of the Swiss Pentecostal Mission.[41]

Apparently the editors feared that such a testimony would undermine
faith. But does faith depend on a selective proclamation of truth? The
tension between belief in divine healing for all, and the apparent
number of actual healings attributed to faith is one area where an
alternative telling of the tale, in the sense Claude BREMOND suggests,
seems appropriate, since bifurcation could be syntactically present in
any narrative. This particular theodicy problem has, by the way, preoccupied Pentecostals for some time.[42] The danger of glossing over the

---

[40] However, suffering as a sense of the tragic is frequently present
when prayer requests are publicly shared. Often, in order to provide
some information to make the request meaningful a short narrative or
explanation is given which sets the tragic in relation to the
expectations of faith.

[41] Walter J. HOLLENWEGER, The Pentecostals, p. 356.

problem of theodicy could be countered by the inclusion of "testimonies of defeat" which in turn would render the "testimonies of victory" more credible, and diminish a trivial rendition of existence.

A starting point in the same direction is already given in the structure of the testimonies so far referred to. It is the function of the **peripeteia**, i.e. the reversal in the plot, **the coup de théâtre**. It is the sudden change in the fate of the hero that gives impact to the testimony. It is the unexpected resurrection that brings power to the passion story. The constant possibility of **peripeteia** is one way of coping with the problem of facing evil and suffering in spite of the proclamation of a loving and caring God. But the sword of this reversal of the plot is double-edged. Anti-testimonies are also part of the plot and would certainly dispel a sense of faith that appears to be a feigned bargain.

4.3. Considerations on the Semantic Level

Whereas a syntactic / morphological approach is concerned with linguistic forms and their inner coherence, a semantic method is primarily concerned with the conveyance of meaning. Some analytic philosophers tend to associate the semantic level of language either with its syntactic or pragmatic counterpart. To keep the three linguistic dimensions of Ch. MORRIS as distinct as possible is not always easy. In the discussion on trivial aspects of testimony the semantic has touched on the syntactic field. Likewise, the semantic and pragmatic dimensions can overlap, especially when language is evocative and performative at the same time. For hermeneutic purposes one can, on the semantic plane, attribute meaning to the narrative as such, whereas on the pragmatic level meaning is studied in the act and result of communication. In principle, however, signification as a whole happens in the interaction of all three dimensions.

---

[42] Cf. Donald GEE, Trophimus I Left Sick, London, 1952. German edition consulted: "Trophimus liess ich krank zurück", Schorndorf, n.d.

4.3.1. The Fundamental Problem of Meaning in Language

A basic semantic structure has been established by Ferdinand DE SAUSSURE.[43] He pointed to the double connotative nature of signs. On the first level a sign consists of a linguistic signifier (**signifiant**, abbreviation: sign*). This signifier points to a conceptual signified (**signifié**, abbreviation: sign°), which in turn denotes or designates a referent. But meaning can also emerge from a deeper level, namely if the meaning of the first level (i.e. conceptual referent) turns into a new signifier and thus sets another semantic order with a new signified into action (e.g. symbolic connotation). It is this double order of meaning that one finds in the parabolic and metaphoric language of the Bible. Now it is in the very nature of religious narratives to make use of the same dynamics. A hermeneutic of testimony would, consequently, also take heed of symbolic meaning. Such an approach is then by necessity polysemic, that is, meaning can be discovered on various levels. One can say that the language of religious testimony has a double function. On the one hand it is informational, it situates the narrator and the audience in a life world. On the other hand it is symbolic, it attempts to share a self-transcending disclosure with the listeners.

This rather complex theory can be clarified by means of illustrations.[44] In the Gospel of Luke chapter 15 we read: "a certain man had two sons." This statement can be understood on a conceptual level, in terms of a proposition, an idea presented. But on a symbolic level it also points to another significance which is unstated, namely that God is compared to a father and that he has two kinds of children. Another example can be drawn from Frank BARTLEMAN's testimony. On the informational level one learns that he suffered greatly through the loss of his little daughter. On a symbolic level one might realize that the pastor found no consolation in his own

---

[43] Ferdinand DE SAUSSURE, Cours de linguistique générale, Paris, 1916, 1922. The German edition was consulted: Grundfragen der allgemeinen Sprachwissenschaft, Berlin, 1931.

[44] Cf. Susan WITTIG, A Theory of Multiple Meanings, in Semeia 9 (1977), pp. 75-103, especially pp. 84-87.

mind. He had to appeal to a reality which transcended him. Someone else, however, might interpret the symbolic significance differently, namely as a pointer to the nature of affective relationships. He might experience a disclosure in which love is presented as outlasting death.

A polysemic understanding cannot therefore be limited to one informational and one symbolic dimension, since the veracity of a testimony might be accepted on many levels. How is this possible? The main reason is that signs do not appear in isolation.[45] It is precisely for this reason that the narrative context of a testimony is significant.[46] It provides certain limits for the meaningful function of signs. Furthermore, the context of the life world must also be taken into account. For example, if a hearer of the parable of the prodigal son had a sadistic tyrant as a father, he could well expect the parable to end in disaster, or he might have difficulties in appreciating a symbolic reference to God. To state the case theoretically, one can say that in a text one is confronted with a limited sequence of signs (synchronic view), but as soon as one moves into the oral domain of language the sequence of signs is by necessity open (panchronic view), for the sign and its use stand, in view of the audience addressed, in a dialectic relationship to each other.[47]

Thus, a semantic study of testimonies is faced with a chain of signs (signifiers and signifieds) which influence each other.[48] In the case of T.B. BARRATT's experience of his Spirit-Baptism one could, for instance, construct the following chain of contexts:

---

[45] Other reasons might be that the receiver of the message does not understand certain signs, or that he attributes to signifiers other signifying functions.

[46] Susan WITTIG, Multiple Meanings, p. 87. The same argument also illustrates the function of narratives in theology as a whole.

[47] DE SAUSSURE would deny the possibility of meaningful panchronic language situations. Ferdinand DE SAUSURE, Grundfragen, p. 114.
However, one may recall Paul RICOEUR's suggestion to consider certain lingustic phenomena as an event in which synchronic and diachronic aspects merge into a panchronic manifestation of "language in celebration" (en fête). Cf. 2.3.1.

[48] Susan WITTIG, Multiple Meanings, p. 88.

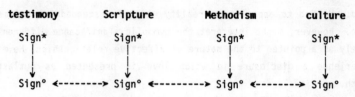

From a cultural point of view, his Cornish background and his
aesthetic education (painting under Olaf DAHL of Bergen; music under
Edvard GRIEG)[49] might be considered. In his case the aesthetic would
certainly play an important role in religious experience. His
methodist background provided a sacramental understanding of grace for
his experience. The Norwegian Bible from which he quoted says that the
believers spoke "in a loud voice" when they were filled with the
Spirit.[50] Furthermore, in terms of his testimony it can be noted that
BARRATT frequently met and corresponded with Pentecostals in the
United States of America; he was concerned that there should be
congruence between his experience and the account given to him by his
American friends. The interaction of these aspects has undoubtedly
lead to a rich semantic field of reference, without which the
interpretation of BARRATT's testimony might seem awkward.

    At this point a semantic analysis is in close proximity to the
pragmatic dimension of language. The creativity of production borders
on the creativity of interpretation. The receiver of the message will,
of course, relate the contents of what is said to his own set of
interdependent signs.

    Before considering some detailed aspects in the production of
meaning one could summarize the general semantic considerations as
follows. First, religious language in general and the language of
testimony specifically is never merely informational. There are also
symbolic dimensions that are bearers of meaning.[51] Second, the

---

[49] Nils BLOCH-HOELL, The Pentecostal Movement, p. 178.

[50] Kilian McDONNELL, The Function of Tongues in Pentecostalism. Roman
Catholic / Pentecostal Dialogue. Papers from the Rome meeting, Oct.
1977, in One In Christ 19,4 (1983), p. 350. The text BARRATT refers to
is Acts 10:46. The speaking "in a loud voice" is part of his
"branding."

function of signs in terms of what they signify is relative to the context in which they appear. Diachronic changes of meaning, for example the problem of religious language games in a secular society, relate also to this aspect. Third, oral testimonies fall not only under the trial of syntactic coherence, but also under that of semantic compatibility. Not all semantic connotations would be understood, but those that are should fall in line with each other. The role of the reception or rejection of a testimony constitutes once more an important factor in the evaluation of a testimony as a whole, and in responding to its intentionality.

4.3.2. The Understanding of Religious Experience

At the present there is much talk about having experiences. The word "experience," however, has a highly complex semantic field.[52] To give an example, one can think of a famous army general who is said to have a lot of experience. Here, the idea is that he has a lot of practice, that he has through time acquired the skill of being a military leader. His experience has a history. In contrast to this understanding of experience one can imagine a drug addict who claims to have had a wonderful experience during his last "high." Here, apparently, the meaning of experience has nothing to do with traditional skill or practice; on the contrary it relates to novelty, that is, something which is beyond the reach of practice, something eventful.

To add to confusion one can differentiate various types of experience. The army general can be said to have pragmatic experience, and the drug addict a subjective one. In addition there is also

---

[51] This statement does not exclude the possibility that symbolic language can also be to a certain degree informational. The aim of this distinction is not to place two linguistic aspects in confrontation with each other, but to facilitate an analysis. The same applies to evocative language, which may very well also be descriptive.

[52] For the multiple aspects of the idea of experience, its secular and theological use see Dietmar MIETH, What is Experience, in Concilium 113 (1979), pp. 40-53.

empirical experience, for instance in a chemical experiment, that
provides repeatedly the same result. But what is of importance to this
study is a hermeneutical type of experience. It is essential for the
interpretation of testimonies that any subjective experience mentioned
does not distract from the deeper hermeneutic experience which is
being brought to words. Thus, when T.B. BARRATT said "immediately the
power of God began to work in my body, as well as in my spirit" it
should be related to "a great concern came over me, not for my self,
but for others," and to "magnifying God in the power of the Holy
Spirit." In other words, he did not only have an experience of
wholeness, but also a disclosure, prompting him to praise and
commitment. Likewise testimonies cannot be "empirical" proofs of God's
existence, not even if they relate to the most glorious miracles, but
they can testify to what can happen if one believes in Him.[53]

When experiences are told, claims are made. In the case of
therapeutic testimonies the temptation is great to locate the claim in
the physical sensation or change that is reported. Theologically, the
physical aspect is only a means and not the end in itself. It is a
sign to the transcendent, and the claim relates to the all-embracing.
But it can only point beyond itself if it remains open, open to wonder
and mystery.[54] Consequently, it would be ill-advised to demythologize
the element of surplus. An experience as disclosure can only suggest
an answer, or offer a diagnosis of a crisis, if it is linguistically
able to formulate heuristic wisdom.

---

[53] Karl RAHNER, in his article Interprétation théologique du
témoignage, in Le témoignage, pp. 173-187, states that the christian
testimony does have a categorical content, but it lies in "the
presence of God in Jesus Christ" (p. 181) and not in the nature of a
miracle. Nevertheless, the intentionality of a miracle can be
understood inter-subjectively as a sign calling for commitment in
Christ, provided it can be read as an event of grace; otherwise it
would be a false testimony.

[54] Dietmar MIETH rightly emphasizes that any experience which claims
to be "definitive" finds an expression in a taboo, a convention, or an
immutable dogma. It leads to a diminution of experience, and as
Raimundo PANIKKAR would say, it invalidates the testimony as such.
Dietmar MIETH, What is Experience? p. 49.

However, the question remains whether the secular person can benefit from the telling of a religious experience if the words used are highly esoteric and the story's meaning is hidden underneath the obvious. First, it can be said that the use of God-talk is to a large extent a matter of culture and learned behaviour.[55] The prominent role of poetic language would be more forceful if communication were mostly straight forward; i.e. if the metaphors used were fresh. Second, the nature of experience, whether secular or religious, is the same. It is, as Dietmar MIETH points out, highly paradoxical[56] and predisposes interpretation favourably. What needs to be understood is the disclosure and the issuing commitment. For this purpose a passive linguistic competence,[57] the capability of listening, is, at first, sufficient. Identification with and differentiation from one's own situation takes place and starts an internal dialogue that hopefully can also find an outward inter-subjective expression.

To summarize, the meaning of communicating experience in testimonies of grace is an affirmation of life and the worth of investing in it. As a result there is an invitation to some form of commitment, for instance, obedience,[58] or the taking up of a new task.[59] Insight can come as a shock or as a consolation, but in either case it broadens and shapes one's horizon of life.

---

[55] There is a marked difference in the use of language between testimonies dating from the beginning of the Pentecostal movement (cf. Appendix II) and contemporary testimonies consulted (e.g. footnotes 76 and 77 below).

[56] Dietmar MIETH, What is Experience?, pp. 44-49.
An experience is at the same time process (skill) and event (impression), directness (situated socio-linguistically) and indirectness (arbitrary and hard to formulate), extensity (generalization) and intensity (concrete), integration (interpreting the world) and hinderance (setting it apart), dialectic (experience as negation) and analectic (experience as relational).

[57] Heinrich STIRNIMANN, Language, Experience and Revelation, in Concilium 113 (1979), p. 121.

[58] Cf. Testimonies (D) and (G) in Appendix II.

[59] The testimonies of Frank BARTLEMAN and T.B. BARRATT in the text, as well as the visions of Dorothy KERIN in Appendix III (C).

4.3.3. The Mythological Dimension: Conversion   and   the   Easter
Experience

Most testimonies of early Pentecostalism focus on aspects which
other churches did not emphasize,   such as spiritual renewal and
healing.   That explains why conversion testimonies are comparatively
rare in early publications.   Furthermore,   the editors might have
considered experiences of maturation and healing more edifying,   since
the readership was generally already committed to a christian way of
life. Nevertheless, conversion stories constitute a fundamental form
of testimony and it seems appropriate in the context of worship to
study the relationship between the disclosure that led to the choice
of a christian fundamental option in life and the mythologizing
aspects relating to it.

Edward SCHILLEBEECKX,   as already indicated (1.3.3.3.),   has
thought about the developmental aspects which led to the Easter
experience of the disciples. In his opinion, the conversion process of
the disciples was a hermeneutic act, by which a disclosure of grace
(and probably of forgiveness since the disciples had deserted him) led
to a experiental reliving of their memories of Jesus before his death
in the light of the present situation.

> These disciples did of course come to realize - in a process of
> repentance and conversion which it is no longer possible to
> reconstruct on a historical basis - something about their
> experience of disclosure that had taken them by storm: their
> "recognition" and "acknowledgement" of Jesus in the totality of
> his life.[60]

Analogous to the Easter experience, the common conversion experience
is "the recognition and acknowledgement of Jesus in the totality of my
life." Phrases like "He still forgives, he must be alive" or "I know
that He lives, I've experienced it" reflect this analogy. But this
mythological analogy must be nurtured, by kerygmatic models previous
to the disclosure, and following it by the celebration of the
Christ-Event in communal worship, as well as in physical involvement
in his name, following it.

---

[60] Edward SCHILLEBEECKX, Jesus, p. 387.

Testimonies cannot be mythical in the strict sense, but they can function as catalytic agents for mythical activity, for as Antoine VERGOTE points out: "myth thinks itself," it needs no witness nor can it, as primordial narrative, have one.[61] But testimonies encode (inchoate) experience metaphorically by establishing new relationships as in the case of the Easter experience. If the religious metaphor survives the test of public confession, if it rings true, brings depth, and is acknowledged by the community of interpretation with its specific criteria (e.g. it must be in accordance with the Scriptures, it must respect the teaching of the Church, etc.), then it has contributed to the enlargement of the horizon of religious experience. This contribution,

> ... not only aids in the specification of experience for a community, but binds the community together in another communicative activity: ritual... ritual, with its episodic structure, allows for regional expansion of a semantic field; in its hymns of praise suggests new forms of multiple predication (litanies); and because of the dramatic and episodic structure, allows one to progress back through the various predications to the 'original experience' as the moment of birth of the revelatory experience itself. Perhaps it is for this reason that the **lex orandi** has always figured so strongly in the specification of experience in the Christian tradition. For generally speaking, semantic innovations occurring within worship have always been of decisive importance for Christians throughout the ages.[62]

From this it should be clear that the mere testimonial practice does not fulfill its purpose unless it is put to work.

---

[61] Antione VERGOTE, Inteprétation, p. 78-81.

[62] Robert SCHREITER, The Specification of Experience and the Language of Revelation, in Concilium 113 (1979), p. 63. Cf. also Henri GOUTIER, Témoignage et expérience religieuse, in Le témoignage, pp. 63-73. "Le témoignage devient créateur de témoins... l'expérience qui en constitue la signification religieuse peut être indéfiniment répétée." (p.73)

4.4. The Pragmatic Level

This aspect of linguistic analysis relates to the intentionality of what is communicated, as the word pragmatic indicates. On one side, it is concerned with understanding the actual use and effect of language. On the other side, it brings up the question of commitment resulting from evocative and performative statements. Since religious speech is closely interwoven with ethical convictions it is worth while to reflect on some basic modalities where creative language undergoes a metamorphosis into action, which in the last chapter will be looked at again in the context of worship.

4.4.1. In the Linguistic Sense

The use of language, in the case of testimony, relates to the teller and to the listener alike. Basically three spheres need to be studied. First, one has to ask which language games are being used. Then, it needs to be clarified what speech acts are involved. And lastly, the speech situation in which meaning is communicated should be examined.[63]

As far as the language games are concerned[64] one can distinguish whether the author is using for example: popular, academic, poetic, religious or political language, or any combination of the above. The clarification of which language game(s) is (are) being used is helpful for the following reasons. For one, it can tell the interpreter about the life world from which the message emerges (cf. T.B. BARRATT). For another, a language game influences the significance of words. In order to give an example one may look at Vladimir PROPP's Morphology. It has been noted that his approach, although it plays an indispensable role in structural analysis, suffers from a formalist fixation. He claimed that the functions follow by necessity the same

---

[63] A useful introduction to pragmatic questions is presented in Anton GRABNER-HAIDER, Glaubenssprache. Ihre Struktur und Anwendbarkeit in Verkündigung und Theologie, Wien, 1975, pp. 155-166.

[64] Language games refer in this case to the socio-linguistic background in which a variety of speech acts can be used.

sequence. Such a view becomes easier to understand as soon as one notices ideological vocabulary such as, "the early stages of the development of human society" or "the appearance of these plots responds to historical necessity."[65] PROPP's system makes perfect sense in an early twentieth century Marxist life world. Similarly, vocabulary like "religion", "virtue" or "God" carries a different significance when it is used by a poet like Ralph W. EMERSON, a priest like Dom Helder CAMARRA or a politician like Adolf HITLER.

The second pragmatic question centers around the speech acts involved. A theory of speech act has first been presented by J.L. AUSTIN. It was later developed by his **protegé** J.R. SEARLE and relates to behavioural rules of communication.[66] It is basically argued that different speech acts fulfill different functions. For brevity's sake it will only be mentioned that religious language has a performative character (constituting an interplay between intentions and conventions) which is due to its illocutionary force (relatively functional to the given situation), and that speech acts such as expressions of faith (e.g. a promise) need not be identical with speech acts of proclamation (e.g. an invitation). It is important to observe that religious speech acts are of an evocative nature. It should therefore be asked what they evoke. On a passive level they might evoke emotions, on the active plane they may call for an answer on the cognitive level.[67] Whereas T.B. BARRATT's account apparently calls for imitation in order to attain a similar experience for a deeper christian commitment, Frank BARTLEMAN's story evokes an attitude of praise as it pictures the power, love and wisdom of God.

Asking about the contents of the evocation is important, since symbolic language leaves the final signified unstated. It is "giving to the system a dynamic, unstable **indeterminancy** which invites, even

---

[65] Vladimir PROPP, Structure and History in the Study of the Fairy Tale, in Semeia 10 (1978), p.65. Cf. Claude BREMOND's critique above.

[66] J.L. AUSTIN, How to Do Things with Words, Oxford, 1962; John R. SEARLE, Speech Acts. An Essay in the Philosophy of Language, Cambridge, Mass., 1969.

[67] Wim DE PATER, Theologische Sprachlogik, München, 1971, pp. 47f.

compels the perceiver to complete the signification."[68] In other words, a testimony does not create one particular meaning, but as with parables, it creates the possibility for

> **the conditions under which the creation of meaning can be defined and examined by each individual perceiver,** who through this examination can come to a clearer understanding of his own expectations and preconceptions - his own meaning system.[69]

The evocative function of a testimony would consequently also have to meet pragmatic criteria of compatibility. For instance, does the speech act agree with the contents of the testimony, and the integrity of the narrator initiating an autobiographical pact? Does it make use of valid conventions? Is its intentionality honest? etc.[70]

Finally, a hermeneutic of testimony would have to consider the speech situation as a whole. The following questions could be asked: Who constitutes the community of interpretation? Is it basically hostile or benevolent? Does it consist of a gathering of adepts or is it a heterogeneous crowd? Are there institutional constraints such as special interest groups? Such factors influence the flow, presentation, and contents of an oral narrative. Accordingly, any hermeneutic activity on this level demands a type of hermeneutic involvement that cannot easily be retraced on paper without a field study.

4.4.2. As Invitation to Response-Ability

It has been mentioned in chapter 2 that the witness pays a price for testifying. One could say that testimonial language is an expression of responsibility in view of values worth living for. The

---

[68] Susan WITTIG, Multiple Meanings, p. 87 (emphasis hers).

[69] Susan WITTIG, Multiple Meanings, pp. 95f. (emphasis hers).

[70] For a discussion of criteria of pragmatic compatibility see: Wim DE PATER, Sprachlogik, pp. 170-174; J. L. AUSTIN, Things, pp. 12-52. In view of the compatibility between speech acts and personal integrity, Hans-Georg GADAMER recalls that according to ancient Greek law the witness was considered reliable not on the ground of what he had to say, but due to the credibility of his personal engagement in society. Hans-Georg GADAMER, Témoignage et affirmation, in Le Témoignage, p. 162.

juridical understanding of testimony, which Richard FENN has shown to be well and alive in secular consciousness, takes this for granted. Nevertheless, in some religious circles, especially those which are acquainted with the practice of confessing faith narratively, a latent tendency to transform the intentionality of the testimony from a social act into a more or less private exercise of (probably unconscious) justification of **Dasein** can be noticed.

If one adds to this the ever increasing influence of the mass media in modern society, with its pluralistic and materialistic rationality , one may wonder if the practice of testifying to a conviction has become meaningless. If the media "thingify" the concerns of secular man and cannot establish relationships to the media consumer's "neighbor," is it not wiser to change strategy? With this in mind, Jacques ELLUL suggests substituting engagement for testimony.[71] It seems, however, that such an attempt would be an attempt to separate two sides of the same coin. Has not testimony always related to engagement **and** a statement of conviction. ELLUL would probably answer to this, "Sure, but let the actions speak!" But one could retort that the world can, in Ian RAMSEY's terminology, be seen as the "model" and the actions of commitment as a "qualifier," so that it would still be necessary for a "disclosure" to be brought to public light through the hermeneutical process of a testimony. In view of the secularizing situation it is more a question of what form a statement of conviction takes, than whether it can be meaningful at all. Furthermore, if it is meaningless to testify about the "thingi-fied," is it not even more important to testify about the ground of being and the vision of wholeness, the redemption of the deeply personal as well as the **humanum** in its social forms? The role of testimony could be expanded from a claim to truth to an invitation to response-ability, that is, an illustration that secular man is still able to live with values which transcend his immediate interests.

Testimony has, in that case, to remain a social, and therefore public, act if it wants to be answerable to the Other/other, remain relevant with regard to the trial of **Dasein**, and truthful to its

---

[71] Jacques ELLUL, Témoignage et société technicienne, in Le témoignage, pp. 447, 452ff.

Source.[72] It seems that the early Pentecostals knew this. In the first
issue of the British pentecostal Magazine Confidence[73] in April 1908
great care was taken to publicize reports indicating that all social
strata were touched by the pentecostal revival. Similarly, it was
common to mention the exact address of the witness or the person
concerned,[74] so that anyone could verify for himself what was claimed
and how it related to the person's life.

But testimony should also be responsible in a more pragmatic
sense. Precisely here lies a basic difficulty for the role of
testimony in secular society. The pursuit of happiness, as Robert
BELLAH pointed out,[75] is at present the most important aim of
biographical activity in the First World. Success, freedom, personal
rights, the creative development of one's personality are the key
notions that emerge in secular life mapping. This emphasis on
individual goals is also strongly present in religious testimonies of
grace. Individuals testify of new found joy and fulfillment.[76] They
see their conversion to a christian life option as beneficial for
their professional career.[77] The problem is that individual goals can

---

[72] René HABACHI, Témoignage et faux-témoignage, in Le témoignage, p.
458.

[73] Cf. Appendix II: especially Testimony (H).

[74] Cf. Appendix II: Testimonies, (H) and (I).

[75] Robert BELLAH, Habits, p. 20-26.

[76] So, for instance a testimony from Volksmissionar Nr. 372, 35,4
(1983), p. 14. "... So habe ich ziemlich alles genossen, was mir die
Welt geboten hat. Jedoch spürte ich in meinem Leben ein unzufriedenes,
leeres und unausgeglichenes Gefühl. Oft hatte ich keine Freude mehr am
Leben... (repeated visits to a "tea bus" and discussions with engaged
Christians are described, then...) Abends brachte ich alles, was mich
belastete, vor Gott hin... Am nächsten Morgen... Halleluja! Ich fühlte
mich frei und hätte am liebsten die ganze Welt umarmen können. Alles
veränderte sich, meine Hassgefühle auf bestimmte Menschen habe ich
verloren."

[77] One could quote testimonies of christian businessmen, or as below
an experience of aesthetic épanouissement of a young musician.
"Nach meiner Hinwendung zu Jesus Christus ist in mir eine viel
grössere Ausgeglichenheit, die mir hilft, mich nach aussen viel freier
und intensiver auszudrücken... Das hat die Voraussetzung meiner
Karriere geschaffen." Volksmissionar, Nr. 355, 33,11 (1981), p. 11.

be achieved without public involvement and concern for the other. Here a prophetic voice is necessary, showing that contemporary individualism is a phenomenon of the modern age and is in stark contrast to the biblical models of moral responsibility and the christian vision of the kingdom of God.

It is, however, one-sided to object to testimonial practice if one forgets the therapeutic value of such experiences. After all, they are significant to those who give them and retain a certain importance in that, as testimonies, they allow the individual to open him- or herself up toward others. It is for many the first step to a way of life that also takes the concerns of others into consideration. For Pierre-Luigi DUBIED such a public biographical account of faith is more therapeutic than a private confession before God, because it represents a movement away from introversion and discourages mistaking one's super-ego for God.[78] The act of telling a life story is theologically significant, because, even if it is individualistic, it is a deeply personal move of reconciliation for the self, to God and to the community. All the same, one may wonder why the early pentecostal testimonies, in spite of their archaic language (which still lingers on), demonstrated more concern (**Sorge**) for the world than contemporary accounts.

4.5. General Conclusion

The purpose of such a hermeneutic is not to reduce a life story into manageable non-entities, but to allow for an honest approach to testimonies in order to clarify the map-making process and its religious significance of the life world for the communicator and the community of interpretation, as well as any other addressed or interested parties.

---

[78] Pierre-Luigi DUBIED, Le rôle du récit de soi dans l'entretien pastoral. Une hypothèse-cadre pour sa prise en compte et son analyse, in Etudes théologiques et religieuses, 60,1 (1985), pp. 45-53.

On the syntactic level the parallels between fairy tale and testimony deserve further study. Three aspects have appeared to be of special significance. First, the structural similarity between the two genres is of symbolic significance. It bridges everyday life and the awareness of the Sacred. One could call testimonies modern forms of tragedy and comedy where good and evil have a name. Second, these structures must leave the possibility of "bifurcation" open. The trial of **Dasein**, if it can be expressed appropriately, is to take seriously the contingencies of life, and from a religious point of view the possibility of a divine "turn of events." Third, as in all personal narratives the problem of self-deception needs to be addressed. Is the autobiographical pact upheld? Is there a community to interpret, to receive or reject the testimonial claims?

In the semantic dimension one ought to note that polysemy does not only refer to signs. It is an equally important factor in the understanding of experiences themselves. Whether religious jargon can still be understood meaningfully, and be related to the events narrated is still a crucial question. It may, if it is limited to the essential and the heuristic, and if mythological activity relates to the here and now.

From a pragmatic point of view it is apparent that orthopraxis and orthodoxy can only come to harmonious celebration **within** the community. The role of testimonies would then be to bridge the gap between values held and values achieved, thus calling for a renewed commitment in the world to the values and the **humanum** that keep on begging for redemption.

5. ON THE VALUE OF VISIONARY NARRATIVES IN PLURALIST COMMUNITIES

STRUCTURE, RECEPTION AND INTENTIONALITY

"Where there is no prophecy the people cast off restraint."
Proverbs 29:18 Revised Standard Version

"Where there is no vision, the people perish."
Proverbs 29:18 King James Version

5.1. Introduction

At first, a definition of vision as something that is seen by the mind's eye[1] seems to be a sufficiently clear and universal concept to set any discussion about it on the right track from the start. But the above quotations indicate that the matter is not univocally understood, because not only a phenomenon but also content is presumed in the word. It is possible that the various references to visions, prophetic visions and visionary narratives in the context of the preceding chapters have already begun to clear the way for an understanding of the matter in this study. However, further clarifications are necessary.

5.1.1. Some General Premises

A large number of instances in the history of the christian church could be mentioned where visionary and prophetic activity have caused problems, tensions and division within the ranks of the

---

[1] So the definition of the Oxford Advanced Learner's Dictionary of Current English, A.S. HORNBY et al. London, 1974, p. 977.

clerical hierarchy and the laity. The list would include second
century Montanism, the activity of SAVANAROLA in Florence, the Zwickau
prophets at the time of the protestant reformation and the 17th
century Camisards in France, to mention just a few. Fortunately, in
the eyes of many, waves of prophetic activity tended to decline with
the reactionary increase of institutional authority.[2] The prophetic
spirit, it is argued, although innovative, was unbridled and had to be
replaced with a controllable form of church politics.

Why then should one attempt a hermeneutic of prophetic visions in
a contemporary liturgical context, as this immediately raises the
question of present suitability and use? One presupposition of this
study is the assumption that there are various levels of prophetic
acuity. Infelicitous examples do not negate the value of prophecy as
such. A second premise is based on the general agreement among
sociologists of religion and biblical scholars that prophetic and
visionary activity is to a large extent socio-historically conditioned. These two points present a challenge, namely that prophetic
activity could be re-examined in terms of Paul RICOEUR's concept of a
second naïveté. That means that new attention can be given to the
depth of poetic language and religious experience without neglecting
the critical demands of 20th century hermeneutics. The same approach
which has re-evaluated testimonies in the preceding chapter will,
therefore, also be used here in relation to visionary practice.

Now it might be argued that such an approach is in order as far
as testimonies are concerned, because they relate to a human context
of production, but are not visions, inspired by the Sacred, claimed to
have a divine origin? To answer this question, two personal
convictions which will be substantiated in the next sections can be
anticipated. First, it is my conviction that religious visions, unless

---

[2] The argument applies to Judaism, early Christianity, the
institutionalization of religious orders in the middle ages, in
general for all socially anchored religious movements. Cf. in close
relation to the topic of this study: David E. AUNE, Prophecy in Early
Christianity and the Ancient Mediteranean World, Grand Rapids, 1983,
p. 338; Ted A. CAMPBELL, Charismata in the Christian Communities of
the Second Century, in Wesleyan Theological Journal 17,2 (1982), p.
14; and with various authors in the periodical Semeia 21, Anthropological Perspectives on Old Testament Prophecy, 1982.

they are attributed to a divine authorship, lose their evocative and prophetic force. Second, visions, no matter how extraordinary, cannot overrule human imagination. They will always reflect to some extent a socio-cultural and linguistic conditioning if they can be understood. These two aspects of the social phenomenon of prophetic activity contribute to a hermeneutic approach that is critical, and at the same time respectful.

It is remarkable in view of the socio-cultural conditioning that where one finds complacency within a certain social level, the prophetic spirit is vanishing.[3] The prophecy based on the parable of the ten virgins (Appendix III, Vision (L)) is a good illustration: a) of the necessity to contextualize prophecies socially, b) that in different socio-cultural circumstances prophecies may fail to be meaningful, and c) that a feeling of anti-worldliness is not necessarily a sign of socially irresponsible religion. To put it differently, the new hermeneutic awareness that secularization has brought about, is an awareness of the limits of human understanding.

Linguistic conditioning is the second social variable to take into consideration when one seeks to understand a prophetic utterance. If a prophecy is wrapped in esoteric language, as for instance God-talk, it will intend to address only a small audience. If, on the other hand, it is formulated in language understandable by the masses, it will have an influence reaching beyond the confines of a church building. Bruce YOCUM, a leader in the charismatic "Word of God Community" in Ann Arbor made an experiment because he wanted to know whether prophecies could be formulated in secular language. Most of the people in the community, he says, had difficulty understanding prophecies given in the archaic language so he asked the people concerned to use normal English instead. Everybody was amazed how the

---

[3] Cf. Thomas W. OVERHOLT, Prophecy. The Problem of Cross-Cultural Comparison, in Semeia 21, pp. 55-78.
    Formerly prophetic movements, once they have been accepted and have gained a certain social status (**Verkirchlichung**) seem to lose the original driving force. A practical example is Pentecostalism in the First World, where prophetic activity is steadily diminishing. The fourth generation Pentecostals have achieved a markedly higher social status since their pioneers began to meet in factory halls and barns.

prophetic utterances gained pertinence.[4] That secular prophetic speech
is possible has been demonstrated in a very different way by the
address of President Corazon AQUINO of the Philippines at the General
Assembly of the United Nations on September 22, 1986.[5] Integrative
social structures are necessary for the sake of translating prophetic
concerns into action. Hence, a conscious choice was made to study
prophetic visions in a clearly defined religious context.

The reason for having focused on pentecostal visions is not
because they would be the ideal genre to promote. They are suitable
for study because as productions of the first part of the twentieth
century they stand at the threshold of secularization. They may show
what potential, if any, prophetic visions could have for christian
churches today. A second reason is due to their liturgical context.
Prophecies in pentecostal and charismatic services are received or
rejected in a very democratic way, in a manner suitable to a pluralist
world.

5.1.2. On the Definition of the Term

That visions and prophecies relate to each other can be seen in
their common function. They confront the receiver with a self-
transcending claim that relates to his or her personal and social
behaviour. As biblical examples one may think of the prophecies of
Jeremiah and Amos, or the visions in the Apocalypse. Two contemporary
illustrations are the visions of Fatima, or the prophecy given to the
first spokesman of the ecumenical charismatic movement, David du

---

[4] Bruce YOCUM, Prophecy. Exercising the Prophetic Gifts of the Spirit
in the Church Today, Ann Arbor, 1976, p. 83.

[5] It was her first speech at the United Nations. It centered on human
rights and peaceful, democratic ways of bringing about new government
in dictarorially ruled countries. What she had to say was not
different from what others before her had said, but her message was
not considered to be morally insincere and cynical like most
diplomatic speeches in this body of power struggle, because there was
apparently a coherence between her words, her character, and her
experiences. Even if one could eventually prove that Mrs. AQUINO's
speech was masterminded by a well trained propaganda writer, one would
still have to explain the favourable reaction of the press.

PLESSIS. The common function of the phenomena suggests that one does not gain much by separating them. Furthermore, the intentionality of the two forms of sacred address also covers much the same ground. Prophecy is known in all forms of socially anchored religion[6] and is primarily a means of exhortation and edification, although the contemporary popular idea of prophecy thinks of it generally as a telling of future events. A similar misunderstanding is prevalent in the common notion of vision as a new revelation. It is more appropriate to say that both phenomena reveal a moral dilemma and indicate, more or less clearly, a way of resolving it. It is therefore not surprising that Yves CONGAR remarks that most prophecies in charismatic circles are little more than edificational exhortations.[7] The Mechelen Document,[8] which CONGAR quotes, underlines this edificational function. People considering visions as "merely" edificational might have to reconsider the role of affirmative narratives in human life. In any case, it is not inappropriate to describe visions and prophecies, as indicated above (4.1.), as therapeutic narratives. They can be treated as such even if they contain elements of foretelling.

To say that visions and prophecies do not essentially differ in their function and intentionality, does not mean that one cannot make distinctions in their modality. Although, both genres begin as private revelations they can be perceived subjectively in different ways. Karl RAHNER distinguishes various kinds of visionary impression. There is that which in the catholic tradition is known as mystic vision, a private revelation for the perfection of religious life. RAHNER sees prophetic visions, which cause the receptor to communicate something

---

[6] That prophecy is an universal phenomenon has been established by researchers in philosophy of religion, as well as by anthropological and folkloristic studies. For the interplay between these disciplines see: Semeia 21, Anthropological Perspectives on Old Testament Prophecy, 1982, Robert C. CULLEY and Thomas W. OVERHOLT (eds.).

[7] "Zwar führt man in der Erneuerung gern einige Fälle von Prophetie an, welche die Zukunft ankündigen, den Grund eines Herzens blosslegen oder einen bestimmten Aufruf der Vorsehung offenbar würden. Zumeist aber handelt es sich um erbauliche Ermahnungen." Yves CONGAR, Der Heilige Geist, Freiburg, 1979, 1982, pp. 287 f.

[8] Published in Lumen Vitae 29, Brussels 1974, p. 399.

to the church, as in contrast to mystic visions.[9] The visions are prophetic in so far as they relate to the behaviour of the faithful in view of a present situation and their commitment to the future. It is these kind of visions that are of interest here as therapeutic visions. Mystic visions, which can be religiously just as genuine, have at best only indirectly a bearing on secular society, namely through the witness of transformed life. They tend, however, to be misunderstood negatively as private, that is, as antisocial and purely subjective experiences.

Other modal distinctions relate to the impression through which visions are received. RAHNER distinguishes between physical, imaginary and purely spiritual visions.[10] The purely spiritual visions are theoretical in nature and do not present themselves in images or narrative sequences. They are comparatively rare and of no interest in this study. Physical visions, for instance appearances of heavenly beings, biblical characters or saints, are in the last analysis also imaginary, because the subject receiving the vision can only appreciate it if it conforms to his or her own interpretative criteria, that is, mental impressions and concepts. The veracity of any vision is consequently not established if it can be claimed to be physical or supernatural in terms of its reception, nor can it be proven by the personal integrity and health of the receptor.[11] How then should imaginary visions be evaluated?

5.1.3. Revelatory Status and Religious Value of Visions

That there are no common objective criteria for the veracity of visions and prophecies can be illustrated by the fact that the Hebrew Bible has no word for "false prophet." It was the Greek version of the Old Testament which began to use this notion. Previous to that there

---

[9] Karl RAHNER, Visionen und Prophezeiungen, Freiburg, 1958, 2nd ed., pp. 18f.

[10] Karl RAHNER, Visionen, pp. 32ff.

[11] That even saints can err is well illustrated in Karl RAHNER, Visionen, pp. 66-69.

was simply the awareness of prophetic conflict,[12] in other words, a situation of trial which always displayed itself in a social context. That Old Testament prophecy was, therefore, a highly ambivalent matter is also shown in a quotation from Deuteronomy 13.[13] Even an objective verification of a speech act by means of signs could be deceptive. It is better to test the reliability of visions and the veracity of prophetic speech in light of the revelation which culminated in the prophetic ministry of Jesus Christ, and in light of the social context to which it is addressed. For it is also possible for a prophetic utterance to be theologically acceptable, but still fail to address itself to the present situation and thus be practically meaningless. Consequently, the revelatory intentionality of visions is not to give insight unveiling new truth, but to relate a christian imperative (from an inter-subjective point of view) to any given situation. Finally, a genuine prophetic or visionary utterance will contain a surplus value due to the dynamics of eventful speech put to practice. This surplus value is not only recognizable in the action that results, but also in the model which the whole process represents. These criteria are in fact identical with the ones established for the ascertainment of responsible christian myths (1.3.3.2.).

The religious value of visions can be deduced from the explanations concerning their function and intentionality. As edificational exhortations they fulfill a therapeutic role; for an individual (one should be careful not to criticize private visions too quickly) or a community. But they are only truly therapeutic if they do not represent a replacement of neurotic or pathological symptoms, but promote the realization of the **humanum**; that is, if they initiate christian action in view of the other and the self. As far as

---

[12] James A. RIMBACH, Prophets in Conflict - Who Speaks for God? in Currents in Theology and Mission 9,3 (1982), p. 174.

[13] "If a prophet arises among you, or a dreamer of dreams, and gives you a sign or a wonder, and the sign or wonder which he tells you comes to pass, and if he says, 'Let us go after other gods,' which you have not known, 'and let us serve them,' you shall not listen to the words of that prophet or to that dreamer of dreams; for the Lord your God is testing you, to know whether you love the Lord your God with all your heart and with all your soul." Deuteronomy 13:1-3.

prophetic visions are concerned, their value can be recognized if they operate as eventful speech, to use Richard FENN's phrase. In other words, if they serve as an address to the church and preferably also to society under the condition that they have ears to listen and eyes to see.

5.2. A Closer Look at Various Visions

This section will attempt to relate the above to concrete situations in which visionary production met a receptive audience. Since visions respond to various situations it is not surprising that they can be classified in different categories. In view of Paul RICOEUR's remark on subjective temporality and the poetic production of insight (2.3.6.1.) the following visions will be considered in two categories. First, there will be a study of discordant visions reflecting the awareness of tragedy and the tornness of the human soul (**distentio animi**). These visions have relatively strong prophetic potential. An example of a biblical discordant vision is Peter's vision in Acts 10:10-16. The second approach will look at visions of wholeness which could be called concordant visions relating to a subjective awareness of unity (**intentio animi**). One could consider these visions as primarily therapeutic. Examples of this type can be found in Revelation 4 and 5 and possibly Stephen's vision in Acts 7:55f.[14]

---

[14] Reservations as to the original nature of the vision of Stephen are expressed by David AUNE. He considers it a literary composition "modeled after stereotypical popular conceptions of oracular speech," and refers to PHILO and the Acts of the Christian Martyrs. David E. AUNE, Prophecy, pp. 319f.

5.2.1. A Case Study of Discordant Visions: Pentecostal Visions in Nazi-Germany. Their Structure, Reception, and Intentionality[15]

5.2.1.1. Examples

(1) Vision of a German Pentecostal in a Polish concentration camp, previous to the German invasion.

The ambiguous value of an invasion

... Emil WITZKE, with him four other men, was brought to the Polish concentration camp Kartuska at the end of August 1939, where he had to suffer indescribably. He was already marked by death. Then he prayed once more to the Lord, humbling himself deeply. Thereupon he saw the following vision (**Gesicht**). HITLER stood proudly astride on a great cylinder (or roller). "Germany" was written on this cylinder. Then another, smaller cylinder, on which "Poland" was written, rolled towards him. He put his foot on it. Then, one cylinder after another rolled towards him, each bearing the name of a nation, and he took them all in turn. He now stood there powerfully, with a threatening hand and the states under his feet. But then the cylinders began to move. One after the other vanished from the feet of the conqueror. Lastly, even the cylinder with the inscription "Germany" was taken from him. Then, he fell down. Brother WITZKE awoke and knew that HITLER would march into Poland and take many countries, but when he had reached the highest point of his power, he would collapse. He said to the fellow prisoners from his village, "Have a little patience, the Germans will come in a few days, and we shall all be freed." Those who had lost their hope gained new courage, and indeed, the war with Poland broke out after some days and they were liberated from the Polish concentration camp.[16]

(2) Vision of a German-born American evangelist, during his military service for the German armed forces on the occupied island of Guernsey.

Seeing his unit - but not as usual

During my stay on the island the Lord gave me several revelations and visions (**Gesichte**) which clearly showed me the outcome of the war. It was on November 19, 1942; I had come back from my leave and slept again in the pillbox. There were three bunk beds, and I slept in the middle one. Between three and five o'clock in the morning, the power

[15] The basic ideas of this section were presented at a conference on "Story and Narrative in the Christian Tradition" in Cambridge, England in 1984.

[16] Gerhard KRUEGER, Erlebte Gottesgnade, Erzhausen, 1970, p. 46.

of God came mightily upon me and woke me up. I saw in a vision
(**Vision**) how I stood among my 22 comrades next to the fourth gun
(**Geschütz**). The gun commander was also present as usual. Some
"Landser" had their hands in their pockets. One said to another, "The
swindle is now over, the war is lost."... This vision (**Vision**) was
powerful for me, because as a few days earlier, while on leave, I had
heard HITLER on the radio saying, "Stalingrad will fall in a few
hours!" The German troops in Africa stood at the Suez Canal. But the
turning point came, it was exactly as the Lord had shown to me...
Although the war did last till 1945, there came defeat after defeat. I
knew with certainty in my heart that we could again preach in freedom
in Germany.
    At the time, as I had this vision (**Vision**), Germany stood at the
peak of its victories. Nobody guessed that the judgments of God upon
this people, which venerated HITLER as God, had already been
determined.[17]

5.2.1.2. Introductory Remarks

    These are two examples of visions as German Pentecostals were
telling them during (and, because they were recorded, also after) the
bitter years of the Second World War. For the general reader, even if
he has religious or literary interests, these might represent a
somewhat unaccustomed kind of narrative. Therefore, it will be
profitable to clarify a few matters before actually tackling specific
hermeneutic questions.

    First of all, it is customary for Pentecostals in the German
speaking areas of Europe to distinguish between a vision (**Vision**) on
the one hand, and what could be called a "sight" (**Gesicht**) on the
other. A **Vision** would refer to a kind of apocalyptic phenomenon, where
the element of prediction would play a essential role. But a **Gesicht**
is a manifestation on a more pragmatic level, where, as it has been
argued, the element of foreknowledge actually plays a minor role.[18]

---

[17] Herman LAUSTER, Vom Pflug zur Kanzel, Krehwinkel, 1964, p. 74.

[18] For a substantiation of this claim see the sections 5.2.1.4. and
5.2.1.5.
    An interchageable use of **Vision** and **Gesicht** is found in the
second vision. This might be due to the fact that LAUSTER received
influential religious training while in the United States of America,
where the pentecostal concept of vision is broader. Incidently, in the
New Testament there seems to be no clear distinction between the use

One could add that the visions the German Pentecostals saw have only certain aspects in common with medieval visions.[19] The catholic tradition knows a wide variety of visionary activity that ranges from popular apparitions of Mary, to a blissful intellectual consciousness of God freed from a undue sense of self and the world, caught up in a union of love with that which can be called the True, Good, and Beautiful.[20] The visions just quoted can also be differentiated from

---

of **horama** and **optasia**; see the article by Wilhelm MICHAELIS in Theological Dictionary of the New Testament, Vol. V, Grand Rapids, 1954, pp. 371-373.
    The pragmatic aspects of "sights" can also be noted in the common emphasis that these visions have been received with full consciousness. The first vision referred to above does contain the phrase, "Brother Witzke awoke and knew," but it is by no means certain that he received the vision while asleep, for it followed intensive prayer. Furthermore, many Pentecostals are suspicious of visions that are not received in a state of consciousness. E.g. "A vision is a divine visual communication (as compared to a mental impression) **received while fully conscious.**" Ray E. SMITH Visions and Dreams, in Gwen JONES (ed.), Conference on the Holy Spirit Digest, Vol. 2, Springfield, 1983, p. 306 (emphasis added); cf. also the title of Vision (D) in the appendices.

[19] In the Middle Ages the term **"visio"** was used rather freely, and the phenomenon was later also referred to as **"revelatio."** Cf. Peter DINZELBACHER, Vision und Visionsliteratur im Mittelalter, Stuttgart, 1981, pp. 45 f.

[20] A difference between popular medieval visions and the "sights" seen by these Pentecostals rests in their contents. The former visions provided an insight into the after-world, the rewards of heaven or the pains of hell, or else the visions had a **pro-domo** purpose, that is they often represented a justification or glorification of the religious institution of the visionary. Peter DINZELBACHER, Vision, pp. 202f., 210-222.
    The content of the pentecostal visions though, as it will be seen, is consciously metaphorical and the temptation to self-justification or glorification could only arise in the subsequent interpretation of the vision, for instance in hagiographic biographies.
    However, a commonality between catholic and pentecostal visions can also be noted. The classical notion of the "beatific vision," whether in is popular understanding as the vision of God in the eternal state of salvation, or explained as a mystic experience, an intellectual charism, of God's love and incommensurability, contains a wholesome self-transcending element. Felice DA MARETO, Visione and Antonio PIOLANTI Visione Beatifica, in Ecyclopedia Cattolica Vol. XII, Vatican City, 1954, pp. 1485-1493; Karl RAHNER, Beatific Vison, in Encyclopedia of Theology, pp. 78-80.

christophanies, common in 19th century evangelical, an early 20th century pentecostal[21] or a contemporary charismatic context in North America.[22] In view of this variety it suffices to suggest that because visions originate from a particular **Sitz im Leben** they should be studied in a specific context, and that generalizations should be sparse and limit themselves to matters of form and intentionality, rather than to content.

Accordingly, the historical context for the present analysis of discordant visions was chosen because the period of Nazism is clearly defined and provides useful limitations for the sake of clarity, and because an academic analysis of these visions is inoffensive since they lie in the past. The weightiest reason though for focusing on that period relates to circumstance. Pentecostals generally consider visions to be of temporal use, that is, once they have fulfilled their function in a worship service, they need not be written down and pre-served, unless, of course, they might be of historical (and biograph-ical) interest. Consequently, it is more difficult to find records of such visions in times of peace and prosperity.[23] It seems to be difficult to maintain the **status quo** and be prophetic at the same time.

The hermeneutical project of this case study can be delineated as follows: first of all, it is concerned with the structural impli-cations that can be drawn from these visionary narratives. Are the syntactic aspects significant and coherent enough for religious com-munication? The second step studies the reception of these stories in the light of linguistic ambiguity, and in view of their recipients' (narrator and hearer) life world. The last section will directly relate to the conclusions reached in the first two. It will center on the intentionality of the visions. If it is the case that a semantic

---

[21] Cf. Appendix III: Vision (F).

[22] Cf. Chet and Lucile HUYSSEN, Visions of Jesus, Plainfield, 1977.

[23] An exception, when visions found their way into the printing press, were the early days of Pentecostalism when the reception of visions was one of the few aspects which differentiated the Pentecostals from other Christians who shared in non-charismatic matters the same theological convictions.

disclosure takes place, in what way can discordant visions contribute
to a religious commitment in and through the community of interpretation?

5.2.1.3. In Search of Structure

At first sight the visions appear to be short surrealist
narratives with some symbolic imagery. One could legitimately ask if
these visions have something in common with the kind of folk and fairy
tales that have been studied by Vladimir PROPP. Don't they bear
elements of the fantastic? Isn't there a similarity between the spirit
/ matter relationship of classical fairy tales on the one hand, and
the object-transcending images pictured in the spiritual day-dreams on
the other? Without attempting to brush aside valid questions, there is
at least one point in which the visions differ radically from PROPP's
subject matter. They do not have the "hero" as their major point of
reference. Accordingly, there is also no clear presence of the famous
functions that PROPP enumerated.

For similar reasons, A.J. GREIMAS' actantial model is practically
inapplicable. The "hero" is, in a very literal sense, out of the
picture. In other words, the discordant visions show the hero (if he
can be called that) to be the one who perceives the vision, rather
than being actively part of it.

Instead, would a scrutiny of the "fantastic" elements in the
vision be more fruitful, since the etymological root of the word
phantazesthai (to make appear) is closely related to the visionary?
For this purpose one might turn to Tzvetan TODOROV's study of
fantastic literature.[24] There the author defines the fantastic as a
state of uncertitude in which the reader or hearer of a tale is
hesitant about making his mind up as to the placement of the
narrative's truth-content.[25] The literature of the fantastic,

---

[24] Tzvetan TODOROV, Introduction à la littérature fantastique, Paris,
1970. English edition: The Fantastic. A Structural Approach to a
Literary Genre, Ithaca, 1975.

[25] "Le fantastique occupe le temps de cette incertitude; dès qu'on

according to TODOROV, exploits this very moment of hesitation between
a natural explanation of events and a supernatural interpretation
thereof. From a religious point of view one might welcome a correlation between such a narrative on the one hand, and the possible
intrusion of the supernatural on the other. But does an analysis of
these pentecostal visions confirm this theory? The opposite seems to
be the case. The recipients of these visions often stated emphatically
that they knew that to which the visions related.[26] They had no
reservations as to how they were to interpret the narrative. Beyond
that, there are inherent reasons why the believers did not even expect
the visionary accounts to contain a tension between the natural and
the supernatural. First, because the supernatural in the narrative is
being conceived of as a vehicle of thought, as a metaphor. Second,
because the intervention of God in history is taken for granted.

But there is another aspect of TODOROV's theory of the fantastic
that needs to be considered, namely the themes of the self (le thèmes
du "je").[27] Studying fairy tales, gothic novels and other "fantastic
literature" in which the supernatural has an obvious role, TODOROV
discovered two basic themes whose structure, according to him, reflect
man's relation to his or her world. The first is metamorphosis. In
tales of the fantastic one encounters human beings changing into all
kinds of animals and even into inanimate objects. On a practical
level, metamorphosis allows man to step out of a given social role and
self-identity, or to consider objects for other-than-material
purposes.

---

choisit l'une ou l'autre réponse, on quitte le fantastique pour entrer
dans un genre voisin, l'étrange ou le merveilleux. Le fantastique,
c'est l'hésitation éprouvée par un être qui ne connaît que les lois
naturelles, face à un événement en apparence surnaturel." Tzvetan
TODOROV, fantastique, p. 29.

[26] So for example, Gerhard KRUEGER, Gottesgnade, pp. 46 + 86;
implicitly the second example in the text; in appendix III vision (A)
line 18f.; and in vision (B) where the meaning of the vision is not
immediately known, but there is no question as to its metamorphical
character in the mind of the receiver, cf. lines 30ff., 43ff., and
52ff.

[27] Tzvetan TODOROV, fantastique, pp. 113-130.

The second prominent theme is pan-determinism. It responds to the constant struggle of the self between conformity and freedom. It is the desire to be in control of events, or at least to have an explanation of the events that shape one's life.[28]

These two aspects fall together in what TODOROV calls "the incarnation of imaginary causality."[29] In other words, the themes of the self represent the mental activity in which the distinction between spirit and matter becomes relative and open to creative violation. From a literary point of view this means that the visions cannot be interpreted as mere allegories, where each object represents a clearly defined referent in a closed context, but they can be understood as extended metaphors that may possibly yield a surplus of meaning. From a psychoanalytic point of view, the themes of the self, so dominant in the visions consulted,[30] are concerned with the basic structuration of man's relationship with the world, namely the relationship between perception and conscience.[31] This relationship would center on the **position** of the human being in his environment, **rather than** on his **action** in the same. Accordingly, it is understandable why the role of the "hero" in the visions is typically passive.

But how does TODOROV's theory compare in concrete terms with the visions of German Pentecostals during the rule of National Socialism? Do the visions reveal a significant structure that could lead to a semantic disclosure? To begin with, what can be said about the theme of metamorphosis in this particular context?

---

[28] One is tempted to draw parallels with a Freudian conception of the human psyche: the understanding of the self, the dream for power, and the dynamics of repressed desires.

[29] Tzvetan TODOROV, fantastique, p. 116. This formulation is obviously highly suggestive in a christological context.

[30] Indirectly in discordant visions and directly in concordant visions; cf. Miss SISSON's vision in Testimony (D) lines 151-168 in relation to metamorphosis and visions (C) and (F) as clear examples.

[31] Tzvetan TODOROV, fantastique, p. 126. An analogous, though independently argued correlation between the psychological and linguistic aspects of metaphor can be found in Paul RICOEUR, Rule, pp. 200-206.

First of all, it is worth while to reflect on the significance of
the objects mentioned in the visions. They are frequently elements of
metaphorical speech that also express moral attitudes. For example,
the German word for cylinder (cf. the first example) also evokes the
picture of a roller used in the construction of roads, and by
metaphorical implication, an obtrusive personality. Similarly, the
house in the vision (A) in the Appendix III stands as a representation
of power (cf. "A mighty fortress is our God"). The boat (in vision
(B)) can be seen as a symbol of safety against depth of evil, just as
the Bible-message is being thought of as sharper than any two-edged
sword, and pure or calm water is contrasted with polluted and excited
water; objects stand as symbols of moral integrity or the lack of the
same.[32] Likewise, the presence of the complete military unit and the
inclusion of the gun in the second example effectively works as an
image of power.

Metamorphosis takes place in so far as objects and events are
representative of subjective issues; on the one hand, the perception
of fate, the intrusion of violence, or the assertion of power, and on
the other, the question of conscience (to what extent one should or
should not identify with these issues).[33]

---

[32] See, for instance Paul RICOEUR, Symbolism, p. 25 and context.

[33] The dialectic between perception and conscience is a constant
element in the visions. In relation to the first example one can
enumerate the following tensions:
   1) immanent invasion versus relative benefit
   2) expansion of one interest group versus the presence of the
other (the German-speaking Poles were faced with the ethnic tension
between allegiance to Germanic or Slavic cultural values)
   In vision (B) in appendix III one notices:
   1) perception of the ethical code of Nazism versus conscientious
perception of its evils
   2) the representation of power versus the underlying influence of
moral motivation
   In a similar vein, Amos N. WILDER considers Christian myths and
dreams to be generated by a twofold mythopoetic impulse. First, the
Christian community has often been faced with the possible loss of its
roots in the light of change. Furthermore, it has the moral obligation
to be answerable to social authority. Amos N. WILDER, Myth and Dream
in Christian Scripture, in Joseph CAMPBELL (ed.), Myths, Dreams, and
Religion, New York, 1970, pp. 68-90.

The second theme of the self, according to TODOROV, is pan-determinism. In the cases referred to above, it can best be understood in terms of a power struggle between forces in a secular context and religious convictions that provide an antithesis. Although running the risk of being accused of confusing syntactic and semantic fields of reference, one could clarify the theme of pan-determinism by referring to I.T. RAMSEY's disclosure theory.

As a "model" one would have the awareness of a force more powerful than the self (e.g. an institution such as the military). The "qualifier" to this model appears as a force, whose appearance is sudden, and whose power is even stronger than that in the model (e.g. fate, unforseen political changes, etc.). The insurrection[34] of this qualifier leads to a "disclosure," which challenges the individual who experiences it to change his or her point of view (e.g. to attribute change to a cause).

Applying this theory to the first vision, one can see the model as HITLER's might, capable of bringing foreign powers under his dominion. The qualifier is that which causes the movement among the cylinders, that which brings about the fall of the dictator. The disclosure could be the realization that HITLER is not omnipotent. For vision (B) in Appendix III the model would be the house, representative of all claims of Nazism. The qualifier (the rock flying onto the house) leads to the disclosure that these claims are liable to collapse.[35]

---

[34] The term "insurrection" has been chosen in order to emphasize that the qualifier appears in an unexpected and sometime even rebellious manner; religiously speaking because of the sudden awareness of divine presence, linguistically speaking because new meaning is understood to be born within the tension between "appropriate" and "impertinent" use of language.

[35] For (B):
    model = water as the moral current
    qualifier = the boat separating the waters
    disclosure = the presence of a moral imperative
For the second example in the text:
    model = the whole unit and the gun (unity/strength)
    qualifier = the statement of fact ("The swindle is now over.")
    disclosure = the statement of truth (i.e. preaching the Gospel will outlast the temporary disruption)

At this point it becomes clear that there is another distinctive difference between the fantastic stories studied by TODOROV and the visions consulted. The supernatural dimension in the former centers around the notion of metamorphosis, (e.g. the change of the hero or magician into animals), whereas in the vision metamorphosis functions only as a linguistic tool (suspending the spirit/matter distinction), while its supernatural element rests in the disclosure of pan-determinism.[36]

But before moving to the receptional aspects of these visions, a summary of what their syntactic aspects yield should be given. First, the structure of the visions shows that there is a link between the experiences in the life-world of the Pentecostal and the articulation of his religious beliefs. There is a linguistic harmony between the two. Second, it is the disclosure evoked by the pan-deterministic theme that allows the believer to take issue with his/her dilemma between the perception of his/her world and his/her convictions of conscience. It can be argued that the poetic structure of visions suggests them to be viable narrative communications of religious concerns within the community of interpretation and their world. An outsider may, however, have difficulties.

5.2.1.4. The Dynamics of Reception

That the semantic function of those visions was not univocal can best be seen in contemporary utterances that testify to the ambiguous response to the HITLER regime on the one side, and to the visions on the other.[37] This ambivalence gives rise to two inquiries. First, the

---

[36] It should be noted that pan-determinism is primarily a structural theme of the vision. It does not necessarily carry theological implications. In (B) pan-determinism has even found its way in the interpretative comments, e.g. "It all depends to which side you are brought... It depends under which law of movement we fall."

[37] I have discussed this ambiguous ethical commitment of Pentecostals during that period in European Reactions to Totalitarianism. A Study of Ethical Commitment in the 1930's, in EPTA Bulletin 4,2 (1985), pp. 40-55; and 4,3 (1985), pp. 88-100.

problem of equivocity may be due to the fundamental role given to the mimetic elements in the visions. Second, their operation must be placed in the context of the role of the narrator's or the hearer's involvement respectively.

As far as the mimetic elements are concerned,[38] it has been pointed out that they are especially relevant in representational (as opposed to illustrative) narratives.[39] They build a bridge between the fictional and the real world. If a vision, as illustrative narrative, were to be interpreted as an allegory, the bridge between the two worlds would be symbolical,[40] and the narrative elements would be illustrative in the sense that they draw a clearly defined picture of a sign, of either the one or the other world. But the mimetic elements do not draw a line of separation, because the description of both worlds makes use of the same linguistic data. They are not an end for the sake of contemplation, but a means for the sake of action. This difference between the illustrative and representational can be clarified with an example. From a symbolical point of view the cross connotes in terms of religious aspects meaningful suffering, but in a secular context it can denote, as a sign, a railroad crossing. From a mimetic point of view, however, the cross refers to a larger context, namely a particular story of a certain Jew, or for that matter to the fate of innumerable criminals and martyrs during the Roman Empire. The point is that the same event can also meaningfully be retold in non-religious terms, albeit not necessarily with the same conclusion.

---

[38] Mimesis, as a creative imitation of human action, functions in narratives as a "referential" to the world. The visions as they are perceived would represent the first mimetic moment (2.3.6.2 and 2.3.6.3.).

[39] Robert SCHOLES and Robert KELLOGG, The Nature of Narrative, New York, 1966, pp. 84 f.

[40] In literary theory, the symbolic refers to an appreciation of signs and should not be mistaken for the rich notion of "symbol" in religious studies with phenomenological emphases. Cf. Robert SCHOLES and Robert KELLOGG, Nature, pp. 106f. as well as Terry EAGLETON, Literary Theory. An Introduction, Oxford, 1983, pp. 21f.

At first it seems preferable to follow the symbolic route, in which one can usually determine if and when a certain object of thought is to be interpreted in a religious way. But then one has to pay the price of alienation, the willed division between the sacred and the secular.

Siding with the other option, one could say that the ambiguity, which the mimetic elements in the visions expose, is in fact the keystone for a possible bridging between the world of thought and the domain of social experiences. It could also be a catalytic agent that allows a secular decision to be converted into a religious commitment and vice versa.

Now that the inquiry into the mimetic ambivalence of visions has produced a working hypothesis, it is also appropriate to ask to what extent functional ambiguity in visions is due to the role of the narrator's and/or hearer's hermeneutical involvement.

Phenomenologists and structuralists alike have stressed the importance of taking into account the subjectivity of the author of a narrative as well as of its recipients.[41] This can be done by the following three steps. First, by trying to delineate the life-world of the communicator of the vision. Second, by searching for the various forms of the "self" in the narrative presented. Third, by deducing possible responses of the "selves" in the audience.

Taking the first step in this particular case is relatively easy. The visions seen and spelled out during the Nazi regime in Germany are set in an uncomfortable context of tension between civil/political and religious/moral imperatives. The people who received the visions mentioned above had all experienced the difficult position of uncertainty between loyalty to the state and religious commitment in view of social or political threats.[42] The religious interpretation of

---

[41] Robert DETWEILER, Story, Sign, Self, Philadelphia, 1978, pp. 199f., 205f., 210f.

[42] In the first example the dilemma was the position of a minority group in a basically hostile environment due to the imminent invasion of Poland. In the second example the pastor had on earlier occasion been expressly forbidden to assemble and threatened with deportation to a concentration camp if he propagated his faith publicly (both of

one's life-world was influenced by fear and uncertainty regarding the present system, and hope in the promise of divine guidance. Beyond that, as in all oral traditions (especially when they are threatened), their narratives would reflect the intellectual, aesthetic and social experience of those groups among whom they flourish.[43]

The second step concerns itself with the various "selves" that are usually contained in any given narrative. Of course, there is the "I" of the narrator. It is especially evident when the vision is decorated with interpretative elements.[44] Then there is the implied author of the vision, namely God. However, it seems characteristic to these visions that God is not explicitly mentioned, except in the interpretative comments. But more importantly, as said before, there is a clear absence of the theme of the hero. That implies that the recipients of the vision cannot take advantage of identification with the protagonist. For, at best, the protagonist is history.[45]

This observation leads to the third step: the possible response of the individual or the audience. As with the believer who described his vision, the hearer faces the challenge of a moral decision.

---

which had taken place by the time the visions was received). In vision (A) in appendix III the pastor was constantly pressured to join the National Socialists abroad. In (B) a major leader of the Mülheim group had to make up his mind in the movement's national convention of elders as to the nature of National Socialism.

[43] Robert SCHOLES and Robert KELLOGG, Nature, p. 56. Cf. also the mutual influence of signifieds (4.3.1.) and vision (C) in the appendix, which reflects the use of rather pre-reformatory symbols for a protestant readership.

[44] Visions (B) and (D) provide good examples of such interpretative inclusions. (E.g. "I saw above the boat-like structure a hand from above, **the hand of God. And the question occured to me: Is this boat the thought of God?**...) In the other examples, the interpretative element follows the telling of the vision. Sometimes there is a revealing change of the pronoun from the first person singular to the first person plural.

[45] It is not helpful to assume that God is the "hero". In popular narratives any self-transcending reality is clearly distinguished from the human hero. Such a claim can be substantiated by Vladimir PROPP's narrative functions as well as by means of A.J. GREIMAS' actantial model, where one would distinguish between the addressor (sender) and the subject (hero) of the narrative.

Evidently, this is a matter of his or her fundamental life option. If he has a self-transcending faith commitment the response to the vision may be an act of hope (cf. pan-determinism). If, however, his fundamental option is bound to a basically ego-centric state of affairs, his response may be one of lack of understanding, confusion or fear, because evil has been objectified in the vision (cf. metamorphosis), and therefore, bears a name.

In view of this, we would suggest that the reception of the visions above is not only dependent on the mimetic use of language, but in fact also fluctuates between the opposite poles of fear and hope, or religiously speaking between warning (exhortation) and edification. In summary, then, the **mimetic ambiguity** relates to the metamorphic elements of the vision and sets the stage for the model of disclosure. The ambiguity arising from the self's **hermeneutic involvement** in the vision can be related to the pan-determinism that works as qualifier in relation to the self's fundamental option. In the end the function of the visions is to disclose a **semantic evocation**. And again, metaphorical language gives rise to thought,[46] especially if it, as eventful speech, intrudes into the secular code of understanding.

Consequently, one is invited to pursue the hermeneutic question concerning visions in terms of intentionality.

5.2.1.5. In Search of Intentionality

So far two interpretative horizons have been briefly discussed. First, there was the horizon of the vision; its literary structure and semantic ambiguity. Second, the horizon of the recipient of the visionary narrative has been touched upon; especially the circumstances of his involvement in gaining understanding of the vision. In this last section an attempt will be made to consider both aspects together in the event of worship, the **Sitz im Leben** of visions.

---

[46] Paul RICOEUR's conviction is also an integral part of the thought-models of linguistic philosophers such as Earl R. MacCORMAC, and literary critics like A.N. WILDER and Michael GOLDBERG.

But first of all one needs to clarify what the term intentionality will cover in this context. As a phenomenological notion
intentionality focuses on the consciousness of the subject appre-
hending an object. It is, therefore, always a consciousness of
something. Consequently, it is suggested that in this particular case
intentionality refers to the consciousness of the believer as being in
dialogue with the world and that which presents itself as a surplus of
meaning. It is consciousness of something **and more.**

This surplus of meaning emerges from two qualities inherent in
the visions. On the one hand there is this semantic ambiguity, and
closely connected with it, the polysemic nature of metaphorical
language.[47] Language carries, or is being carried by, a dynamism that
allows for new constellations of sense. On the other hand, surplus of
meaning is also generated by the typically religious implications of
visions. As can be noticed in relation to pan-determinism, the visions
disclose self-transcending aspects of life, whether this be in terms
of the "other power" changing the course of events, or the freedom of
choice offered to the recipient of the vision in terms of a moral
decision.[48]

One can say that in trying to understand the vision, the believer
moves from a given perspective (**his** vision) to an act of hope (in a
certain sense the common vision of all believers in, and theologically
never independent from, Christ).[49] Thus, the interpretation of visions

---

[47] Polysemy, or the capacity for multiple meanings, can be seen on two
levels of language. First there is lexical polysemy which is already
codified and culturally accepted, e.g. a square can refer to a
rectangular figure, a public place, or it may also denote a person
with an old-fashioned mentality, being out of touch with new ideas,
styles, etc. On the second level polysemy can arise from new
metaphorical usage, as is frequently the case in modern poetry. It is
this second level that is of interest here. Cf. (2.3.6.5.)

[48] Cf. Ian T. RAMSEY, Freedom and Immortality, London 1957, especially
pp. 63-90, where RAMSEY discusses the relationship between freedom of
choice and the awareness of a self-transcending value (e.g. immortality).

[49] For a stimulating discussion on the role of stories in the context
of worship and ethical commitment see: Dietrich RITSCHL, Zur Logik der
Theologie. Kurze Darstellung der Zusammenhänge theologischer
Grundgedanken, München, 1984, pp. 300-314 and 329-338.

yields a pragmatic substance.

This pragmatic substance can be described in two movements. There
is first the impulse of doxology, and second the challenge of
religious commitment. Each aspect reflects, by the way, the biblical
function of visions. The main emphasis lies not in foretelling, but in
pardoning, encouraging and commissioning.[50] In short it is therapeutic. It also has been argued that the function of such visions is
fundamentally diagnostic, especially when they emerge in a commu-
nitarian dimension, reflecting the state of the particular congregation concerned.[51] But in spite of this focus on the human predicament, the visions do not lose sight of their ultimate point of
reference, God, from whom they are believed to come, and to whom they
point in turn.

The doxological movement arises when the disclosure of the vision
is interpreted as a sign of God's faithfulness and love. The visions
then find a resolution. If they have a hortatory emphasis, resolution
is found in forgiveness. If their accent is edificational, encouragement and commitment is the response.[52] Finally, these visions received
during the years of Nazi terror have a doxological element because
they make the conviction possible that good can be achieved regardless
of the overwhelming presence of evil. Divine action, although
perceived as having an independent origin, assumes its meaning in
correlation with human action.

This acknowledgement of divine and human interaction allows for
an appropriate christian commitment. The response to the vision is an
act of faith, in the light of hope evoked, the inner coherence of the

---

[50] See Karl DAHN, oraô, in The New International Dictionary of New
Testamet Theology, Vol. III, p. 515.

[51] Arnold BITTLINGER, Die charismatische Erneuerung der Kirchen.
Aufbruch urchristlicher Geisterfahrung, in Claus HEITMANN and Heribert
MUEHLEN (eds.), Erfahrung und Theologie des Heiligen Geistes, München,
1974, p. 28; cf. section 5.2.3.

[52] - "Those who had lost their hope gained new courage..." (first
example) - "This vision was powerful for me... I knew with certainty
in my heart that we could again preach in freedom in Germany." (second
example) - "We waited confidently for the things, which were to come."
(vision (A))

vision, and the believer's world-view. The gained insights, religious
and secular, make the wager of a faith commitment reasonable. As the
Pentecostals lacked political training, their commitment was to their
God, flock and neighbors. But it might just as well have been a
commitment to God's cause in a world that had lost its vision of the
true, good and beautiful.

5.2.2. The Concordant Visions

The second group of visions does not emphasize the tornness of
existence (**distentio animi**). The self does not stand between the
tragic and pan-determinism. Rather, it draws its momentum from a
proximity with, or a personal address from the Sacred. One can say
that these visions place the "themes of the self" in a regressive
movement (for examples see Visions (C), (D) and (F)). In a sense they
are visions of innocence, but it is not appropriate to dismiss them as
mere psychological expressions of avoidance of pain and search for
sheltered pleasure. After all, as poetic perceptions of self-
transcendence, they are bringing awareness of wholeness **and more**. For
it is an experience of healing or blessing relating to a purpose,
indicating a directive task to the individual or to the community. In
the case of (C) it is a ministry of edification and intercession. As
far as (D) is concerned it is a call for commitment in view of the
costly price of grace. And in vision (F) it is the realization that
the foreigner speaking a strange language is just as much an addressee
of grace as the "White Anglo-Saxon Protestant." This double movement,
the wholesome apprehension of the Holy and the ethical prescription,
situates concordant visions within the same field as a large section
of New Testament prophetic oracles, as David E. AUNE has demonstrated.[53] The apprehension of the Holy is classically expressed in
extraordinary theophanies (or visions of heavenly beings). The
experience of the "healing touch," which is typical in contemporary
visions can be understood as a secularized form of theophanies. In
either case the presence of the Holy is never an end in itself. For

---

[53] David E. AUNE, Prophecy, pp. 320 ff.

the promise of the salvific is related to a mostly ethical prescription (cf. visions (C 1,2,3), (D), (F), (and diagnostic visions
below). The trend towards secularization can also be noticed in so far
as another group of visions, namely the diagnostic ones, seem to gain
importance. Concordant visions display the same syntactic structures
as the discordant ones. They are basically narratives containing
surprises (**peripeteia**), which depend on metaphorical meaning, and
culminate in disclosures, whose model and qualifiers are rooted in the
text and its plot, and are not simply superimposed. The metamorphosis
is directly experienced (e.g. voyage into outer space), and pan-
determinism has primarily a religious focus (e.g. being in the
presence of Jesus). Perhaps concordant visions appear to be less of a
riddle, because the recipient is in a more passive role, as visions
(C), (F), and (G) seem to indicate; on the other hand vision (D) calls
for the recipient's active interpretative involvement.

5.2.3. Diagnostic Visions

Another common category of visions in pentecostal circles are
those of a diagnostic type. Unlike visions where "themes of the self"
are central, these visions have their receptive function in the
community, although they can also contain elements of the fantastic
and contribute to the resolution of a personal dilemma. Arnold
BITTLINGER calls them "diagnostic visions," because they have a
distinct didactic and hortatory purpose. They compare with David E.
AUNE's "parenetic salvation-judgment oracles," especially those found
in the Book of Revelation.[54] Like their apocalyptic predecessors, they
exhibit a strong emphasis on moral and behavioural exhortation and
arise as a result of a crisis situation. In the Apocalypse it was a
pagan environment and moral laxity. In contemporary circumstances it
may be the awareness of a transformation of values through the process
of secularization.

---

[54] David E. AUNE, Prophecy, p. 326.

These visions can be classified into two types. First, there are
what one could call the "I know you... but I have this against you..."
visions.[55]
They start with a positive description. For example:
      "I see a forest where many people are chopping wood. Everybody
      is happy and working with vigour."
But then a second look reveals a peculiarity.
      "...but suddenly I notice that no trees are falling to the
      ground. Everyone just hews a few times on a particular tree and
      then walks off to another one."
Then follows an application.
      "...They are busy, but the work remains undone. - Perhaps the
      Lord wants to point his finger on our activities and say, 'You
      are very active indeed, but you are wasting your energy. I'd
      rather you'd stay with a particular task till you're done.'"
This type of vision is perhaps common because it is easy to understand
and does not call for any particular skills, save a charismatic gift
of creative imagination. It is most likely learnt behaviour, but so
was prophetism in the Old Testament. In pentecostal and charismatic
circles diagnostic visions promote soul-searching in an unobtrusive
way. As the example (H) shows, there is little or no concern for a
secular context. This is understandable in view of the great influence
that the "holiness tradition" of Methodism had on Pentecostalism in
the early twentieth century. Nevertheless, it is a pity if such
visions have only a **pro domo** use. This need not be, as the next type
of diagnostic visions show.

The second type can be called parabolic visions.[56] They are very
similar to the parables in the gospels, and display the same
sensibility for popular story telling. The functions are identical:
they evoke an image with which one can identify, and emphasize
generally one basic point. In the earlier years of the Pentecostal
movement, at least in German speaking Europe, this type of vision was
told as a form of invitation after the sermon to the unbelievers who

---

[55] For a typical example see vision (H).

[56] For examples see visions (E 1,2,3), (I), and (K).

had come to evangelistic meetings. Probably concern for social respectability has made them vanish from public meetings and official publications. Sometimes they are shared in prayer meetings. This is indeed paradoxical because their parabolic character allows them to be exceedingly flexible. In other words, they would allow for eventful speech and at the same time be understandable to non-religious people. Visions (E 1,2,3) are an example of such secular visions, whereas visions (I) and (K) represent a traditional style. Especially in (K) one would have to ask, as a member of the community of interpretation, whether the vision fulfills its kerygmatic purpose, or if it represents wishful thinking.

As a whole, these diagnostic visions retain a value as pre-reflective communications. Of course, it is possible to consciously invent such narratives and to misuse them. But as with testimonies the narrator's "person" is under trial, and the visions are received or rejected by the audience, or at least individually by those present.[57] That means, they are not harmful because, unlike apodictic statements, they are open to interpretation.

5.3. Anthropological and Theological Concerns

"Do not quench the Spirit, do not despise prophesying, but test everything; hold fast what is good." The pentecostal minister, as well as many lay people, are well aware of these words in I Thessalonians 5:19-21. Step by step they are learning to put them into practice.

---

[57] At a large hotel in Germany an ecumenical retreat was held for U.S. soldiers who were affiliated with pentecostal and charismatic communities. One evening was devoted to sharing personal experiences. Testimonies were given and hymns sung. The service had already lasted for more than an hour. It seemed that the participants began to respond to each testimony with an automatic clapping of hands, without displaying a conscious dialogue with that which had just been said. Then a Vietnam veteran came forward and announced that he had recently seen a vision, which he wanted to communicate. He did. It was a strange mixture of apocalyptic trauma and biblical quotations. He was allowed to finish (as therapeutic concession?), and I wondered whether the audience would again clap inattentively their hands. But no, there was silence.

This chapter on visions cannot fulfill the role of a handbook. The main intention was to present the possibility for a responsible use of visions in a christian context, and to consider its chances of survival in view of a changing world. Some general remarks of what visions can and cannot do will bring this chapter to a close.

5.3.1. Reservations

The fact that deceptive visions can emerge is certainly beyond any doubt. It is, therefore, important to consider their role in worship in an integral fashion. The character of visions is relative to the nurturing ground they find,[58] just as, in the Third World, theologies emerge in relation to the present needs and local socio-ideological convictions. The importance of theological guidance cannot be underestimated. Sound teaching and pastoral sensibility are a prerequisite for a responsible practice of visionary communication. There is no guarantee that through visions christian commitment is brought to bear on everyday life and the world community. The opposite may well be the case, namely that they drift to a preoccupation with non-essentials or spiritualized concerns. The visions in the third appendix show, however, that therapeutic and ethical language hold the balance. Prescriptive language is most of the time expressed as commands, rather than calls to responsibility, and as such indicates basic rather than complex and corporate ethical awareness. The intentionality of visions could also relate to the public **Dasein**. This is the challenge that religion can bring to a secularized world, which due to its pluralism tends to focus on the individual.

Another question which needs to be kept in mind is, as James M. GUSTAFSON has pointed out,[59] that prophetism has two forms of appearance. Borrowing terminology from Max WEBER and Ernst TROELTSCH

---

[58] Visions were often told following the homily, and reflect the tenor of the liturgy of the word.
"In nachfolgendem geben wir einige Botschaften wieder... diese werfen Licht auf die Bedeutung des Todes Jesu am Kreuz für die Gläubigen und waren eine kraftvolle Bestätigung der vorangegebenen Predigt gestanden." Pfingstgrüsse 6,23 (8. März 1914), p. 179.

[59] James M. GUSTAFSON, Decision-Maker, p. 31.

there is a distinction between prophetism which puts an ethic of individual conscience to practice, and emissary prophetism whose ethical concern reflects and reacts to cultural responsibility. The pentecostal visions discussed indeed tend toward a more personal (i.e. exemplary) form of ethical commitment, but there is no reason to assume an exclusive necessity for this in their visionary activity. Much depends on catechetical, homiletical, and practical teaching in the church.

Besides, even if one would welcome the practice of sharing visions, one should remember that they remain a **charisma**, a gift which wants to be received and which cannot be integrated at will. Visions are not a tool to be used as long as there is a fashionable impulse. They are a devotional and solemn channel of religious communication as fragile as the threatened **humanum** itself, in which God is acknowledged, as in the autobiographical pact, as **auctor** (creator of surplus, author, authority) of prophetic speech by means of human imagination.[60] That means that in visionary activity, God is not postulated as the author in order to provide an explanantion of the extraordinary, but he is apprehended as the **auctor** in the sense that he brings more to that which is, and because he is acknowledged as standing at the origin of visionary insight he is also considered as authority,[61] and consequently, as the primordial witness to what is being reported. As with the communication of a testimony, the telling

---

[60] On the innate urge to relate any textual production to an author see Harald WEINRICH, Der Autor des Lesers. Ueber eine Beziehung im Geiste, in Neue Zürcher Zeitung (October 13/14, 1984), pp. 65f.
    "Beobachtet man nämlich etwas genauer, wie Leser tatsächlich mit der Literatur umgehen, so stellt man fest, dass der Autor, wie er für den Leser existiert, nicht nur eine bequeme Chiffre für das (Gesamt-) Werk ist, sondern über das literarische Werk hinaus einen Mehrwert hat, durch den dieses überhaupt erst existenziell beglaubigt wird. Denn der neuzeitliche Leser braucht den Autor, und zwar den Autor-im-Fleische, als den ersten Zeugen für die überindividuelle Bedeutung eine (sic) Textes - der zweite Zeuge ist er selber." (p. 65)

[61] That God, as author, is considered as authority on etymological grounds, brings along the realization that whenever God is said to speak, he is said to speak with ethical importance.
    Cf. also Jean STAROBINSKI, Der Autor und die Autorität. Notizen über Dauer und Wandel einer Beziehung, in Neue Zürcher Zeitung (October 13/14, 1984), pp. 67f.

of a vision thus relates to a minimum of three parties. It would be the task of liturgy to bring the relationship between the parties to light.

5.3.2. Prospects

What visions can do can be summarized as follows. They can be a pedagogic means to promote spiritual maturation. In James W. FOWLER's scheme concerning the structural development of faith, the promotion is one from intuitive-projective faith to a synthetic, reflective and eventually consolidative faith.[62] Discordant visions challenge a decision-making process in which moral conflict plays an important role. Concordant visions affirm human existence in spite of the contingent, and diagnostic visions can set an individual or a community in front of a disquieting mirror.

The second basic function of visions is that they invite people to wholeness. This may be in the form of inner healing and equally important in view of personal existence with others. In the form of inner healing it is wholeness in spite of **and** because of change and diversity (i.e. secularization). In view of personal existence it is a holistic world view, because just as the matter/ spirit distinction can vanish in the visions (metamorphosis), so the mental barrier between the sacred and the secular can also be broken down. In terms of secularization it can encourage non-religious persons to learn the "second language" as Robert BELLAH called it. It is a language of praise and self-transcending commitment in a world of self-interest and dominating material values.

---

[62] James W. FOWLER, Life Maps, pp. 39-99. The final stage of universalizing faith has not been referred to because it is exceedingly rare and (although it could be strived at in and through the myth of the Christ-Event) tends to cloud the putting into practice of faith in an ordinary liturgical context because of its overwhelming horizon. In other words, the existential inability of 99 % (?) to appreciate the last stage makes the celebration of myths even more important. The universalizing stage is a vision of being that cannot be communicated in any other way than through a life's example. (cf. especially pp. 87-95)

Third, prophetic visions have an important role in the decision-making process of the church as an institution. They can bring creative change to the community of faith, provided that prophecy has access to the definition of key notions like the mission, purpose, and order of the church.[63] In that case prophetic activity is not an **addendum** to church life, but a vital part of it. It has, when it addresses the world, the ability to unmask God-less forms of secular subsitute religion.

Finally, visions do fulfill a mythological function. They generate hope, spanning the restoration of the self and of the world. A good example of this mythological function is Dr. Martin LUTHER KING's vision, for which his life had to be on trial. It all came to focus when he said, "I have a dream - that one day - we shall all sit together at the table of brotherhood."

5.3.3. Visions as Supplementary Aspects of the Prophetic Ministry of the Church

Visions do not replace the "testimonies of justice and love," but as with "testimonies of grace" they may motivate to christian action, with a global view of the **humanum**, sharing and practicing the vision for God's kingdom as Jesus Christ taught and exemplified it. Visions, because they intrude unexpectedly, may stir those who are morally self-satisfied to repentance, and may lead those who despaire in face of human finitude to an affirmation of life.

---

[63] James M. GUSTAFSON, Treasure, p. 34. The question at the end of section 1.3.3.2. can thus be answered. A mythological paradigm shift is a real possibility.

6. ACCESSIBLE LITURGY

THEOLOGICAL AND LITURGICAL CONSEQUENCES

"Quod omnes tangit ab omnibus tractari et approbari debet."

Innocent III

6.1. Introduction

The christian voices in the New Testament have emphasized in various ways that mankind has found access to God's grace through the life and work of Jesus Christ (e.g. Rom. 5:2; Eph. 2:18; 3:11,12; Heb. 10:19ff.). This theological claim, however, is only meaningful if it can be experienced religiously. The liturgies of the christian churches have traditionally been regarded as the appropriate context for such an experience. In view of the many cultural changes that have taken place through the years, it is legitimate to ask whether such liturgies still represent for the general population in christian cultures a credible invitation to, and a celebration of faith in God.

The aim of this chapter is to tie together the results of the research in the preceding chapters by placing testimonial and visionary narratives into a meaningful liturgical context. Accordingly, the focus will be on the theological and hermeneutical consequences that the use of oral narratives, as they have been described, imply. Three areas where these consequences are of vital importance will be emphasized specifically. First, and perhaps most importantly, a narrative praxis begs for a theology of laity. Second, the nature of the christian narratives discussed call for a re-evaluation of a theology proper, that is a renewed appreciation of divine activity. The third area relates to the praxis of worship itself. The liturgical activity will first be discussed from an anthropological point of view in a short excursion, and will for a

last time pick up the curious relationship between the religious and
the secular. Some practical reflections will bring the discussions in
this chapter to a close.

6.2. The Need for a Theology of Laity

The attempt to interpret testimonies has shown that the witness
does not simply make a religious statement which can be understood as
a formulation of his or her affiliation to a certain group or
institution. The witness, claiming an experience of self-transcendence, makes a theological statement. In fact, such a claim is not
very different from the propositions of faith at the heart of the
making of Christianity, as Edward SCHILLEBEECKX has pointed out.[1] It
is inconceivable that in the christian beginnings there was a strict
distinction between a group of official theologians and another group
of more or less passive consenters.

The conflict in Corinth, as described in the Pauline correspondence, is a lively example of common theology in the making. The
conflict, because it touched the foundation of faith, was wrestled
with on all levels represented in the church. Paul acknowledged the
valid concerns of the different parties and mediated a consensus which
found its expression in the common meal and in the celebration of the
eucharist. Historically however, Christianity developed from a
charismatic movement in which every believer, by virtue of his or her
disclosure of faith in Christ (theologically: baptism with / or
fullness of the Holy Spirit) was entitled to participate in the
formulation of faith, into an institutionalized religion in which
statements pertaining to faith were issued by a specialized minority.
Although the protestant reformation emphasized the common priesthood
of all believers, both branches of western Christianity found it
potentially dangerous to "democratize" the formulation of faith to the
extent where it would have a tangible effect on the life of the

---

[1] For instance, his description of the Easter-Event (4.3.3.), but also
in The Teaching Authority of All - A Reflection about the Structure of
the New Testament, in Concilium 180 (4, 1985), pp. 13f.

church. The academic and clerical elite thought their role would be threatened if the "common" faithful had a programmatic voice. They thought that the people should be satisfied with living out what the creeds, the devotional tradition, the doctors of theology, or the magisterium proclaimed in matters of faith and morals. The secularization of the West forced a change of attitude. The "common" person today, if he professes to believe at all, wants to make up his own mind. Having come of age he consents to authority only if it is convincing to him.[2] As a result, a **sensus fidelium** can only flourish if it can be elaborated from the base. A theology of the laity becomes a necessity.[3]

The conviction that theology had to be not only **for**, but also **of** the laity dawned only in the second half of the twentieth century. The ice was broken by Yves CONGAR's pre-Vatican II publication Jalons pour une théologie du laïcat[4]. Hendrik KRAEMER reacted to CONGAR's proposals by approaching the topic from a protestant point of view.[5] Whereas CONGAR's work is still important in terms of the elaboration of basic ideas, KRAEMER's book is worth discussing because of the applications it suggests.

6.2.1. Yves CONGAR: A Catholic Approach

Yves CONGAR wrote his book at the beginning of the fifties. It is, therefore, to be considered in a context where the distinction between the religious hierarchy and the laity was still dominated by ontological prejudices; the distinction was stronger than the christian message could warrant. He had to mediate between a **de facto**

---

[2] A good example is the practical disregard by western Catholics of the moral unacceptability of contraceptives as taught by Pope Paul VI in **Humanae Vitae.**

[3] This is also the logical consequence of Robert BELLAH's and James GUSTAFSON's ideas, cf. sections 3.5.1. and 3.5.2.

[4] Yves CONGAR, Jalons pour une théologie du laïcat, Paris, 1952.

[5] Hendrik KRAEMER, Theologie des Laientums. Die Laien in der Kirche, Zürich, 1959; originally published as Theology of Laity.

situation and the **de iure** propositions of canon law and tradition[6]. He nevertheless succeeded in bringing attention back to essentials, namely to that which all Christians have in common.

6.2.1.1. The Basic Dilemma

The faithful, in view of the problematic gap between the officers and the people of the christian body, became conscious that they organically constituted the church. The clergy as representatives of the hierarchical priesthood, on the other hand, considered it important to maintain an ontological difference with regard to the believers representing the common priesthood. Nevertheless; CONGAR insisted on theological grounds[7] (the sociological changes were only a catalytic agent) that all believers shared fully in the christian vocation. Consequently, a new ecclesiology would sooner or later have to emerge where the distinction of the church as a **societas fidelium** and the church as a **Heilanstalt** would only be functional. CONGAR also argued that the church official was first of all a lay person; his fundamental christian option developed before he was ordained.[8]

---

[6] Only in that light can one understand double affirmations like: "Les laïcs formeront toujours, dans l'Eglise, un ordre subordonné, mais ils sont en train de retrouver une plus pleine conscience d'en être organiquement des members actifs, de plein droit et de plein exercice." (Yves CONGAR, Jalons, p. 7) The problem then was obviously how to reconcile the idea of subordination with the theological insights of full integration, full rights and full exercise of being a Christian. A solution was indicated in the Vatican II document Lumen Gentium where the "people of God" are spoken of prior to the official leadership of the church. (See also below on the idea of reception.)

[7] Yves CONGAR mentions for instance the fact that the New Testament does not explicitly refer to a distinction between a christian clerus and the laity. (Jalons, p. 20). The strong distinction (from an originally functional to an ontological difference) between the clerics and the laity took place relatively late, namely between the 11th and the 13th century. GRATIAN in the 12th century was the first to make a definite distinction, **"Duo sunt genera christianorum"** (cf. Jalons, p. 27-36).

[8] "Et d'abord, affirmons une vérité très importante et qu'il ne faudrait jamais perdre de vue: le prêtre (l' évêque, le pape) est d'abord un laïc." Yves CONGAR, Jalons, p. 234.

Without sounding "protestant," he could now develop a theology of the
laity based on the common priesthood of all believers.[9] He illustrates
his convictions through the threefold messianic ministry of Christ.

6.2.1.2. The Common Priesthood

The messianic ministry of Jesus Christ is classically described
as priestly, royal, and prophetic. CONGAR discusses first the priestly
function. The important areas are moral responsibility, testimonial
engagement and liturgical participation.[10] The royal function is
second. It is described as a way of life (in the power and in
anticipation of the kingdom of God) and as an exercise of power.[11] The
third function is the prophetic one. It is the participation through
the power of the Holy Spirit in mystical knowledge and in teaching.[12]
These aspects of the common priesthood must be mentioned because they
also cover central issues which surfaced in the discussion of
testimonies, prophetic visions and the hermeneutic activity which they
provoke. It is interesting to note that Yves CONGAR brings these

---

[9] CONGAR prefers to speak about a "spiritual priesthood" (Jalons, p.
242) but his terminology has not found many imitators, perhaps because
it is virtually a pleonasm.

[10] Yves CONGAR, Jalons, pp. 246-308. Liturgical involvement is seen in
the participation in the eucharist, in emergency baptism and in lay
confession, thus not in the shaping of liturgical content, as for
instance in the kerygmatic activity (Liturgy of the Word).

[11] Yves CONGAR, Jalons, pp. 314-366. The exercise of power relates
mostly to the church as an institution (e.g. elections, cosultation in
coucils, executive administration); it is not presented as power to a
rightful claim, or as consensus formation borne by faith.

[12] Yves CONGAR, Jalons, pp. 367-453.
"... la fonction prophétique de l'Eglise comprend tout l'activité
suscitée en elle par le Saint-Esprit, par laquelle elle connaît et
fait connaître Dieu et son propos de grâce..." (p. 367).
The distinction between mystical knowledge and teaching, although
valid because of their different vantage points, is no longer very
meaningful to the secular person, for he does not consider subjective
experience as such as inferior to generally accepted and taught
opinions. The two aspects fall together for many. The same happens in
religious narratives; cf. Appendix III, visions (D) and (E).

various aspects of lay activity together, not in a postulation of some
higher institutional order, but in a hermeneutically significant
notion based on communicative harmony.

6.2.1.3. Sobornost' as Theory of Reception

The French dominican appeals to the slavonic notion of
Sobornost', a term primarily used in 19th century Russian literary
circles to denote consensus and identity formation in spite of
plurality.[13] For orthodox Christians this term became the paragon of
communion in Christ (the pancrator) through the participation of all.
This idea is important for CONGAR, because for him it truly reflects
the etymological meaning of ekklesia.[14] As a consequence of this
ecclesiology of all, a door is opened to the theory of reception, a
theory in which the "law of faith" is received or suspended through a
communal praxis which is the "law of praise" and that of "commitment."
To put it differently, christian truth, because of the itinerant
nature of human understanding, is not static but is to be received
continually by the community as a whole in view of the past (the
revelation of God in Jesus Christ and the lessons of church history),
the present (the tragedy of unredeemed life), and the future (the
anticipation of wholeness in and through faith in Christ, but also the
reservation with regard to projects of human finitude).[15] Another

---

[13] "il nous semble qu'il y a, dans le Sobornost', un grand fond de
vérité ecclésiologique... Il est, en sous-sol, de quelques principes
généraux qui traduisent des valeurs proprement dogmatiques: celui de
l'unité de l'humanité depuis Adam d'abord, dans le Christ et par lui
en suite; celui de l'Eglise comme finalisée par un idéal de communion
où plusieurs soient un, tout en restant des personnes libres: cette
idée d'unipluralité ou d'unitotalité... se retrouve, d'une manière ou
d'une autre, chez tous les auteurs que nous avons cités." (Yves
CONGAR, Jalons, pp. 381f.)

[14] "... l'idée de Sobornost' reflète une ecclésiologie construite à
partir de la notion d' ecclesia, d'unité du corps, et non à partir de
la notion de pouvoirs hiérarchiques." (Yves CONGAR, Jalons, p. 382.)

[15] The notion of Sobornost' as reception has in fact been integrated
in Lumen Gentium § 12.
    "The holy People of God shares also in Christ's prophetic
office... The whole body of the faithful who have an anointing that

consequence of **Sobornost'** is a renewed appreciation of the history of the church in its pluriformity, and at the same time a deeper sense of ecumenism. But all is subject to the common reception of faith and the simultaneous acknowledgement of Christ's lordship.[16] In other words, the reception of dogma is subject to a common trial and a mythologically celebrated consensus in Christ.

CONGAR then concentrates his theology of laity in a **sensus fidelium**, a sense of faith shared by all believers which on the one hand aims at the conservation of doctrines and tradition, and on the other hand has the task of developing doctrine. He illustrates this by referring to the various activities of the "Action Catholique." However, he remains vague as to the development of doctrine, which after all is the key issue for a realistic theology of laity, and the pivotal point for a theory of public interpretation of religious narratives. The ideas of Hendrik KRAEMER may be of use here.

6.2.2. Hendrik KRAEMER: A Protestant Approach

KRAEMER begins his response to CONGAR's book with a short review of lay influence in church history.[17] He notices a diaconical and

comes from the holy one (cf. 1 Jn. 2:20 and 27) **cannot err in matters of belief.** This characteristic is shown in the supernatural appreciation of the faith (**sensus fidei**) of the whole people, when, 'from the bishops to the last of the faithful' **they manifest a universal consent in matters of faith and morals.** By this appreciation of the faith, aroused and sustained by the Spirit of Truth, the People of God, guided by the sacred teaching authority (**magisterium**), and obeying it, **receives** not the mere word of men, but **truly the word of God** (cf. 1 Th. 2:13)..." Austin FLANNERY (ed.), Vatican Council II, p. 363 (emphasis added).

[16] Yves CONGAR is well aware that this slavophile notion was strongly influenced by German idealistic romanticism and Russian culture (Jalons, p. 383). An appreciation of **Sobornost'** in light of contemporary critical theory would not invalidate the notion of pluriform unity, but it would take divergence and rejection of unity seriously in their own right. For instance, the bond with tradition would have to be a critical rather than an unreflected one. Furthermore, as Hendrik KRAEMER rightly emphasizes, the idea of plurifom unity is not to be isolated as a spiritual notion from its **Sitz im Leben**. Hendrik KRAEMER, Theologie, p. 78.

[17] Hendrik KRAEMER, Theologie, pp. 14-24.

charismatic function fulfilled by the laity in various renewal movements, which eventually vanished through the consolidation of new ecclesial structures. In the Anglo-Saxon protestant world various religious communities drew on the resources of gifted lay people and committed to them active ecclesial functions. It was a participation in the spiritual realm. Only in this century, however, has the lay issue been addressed in terms of the worldly realm, i.e. in view of secularisation.[18] Hendrik KRAEMER suggests a radical theology of laity, not only on basic theological grounds, but also because the process of secularization sheds light on the relative character of history and the prominent role of ethics in public life. It challenges the church to be true to its vocation as an ek-klesia.[19]

6.2.2.1. Accents of a Theology of Laity

Basically, the whole idea centers on lending credibility to the church as an article of faith. Its mission, its worship and its actions should again be recognized as a testimony of christian faith. This testimony is mediated through the church as community to the world in a language understandable to all. It is a language with pragmatic repercussions, born of a sense of responsibility and participation. It is a language of faith because it is not anthropocentric but christocentric.

---

[18] Hendrik KRAEMER, Theologie, pp. 24, 28-36. As milestones promoting an engagement between christian convictions and involvement in the world are mentioned the flourishing of evangelical academies, the "Action Catholique," the introduction of a "Kirchentag" in Germany, the opening of centers such as "Kerk en Wereld" and the Ecumenical Institute in Bossey.

[19] Hendrik KRAEMER, Theologie, pp. 71-75.
    "Erst wenn die Verhältnisse der Welt ganz in den Wirkungskreis einer kirchlichen Doktrin treten, wenn dem anhaltenden Ruf nach einer Erneuerung völlig Rechnung getragen wird und die Direktiven für das kirchliche Leben aus ihrem eigenen Wesen und ihrer Berufung abgelesen werden, und zwar im vollen Bewustsein dessen, was dies für einen wagemutigen Glauben voraussetzt, ist eine echte Theologie des Laientums - als unentbehrlicher Bestandteil der ganzen kirchlichen Doktrin - möglich." (p. 73)

The first accent KRAEMER discusses is the mission of the church.[20] If the church only **had** a mission it could be taken care of by a professional elite. The point, though, is that in Christ the church **is** a mission in which all believers are summoned to partici- pate. Only the fusion of the mission and the corporate unity of the church brings, according to KRAEMER, wholeness, healing, and salvation in Christ. An immediate consequence is naturally of ecumenical significance, i.e. that the mission of the church is only truly lived if the church is one.[21] It is noteworthy to realize that the laity in practical terms is already bound to live ecumenically in various ways,[22] whereas the officers of the churches mainly try to tackle theoretical problems of oneness in Christ.

The second accent is the participation of the whole church in worship and is closely related to the third aspect, namely that of committed action issuing from an awareness of faith. To put it briefly, worship as "ascribing worth to God" is a form of **diakonia**, a service. In a secular context the service of worship, if it is genuine, will have repercussions in the world. The melting of the two aspects, is in fact mythologically represented in the incarnation of the will of God in Jesus Christ, whose whole life was an act of **diakonia**. It is in this sense that Hendrik KRAEMER sees the charis-

---

[20] Hendrik KRAEMER, Theologie, pp. 108-111.

[21] It is quite evident that an increased narrative activity will influence the ecclesiological image of the church. In the historic churches, because of their traditional tendency to see themselves as (the) one identifiable church, narrative pluralism could relativize their self-understanding. But also the smaller independent communities and protestant free churches would, through the communication of shared religious experience, suddenly find themselves confronted with question of ecumenicity and visible participation in the universal church. This happened, for instance, in pentecostal circles when catholic Charismatics began to share testimonies that reflected a compatible faith experience although some theological presuppositions were later understood to be different.

[22] Most illustrative are the consequences issuing from inter-marriage, and the religious education of children born into a dual confession. Another example is the cooperation in interest groups pursuing political, moral and/or ecological aims based on common religious convictions.

matic function of the early church.[23] The liturgical roots of the service of the church make it clear that the church in effect **is** and not just **has** a **diakonia**. But the service in word and deed must be mediated religiously and communicatively. One basic means for this mediation is the narrative participation of the laity. As a royal priesthood they celebrate and invite to wholeness in Christ, as messianic prophets they bring it into the world.

6.2.3. Towards a **Consensus Fidelium**

It might be added that more recent studies on the participation of all in defining the church's faith have emphasized three important areas. First, there is a consensus on the importance of testimonial activity. The laity does not feel involved if their status of witness is not taken seriously.[24] Furthermore, testimony "...forms an essential part of the answer to the question as to who Jesus was and who he can be for us today."[25] Second, it is realized that from a dogmatic point of view theologians should rediscover the far-reaching implications of pneumatology in the life of the faithful. Early Christianity developed under the bond of unity and solidarity in Christ and through the Spirit.[26] The same Spirit, in the Old Testament sense as God's **force vitale**, and in the New Testament sense as the "Spirit of the Lord" could illuminate today's Christians. The community is brought to unity, not through an institution but by the Spirit of God.[27] Lastly, there is an awareness of the non-functional authority of the laity. It is an authority born out of suffering, finding moral consensus and fulfilling a regulatory role analogous to

---

[23] Hendrik KRAEMER, Theologie, pp. 113-116.

[24] Christian DUQUOC, An Active Role for the People of God in Defining the Church's Faith, in Concilium 180 (4, 1985), p. 75.

[25] Edward SCHILLEBEECKX, Teaching Authority, p. 14.

[26] Edward SCHILLEBEECKX, Teaching Authority, pp. 15-18.

[27] Herbert VORGRIMLER, From **Sensus Fidei** to **Consensus Fidelium**, in Concilium 180 (4,1985), p. 7.

that of public opinion in a democracy.[28] A theology of laity would
have an authority emerging from the grassroots. As Herbert VORGRIMLER
put it,

> 'Ordinary' believers are only beginning to find courage and their
> own language. Their 'teaching' will be presented in a form and
> with methods different from those known to us from intellec-
> tualized theology. It will be proposed in 'narrative' form or as
> 'oral history', as we see from its first attempts in feminism, in
> Latin America and in Africa.[29]

These aspects affirm the intentionality of this study: to invite
testimonial and prophetic activity on the part of the laity into the
heart of communal religious expression.

6.3. The Divine Subject of Worship

If the **locus vivendi** of religious narrative is worship, then it
is not enough to delineate a feasible linguistic structure. It is also
important to be aware of the communicative relationships involved. As
previously mentioned (3.5.3.) these relationships are: a) between the
self and the community, b) between the community and the world, and c)
between the believer(s) and God. The interaction between the various
communicative partners has to be taken seriously if a proposition is
to have a value. The presence of any one partner cannot be taken for
granted (e.g. the presence of God), nor can it be played down (e.g.
the participation of the world). This section will pay close attention
to the narrative perception of the divine, and suggest a fresh
approach to pneumatology in light of the hermeneutical activity of the
church. Matters pertaining to other communicative partners (i.e. the
believers and the world) will be picked up in section 6.4.

---

[28] Edward SCHILLEBEECKX, Teaching Authority, p. 18-21; Christian
DUQUOC, Active Role, p. 76.

[29] Herbert VORGRIMLER, **Sensus Fidei**, p. 8.

6.3.1. God

A person making statements about God has to be careful. First, because an image of God (**Gottesbild**) is always fragmentary. One cannot codify and delineate the essence of the divine as Meister ECKHART, Nicolas of CUSA, as well as Immanuel KANT, among others, have emphasized. Second, because an image of God is subject to change as, for instance, the notion of progressive revelation indicates.[30] But an awareness that every image of God is fragmentary and subject to transformations does not make a human conception of God meaningless.

Furthermore, it has been argued above (5.4.1.) that an image of God is essential in visionary narratives. As visions emerge in a context of prayer, God is acknowledged as author of visions; he is seen as a communicator and giver of meaning. In this respect it is rewarding to take note of a study by Edward H. HENDERSON. He compared the personal conceptions of God in the writings of Austin FARRER with a non-personal conception of the divine elaborated by D.Z. PHILLIPS and comes to affirm traditional teaching on prayer with a twofold conclusion. First, the ability to address a personal God is essential to the exercise of christian faith. Second, God should be seen as effecting change in the world.[31] God is considered as an important "actant" in both cases. He is addressed as a person (at least in the literary sense).

---

[30] In the beginning of the Old Testament, images of God are described in relation to power over natural forces, or a bountiful garden; the images are understandable to nomadic people. Later God is the God of Israel, then God is recognized as God of the living as well as of the dead. The later prophets proclaim a God who wants justice for all nations. In the New Testament God reveals himself in the man Jesus and as a living Spirit in the church. Indeed a tremendous change.

[31] Edward H. HENDERSON, Austin Farrer and D.Z. Phillips on lived Faith, Prayer and Divine Reality in Modern Theology 1,3 (1985), pp. 223-243, esp. pp. 240-242. HENDERSON unfortunately does not distinguish sufficiently the different presuppositions (christian or buddhist) of the authors he discusses. Nevertheless, in a christian frame of reference the argument for an image of a personal God seems valid.

6.3.1.1. Is it still Meaningful from a Narrative Point of View to
Retain a Trinitarian Portrait of God?

In a secularized world it seems easier to imagine God as the
ground of being, than to dissect divine existence as it were into a
systematic theory of a trinitarian God who, at the same time, manages
not to be tri-theistic. However, a narrative comprehension of God
favours not only a personal but even an interpersonal model of the
divine.[32] For instance, the statement that God is love is easier to
understand (in spite of all suffering existing in the world) when it
also finds a dynamic function within the divine itself. In the end,
one is possibly faced with a wager. Either one rejects an interpersonal model of God as anthropocentric, or one consciously approves
of it because of its heuristic value, already demonstrated in essence
in the Scriptures. Christian narratives prefer the second option, and
formalist theories indicate that a secular person can very well follow
a plot in which the Sacred is a "Donor." But to avoid tri-theism a
fluid notion of the Trinity may be suggested.[33] A fluid notion is,
however, not identical with a vague notion. At least, the visionary
narratives of Pentecostals containing the theme of metamorphosis
reflect a comprehension of the self in dialogue with a pluriform
presence of the Sacred.[34] Furthermore, a mythological presencing of

---

[32] It is the paradoxical nature of the transcendent as containing the
one (undifferentiated essence) as well as the many (differentiated
essence) that preoccupies all world religions. Cf. Carl A. KELLER,
Verlangen nach Offenbarung in der heutigen Zeit, in Neue Zürcher
Zeitung, 4/5 Oktober 1986, p. 37. Because a negative theology describing the divine in terms of what it is not, is as dissatisfactory
as a theology speaking about God in positive terms, i.e. in terms of
what he can be said to be, a metaphorical apporach seems to be a
productive alternative; namely, to speak of God as what he "is" and
"is not" at the same time. To speak of the christian God as "three in
one and one in three" remains such a paradox.

[33] A secular person will understandably find it even more difficult
than the average religious person to make sense of the Sacred in the
theoretical formulations of Constantinople and Chalcedon. A narrative
approach has the advantage of allowing overlapping semantic fields to
interact.

[34] Cf. Appendix III, vision (F) lines 11-19, and for a contemporary
example vision (D).

God's grace in a sacramental liturgy seems to depend on a polysemic appreciation of the divine.

6.3.1.2. A Narrative Comprehension of God

In the Bible, God appears within the tissue of history as it has been mentioned in chapter one. Human beings seem not to be able to speak about divine activity without contextual reference. A convincing example is God's act of grace in the incarnation of the Logos, the life of Jesus, and the resurrection of Christ. Basically, such a contextual reference would be narrative in type. One may well speculate about the essence of God without narrative reference, but that, as abstract exercise, is quite a different matter. The "religions of the Book" believe in a God that has made His-Story. Furthermore, in worship God is actively addressed, and more or less consciously experienced by the believer as present. Narratives help to interpret such experiences with the ground of being, whether they take place in the liturgy or in secular life.

6.3.2. The Narrative of Jesus, the Christ

The power of the Gospel rests in the story of Jesus, in his generally narrative teaching, and in the mythological celebration of his victory over death. One can say that narrative stands, from a christological point of view, with one foot in the domain of the word and with the other foot in the realm of the sacramental. The central role of Christ in worship is also the primary hermeneutical criterion for testimonies. In theological terms, the message of God is only fully incarnate when the story of Jesus Christ has a clear reference point in the world. From a literary, non-religious and secular point of view it can be maintained that the life of Jesus of Nazareth makes perfect sense as a human tragedy. But as Paul RICOEUR noted by referring to ARISTOTLE, true tragedy yields a moral surplus.[35] It is a surplus which cannot be contained in finite human action. As a result

---

[35] Paul RICOEUR, Temps, Vol. I, pp. 58, 64f.

the pivotal role of the narrative of Jesus Christ constantly mediates between the Sacred and the secular. This mediation is most clearly brought to bear when stories of everyday experience and the mythological presence of Christ meet in worship. Here the starting point can be placed for a pneumatological awareness of the laity.

6.3.3. A Pneumatological Blueprint

There are at least two reasons which indicate the need to study afresh the pneumatological teaching of the Bible. One general reason is the close connection between the biblical perception of the Holy Spirit and the practice of worship.[36] The other, more specific, reason is linked with the difficulty of interpreting metaphorical statements of transcendence with the belief in the divine on one side, and daily experiences on the other.

This section will survey some pneumatological aspects which may be helpful in a praxis of worship taking an interest in the oral communication of religious narratives.

6.3.3.1. The Spirit as **Force Vitale**

The Old Testament presents a picture of God's Spirit as a live-giving power. The **ruach elohim / yahweh** is more than the breath of God, or the wind that blows over creation; it is the principle conveying and sustaining life. But the Spirit of God is not only life-giving in the physical sense. The books of the Old Testament also portray him (it? or her) as a creative force enabling human beings to produce works of art[37] and make wise and discerning decisions.[38] The Spirit of God not only empowers people to a specific task, but in post

---

[36] Jean Jacques VON ALLMEN, Worship and the Holy Spirit, in Studia Liturgica 2,2 (1963), pp. 124- 135.

[37] So in Exodus 35:30-35, or Phoenician craftsmanship in the construction of the temple.

[38] The Persian king Cyrus even being refered to as messiah in Isa. 45:1.

exilic Judaism he is believed to be a gift to change man's life
option, as the passage in Ezekiel 36:26f., speaking about the Spirit
turning hearts of stone into hearts of flesh, illustrates.

Similarly, the New Testament word **dynamis** emphasizes a power in
relation to the Holy Spirit that speaks of authority and might in a
constructive way.[39] The Evangelists Matthew and Mark relate the
Spirit's influence on Jesus in the Old Testament way. Jesus is not
presented as a pneumatic person, but rather as a prophet on which the
power of the Spirit of God falls.[40] It is the classical way in which
God encounters his people.

But to recognize the Holy Spirit as a **force vitale**, especially
from an Old Testament point of view, implies recognizing this
invigorating power as a creational gift of God to all of mankind. In
that sense all people, whether attentive to the Spirit or not, have
this gift from God without which they could not live. Consequently,
they could also be gifted to convey matters of spiritual (i.e.
fundamentally human) importance. This implies in our discussion that
the liturgical activities would have to be open to such contributions,
at least to the extent that redeemed and "unredeemed" voices can
introduce an image of the world which asks for secular meaning **and
more.**

6.3.3.2. The Spirit as Divine Agent

It follows from a Hebrew understanding of the divine that the
Spirit of God is a manifesting Spirit. This idea has been carried into
the New Testament. In the Gospel of Luke and the Book of Acts God's
pneuma appears visibly and demonstrably.[41] The Spirit comes with power
and authority. It is typical for Pentecostals to identify with this

---

[39] The author of the book of Acts describes the first Pentecost in
these terms. It would also be of great interest to study the New
Testament pictures of the Holy Spirit in the light of his public
function.

[40] Eduard SCHWEIZER, **pneuma**, in Theological Dictionary of the New
Testament, Vol. VI, p. 403.

[41] Eduard SCHWEIZER, **pneuma**, p. 407.

Lukean view, especially in their preaching. The testimonies and visions studied confirm this aspect to a certain point.[42] Prophetic awareness especially is much more concrete and public. Eduard SCHWEIZER describes the Lukean view as follows,

> Luke took an important step beyond Mark and Matthew. He did not think it enough to represent Jesus as a bearer of the Spirit by pointing to individual pneumatic features or to the birth and baptism stories. His special concern was with the time of the Church. Here the promises are fulfilled by the people of God, to whom the Spirit is given in totality. The prophets are no longer isolated individuals. All the members of the eschatological community are prophets.[43]

By being potentially common to all, due to the Christians' baptism in Christ, spiritual agency is brought to a human level; that is, it is not supernatural in the Old Testament sense that the prophet is overpowered by it, but rather takes the form of a cooperation analogous to the idea of the incarnation. That is why Karl RAHNER can state that,

> Spiritual experience... is not the result of a single action of God 'from outside' on the human spirit regarded as definitively constituted. It means that God, through his self-communication (uncreated grace), becomes always and everywhere in grace a co-constitutive principle of the human spirit in its transcendence.[44]

This statement emphasizes, first, that human mental activity is always involved in the production of spiritual insight. This has perhaps best been evidenced in the hermeneutic activity of visions. Therefore one can speak of a contextualization between mundane and spiritual

---

[42] In the testimonies the Spirit is related to branding, disclosing, and healing (or empowering), but the Spirit is also identified as agent where he cannot be identified demonstrably, that is when he is seen in a hermeneutic role. This is even more the case in the visions. The Holy Spirit is portrayed as dialoguing with the human spirit and is often recognized as a strong or commanding voice. Besides the testimonies of Frank BARTLEMANN and T.B. BARRATT in chapter 4 consult among the testimonies: (D) lines 163f., 167, 214, 266, 313 (and indirectly references like lines 96, 103f., 112f. etc.); (E) lines 55f., 71, (indirectly line 80f.); (G) lines 31f., 36f. 43f., 48f., 57f.; and among the visions: (C) lines 19ff., 38, 44ff.; (D) lines 56, 111f., 136f., 143f.; (E) lines 16f., 22; (K) lines 24f.

[43] Eduard SCHWEIZER, pneuma, p. 412.

[44] Karl RAHNER, Experience of the Spirit and Existential Decision, in Concilium 10 (1974), p. 41.

knowledge. Second, spiritual agency, as an act of grace, is understood as prompting a disclosure of transcendence. It is no accident that a sense of spiritual agency is felt in testimony (D) in the Proppian functions of "transference," the "struggle with the villain," the "new provision," and the "helper/donor."

This second aspect gains depth when the inspiring activity of the Holy Spirit is explained with the whole etymological breadth of the notion of authorship. The Spirit as **auctor** is originator, authority, and agent of surplus in one. He is a) the originator of faith in Christ, the author (**Verfasser**) of "visions" of hope in the promise of God; b) the authority of the divine, representing the cause of Christ in an uncompromising fashion, for instance in "dangerous" testimonies of suffering; and c) the agent of love within the community of mankind bringing mercy and reconciliation in spite of its pluralistic preferences and individual life stories.

There is a challenge to use public liturgical narratives as they have been described with an explicit confidence in the sovereign activity of God's Spirit as guiding principle and hermeneutic arbiter within human dialogue. Such a confidence could only make sense today through a "**second naïveté**" brought to light in a mythological celebration where the Holy Spirit is welcomed as the sacrament to the church, and the church is actively typified as the sacrament to the world. But this presupposes already the paracletic representation of Jesus Christ through the Holy Spirit.

6.3.3.3. The Spirit as Paraclete

Although the Gospel of John has Jesus refer to the Holy Spirit as paraclete it is Paul who, writing at an earlier date, develops the idea that in the Holy Spirit there is intimate communion with Jesus Christ. He does this by relating the message of the Spirit to that of the crucified, risen and coming **kyrios**.[45] It is a marvellous synthesis of Jewish concern (i.e. being controlled by the Spirit), Hellenistic vocabulary (i.e. "spiritual body"), the Lukean insistence that all

---

[45] Eduard SCHWEIZER, **pneuma**, pp. 415-437.

Christians are bearers of the dynamic Spirit, and the decisive point in history (the Easter-Event) illuminated through the life and words of Jesus Christ. This synthesis brings forth a pneumatological point which is often neglected, namely that the ethical and soteriological functions of God's Spirit cannot be separated.[46] Eduard SCHWEIZER boils Paul's theology down to the following statement,

> If the knowledge given by the Spirit is knowledge of God's saving work, it liberates man from himself and opens him to others. It also restores his individuality, not in such a way that he can only contemplate it, but in order that he may stand before God and others therewith, and live for others therein.[47]

It is precisely in a communal testimonial activity where a spiritual orientation can take place which liberates, restores, and directs not only the individual, but the individual and the community.

The therapeutic and the prophetic go hand in hand. The testimonial stories illustrate this through their plot. For testimonies and (auto)biographical accounts demonstrate that life is full of interruptions. What the morrow brings is imaginable but by no means predictable. The peripeteic changes in the plot of life cause either sudden surprise, awe, and joy, or else bereavement, fear, and affliction. The presence of Christ through the Spirit can be perceived by the believer as such interruptions, and the reactions they cause are spelled out in faith, because the community and the liturgical atmosphere provide a context for a disclosure as speech-event and symbolic action.

The question remains, can the Spirit of God also be an advocate or comforter to the secular person without professed religious affiliation in the traditional sense? The answer may be yes, when the worshipping church has "windows" to the world through which such a person may recognize himself **and more**, and be lead to a deeper understanding of his existential situation by the community (now paraclete in the Name of Christ) that demonstrates solidarity as well

---

[46] Eduard SCHWEIZER, **pneuma**, pp. 430-432.

[47] Eduard SCHWEIZER, **pneuma**, p. 432.

as a self-transcending outlook on life. Testimonial narratives of positive and negative experiences alike can be such "windows" to the world and to the kingdom of God.

It may be considered to be too easy a solution to delegate a hermeneutic responsibility to the Holy Spirit. After all, does not the secular world demand a less hypothetical, and non-miraculous solution in the search for meaning? An answer to this question depends heavily on how one understands spiritual participation in the human project of interpretation.

6.3.3.4. The Spirit as Deliberator

If, as Karl RAHNER said, spiritual experience and insight is only possible as a moment of co-constitutive grace in the human mind, then the participation of the Holy Spirit in the search for truth need not be a seen as the invasion of a totally foreign element.

Speaking theologically, the Spirit can be thought of as a deliberator.[48] First of all, a deliberator from sin and guilt in view of human shortcomings and the salvific work of Christ, which now, in its programmatic aspect is continued in the christian body. Second, the Spirit can be conceived as a deliberator of the dialoguing community. It is the second aspect that is to preoccupy us now.

The deliberation happens as a careful play between two levels. There is, on the one hand, the level where cultural knowledge still bears the mark of the divine **force vitale**, the creational power of the Spirit. On the other hand there is the level where the Holy Spirit is active through the Word of God and the church. It would not be helpful to see a competitive dilemma between the two movements if one presupposes that truth as such is perceived as indivisible although many-faceted. The deliberation of the Spirit would be recognized in a double consensus formation (as a theology of laity would also suggest), in dialogue with the world on the one side, and through theological insight and reception within the christian church on the

---

[48] The pneumatic deliberation is not merely thought of as careful counsel, but also as a freeing word.

other.[49] The lay person would gain true ecclesiological status, for the church would be acknowledged as the community of the Holy Spirit in which the believers realize in communion with others a hermeneutical responsibility in which the help of the Spirit, the legacy of Christ, is called upon.[50] Such deliberation in the church would not be anthropocentric or anticlerical. It would not be anthropocentric because it would be embedded in the acknowledged authority of the Bible as divinely inspired (expressed for instance in an eschatological reservation) and existentially exemplified in the life, death and resurrection of Jesus Christ. Furthermore, the reciprocal **lex orandi, lex credendi** principle, conveys a dimension to worship in which spirit and truth are recognized as historical values that remain open. In other words, the deliberation of the Spirit would always be mythological in the sense Walter HOLLENWEGER suggested it. That the involvement of the laity of a secular society is unlikely to produce a type of anti-clericalism as was known in the 19th century, and how the classic tension between charismatic and institutional action is not an insoluble dilemma will be touched on in the following section.

6.3.3.5. The Charismatic Activity of the Spirit

It can be deduced from Pauline correspondence that the deliberating activity of God's Spirit brings about a structuration of the church which is very different from the set up of an institution in

---

[49] As to the second aspect, see footnote 42 in this chapter, specifically the remarks concerning visions.

[50] Leonardo BOFF, Kirche, p. 223.
According to BOFF, the historic churches in the First World could develop from churches exclusively depending on an élite, to churches of God's people in dialogue, from institutions to communities putting faith, hope, and love into practice, and finally from ritual churches to prophetic churches. In other words, he suggests a development similar to the basic christian communities in Latin America. L. BOFF, Kirche, p. 234.
The non-white indigenous christian churches in Africa present a different case, because the differentiation between the shaman type priest and the adepts is strong. Nevertheless, even there seems to be more "lay" involvement as the ministries of "prophet," "spiritual mother," "evangelist" and "story teller" indicate.

which the ontological division between amateurs and professionals is
the fundamental driving force of perpetuation. It is a structuration
based on **charismata**, gifts of God's grace in view of the common good,
signs of the Sacred's presence visible to the public.[51] A charism
situates God's gift of salvation or wholeness into the context of
existence. That includes the consequence for Paul that the charisma
are not supra-natural impositions in the Old Testament sense, but
co-natural gifts as a result of new life in Christ. In other words,
the charisms are essential in the everyday affairs of the believers
and the mission of the church; they are not presented as esoteric
gifts of a few elect as Gnosticism would have it.[52] It is therefore
not surprising that the Pauline teaching on charisms goes hand in hand
with the teaching on diaconical activity.[53] There are "varieties of
gifts, but the same Spirit, and there are varieties of service, but
the same Lord." I Cor. 12:4,5. The charismatic structure of the
church, which to a large extent serves hermeneutic aims, can

---

[51] Leonardo BOFF says (Kirche, p. 271) in the language of Gotthold
HASENHUETTL, "Für (Paulus) bildet das Charisma die strukturierende
Struktur der Gemeinde. Die theologische Rechtfertigung beruht auf
seiner Ueberzeugung, mit der Gründung der Kirche sei das Ende der
Zeiten angebrochen und deshalb sei mit aller Macht auch die Fülle des
Geistes über sie herabgekommen. So verstanden gehört das Charisma
nicht mehr in den Bereich des Ausserordentlichen und
Aussergewöhnlichen, sondern ist die Regel bei der gemeindlichen
Strukturierung. Damit bedeutet das Charisma schlicht die konkrete
Funktion, die jeder zum Wohle aller in der Gemeinde ausübt..."

[52] This does not stand in contradiction to extraordinary charismatic
manifestations as they are described in the Book of Acts and in I
Corinthians 12-14. For these too, according to Paul serve the common
good, and this only if they relate to living out of the christian
option; I Cor. 12:3, 7; 13:1ff., 14:12, 26.

[53] "Charisma ist die durch das Heilsgeschehen geschenkte, (Zeit und
Ewigkeit umspannende) je konkrete Berufung, die in der Gemeinde
verwirklicht wird, sie konstituiert und dauernd aufbaut und dem
Mitmenschen in Liebe dient." Gotthold HASENHUETTL, Charisma.
Ordnungsprinzip der Kirche, Freiburg, 1969, p. 238.
        "Ein echtes Charisma blüht dann auf, wenn die Menschen das
bieten, was sie sind, was sie haben und was sie im Dienste Gottes und
im Dienst an ihren Brüdern und Schwestern können." Leonardo BOFF,
Kirche, p. 273.

accordingly be studied from three angles: as a gift of grace, as a service to the neighbor, and in its holistic intentionality. These three angles shed light on the understanding of life as meaningful.

First, the "charismatic" church, because it lives consciously by the grace of God in Christ, understands itself as a gift. It stands in strong opposition to an institution that arrogates its existence by an act of hybris.[54] It is through God's Spirit that the believers are baptized into the body of Christ, and are made partakers of his presence, I Cor. 12:13. Participation in the Gospel is typically experienced as a gift. This is why a testimony of a religious disclosure is structurally similar to the encounter with a donor of a magical agent in the fairy tales. The fact that those who received such a gift of wholeness share in a common experience disposes them for living for the common good they recognize as an answer to the christian message, for it is the source (in secular terms say: reason) and the aim, the receiving and the giving, that come together in the model of Christ, I Cor. 12:4-7. Since all Christians have been made to drink by and of the same Spirit, they share a common mission. As with PROPP's magical agent, their natural talents are turned into talents for a new task.[55] A charism is a vocation to minister. The Spirit dwelling in man deliberates him to authority, but only if he gives up the attempt to own power and control.[56] The presence of the Spirit

---

[54] Although the testimony of Jesus Christ is the testimony of a man called the Son of God, it is the account of suffering and weakness (even of foolishness) that puts a claim on its listeners, and not the exercise of influence and power.

[55] A secular equivalent to the magic potion is, for instance, a new motivation as a result of tragedy (e.g. the Tchernobyl trauma). On the relationship between charism and human talent see Leonardo BOFF, Kirche, p. 279.

[56] Dem Menschen ist die Macht des Geistes zwar gegeben, er verdankt sie aber nicht sich selbst, sondern sie ist ihm geschenkt, und zwar so, dass der Mensch dem Herrn gehört (Röm. 8:9-12). In antiker Terminologie kann dieses Eigentumsverhältnis mit der "Einwohnung" ausgedrückt werden. In der Gemeinde, im einzelnen "wohnt" die Kraft des Geistes. Diese Vorstellung schützt davor, das Vollmachtsereignis als ein menschlich begründbares und daher zerstörbares zu verstehen. In wem der Geist wohnt, der lebt nicht nur aus der Macht heraus, die ihm geschenkt ist, sondern gleichsam in ihr: sein Sein ist "im Geist"... Zugleich kann dieses sein im Geist mit dem Sein-in-Christus

then is the essence of Christ in and through the believers.

Second, the "charismatic" structure of the church aims at service for the common good. In such a circumstance even power becomes a charism because it does not seek itself.[57] The charismatic power of a testimony and of a prophetic utterance is only unleashed if it passes the public trial. In secular terms one could say that metaphors only remain or become meaningful if they are allowed to interact with juridical, i.e. rational, thought.[58] For the church the metaphor **par excellence** (its form **and** content) is Jesus Christ, communicated on the stage of the world in view of the threatened **humanum**. To bring it to a point one can say that the grace of God does not make sense unless it leads mankind to wholeness.

The third structural aspect of the "charismatic" church centers therefore on the holistic intentionality. There is no place for private religion where the Spirit of Christ is the cornerstone for the edification of all.[59] A good example of this proposition is given in the discussion on the use of prophecy and speaking in tongues in I Cor. 14:1-5, 12, 16f., 26, and the analogy of the body in I Cor. 12:4-7, 12-26. Again, the edification of the body of Christ has, to a certain degree, its secular couterpart: solidarity with the sick and powerless for instance. But in all this it must not be forgotten that the Spirit of God is only a deliberator to meaning if Jesus Christ is subjectively experienced, and objectively confessed in word and deed, as the prism through which the light of the world is reflected in the colors of the covenant.

---

identifiziert werden, denn beides bezeichnet die Existenz des Glaubenden. Anders ausgedrückt: Jesus Christus wird im Geist offenbar im Raum seines An-wesens, der Gemeinde." Gotthold HASENHUETTL, Charisma, p. 88 (emphasis his); cf. also p. 122.

[57] Leonardo BOFF, Kirche, p. 278.

[58] Here the contributions of Richard FENN and Hans BLUMENBERG are dialectically brought into play. On the one hand the tension between liturgical language and language of trial is maintained. On the other hand the notion of metaphor is not reduced to a matter of form. In short, a "living metaphor" remains always also a matter of content.

[59] Gotthold HASENHUETTL, Charisma, pp. 125ff.

A theology of laity, thus, cannot do without the charismatic presence of the Spirit of Christ as hermeneutical deliberator between orthodoxy and orthopraxis. Where the two meet, there is life - and true prophecy.

6.4. The Human Subject of Worship

If worship is truly a communicative process, then it is not only the Sacred that is addressed. The other poles in the triangle of communication are the community of believers and the world at large. For both an interpretative framework cannot be taken for granted, but must be explicated.

6.4.1. The Community of Faith

Considering what has been said concerning the fragmentation of contemporary society in chapter three, one faces a difficulty in view of the image of homogeneity formerly associated with the "Lord's flock." It once was common practice to refer to a triangular relationship between God, the church, and the world. But this will not work any longer and this for at least two reasons. First, to be precise one should take into account the communicative dynamics which function within the community itself. The secular emphasis on the subject in the West no longer allows for a homogeneous notion of community. Second, a member of a church is simultaneously a member of a far more intricate institution, that is, the society in which he lives and attempts to realize individual and integrative ambitions quite different from those in the religious community. Consequently, if worship is seen as a communicative act of faith, one will have to provide a fairly open horizon for the expression of the same, a horizon that allows for individuation as well as integration.

6.4.1.1. The One

The particular problem in mentioning individuation is the latent possibility of encouraging a private expression of faith that is asocial and has little in common with a christian option of justice and love. An individual testimony if freely shared in a public context can set dynamics free which allow for a harmonious and unpretentious interplay between individuation and integration.

The particular challenge in taking the individual seriously as a communicative partner rests in the christian **diakonia** which can generate a commitment to others. Even a testimony of individuation will acknowledge the instrumentality of others (PROPP's "helper"), and testimonies of integration would point to a "home coming" with purpose. The practice of worship then, would not limit itself to ascribing worth to God, but would also ascribe worth to man in view of the redemption that Christ has availed for him. From this point of view one can say, man is not made for liturgy, but liturgy is made for man.

6.4.1.2. The Many

The particular problem here lies in the institutionalization of communication. If liturgy becomes **the** liturgy, and communication is reduced to the sacramental realm then liturgy has become a means for the justification of faith and can no longer function as generator of the same, at least not in a pluralistic society. This, of course, does not deny the value of a common profession of faith, but it does point out that the common voice has to be born from the convictions gained by the individual in interaction with others **and more.**

The particular challenge of a common testimony is that it can be recognized as a statement of conviction of a **communio sanctorum** (the religious element being positively recognizable by the secular audience) to corporate response-ability towards God and the world. Another communicative challenge relates to the prophetic spirit in the church. It could fulfill an important function not only as a critical and programmatic voice, but also as "master of ceremonies" giving the right of speech to those unheard and unasked.

6.4.2. The World at Large

Finally there is the communicative pole, which traditionally has been dealt with only from a missionary point of view. But Christianity has had since its beginnings an ambivalent attitude towards the mundane. On the one hand, Jesus is said to have criticised exclusivist religious circles. He is portrayed as ministering to and living among all. On the other hand, Christians have always been careful not to spoil the "pure" doctrine and worship of God. That the "world" is a point of reference in christian life has never been denied, but what exactly is the relationship between the "chosen" and the "others"? And why should certain narratives play an important role in the dialogue between the two parties?

6.4.2.1. Recognition of a **Weltbewusstsein** in the Act of Worship

It is clear that not every pluralistic innovation should be introduced into the activities of the christian church. There are ethical and pragmatic reasons which see some secular convictions as counter-indicative to faith.[60] At the same time, a strong fostering of religious solidarity, a liturgical justification of the religious status quo, and a ghetto mentality shying away from any contact with other social realities, have been counter-indicative to the life of the church. In view of this problem, William EVERETT has attempted a sociological sketch of a balanced field of reference for liturgical activity.[61] After discussing the theories of Donald SALIERS and Paul RAMSEY, who in their own ways try to maintain the integrity of

---

[60] If there were no partisan standpoints, Christianity would be indifferent to secular developments and lose not only its religious, but also its social significance.

[61] William W. EVERETT, Liturgy and Ethics. A Response to Saliers and Ramsey, in The Journal of Religious Ethics 7,2 (1979), pp. 203-214.

worship, he suggests the notions of "publicity" and "profession" as a basis for liturgy to maintain identity as well as openness to social pluralism.

His argument for publicity runs as follows. First, the concept of the public realm is defined as cutting through all institutional barriers.[62] Public places and buildings are, in theory at least, accessible to all; a public park is not the same as the neighbor's garden. Similarly, public figures deserve the adjective because their presentation is not esoteric.

The second argument for public worship is based on the biblical presentation of "God's dwelling place".

> Biblical faith gives God a specific character and address. God has a "dwelling place" described variously as "most high," heaven, heavenly kingdom, heavenly court, or throne. This spatiality may strike sophisticates as quaint, unless they realize that the biblical authors are claiming that God dwells in perfect public - a place of light, of open disclosure, of persuasive truth, of judgment in the light of all the facts.[63]

To that one could add the familiar notion in the Old Testament of "God dwelling among his people," or "the Word became flesh and dwelt among us, full of grace and truth" (John 1:14).

EVERETT's third reason for advocating the notion of the public realm arises as a contrast of the fallen human condition, which retreats into privation, isolation and darkness, selfish coercion and death.[64] Ironically, the pluralistic concept of the "public" becomes a symbol of wholeness and salvation.

The argument for profession tries on the other side of the scale to maintain the value of identity formation. The sacrament or the celebration of confirmation, and even more so the personal testimony, is seen as a achievement leading to a religious confession (belonging

---

[62] William EVERETT, Liturgy and Ethics, p. 209. In this context he also discusses public stories and notes that these are more likely to be stories of the present than stories of the past, since the past is not common to all participants. However, it seems to me that Christians have a responsibility to publicize the past, both religious and secular, as well as a vision of the future.

[63] William EVERETT, Liturgy and Ethics, p. 209.

[64] William EVERETT, Liturgy and Ethics, p. 210.

to a cultic vision), and later to a profession of faith which is nothing less than the ethical conviction going public.[65] Thus the circle is closed, or rather opened to a dynamic life of faith in modern society. If acts of worship take the challenge of the public realm seriously, then the mundane may have access to the Sacred, and in turn, God's grace (presence) may pervade a world in need of restoration. A consciousness of being in the world is fundamental to liturgy, for both the believer and the non- or otherwise committed person, if the secular realm is to be addressed in the Name of the Author of Life.

6.4.3. A Twofold Consequence

The consequences discussed here are, naturally, limited to the pertinence of narrative in liturgical activity based on the thesis that testimonial and visionary narratives are especially suited to bridge the communicative gap between the Sacred (of ultimate value) and the profane (of fragmentized, pluralistic, but nevertheless sometimes penultimate value).

The figurative connotations implied in the use of "Sacred" and "profane" help to illustrate a central point, namely, that every person who intends to stand in the presence of the Holy in the "sanctuary" has first to pass through the "court of the gentiles".

6.4.3.1. "Crossing" the Profane in Order to Stand Before the Sacred

First, the testimonies consulted indicate that there is no experience of the Sacred without everyday experience. What has been labelled as trivial, can indeed refer to a stereotyped description of popular religious motives, but more importantly, it points to the necessity of a **nexus** to ordinary everyday experience.

Second, a testimony arising from a common context is not a christian testimony unless it reflects a fundamental option which is born of the primordial witness of Jesus Christ. That implies that the

---

[65] William EVERETT, Liturgy and Ethics, p. 211.

profane must bear the potential of being interpreted in view of the cross. Hence the "crossing" of the profane is understood in a double sense, as a passage and as a marking. Furthermore, the notion of the profane is not to be defined in a narrow negative sense, but as the matter in which penultimate values can arise;[66] that is, values without which the ultimate (religiously speaking, the Kingdom of God) is not brought to bear, because it is not recognized as such.

The trial of testimonies exemplifies the tension between the ultimate and the penultimate values. It is the traffic that goes on between the awareness of Wholeness and the market square of profane opinions. As negative possibility a testimony may lack credibility if there is a denial of the profane anchoring of existence in this world, if an experience of the Holy is detached to such an extent from common existence that one no longer knows specifically from what it is detached. As positive possibility, the trial can result in an affirmation of the paradox "already and not yet," that is of the ambivalence which affirms life in spite of the defeat of existence experienced through the lack of justice and love.

6.4.3.2. Stepping Down from the Sacred in Order to Bring Wholeness to the Profane

It follows that christian liturgy is not only an involvement with the holy mysteries. It needs a sense of mission in order to be meaningful.

As the visions consulted illustrate there can be an ethical dimension which joins the actual proclamation of Christ's love. As a negative possibility visions can operate as a purely regressive retreat into the bosom of the uncontaminated community.[67] Then

---

[66] Cf. Dietrich BONHOEFFER, Ethics. London, 1955, pp. 103-119.

[67] This, of course, is an illusion which sooner or later is uncovered. If the christian community is aware of its role as a community of interpretation such ideologies and utopian images can be pointed out. Cf. 3.2.3.1.2.

wholeness to the profane is denied. As positive possibility, a vision generates commitment and action for the healing of the profane by drawing it into the influence of the kingdom of God.

The double movement between the Sacred and the profane thus affirms the importance of elaborating criteria for a hermeneutic of religious narratives which are "bilingual." Either pre-reflective thought originates primarily but not exclusively[68] from a worldly context (generally, testimony), or it is largely drawn from a religious matrix (generally, visions). Liturgy, since it consists of this double movement, is the necessary contextual reference which allows the mimetic representation of life to be interpreted in a christian way. It may be as the recital of root experiences (tragic or "comic," but in any case peripeteic) or as a re-enactment and celebration of myths, though ideally of both.

6.5. A Short Anthropological Excursion

So far the argumentation for bilingual communication between the religious and the secular has mainly been based on linguistic grounds. Other avenues of reasoning, psychological or anthropological, could just as well be followed. On the anthropological level the challenge of bilingualism could be transposed to the relationship between modern society and religious ritual. In the context of this study two areas of interest would in that case deserve special attention. First, what are the social dynamics in the ritual process? Second, in what way can ritual effect social change?

---

[68] The first mimetic moment, because it arises from a culturally conditioned understanding of temporality, contains in a pre-reflective way already religious ideas. (2.3.6.3.)

6.5.1. Victor TURNER and the "Liminal" Phase in Ritual

In his book The Ritual Process Victor TURNER discusses in great
detail central African rites and their relationship to social
structures.[69] His starting point is Arnold VAN GENNEP's well known
study on "rites of passage."[70] These rites accompany mankind through
fundamental changes in life and provide guidance in crisis situations.
According to VAN GENNEP they facilitate the transition to a new stage
of life (e.g. from celibacy to marital responsibility) by means of a
three-phase ritual. The first phase separates the individual or group
from the "normal" cultural conditions. The second phase brings the
ritual subject to an ambivalent marginal situation, a "threshold" to a
new awareness of existence. This phase is called liminal in reference
to the Latin word limen, "threshold." The third phase is referred to
as "reaggregation," a reincorporation into the established social
order. Now it is not only interesting to note that formally the plot
of a testimony, as well as its liturgical setting, contain parallels
with the three phases of a rite of passage.[71] More importantly, the
liturgical giving of a testimony (and in a certain sense the
prophetical utterance) is in itself bearing the marks of a rite of

---

[69] When Victor TURNER refers to "structure" he means basically social
customs and conventions as opposed to anti-structures of socially
"deviant" behaviour, not to the logical categories and relational
forms of structuralists such as LEVI-STRAUSS. Victor W. TURNER, The
Ritual Process. Structure and Anti-Structure, London, 1966, pp. 166f.

[70] Arnold VAN GENNEP, The Rites of Passage, London, 1960 (1909).

[71] As far as the testimony itself is concerned, the separation phase
formally corresponds to the "journey," the detachment from the story's
initial situation. The liminal phase relates in the analysis of fairy
tales and testimonies to the existential experience of the protagonist
(e.g. the transfiguration, the branding, or the fulfillment of the
task). Even the theme of metamorphosis in the visions can in fact be
interpreted as a liminal experience. Cf. the vision in Testimony (D)
lines 161-180, and Vision (F) lines 11ff. The reaggregation phase
parallels the hero's journey back home. In terms of the liturgical
frame of reference, the phase of separation is represented in the
frequently different geographical location or architectural setting.
The liminal phase is seen in the transitional aspect of rituals as
such. Finally the phase of reincorporation is evident in the
benediction and exhortation to pragmatic commitment.

passage. It is liminal in so far as the content of what is being said is momentarily marginal. The narrative disclosure is, in its symbolic representation and metaphorical power, lifted from the hinges of socially dictated references and yet it can be understood in relation to social life. This statement can be explained by Victor TURNER's insights into liminality.

TURNER observed in his anthropological studies that the liminal phase did something peculiar to established social structures. Liminal entities (the ritual reversal of roles, for instance, or a religious status elevation[72]) temporally suspend social norms, because they are ambiguous and between the positions assigned by convention. TURNER describes it as follows,

> We are presented, in such rites, with a "moment in and out of time," and in and out of secular social structure, which reveals, however fleetingly, some recognition of a generalized social bond that has ceased to be and has simultaneously yet to be fragmented into a multiplicity of structural ties.[73]

This "'moment in and out of time' and in and out of secular social structure" can lead to a spontaneous sense of community where status systems become irrelevant. Distinctions of wealth, rank, and rights give way to homogeneity, totality, and equality.[74] And yet, the liminal aspects of ritual do, by displaying an anti-structure, relate to the social reality of the participants. Liminality gives "recognition to an essential and generic human bond, without which there could be no society. Liminality implies that the high could not be high unless the low existed..."[75] In other words, a ritual which has a "threshold experience" as its center is mythic in character.

---

[72] An example of the former would be an annual college dinner where the students are served by faculty members. An example of status elevation can be noticed when lay people fulfill religiously sophisticated functions on special occasions.

[73] Victor TURNER, The Ritual Process, p. 96.

[74] Note the comments on the liminal phase of early Pentecostalism in Appendix I.

[75] Victor TURNER, The Ritual Process, p. 97, emphasis his.

One can apply this anthropological interpretation of the liminal
phase in a specific sense to the tension between the religious and the
secular.[76] When the threshold of the deeply personal is crossed, then
the distinction between the religious and the secular have become
irrelevant. In other words, if a personal narrative is communicated
eventfully (cf. Richard FENN), then the secular and the religious have
found a common denominator because both are being addressed. For a
short period the problem of bilingualism is suspended into one
linguistic expression, not because the two domains[77] flow indis-
tinguishably together, but because they constitute together a new
narrative horizon. If a ritual context is given then a spontaneous
community (in the sense of V. TURNER's **communitas**[78]) is formed and the
individual is involved in a hermeneutic process with others. This
hermeneutic process is the social result of a liminal disclosure,
which does not exclude, theologically speaking, that this process can
also be interpreted as a gift of God's Spirit.

---

[76] Liminality, as Victor TURNER has defined it, is used as a designation of ritual paradoxical behaviour. I have chosen to emphasize one
aspect of liminality, namely the temporal overcoming of social
conventions, specifically the overcoming of the conventional contrast
between the religious and the secular.

[77] The classical distinction between the secular and the religious (or
the sacred and the profane popularized by Emile DURKHEIM) is
conventional, as Sally F. MOORE and Barbara G. MEYERHOFF are careful
to point out. For in some societies the mundane itself is contained by
the sacred, and in others the sacred is not an inherent quality, but
an attribution given to things. Sally F. MOORE and Barbara G.
MEYERHOFF Secular Ritual. Forms and Meanings, in Secular Ritual, Sally
F. MOORE and Barbara G. MEYERHOFF (eds.), Assen, 1977, pp. 22f.

[78] Victor TURNER distinguishes three forms of community that are at
variance with given structures of society. First, there are
spontaneous communities that represent an anti-structure to society
(e.g. a "happening" in the language of the hippies of the 1960s, or
the original fellowship around St. Francis of Assisi). This type of
community is closely related to liminal phenomena. Second, there are
normative communities representing an attempt to preserve the charisma
of former spontaneous communities (e.g. pentecostal denominations, or
certain labour unions). Third, there are ideological communities that
try to formulate an utopian social structure (e.g. secret societies).
The second and the third type already stand in some relation with
structured society. Cf. Victor TURNER, The Ritual Process, pp. 132f.
and Variations on a Theme of Liminality, in Secular Ritual, Sally F.
MOORE and Barbara G. MEYERHOFF (eds.), Assen, 1977, pp. 46.

The point to be made is that the subject is willing to make concessions regarding the existing social structures (or secular conventions) in a liminal phase, provided it is surrounded in an appropriate ritual setting.[79] This has little to do with psychological kidnapping, rather it is a peripheral social legitimation to "bracket" the norms in order to reappropriate them. But what happens from an anthropological point of view if the norms are not reappropriated?

6.5.2. The Relationship Between Ritual and Social Change

Emile DURKHEIM expressed the conviction that social conditions would influence ritual behaviour and not the other way around. The collective consciousness of society, he believed, was the generator of universal reason. Secular man would strip off the aura of mystery that religious reason still provided.[80] More recently, however, scholars like Robert BOCOCK question the validity of this point of view. In his sociological analysis of ritualism in modern England[81] BOCOCK claimed that the emergence of recent counter-cultures with their specific rituals (e.g. the psychedelic pop culture of the late sixties) had a definite influence on society as a whole moving it toward a simpler life style and a re-valuation of creative activity as differentiated from organized work.[82]

Basically the relationship between ritual action and the social state of affairs is twofold. "... either it can provide a process whereby people become more attached to the basic way of life and

---

[79] A "cryptic" form of liminality, where only the insiders can benefit from a particular ritual, is conceivable. A constructive form of liminality could be called "open," and understood to lead to an atmosphere of wholeness. There, the secular person could encounter lay participation, the presence of various social strata and the coherence of temporality with mythic time in relation to an ethical paradigm.

[80] Emile DURKHEIM, Les formes élémentaires, pp. 631-638.

[81] Robert BOCOCK, Ritual in Industrial Society. A Sociological Analysis in Modern England, London, 1974.

[82] Robert BOCOCK, Ritual, p. 185f.; see also Victor TURNER, Variations, pp. 39-43, where he discusses the relationship between work and leisure with regard to liminal action.

values of the society,... or ritual can lead to people making new
demands on the way of life in their society, and a desire to see
change both in action and in the values the society pursues."[83]
Testimonial activity as it has been analyzed in this study can be
associated with the first case. Problems of theodicy are lifted with a
peripeteic turn in favour of the believer's faith as well as his
situation in society. Visionary activity, when it is prophetic, would
qualify as an element for change in society. This deserves further
attention.

A number of sociological studies suggest, according to Léo
LAEYENDECKER and Mady THUNG, that it is to be doubted that churches
are able to act as an ameliorative agent in society.[84] They advance
various reasons to underline this assumption. First, if the churches
are courageous and advocate ethically responsible but unpopular forms
of social behaviour, then society is unlikely to pay much attention.
On the other hand, if the churches make no demands at all, then
society has nothing to respond to positively. A second reason is that
within the churches there is little consensus - even among the church
members of the same congregation. A third possible argument is that
participation in church activities is generally based on other
motivations than social reform.

If one shares the premise that sociological structures shape the
dynamics of religious bodies and their ritual activity (E. DURKHEIM)
then one can argue that if the churches would adapt their organizational set-up to a pluralist society they might gain more social
pertinence. Along this line one understands the efforts of certain
priests to involve themselves in social action. This idea, as far as
Europe is concerned, had little impact on the social relevance of the
church as a whole, for those committed to reform did not deem it

---

[83] Robert BOCOCK, Ritual, p. 174.

[84] Léo LAEYENDECKER and Mady A. THUNG, Liturgy in a Politically
Engaged Church, in Actes de al 14ème conférence internationale de
sociologie des religions Strassbourg 1977, Lille, 1977. p. 109. The
same conviction is shared by Gerhard Schmidtchen based on a demoscopic
study indicating that the value of liturgical reform stands in direct
relation to the reforms taking place in society; in Gottesdienst in
einer rationalen Welt, Stuttgart, 1973, pp. 147f.

necessary to consult a minister to aid in achieving their aims. Adversely, the community of the faithful asked for spiritual assistance, and not for political programs.[85] But the idea of a change in the organizational set-up need not be limited to a modified job description of the clergy. It can also evolve around the use of language and the means of communication, and then it becomes an issue of the whole body of believers. What then can be said about a communicative organizational set-up?

It has been argued that the effects of secularization on worship are strongly felt with regard to the increased attention paid to the liturgy of the word as opposed to sacramental celebration.[86] In other words, the laity can cope with the diversification of opinions by means of communication, but it is a different matter to reunite the various elements in the church under the common bond of, for instance, the eucharist. This is not to say that the sacramental aspects of worship become less important, but it does indicate that if the church wants to be relevant as a reforming agent in society, it can not allow herself to maintain a mystic fellowship assuming that the rituals **ex opere operato** establish the necessary ferment of the Gospel in twentieth century western society. A relationship between word and sacrament that the religious as well as the secular man can appreciate has to be established.[87] In view of what has been said about the ritual process, it is easy to understand why Georges DE SCHRIJVER believes that the secular person is most likely to appreciate a correlation between word and sacrament if initiation rites relate more directly to his biographical experiences (in both the sociological and

---

[85] In Europe a catholic priest can hardly, from an organizational point of view, be the administrator of sacraments and the revolutionary social worker at the same time. The problems are discussed in Jean REMY, Emile SERVAIS, and J. Pierre HIERNAUX, Formes liturgiques et symboliques sociales, in Social Compass 22,2 (1975), especially pp. 186-192.

[86] Rainer VOLPE, La liturgie en tant que comportement social, in Social Compass 22,2 (1975), pp. 159f.

[87] However, it is clear that the church can not comply with every wish of society without compromising its **raison d'être**. Louis-Marie CHAUVET warns in this respect that worship is not to degenerate into another commodity of consumption on the secular market, Du symbolique, p. 278.

narrative sense of the word).[88] That means that fundamental religious
concerns should be brought into relationship with serious secular
concerns; a relationship between the ultimate christian response-
ability and the penultimate social response-ability.

Two problems must be kept in mind. The first has already been
mentioned in relation to Robert BELLAH's contribution evolving around
the trend to privatize religious experience (3.5.1.). The second is
taken up by Léo LAEYENDECKER and Mady A. THUNG in dialogue with Basil
BERNSTEIN,[89] who distinguishes between two speech-codes capable of
verbalizing explicitly symbolic intent: a restricted and an elaborate
one. The restricted code is characterized by a high degree of
predictability. That means that the speaker has a limited range of
formulations, notions, and formal elements with which to converse,
because they are limited by the communicative circumstance and
content. BERNSTEIN gives three examples: the conversation in a
cocktail-party, the telling of a fairy tale, a liturgical celebration.[90] The elaborate code, on the other hand, has a low degree of
predictability. The range of possible alternatives is fairly large;
the number of commonly shared indentifications, assumptions, and
expectations is accordingly low. Secularization and pluralism in
society seems to have brought about a move from the usage of
restricted codes to elaborate ones. This can, for example, be noticed
in the socializing function of the family. In earlier generations
socialization was often positional, the "we" was highly valued in view
of clearly defined social boundries (e.g. the father was the head of

---

[88] "In een cultuur die, post-traditioneel, een bijzondere waarde hecht
aan de eigen levensgang en de biographische expressie van de persoon,
is de natuurlijke ondergeschiktheid van de persoon aan het collectivum
zoek... Dit maakt dat de inzet voor bekommernissen (**concerns**) van heil
en heilzaamheid een intensere persoonlijke en existentiële noot zal
kennen... Als er dan een opeenvolging van 'fasen van initiatie' is,
zal die in hoofdzaak te zoeken zijn in de persoonlijke levens-
geschiedenis en in de bewogenheid van telkens nieuwe levenskeuzen."
Georges DE SCHRIJVER, Initiatie in het heilige in een post-theïstische
religiositeit, Katholieke Universiteit Leuven, 1984, pp. 14f.

[89] Léo LAEYENDECKER and Mady A. THUNG, Liturgy, pp. 118f.

[90] Léo LAEYENDECKER and Mady A. THUNG, Liturgy, p. 119, quoting Basil
BERNSTEIN, Class, Codes and Control, Vol. I, London 1971, pp. 126ff.

the family). Contemporary family life, however, is characterized by a high valuation of the individual. A strong degree of differentiation and communication is assured, the "I" is placed above the "we."

Basil BERNSTEIN's analysis clearly poses difficulties for a re-valuation of narratives in worship in view of social secularization. The restricted form of communication through testimonies (the Proppian analysis is an example thereof) and the limited scope of sacramental reference in liturgy could discourage the church from being prophetic in today's society. But a second look at the issue brings useful and positive insight into the matter, provided the parameters of worship and of the role of the church are widened.

I would suggest that the christian churches should pay increased attention to a fruitful dialectic between the "we" and the "I," that is, between restricted communication with a strong communal emphasis, and an elaborate code which has the ability to take up specific issues for the sake of the threatened **humanum**. Narrative communication could be a valid currency in this dialectic because it can relate to both aspects. It is person-oriented because testimonies and visions reflect personal struggles, and given the possibility of bifurcation (cf. Claude BREMOND and **peripeteia**) it is able to widen the restricted code. The fact that religious narratives have their **Sitz im Leben** in worship suggests that they could mediate between the material aspects of daily life and the symbolic dimension of existence.[91] The two factors could contribute to a wholesome fusion of a) a proclamation and celebration of ultimate values, b) a reflection on ethical conduct, and c) the engagement in carefully chosen social action.[92]

---

[91] Louis-Marie CHAUVET considers sacramental worship as a chance for secular man to re-enter a liberating symbolic exchange, Du symbolique, p. 277ff. Similarly David HOLLENBACH, A Prophetic Church and the Catholic Sacramental Imagination, in John C. HAUGHEY (ed.), The Faith that Does Justice. Examining the Christian Sources for Social Change, New York, 1977, pp. 249-260.

[92] This threefold activity of the christian church is not only mentioned in Léo LAEYENDECKER and Mady A. THUNG, Liturgy, pp. 121f., but is the general tenor of recent forms of liberation theology. Especially the maintenance of the sacramental dimension in worship to give due attention to the affective dimension of life is now frequently advocated; cf. David HOLLENBACH, A Prophetic Church, pp. 234-263 (cf. the various reasons and examples mentioned).

This fusion would do justice to a responsible handling of myth (chapter 1), to a hermeneutic considering syntax, semantic meaning, and pragmatic commitment (chapter 2), and to a correlation between christian and non-christian communication (chapter 3).

The insights gained from an anthropological point of view as they relate specifically to a liturgical context can be enumerated in order to conclude this excursion. Firstly, the discussion on liminality has shown that the nature of a rite of passage disposes the participants to "bracket" certain social conventions which are often put forward as a hinderance to a dialogue between the religious and the secular domain of experience. Secondly, if the church wants to be prophetically active as a salvific/ameliorative agent in society, it can only do so if the prophetic ferment is present in the whole church, that is, if the ministers **and** the laity can meditate, formulate, and actively participate in bringing about wholeness in the name of Christ. Otherwise society is likely to disregard a call to conversion.

6.6. <u>A Liturgical Blueprint</u>

At this point the liturgical consequences can be discussed. Should participants of worship be encouraged to express themselves in ways similar to the narratives studied in chapters 4 and 5? As was the case in the biblical traditions,[93] one can recognize a basically dual narrative function in worship; first a catechetical, and second a doxological one.

6.6.1. <u>Liturgy as a School of Faith</u>

The famous roman catholic liturgist Josef Andreas JUNGMANN presented in 1957 a speech with the title "Liturgy as a School of Faith".[94] Although much has changed on the catholic scene since the

---

[93] Cf. the various sections in 1.1.

[94] Josef Andreas JUNGMANN, <u>Liturgie als Schule des Glaubens</u>, in <u>Liturgisches Erbe und pastorale Gegenwart</u>, Innsbruck, 1960, pp. 437-450.

liturgical reforms of the Second Vatican Council, and much is different in other christian contexts, it seems that JUNGMANN has set significant accents. He recognized the potential of liturgical activity as **Menschenführung, Lebensorientierung** and **Lebensmeisterung.** In short, he saw in liturgy a pedagogic tool assisting the believer to find genuine fulfillment in life.

In this task he discerned three basic goals. The first was a general orientation of the believer to God. A liturgical celebration could be understood as a "counterpoint" to a materialistic "dominant" in daily life.[95] One could add that the practice of worship is also a "counterpoint" to an individualistic "dominant" in daily life. JUNGMANN considered the second goal to be that the liturgy would represent an image of the christian world view. Prayer, the eucharist, and proclamation should constantly bring the reality of the risen Christ to mind. For JUNGMANN this was not so much of dogmatic importance as it is intended to clarify the religious experiences of daily life.[96] The third goal was to re-evaluate liturgy as common act of the church. Liturgy was not to be the performance of the clerics, but a gathering of the people of God who live in the world.[97] To rephrase JUNGMANN's pastoral approach one can say that a) liturgy is only meaningful if it relates to man's existence in the world, b) that the church is only church if the whole "body" is involved, and c) that worship can help to bring the religious experiences of daily life to a positive trial.

A compatriot of JUNGMANN, Hans HOLLERWEGER, has indirectly taken up the theme of liturgy as school of faith and tried to relate man's existential situation to liturgical celebration.[98] According to him,

---

[95] Josef A. JUNGMANN, Schule, p. 441.

[96] Josef A. JUNGMANN, Schule, pp. 444ff.

[97] "Wenn so die Kirche lebendig wird in den Teilnehmern an einer lebendig gefeierten Liturgie, da entsteht auch ein neues Verhältnis zur umgebenden Welt, auch zur materiellen Welt, auch zur Welt der Arbeit und des Berufes. Denn es ist ja der konkrete Mensch von Fleisch und Blut, der hineingenommen wird in den Vorgang der Liturgie."
Josef A. JUNGMANN, Schule, p. 448.

[98] Hans HOLLERWEGER, Die Liturgie als Antwort auf die Grundsituationen

man is thrown in a Heideggerian fashion into temporality and space where he is challenged to live as a free being. In his temporality, man "is unto death"; living in space, he is bound to relationships with fellowmen; faced with freedom, he is aware of a fundamental task.

HOLLERWEGER believes that in the eucharist the liturgy should answer man's existence unto death by celebrating the victory of Christ. Furthermore, the liturgy (presumably the celebration of the mass) should be a demonstration of christian unity in order to be an example to man's spatial existence, that is to his social reality. Finally, HOLLERWEGER would like to see man's task to use his freedom constructively encouraged by meaningful sacramental celebration. This is, however, only possible according to him if the sacraments are in a certain sense secularized.[99] This means that sacraments are to be explained from the context of human existence and the life and work of Jesus, and not simply in terms of metaphysical mysteries and the glory of the risen Christ. HOLLERWEGER has made an important contribution in so far as he has tried to introduce those aspects into the praxis of worship which concern human beings existentially every day in their lives. He has done so by relying on the narrative of Jesus Christ.

A third contribution to liturgy as a school of faith has been advanced by Rudolf SCHLENDER.[100] His aim is to establish a dialectic between the fundamental ambivalences of human life and the foundational symbol of Jesus Christ. These two ambivalences, following the theory of K.E. NIPKOW, are the tension between repetition and renewal and the tension between action and contemplation. At the intersection of these ambivalences Jesus Christ figures as integrative principle, as symbolic catalyser of human experience and christian life. But how can liturgy provide access to Christ as foundational symbol? SCHLENDER gives random but significant suggestions: by communicating Jesus as a storyteller, as a person ministering healing, and as a reformer of

---

des Menschen, in Zeitschrift für katholische Theologie 107, 1+2 (1985), pp. 64-75.

[99] Hans HOLLERWEGER, Liturgie als Antwort, p. 74.

[100] Rudolf SCHLENDER, Lernen im Erfahrungsraum Gemeinde, in Erfahrungen in religiösen Lernprozessen, Göttingen, 1983, pp. 191-200.

societal structures.[101] These suggestions are significant because, a) they favour the narrative communicability of Jesus Christ as master over the ambivalences of human life, and b) such a manner of communication is likely to be understood by all, even the secularized person not trained in religious language games, for he is faced with the same questions and is acquainted with the same basic structures through which the ambivalent tensions of his own life are brought to words.

The three theologians referred to have related the catechetical value of narratives to the story of Jesus Christ and its sacramental dimension. Their concern was to relate the **cantus firmus** of the christian faith to secular reality. The study of religious testimonies and visions has brought another pedagogic dimension of faith to light, namely the personal articulation of what is believed to be of ultimate concern. And the question arises whether such articulations have a right to be uttered only in the class room, the family table, the sick bed, or the counsellor's office. Pentecostals would answer that testimonies and visions fulfill a kerygmatic and edificational function which is essential to church life and therefore belong to the liturgy just as much as hymns and prayers. Further, they would argue that these elements have an essential place in worship, since Judaism and early Christianity practiced a narrative communication too. Seeing the issue with the eyes of a **second naïveté** one would, however, be bound to ask whether such narratives should, besides the kerygmatic and edificational, not also include a critical function.

Liturgically speaking, the catechetical function of religious narratives finds its suitable place in the Liturgy of the Word. Since God is understood to be an authorial participant in the communication of faith, it follows that testimonial or prophetic narratives cannot precede the invocation of God, an invocation which would include an epiclectic request.[102] The call upon God (the Holy Spirit) to bless

---

[101] Rudolf SCHLENDER, Lernen, p. 193.

[102] Although an epiclesis has traditionally been associated with the eucharistic prayer, and there it does indeed play a central role (see below), it would be shortsighted to fail to perceive that the whole liturgy is celebrated in the presence and power of God's Spirit. Cf. J.D. CRICHTON, A Theology of Worship, in Cheslyn JONES **et al.**, The Study of Liturgy, London, 1978, pp. 16f.

human gifts for the sake of worship, in this case the gift of communicating the secular Gospel (i.e. the christian reality in everyday life), is a necessary pact acknowledging self-transcending reality. For the non-religious person the epiclesis is a comprehensible sign of serious intention and responsibility comparable to the oath in the court of justice. In sum, testimonial confessions of faith (or the struggle with the same) are of catechetical value because they reflect christian response-ability and provide a living context for praise, the homily, and the communal proclamation of faith.

The critical function of a narrative is of catechetical value because it discourages the pretensions of absolute knowledge, and because it underlines the fact that a christian conscience does not allow an unreserved embracing of any **status quo.** It can be brought to bear when the minister has made an invitation to a confession of sins. This is not to be misunderstood as a public stripping of one's self by sharing an deeply personal testimony with grave aspects with which the witness has not yet come to grips. This would be tantamount to tasteless boulevard press voyeurism. The inclusion of testimonies as a non-violent appeal to faith and the convictions thereof would have to be non-violent in its own mechanism and carefully respect personal integrity. But where they can be brought to bear, the critical function of narratives would have a prophetic role which would express itself initially as a confession of failure to live up to christian values.

In addition, it is possible to tell "dangerous stories" (à la J.B. METZ) as a response to the readings and the homily. In such a case the performative aspect of narrative language would build a bridge between proclamation and application. One should remember that personal "dangerous stories" are only fruitful if they can relate to scriptural "dangerous stories." A personal account would be negatively dangerous if it were be self-centered.

Finally, worship as a school of faith would have to point to the delicate relationship between the three parties involved in the communication of testimonial and visionary narratives. As all parties (the narrator, God, and the interpreting community - religious and

secular) are addressed (**angesprochen**), they also have a claim
(**Anspruch**) to an answer. One cannot act **as if** the presence of God is
acknowledged, **as if** the secular domain is addressed, or **as if** the
witness is brought to trial. That means that the differentiated roles
come into play only if they are respected. If "faith comes from what
is heard and what is heard comes by the preaching of Christ" (Rom.
10:17), then the preaching of Christ has to contain the communicative
paradigm which elevates all who are involved to the stake that is at
play; that is the story of Jesus Christ as a metaphor of life.

6.6.2. The Doxological Function of Religious Narratives in Liturgy

Elie WIESEL is quoted as having said that he is telling stories
in order that prayers could be made.[103] In view of his experiences
with the Holocaust it is a negative experience that has to remain the
subject of prayers lest the memory of atrocities vanish from the
public mind. Positively speaking on the other hand, faith experiences
because they have found a resolution in that which can be said to be
true, good and beautiful, are an incentive to self-transcending praise
and the edification of the whole community. A structural parallel to
edificational narratives in liturgy can be found in many evocative
miracle stories of the gospels where the audience is said to have
responded by praising God. Naturally, the comparison is limited, for a
common belief in God cannot be taken for granted today. In belongs,
therefore, to the hermeneutic responsibility of the community to
relate faith to the public involvement in the world, and not to a
search for esoteric gratification.[104] To bring it to a point,

---

[103] To include prayers as a form of "narrative theology" seems to be
well established in Jewish thought; so for instance argues Schalom
BEN-CHORIN, Narrative Theologie des Judentums, p. 29.

[104] The contents of the liturgy would find a more popular
(**volkstümlich**) expression through the narrative activity of the common
priesthood, because every day vocabulary would find considerably more
usage. (Rudolf SCHLENDER, Lernen, p. 193. Cf. also: Rolf Dieter BRAUN,
Charisma und Liturgie) This would work against the tendency existing
in some historic churches which lean towards changing the contents of
liturgy into a culturally sophisticated aesthetic experience
(wonderful rhetoric, beautiful music). Of course, the dangers of

testimonies can only be metaphors of hope if they re-enact
(**nachvollziehen**) the incarnation. Precisely where faith touches on the
issues of life in this world, there a religious disclosure can take
place in the sense Ian RAMSEY suggested it. The reaction to such a
disclosure is not exhausted in a humanitarian commitment. There
remains a surplus which points to the presence of the Sacred, which
for the People of the Book is the God of Abraham, Isaac and Jacob.
Such a moment of surprise and awe finds then a doxological expression,
comparable to the Proppian function of "wedding."

6.6.3. Lay Participation Versus Order?

In all of this, fears that the christian message and worship are
lost in an ocean of words is justified. There is no doubt that an
order of worship is of prime importance so that a meaningful context
for those narratives and a christian intentionality can be maintained.
In the historic churches the liturgical order is so established that
changes for the benefit of lay participation are expected to be
suggested by the minister himself. In a similar way the participation
of para-church groups would in most cases be easy to integrate into an
act of worship. But the real question of order relates to the often
unannounced contributions of individuals and outsiders. For the goal
cannot be to incorporate prophetic activity in the proclamatory
apparatus of the church; this would institutionalize it and render it
meaningless. But the church at worship can foster prophetic consciousness by encouraging moral commitment[105] and providing the

popularized religious language must be remembered. Especially the
possible trivialization of religious experience must be avoided in so
far as it could weaken the theological message as well as the concrete
understanding of the problematic of life. The positive potential of
the democratization of faith is seen in expanding the "school of
faith" by making the borderline of communal worship and everyday life
less pronounced.

[105] Paul LOEFFER (in his article Das Zeugnis der Laien in der
säkularen Welt, in Gerhard SCHNATH (ed.), Fantasie für die Welt.
Gemeinden in neuer Gestalt, Stuttgart, 1967) knows that a description
of the task of the laity in the church is difficult to formulate. He
quotes from the Galayatetö Declaration of the World Council of
Churches, "Niemand von uns versteht im letzten Grunde, was der Dienst

structures for contextualizing prophetic pertinence religiously and socially.[106] In that case the resolution of the tension between spontaneous contribution and order would depend on courage and the charism of leadership. The history of the Church has shown that the balance between the two is hard to keep.

However, exaggerated fears are not helpful. First, to speak with the words of Raimundo PANIKKAR, the interplay between rubrics and "nigrics," just **because** it is a play, follows an established set of rules which define worship as such. To give a practical example: even a prophetic interruption is only understood if it retains by contrast ties to the "normal" order of worship.[107] Second, the study of Rolf-Dieter BRAUN emphasizes that the order of worship, even in an narratively enthusiastic liturgical context, as for instance in charismatic circles, is in so far guaranteed that the adepts learn "to play the game" and know when there is an opportune time for a narrative contribution.[108] The variations allowed for could be

des Laien in unserer so komplizierten modernen Welt eigentlich ist," and suggests that Christians should be animated to participate in the historical process of our time, recognizing hereby God's own encounter with the world (p. 123f.).

[106] Practically that would mean from a religious point of view that people are allowed to dream dreams and to share them in the light of the past heritage and the present situation. A catalytic agent, so that the dreams do not degenerate into utopian wishes or ideological impositions, is a celebration like the eucharist, provided it relates mythically to a presence of Christ in the world today. It is interesting to note that Carlo MOLARI also ends by relating witness and prophetic activity with sacramental worship and emphasizing the role of the community of interpretation. The Hermeneutical Rôle of the Christian Community on the Basis of Judaeo-Christian Experience, in Concilium 113 (1979), pp. 93-105.

[107] Besides, religious communities in the West by virtue of their institutionalized form already practice the game of talking as an institution as well as a "person." Various theologians have, because of this dual role of religious communication, referred to the notion of serious play. Cf. among others, Jerome W, BERRYMAN, Becoming Fundamentally Scriptural Without Being Fundamentalistic, Houston, 1984; Jean Jacques VON ALLMEN, Worship and the Holy Spirit; Hans Georg GADAMER's understanding of play as a basic hermeneutic notion (2.2.1.). All that is asked is the logical extention of the "odd" rules of communication.

[108] "Das Problem, wie das Bedürfnis nach vertrauten Abläufen und die

estimated at 5-10 %. More freedom is not desired since it would
destabilize the social dynamics within the community, dynamics which
believers experience as essential for retaining their sense of
communal integration. Furthermore, those who lead the worship service
have, due to their ministerial function, in most cases an acknowledged
authority to guide the liturgy with spiritual sensibility and
discipline.

Finally it must be admitted, any minister allowing for the
intrusion of testimonies and prophetic utterances will be taking a
risk.[109] The outcome of such speech situations and of the ensuing
communal response are not predictable. But risks are part of the
contingencies of life,[110] and make a liturgical celebration far more
credible than a pre-definded "mock trial" as Richard FENN dared to
call it.

The theoretical implications of the use of oral narratives in
worship have consciously been kept within a ecumenically open
framework. Only basic accents have been pointed out. In order to

angestrebte Spontaneität der verschiedenen Beiträge von Gemeinde-
gliedern verbunden werden können, hat man durch die Gliederung des
Gottesdienstes in mehrere Teile gelöst: Innerhalb des jeweiligen
Rahmens besteht eine ausreichende Entfaltungsmöglichkeit für die
einzelnen Charismen; andererseits gibt es eine Grundstruktur und
jeweils einführende Ueberleitungen, so dass Unsicherheiten bei den
Gottesdienstteilnehmern vermieden werden." Rolf-Dieter BRAUN, Charisma
und Liturgie. Die liturgische Praxis in laikalen Gemeinden mit
charismatischer Prägung dargestellt am Beispiel der "Freien Christen-
gemeinde in Altensteig", Tübingen, 1983, p. 29.

[109] "Kein Fest ohne Risiko. Wer narrative Zeugnisse im Gottesdienst
zulässt, auch in Form einer Berichterstattung nach einem 'Gespräch in
allen Bänken'... muss mit Ueberraschungen rechnen. Die Predigt 'aus
vieler Zeugen Mund' ist nicht glatt geschliffen, aber glaubwürdig.
Selbst was peinlich berührt, ist menschlich. Und Menschlichkeit kann
das Fest als 'Erweiterung des Bewusstseins- und Lebensfeldes' nicht
behindern. Es sei denn, unsere Feste sollten vom Alltag ablenken. Und
das sollen sie gewiss nicht." Dieter TRAUTWEIN, Mut zum Fest, München,
1975, p. 67.

[110] Any gap that might appear between the use of language and the
perception of reality can, because of the secularizing influence of
trial (cf. 3.2.5.2.1.), help to guarantee the seriousness of worship.

illustrate practically what could be implied, a narrative has been added as Postlude at the end of this study. It is based on actual research in a Nigerian Church in Birmingham, England. At the same time it is a piece of mimetic poetry; an image of how a worship service that takes the narrative expression of its community serious could be described.

6.6.4. The Liturgical and Secular Celebration of a Christian Myth

It had been mentioned on occasion that testimonial and visionary narratives could contain mythologizing potential and that it is therefore appropriate to place these narratives on the middle ground between the classic word/sacrament distinction.[111] That does not mean that one could call such narratives fullfledged myths in the literary or socio-religious sense, but it does indicate that they have a liturgical home, and more specifically that they would play an important role in providing substance to the presencing of myths; allowing for a movement from pre-reflective awareness to ethical responsibility, and the restructuration of human experiences. To bring the issue into focus, the thesis can be postulated that these narratives are able to function as a heuristic interpretation of a mythological tradition which otherwise can no longer be understood by secular man.[112]

---

[111] As the definition in chapter one already indicated, religious narratives tend to express an experience of grace. Along the same lines one may recall what has been said by Johann B. METZ (1.2.1.) and Langdon GILKEY (2.4.2.), namely, that life-stories should be integrated in sacramental action in order to acknowledge God's salvific activity in the individual and the community. As a consequence, the Christian becomes aware of his role as a symbol of God's love and presence.

[112] Louis-Marie CHAUVET argues, for instance, that the classic values of the sacred undergo a metamorphosis in secular society serving to the attribution of sacredness for non-religious values such as the history of progress and proletarian liberation. The challenge would lie in a prophetic contextualization of this tendency with the sacramental celebration of the liberating Easter-Event. Du symbolique, pp. 277-281.

In order to substantiate this claim I would like to illustrate how the celebration of the eucharist, as an act of worship, can integrate and energize narrative activity, orthodox reception and christian commitment. It is an example of what was referred to as "testimony of life" in chapter four.

In chapter one Walter HOLLENWEGER suggested interpreting the passages of I Corinthians 10-14 in the light of a social tension between the literate upper class, who had recourse to the writings of Paul, and the mostly illiterate middle and lower classes, who claimed inspiration due to the oral charisms. In this light the celebration of the unity of the christian body gains prophetic significance. Paul exhorts the factions in Corinth that in Christ there is no division, that the various members belong to the same body, and that it is the same Spirit who calls the believers, whether free or slave, whether educated or illiterate, to live out their faith by the grace of God.[113] The **agape** meal and the Lord's supper become the atmospheric medium for the sublimation and transformation of aggressions,[114] from socio-cultural inequality to reconciliation and common orientation based on the example and re-presented life of Jesus Christ.

---

[113] "Or, ce qui est intéressant à Corinthe, c'est que 'la maison de la culture des chrétiens', leur 'association culturelle' ne se séparait pas en deux fractions: une pour les illettrés et illuminés et une autre pour les bourgeois et les lecteurs. C'est là l'attrait fascinant, et je dirais révolutionaire de cette aventure inter-culturelle, que ces deux cultures opposées aient trouvé un terrain commun. Pas pour longtemps, evidemment, parce que bientôt l'Eglise subit les divisions culturelles habituelles. Cet échange culturel - que Paul illustre par le mythe du corps du Christ avec les différents organes - était au temps de l'Empire romain aussi étrange, nouveau, "socialement dysfonctionel" et peut-être même politiquement subversif qu'il l'est aujourd'hui; c'est pour cela que ce mythe a disparu, et c'est justement pour cela, je pense, qu'il faut le redécouvrir." Walter J. HOLLENWEGER, Le livre oral, p. 126.

[114] The social tensions between Greek and Barbarian, between rich and poor, high and low, are transformed, in the light of the suffering and final victory of Jesus Christ, to a commitment of reconciliation and love. The Lord's supper is a successful myth because it is not merely experienced as the mystical body of Christ, but rather as the social body here and now. Cf. Walter J. HOLLENWEGER, Prophetische Verkün-digung, in Das missionarische Wort 31,2 (1978), pp. 55-57.

It is self-evident that the Corinthian example did not survive in its ideal form for very long. The social, inter-cultural, and perhaps the political, pressures were too strong to maintain the heterogeneous group of bankers, merchants, house slaves, port officials and dockers.[115] But this is no sufficient reason to speak of a failure. On the contrary, the celebration of Christ in Corinth underlines the necessity to encourage the witnesses to come to trial, and the prophets to interrupt the normal flow of affairs so that the sustaining myths are continuously re-interpreted in the light of the present circumstances (the musical "counter point" as Dietrich BONHOEFFER called it) and the **cantus firmus** of the christian faith.[116] Only then is a **metanoia** possible that saves mankind from **hybris** and brings healing to the unredeemed.

The celebration of the eucharist, then, is only one, but perhaps the most important, example of how the community can mythologically reflect on, and publicly demonstrate its mission in the world by being a witness of the world to the church, and in turn by being a witness to the world in the name of Christ.

6.7. Concluding Remarks

6.7.1. Coming Back to the Suggested Definition of Worship

The definition explained worship as a dialectical movement between God and the believer underlining the dimensions of, a) ascribing worth to God, and b) inviting to an encounter with the

---

[115] A heterogeneous compilation of the Corinthian church can be deduced from the name lists, references to housing, and travel descriptions in the Pauline correspondence. Cf. Gerd THEISSEN, Soziale Schichtung in der korinthischen Gemeinde. Beitrag zur Soziologie des hellenistischen Urchristentums, in Zeitschrift für neutestamentliche Wissenschaft 65 (1974), pp. 232-272.

[116] For the context of Dietrich BONHOEFFER's terminology and the possible application to myth see Widerstand, pp. 142-144, 162, 166f., 183. Incidently, Dietrich BONHOEFFER's life and tragic death is also an illustration of a "testimony of life," or of "biography as theology" in the words of Johann B. METZ.

Sacred. It is clear that both aspects only bear meaning if they are able to communicate via a religious disclosure. The central question was, are such disclosures still possible when a process of secularization has clouded the evocative power of formerly agreed upon God-talk? As it has been stated on several occasions, no language game is immune to the "usure of meaning,"[117] but it might be that existential narratives, i.e. life stories or plots tackling human fears and aspirations, can at least partially bridge the problem because they are not **a priori** religious, but make a religious interpretation possible or even desirable.

Closely related to the linguistic problem is the necessity of nursing symbolic perception.[118] Since many religious symbols are no longer understandable to a large segment of society, it could be fruitful to school symbolic perception on a more general level. The symbolic elements in narrative language are still accessible to secular man, because they relate to fundamental experiences of life. At the same time they open a way towards the appreciation of symbols of the Sacred in worship.

If the Christian is made aware that he is creator of symbols as well as a symbol himself, he may learn to appreciate his situation in time and space and be liberated from his individualist enclave to commit himself to action in the name of Christ, and to the benefit of his neighbor. Narratives of the past, present, and future allow him to find a place in society within "the will of God."

But there must be symbolic order **and more**, otherwise participation in worship could degenerate to a mere aesthetic experience. Testimonies ascertain that basic human concerns can be voiced and that a christian answer can be expected. They are open-ended. Ideally then, worship is a **locus vivendi** of religious narratives as well as of divine grace. Theologically, and from a human point of view, this can

---

[117] Cf. Jacques DERRIDA, Edward SCHILLEBEECKX and Richard FENN above.

[118] "In einer Zeit fortschreitender Desymbolisierung kann der Erfahrungsraum Gemeinde zu einem Ort werden, Erfahrungen gegen den Erfahrungsverlust zu machen.... Mit der Zerstörung von Symbolen geht auch die Zerstörung von Erfahrung einher, Ambivalenzvermeidung beinhaltet Erfahrungsverlust." Rudolf SCHLENDER, Lernen, p. 198.

be formulated as follows. Religious narratives in worship should contribute either to a confession of faith in view of the transcendent, to an active commitment as a sign of christian love, or to an affirmation of hope and healing in the face of suffering. Speaking in a secular way, this means that the contingencies of life are seen in communal celebration as an integral challenge towards wholeness.[119]

6.7.2. The Contribution of a Narrative Synthesis between the Terrestrial and the Celestial

Various and many have been the attempts for liturgical renewal in this century. First by the Roman Catholic church and the Anglican communion, later in the other historic churches; recently even the independent free churches and christian groups, which frequently do not profess to have an elaborate liturgical apparatus, have begun to search for more meaningful ways of worship, either because there has been renewed reflection on the biblical roots of christian doxology, or because it has become evident that many forms of worship are no longer understandable to a large segment of the population. But the anthropological excursion on ritual and the prophetic impact on a secular world has shown that liturgical reform cannot be achieved simply by integrating stories into the order of worship. The aim of this thesis, then, was to study the value of certain oral narratives in view of the criticism posed by the circumstances of a secular society, and in view of christian values that are traditionally considered to be timeless.

Raimundo PANIKKAR's dictum that only worship can prevent secularization from becoming inhuman, and only secularization can save worship from becoming meaningless points to the necessity of a theological approach that is contextual. In a similar way Romano GUARDINI has pleaded for a "theology of life" and secular sainthood.[120] The incarnation of theological claims into the fabric of

---

[119] In the final analysis, the explanation of what wholeness contains will depend upon the one or the other thought model. As a Christian I would, therefore, not be able to construct a purely secularist concept of wholeness.

daily life, or the contextualization of mundane experiences into a framework of faith is the aim envisaged. It corresponds to Paul RICOEUR's open dialectic between ideology and utopia. Narratives that are born in the world, trans-valued in the communal celebration of faith, and brought back in form of a practical response are a valid tool for such an approach.

Mundane stories, if they lead to a disclosure in a religious context, may also lead into prayer and confession of faith. The evocative power of narrative could transform moments of existential anxiety into an incarnation of creeds, that is in a congruence between dogma and praxis, and thus suggest an answer to theodicy, a moment of praise, a call to action.[121] Along the same lines one can also understand a claim to the everlasting value of divine words in spite of the transitory nature of language. Even if expressions become encrusted and incomprehensible, even if religious phraseology suffers under the usure of time, the words of Jesus do not pass away precisely because they are embedded in a story line which by means of its structure and the surplus it creates resurfaces again and again even if individual words lose their currency. The plot of life always comes up with new questions, and God's story with Israel and the nations, with Jesus and the church, constantly provides pertinent and sometimes also impertinent answers.

Another reason why I believe in a contribution of narrative to a synthesis between christian faith and secular values explains itself by the dialogue that it creates. Sacred narratives or myths represent the divine side, and the dialectical appearance of truth in dialogue stands for the human side in the temporal interpretation of the

---

[120] This idea has been taken up and elaborated upon in James. W. McCLENDON, Jr., Biography as Theology. How Life Stories Can Remake Today's Theology, Nashville, 1974, cf. especially pp.179-203.

[121] Karl Ferdinand MUELLER has triggered this insight although he has a more pessimistic view of prayer and the role of creeds. When he says, "Perhaps to modern man today prayer often means nothing more than a conscious but helpless standing before God with all that this entails, i.e. with empty hands"(p. 92) he may be right, especially in those circumstances when "modern man" is not allowed to carry his daily preoccupations and dreams into church. Karl Ferdinand MUELLER, Living Worship, in Studia Liturgica 7, 2-3 (1970), pp. 86-95.

Gospel. However, such an approach is only possible if, on the divine side, one allows for a more dynamic role of the Holy Spirit in the life of the church,[122] and on the human side, when liturgy is made public. Here is a chance for the christian church to draw positive potential from the pluralistic cross-section of religious opinions, because the public realm, even if it is fictitious, is at its base neutral and a concern to all.

6.7.3. A Contribution to Theory Formation

An unstated presupposition which initiated this study was the conviction that human life and relations are quite fragile. Modern society makes a lot of tough demands on the individual, and the need for gentleness in human relations is often overlooked. The fundamental question arises, is there room for a nonviolent hermeneutic? Without trying to answer this aporetic question, I have tried to delegate power to the word, rather than to the interpreter, to allow the narrative to make claims, rather than to allow the narrator to speak for himself. As a logical consequence, the act of interpretation had to be made public, that is, accessible to all who can and are willing to listen to what is being claimed or proclaimed.

---

[122] As varied as are the emphases in the different pneumatological models in the New Testament are, there are, according to Piet SCHOONENBERG, a number of effects of the Spirit that they have in common. (Piet SCHOONENBERG, Baptism with the Holy Spirit, in Concilium, 10 (1974), pp. 25f.) Two of these relate directly to what has been referred to above as hermeneutic activity of the Spirit. The first allows for a conscious and identifiable christian experience. The second affects the physical perception of man. Fullness of the Spirit in the New Testament is an experience that transcends the separation between spirit and matter and builds unity.
It is for this reason that I see an ecumenical impact emanating from an appropriate use of religious narratives. If there is a sensitivity to spiritual guidance in the different christian churches, then it seems inevitable that genuine experiences are shared beyond the local and institutional boundries. The effects of sharing the same stories in spite of diverging theological models would eventually lead to an active recognition that no **one** institution has a definite claim on pneumatological and dogmatic activity.

It is important, as the first part of this study has indicated, to understand the bilingual nature of existential concerns if ideas are to be communicated between two or more value systems. Language fluctuates between self consciousness and social institution, between metaphor and discursive language, between structure and intentionality. Since narratives have the ability to be symbolic as well as relational, it is reasonable to apply them to the dilemma existing between transcendent values and immanent perceptions.

A theory of hermeneutics is meaningful if it can be applied to the institutionalized form of language, that is, society. Otherwise, the interpretative system is caught in an ideological or utopian vacuum. Personal testimonies and visions, at least if they meet basic communicative criteria, happen to have society involved as **object** of concern. The essential theological point was to involve society as **subject** in dialogue, and to keep it in mind as **project** of wholeness. All that has been said so far underlines the fact that a hermeneutic act cannot be complete unless a pragmatic response is evident. It is not enough to understand, if one can understand at all, for to understand is to modify one's ways.

That implies that a structural analysis is incomplete even if one adds phenomenological, theological, or socio-religious explanantions. Interpretations are of pen-ultimate value and, therefore, a hermeneutic circle remains necessary. Unlike in the exact sciences, where an explanation of a repeatable experiment is sufficient, in the human sciences an explanation is only of temporal value. Nevertheless, as the analysis of religious narratives has shown, an interpretation is important. It can point to something unsaid. It may help the subject relate to others. It can disclose the next step of action. If a religious interpretation could be absolute, one could argue that specialists should be delegated to put it to use. But since the value of self-transcending interpretations are inter-subjective it follows that all participants must be involved. Theologically speaking, that implies that the primacy of God's grace is acknowledged through his Spirit, as a **veto** or as a heuristic disclosure. And finally, praise is part of a religious hermeneutic act. Doxology is the bridge between orthodoxy and orthopraxis.

Concretely, an interpretation is only valid if it is contextualized. For this reason, emphasis was given to the oral nature and
the trial of testimonies and visions. Likewise, I considered it
important to point to the setting of worship, even if liturgical
notions have for ecumenical reasons been kept to a minimum.

Since the provisional nature of this study has been stressed
repeatedly, it might be appropriate to close it with a few theses that
might stimulate further research.

(1) Testimonies are therapeutic and visions prophetic to the
extent that the self is reflected in the other.

(2) It is not possible to tell an ethically neutral narrative.

(3) If the structural emplotment of the testimony does not relate
to society, then it is a phantasm.

(4) The meaning of a vision cannot be syntactically deduced. It
rests on its content in conjunction with the response of the
recipient or the interpreting community.

(5) Any mental disclosure of the Kingdom of God in the world will
be poetic.

(6) A truly religious narrative is always to some extent the
product of socialization and therefore also has significance
for the secular person.

(7) A responsible interpretation of religious narratives can be
said to fluctuate between a first and a second **naïveté**. If
this movement is maintained, a hermeneutic of self-
transcending experiences avoids the danger of either being
negatively regressive or violent.

POSTLUDE

A Commission for Peter PRINCIPAL

"Frankly, what liberties do I have as a civil servant?" muttered
Peter PRINCIPAL to himself as he was driving towards Edgbaston looking
nervously for Gillott Road. He had been given an order by the Ministry
of Inter-Racial Affairs to establish contacts with the black
community, and to assess possibilities for the reduction of the street
violence largely attributed to unemployed youth. The statistics
claimed that 50% of young blacks in Birmingham were without a job.

Mr. PRINCIPAL had received the address of a indigenous Nigerian
church from a sociology professor, who studied the acculturation and
identity formation of socially unfavoured minorities, but he had no
idea what to expect. As a matter of fact, he did not like the
assignment. First, he did not think much of religion, and wondered
whether he would be able to evaluate the situation properly. In theory
he was Anglican, in practice his only religious exercise was to listen
at Christmas time to a record of carols by the Kings College Choir.
Second, he had a strong preference to speak about black people, rather
than talking with them.

John OLANREWAJU, the "Senior Apostle" of "The Church of Cherubim
& Seraphim United Kingdom" had received a telephone call from the
Ministry informing him that Mr. PRINCIPAL would be coming. His
thoughts, though, were focusing on another matter. How could the
church afford to pay the rent for the old methodist church which they
were using for their gatherings? Only 20% of the congregation had a
steady income. As far as he was concerned he had never been paid a
salary by the church. He was a bus driver for the city's public trans-
portation system, but since the local government had slashed subsidies
and "readjusted" the number of employees three months ago, he had been
without paid work.

And then there was Gloria NGOZI, she was the "Spiritual Mother" of the community and known for her fervent prayers and prophetic wisdom. During the week she worked as a charwoman for several companies. On Sunday's, though, she was dressed in a richly embroidered white robe, and the believers honoured her like an elder when she walked to the altar wearing a mitre, equipped with a Bible and her staff. She had prepared everything for the holy service and had now withdrawn to the vestry in silent meditation.

Peter PRINCIPAL was just driving into Gillott Road and looked on his watch. Five minutes to three. As a conscientious civil servant he was pleased to be there on time, and found to his surprise a parking space next to the modest, little church. The adepts of this congregation apparently came on foot or by public transport. He joined a group of black people who were walking to the house of prayer and was courteously greeted. As Mr. PRINCIPAL entered the church he noticed that the women and children withdrew to a little room to the left, and that the men took off their shoes and put on white robes in the cloakroom. John OLANREWAJU, who had just come from the vestry, noticed Peter's hesitation and said, "Mr. PRINCIPAL, I presume," and introduced the civil servant to the customs of the faithful. The Englishman was embarrassed. Had he known, he would have chosen a pair of socks that had matched his suit.

A few minutes later, he was seated on the left side of the sanctuary like all other men and felt slightly intimidated because he was the only one without a robe, like a black sheep as it were, and he wondered whether it was them or him that was out of touch with reality. But suddenly there was movement coming into the simple place of worship. The introit of the ministers together with the choir had begun. They moved very slowly through the aisle, to the rhythm of a tune, playing the tambourine, shaking hand bells, and singing,

> God is a Spirit
> They who worship Him,
> In Spirit and in truth
> Must bow their heads,
> O Thou who dwellest
> Mid'st the Cherubim Seraphim
> Draw nigh to us while
> We draw nigh to Thee. Amen.

The hymn was repeated, because the band had not yet arrived at the altar. This time the whole congregation joined in, "O Thou who dwellest mid'st Cherubim Seraphim draw nigh to us while we draw nigh to Thee." And the room was be filled with sound, incense and a sense of worship.

One of the elders greeted the congregation in the name of Christ and more hymns were sung and prayers said. Peter PRINCIPAL did not understand what was going on, but he sensed that there was a liberating atmosphere. He did not notice that time was passing. John OLANREWAJU now invited anyone in the congregation to share an experience relevant to their faith in the Lord Jesus Christ.

A middle-aged mother stood up and said, "I'd like to praise God for His goodness to my family and myself. Last week my four year old Thomas got an ear infection, but I could not bring him to the hospital, because I just got a new job and did not dare to ask for a leave. Missus THOMPSON, my neighbour, who up to now did not care about us at all, was willing to help and took Thomas to the doctor on my behalf. I want to praise God for her help - and Thomas, as you can see, is doing much better."

Someone in the congregation intuitively responded by beginning a chorus entitled "Thanks we give unto our Saviour." Peter looked helpless, since he did not know the words. The man next to him had apparently noticed that and said, "We are singing hymn number 31." Peter was grateful, as now he could at least pretend to be participating. And in a way he did participate, when he noticed the words. Somehow they bore the marks of life. One verse said,

> God provide for jobless brethren
> To the barren give Children
> Save the life of all our Children
> Let not any suffer death.

It began to dawn on Peter that the people who had gathered here came to worship because it was life-sustaining.

Now a young man, named Blake, stood up and told the congregation that he had been invited to go to the police station for a confrontation with a plaintiff. Blake lived in Handsworth where street violence was highest in Birmingham. The owner of a chemist shop which had been looted had given a description of the vandals he had seen

running away when he approached the shop, and Blake happened to suit
the description. He asked the congregation for prayer and a blessing.
He was called forward to kneel in front of the alter and the whole
community, except Peter PRINCIPAL, gathered around him and raised
their hands in intercession. Gloria NGOZI touched Blake's head with
her staff and said, "You shall overcome in the power of the Holy
Spirit of Jesus. When they falsely accuse you, you shall overcome;
when they have no respect for you because you are black, you shall
overcome; when you face temptation to avoid the truth you shall
overcome, because you are a child of the Lord, and He has overcome."

At first, Peter felt mildly threatened by the solidarity
demonstrated - what would happen if all of Britain's immigrant workers
would manifest such a solidarity? But then, on second thought, he
sensed a feeling of harmony, and did not quite know what to make of
it. More hymns were sung.

At last, the "senior apostle" opened his Bible an preached from
the Gospel according to Matthew, chapter 25, where it says,

> "for I was hungry and you gave me no food, I was thirsty and you
> gave me no drink, I was a stranger and you did not welcome me,
> naked and you did not clothe me, sick and in prison and you did
> not visit me."

The civil servant felt personally attacked, but John OLANREWAJU
addressed the believers, saying that one should not expect any special
favours from others if one is in misery. The art of being Christian
was to remain a faithful witness in spite of adverse circumstances.
Peter thought that he had now understood: the preaching was conformist
and had the aim of soothing the wounds of social inequality. But John
continued, "We do not always understand God's plans, but we **do**
understand that he loves and cares for us. Think of the children of
Israel, they worked in misery for 70 years, but then - then came the
great day of deliverance." And again Peter felt threatened, but
fortunately the "senior apostle" had ended his homily.

A time of prayer followed. Then a woman stood up and turned
toward the congregation saying, "I see in a vision the face of Mrs.
Indira GHANDI. I see now that she is standing in front of the altar of
our church and she is pleading, "Please pray for my son, pray for him.
He has a heavy burden to carry, it is difficult to lead my people,

please pray for him." A man from the congregation responded, by praying for the leaders of this world and especially for those in India, Nigeria, and the United Kingdom.

Then, Gloria NGOZI walked to the altar for she had felt compelled to share another vision, "I see a man working in a mine, his back is bent and he is digging coal - slowly. As I come closer I see that the man has passed his fifties. His face shows the marks of hard labour and suffering. He is coughing and I can hear that his lungs are full of coal dust. Then he is turning toward me and I see his face fully. There is something peaceful about him, his eyes convey a sense of integrity. He tries to smile, but it remains a feeble attempt. Then suddenly, I am in downtown London. I think it's Regent Street. I see from some distance a black brother in white clothes walking confidently toward me. He is dressed fashionably and probably in his thirties. He stops and looks at a display window. As I come closer he looks at me and smiles. And - I can hardly believe it - it is the same face as before."

There was silence in the congregation. John asked if there was anyone who could interpret this vision. The silence continued. Gloria interrupted it, commenting, "I can but think of the verse that says, 'And he died for all, that those who live might live no longer for themselves but for him who for their sake died and was raised.' It seems to me that the fate of Jesus and that of the man in the mine converge somewhere."

As far as Peter was concerned Jesus had died on the cross because he was a fool; he had failed to come to terms with the political powers. Unexpectedly John OLANREWAJU turned to Peter and asked, "Mr. PRINCIPAL what do you think this vision means?" Of course, Peter couldn't say what had just crossed his mind. Besides, he had come as an observer, and not as a participant. But John repeated his invitation for Peter's comment. So he hesitantly remarked that the vision had brought to mind that those who work themselves to death, and those who are without employment do pay the price for those who live in comfort and luxury. He added that, obviously, this was not a religious interpretation and Peter excused himself in this regard.

Gloria picked Peter's comment up and said, "This is the very point Mr. PRINCIPAL. We believe that everything which in the end pertains to our lives is religious, and that includes the way in which we live together. Just as the memory of Christ is alive in us today, and we commit ourselves to live for him, so also is the memory of our past kept alive in our conscience. We thank you for having come to visit us, for now you have begun to share in this memory. Your life will never be the same again." It dawned on Peter that if he wanted to be true to himself, he would have to draw conclusions. What exactly they were, no one could tell, but the whole congregation agreed to pray for Mr. PRINCIPAL. He was asked to kneel in front of the altar and the whole congregation gathered around him, and prayed that God's wisdom and goodness would be with him.

Before the ministers and the choir concluded the service with the slow and rhythmic exit through the nave all sang another hymn. The simple words brought healing to Peter's mind. They were,

> The wise may bring their learning,
> The rich may bring their wealth
> And some may bring their greatness
> and some bring strength and health
> Ye too will bring your treasures
> To offer to the King,
> We have no wealth or learning
> What shall we children bring?
>
> We'll bring the heart that loves him
> We'll bring Him thankful praise
> And young souls meekly striving
> To walk in holy ways
> And those shall be the treasures
> We offer to the King
> And those are gifts that even
> The poorest child may bring.

APPENDIX I

A SHORT ESSAY ON PENTECOSTALISM

The Pentecostal movement is known for its emphasis on the charisms of the Holy Spirit, its popular tradition of worship, and for the kerygmatic zeal typical of the protestant free church tradition. The movement is usually described as a public phenomenon which began at the beginning of the twentieth century in the United States and gained general acceptance when the ecumenical Charismatic renewal brought similar accents to the historic churches of the West.[1] Those accounts which are largely biographical in character tend to forget that there was a historical antecedent to this revival.[2] Some recent works have stressed that the Pentecostal movement grew out of the Holiness tradition of Methodism, but even here many an author is satisfied with mentioning that the emphasis on personal sanctification arose from the theology of John WESLEY and the subsequent ecclesiological developments in the Holiness movement.[3]

---

[1] In encyclopedic entries such as Evangelisches Gemeindelexikon, Erich GELDBACH, et al., Wuppertal, 1978, p. 402; or histories like John Thomas NICHOL, The Pentecostals, Plainfield, 1966, pp. 25-39, 240ff.; and René LAURENTIN, Catholic Pentecostalism, New York, 1978, pp. 21-29.

[2] See for example Frank BARTELMAN's Another Wave Rolls In.

[3] For instance Vinson SYNAN, The Holiness Pentecostal Movement, Grand Rapids, 1971, pp. 13-32. Nils BLOCH-HOELL observes that the nurturing ground of Pentecostalism is as pluriform as the various nationalities and religious traditions of immigrants to the United States. Attempts to create a state church system were unthinkable at the time of the Pilgrim Fathers and proved to be as unsuccessful thereafter. The sectarian origins of the Pentecostal movement are just another indication that the American Christian was, at least at the beginning of this century, not able to appreciate the idea of a una sancta ecclesia. Cf. Nils BLOCH-HOELL, The Pentecostal Movement, Oslo, 1964, p. 5. Two excellent publications concerned with the historical developments leading up to the Pentecostal revival are: Daniel

It comes as a refreshing change that Walter HOLLENWEGER has searched for the roots of this religious phenomenon in more than abstract historical and theological terms. According to him there are two essential aspects that shaped Pentecostalism pragmatically. First, he mentions the catholic devotional spirituality which was carried over by Anglicanism and Pietism to form a Holiness tradition in a number of protestant free churches.[4] John WESLEY encouraged his lay preachers to search for sanctification and a second experience of grace by translating for them the writings of the Italian Lorenzo SCOPULI, the Spanish Benedictine Juan DE CASTANIZA, the Spanish writer Gregor LOPEZ, the French nobelman Jean Baptiste DE RENTY, and promoting the writings of a number of Anglican divines such as William LAW and Jeremy TAYLOR. It was their common plea for a second religious crisis experience that characterized the religious teaching of the Holiness movement on both sides of the Atlantic in the nineteenth century, and which helped to interpret the charismatic "outpouring" of the Holy Spirit as the prayed for cleansing and endowment with power. This devotional sensitivity to the work of the Holy Spirit predisposed believers in the Holiness movement not only to a personal reading of mystical experiences, but more importantly, it made, because it was public, a communal interpretation of God's will for the church and the world possible.[5] Such an openness to the divine mandate did not at first separate social and missiological responsibility, since many adepts came from the most humble social milieus; in other words, their lack of material possession was compensated for by spiritual wealth,

---

BRANDT-BESSIRE, Aux sources de la spiritualité pentecôtiste, Genève, 1986; and Donald DAYTON's book Theological Roots of Pentecostalism, Grand Rapids, 1987. Both authors are careful to show why the Pentecostal movement cannot be explained without reference to various phenomenological and theological factors preceding it.

[4] Walter J. HOLLENWEGER, After Twenty Years' Research on Pentecostalism, in Theology 87 (1984), p. 404.

[5] For a typical description of a black pentecostal church service, with its various expressions of spiritual sensitivity, see James M. SHOPSHIRE, A Socio-Historical Characterization of the Black Pentecostal Movement in America, Ph.D. dissertation, Northwestern University, 1975, the section entitled, "Visit to a Typical Black Pentecostal Worship Service," pp. 170-183.

and their sense of justice did not differentiate between "having" and "being," for the mere thought of existence was their common denominator.[6] This is especially true for early Pentecostalism, where a shared experience was more important than differences in social status.[7] In theory this is still emphasized by Pentecostals today, and the Gospel is understood as addressing the physical just as much as the spiritual.   In   practice   however   it   seems   that   the institutionalization   of   pentecostal   denominations   has   shifted attention   from   public   social   responsibility   to   internal   church matters, that is, to a representation of order and status.

The second basic influence shaping Pentecostalism that HOLLEN-WEGER is careful to mention is the black spirituality of the former slaves of the United States. Not only did the black hymn-writers and evangelists like William SEYMOUR introduce negro spirituals and black rhythms into the liturgy at a time when this music was considered "inferior and unfit for christian worship,"[8] but they led a revival which was definitively interracial during a period when an average of two black persons were known to have been lynched a week.[9] Black

---

[6] For an exposé of the social and educational background of early American Pentecostalism see Robert Mapes ANDERSON, Vision of the Disinherited, pp. 98ff.; for Europe, where significant differences can be found see Walter J. HOLLENWEGER, The Pentecostals.

[7] Testimonies and visions of early Pentecostalism have been chosen precisely because they relate more directly to the communicative tension between religious and secular concerns.

[8] Walter J. HOLLENWEGER, After Twenty Years, p. 405.

[9] HOLLENWEGER writes "In the revival in Los Angeles white bishops and black workers, men and women, Asians and Mexicans, White professors and black laundry women were equals (1906!)," After Twenty Years, p. 405; cf. also Douglas J. NELSON, For Such a Time as This. The Story of Bishop William J. Seymour and the Azusa Street Revival. A Study of Pentecostal Charismatic Roots.   Ph.D.   dissertation,   University of Birmingham, England, 1981.
    Vinson SYNAN states "The fact that the Pentecostal Assemblies of the World was an interracial church, with roughly equal numbers of Negroes and whites as both officials and members, points to the interracial character of the early pentecostal movement. Since the years from 1901 to 1924 were years of growing racism in the United States, this phenomenon of interracial worship by the lower classes of white and Negroes was a significant exception to the racial mores of the times." The Holiness Pentecostal Movement, p. 221.

spirituality combined a spontaneous way of worship with a prophetic manifesto. Communication by means of hymns, dreams and charismatic messages helped to build community and fellowship without losing sight of its christian focus.

A parallel development can be noticed in the history of European Pentecostalism. At the turn of the century large revivalist circles were seeking spiritual guidance and growth.[10] The changes in society that the nineteenth century introduced, especially those in politics and the economy, had brought insecurity and a loss of stability to those most affected. The pentecostal revival brought back a sense of purpose to the poor, a "vision to the disinherited" as Robert M. ANDERSON would say. Interestingly enough there was an inter-cultural community in European pentecostal churches not unlike the interracial contacts in the United States. People of all grades of life could be found in the early years of the movement. Many of the first generation pastors belonged to the middle and upper class.[11] There was no sexual prejudice in ministerial roles. Artists and aristocrats shared the "cup of life" with those who would have qualified for social welfare had it been institutionalized.[12] The social structure of the early pentecostal groups was, in the words of Victor TURNER, typically

---

Similarly, Lawrence Neale JONES, The Black Pentecostals, in The Charismatic Movement, Michael P. HAMILTON (ed.), pp. 145-158, especially p. 147; and James M. SHOPSHIRE, A Socio-Historical Characterization, pp. 64ff.

[10] Already the ministry of Johann Christoph BLUMHARDT had established a dual accent in protestant piety. On one hand there was the assuring confidence of resting in the grace and love of Jesus Christ, and on the other hand the practice of faith called for great spiritual expectations and sanctification. All came to focus in BLUMHARDT's repeated prayers for the coming of the Holy Spirit. See Johann Christoph BLUMHARDT, Seelsorge, Zürich, 1949, pp. 20, 25, 29, 31, etc. See also Jost MUELLER-BOHN, Entscheidende Jahrhundertwende 1895-1905, Reutlingen, 1972.

[11] For a detailed study see Walter J. HOLLENWEGER, The Pentecostals, the chapter entitled "Modern Shamans: The Origin and Environment of Pentecostal Pastors as an Aid in Interpreting Pentecostal Belief and Practice," pp. 474-492.

[12] Anna Larsen BJORNER, for instance, was an opera singer before she became the main pastor of the pentecostal church in Kopenhagen.

"liminal."[13] The believers who could indentify with the pentecostal blessing experienced a transition into a new "order" where a sense of community and sacredness made distinctions of wealth, status, and sex seem trivial. They had crossed a "threshold" which for a moment detached them from fixed social structures. It seems that the kind of "atmospheric communication" peculiar to narrative communities provided a symbolic frame of reference for the barrier-breaking fellowship of those Pentecostals. Man was addressed in therapeutic wholeness, and could eventually find his way back to society with a regenerated sense of being.

Today most pentecostal churches in the First World are homogeneous, ethnically as well as economically. They may be middle class churches as in Switzerland, or the haven of the "proud poor" as in southern Italy. In the United States pentecostal denominations are either predominantly black or white, representing the working class or those socially upward mobile. The segregation which began between the two World Wars is complete.[14] In the Third World and in comparable situations (as in the churches of the immigrant communities of the West) the mythic, and therefore also social, unity in Christ is still part of the message of the Gospel.

Three general questions can be asked in this context: First, is this communicative unity due to a common language game, and if so can it be practiced naively enough to respect spiritual intuition, and critically enough to respect universal reason? Second, has the **Verkirchlichung** of the pentecostal communities in the West led to a point of no return, where the myth of Pentecost, that is, the myth of heterogeneous unity in Chirst through the Spirit, can no longer be re-presented and acted upon, - or are there perhaps global social developments and problems which call for renewed communal concern and

---

[13] Victor W. TURNER, The Ritual Process. Structure and Anti-Structure, London, 1966, especially pp. 94-113.

[14] The influential evangelical School of World Missions and the Institute of Church Growth at Fuller Theological Seminary in Pasadena, California openly advocates a homogeneous church growth principle given the pragmatic rational that the conversion of five hispanics is worth more than the conversion of a white anglo-saxon and a hispanic.

for prophetic acuity. And third, does not the experience of liminality (the religious journey from a given social context, to the realm of the Sacred, and back again) remain relevant beyond the myth of an all-embracing union in Christ, precisely because it is there that the **humanum** stands at the threshold between the religious and the secular and thus there that the story of Jesus Christ can be told.

APPENDIX II
TESTIMONIES

(A)

The Tale of the Swan-Geese

Taken from Vladimir PROPP, _Morphology_, pp. 96-98.

There lived an old man and an old
woman; they had a daughter and a
little son.   Initial situation
"Daughter, daughter," said the
mother, "we are going out to work
and we will bring you back a
little bun, sew you a little dress
and buy you a little kerchief.
Be wise, take care of your little
brother, and do not leave the   Interdiction
courtyard."
The elders went away, and the daughter   Departure
forgot what they had ordered her to
do. She placed her little brother on   Violation of the
the grass under a window and ran out   interdiction
into the street and became absorbed
in playing and having fun.
The swan-geese flew down, seized the
little boy and carried him away on
their wings.   Villainy
The little girl came back, looked,
but her brother wasn't there. She
gasped and rushed hither and thither,

but he wasn't anywere. She called out;
she burst into tears, wailing that
harm would come to her from her
father and her mother, but her little
brother did not answer. She ran out
into the open field; the swan-geese   Departure
sped away into the distance and
disappeared beyond the dark wood.   Dispatch due to
The swan-geese had long before ac-   seen misfortune and
quired an ill fame, caused much   previous knowl-
mischief, and had stolen many a little   edge of evil
child. The girl guessed that they had
carried off her little brother, and she
set out to catch up with them. She ran
and ran until she came upon a stove.   Appearance of
"Stove, stove, tell me: where have   tester
the geese flown?"
"If you eat my little ryecake, I'll
tell."   Trial
"Oh, we don't even eat cakes made of
wheat in my father's house."   Negative reaction
(A meeting with an apple tree and
a river follows. Similar proposals   Trebled repetition
and similar insolent replies.)
She would have run through the
fields and wandered in the forest
a long time if she had not by   Appearance of
good fortune met a hedgehog.   thankful helper
She wished to nudge him, but was   Helpless status of
afraid of pricking herself.   helper and mercy
"Little hedgehog, little hedgehog,"
she asked, "did you not see where   Dialogue
the geese have flown?"
"Away, over there," he pointed.   Thankful help
She ran and came upon a hut on
chickenlegs. It was standing

and turning around.   Dwelling of villain
In the hut sat Baba Jaga, hag-
faced and with a leg of clay.   Physical appearance
The little brother also sat   Appearance of sought-
there on a little bench,   for object
playing with golden apples.
His sister saw him, stole up,
seized him and carried him away,   Receipt and return
and the geese flew after her
in pursuit; the evil-doers were   Pursuit
overtaking them; where was there
to hide?
(Once again a triple testing by
the same characters, but with a
positive answer which evokes the
aid of the tester himself in the
form of rescue from pursuit. The
river, the apple tree, and the
stove hide the little girl.   Deliverance
The tale ends with the little
girl's arrival home.   Arrival

(B)

The Joseph Story (Genesis 37-47)

From a Structural / Formalist Point of View

Main plot:

Joseph's dream (37:1-11)   Initial situation of future
                                             hero and his family relations,
                                             with forewarning.

Hated by his brothers (37:12-24)   First villainy

Sold to Egypt (37:25-36)   Departure

     Sub plot: Complication

Joseph's prosperity (39:1-6)   Initial situation

His temptation to sin (39:7-18)   Second villainy

Joseph cast into prison   Journey to donor
(39:19-20)

The Lord's help (39:21-23)   Appearance of donor

Joseph the interpreter of   Double test
dreams (40:1-23)

Pharaoh's dream (41:1-8)

Butler remembers Joseph (41:9-13)	Thankful helper
Joseph's interpretation (41:14-36)	Third test
Pharaoh makes Joseph ruler (41:37-45)	Reward
Restoration of Joseph (41:46-52 and return to primary plot (41:53 - 42:1a)	
Dispatch of 10 of Jabob's sons (41:42:1-5)	Dispatch of false hero
Joseph meets his brothers (42:6ff.)	Testing of false hero

The primary plot continues in a similar fashion as the sub plot but with reversed roles as logical consequence of the first villainy (42-45). Tests, complications etc., the eventual transfiguration of the hero, the liquidation of misfortune and the reunion of the family bring the story to a harmonious end.

(C)

The Mission of Jesus Christ from a Morphological Point of View

Absentation from home (kenosis)
First function of donor (baptism)
Provision of magical agent (Holy Spirit)
Appearance and trickery of villain (temptation)
Successful completion of test (helpers / angels)
Beginning of the hero's task (introducing the Kingdom)
Struggle (opposition)
Branding (crucifiction)
Apparent victory of villain (death of Jesus)
Defeat of villain (resurrection)
Return of the hero (firstly: to the Father, secondly: second coming
of Christ and the wedding feast of the Lamb)

(D)

Miss SISSON's Miraculous Healing
taken from Confidence 2, 3 (March 1909), pp. 55-58.

The headings indicate parallels to PROPP's morphology. The footnotes
5 relate to semantic and pragmatic aspects of this testimony. No
attempt has been made to note and correct grammatical and syntactic
errors. This testimony, written by the witness herself, still shows
aspects of an oral presentation; for example the ommission of
articles and conjunctions, or the frequent use of the exclamations.

10   Initial situation, misfortune and worsening of the situation

*It was the 1st of August 1908, that in St. Andrew's, Scotland,
whither I had gone to join other Christian workers in a Gospel
campain, I was seized with a very heavy cold, aggravating an
asthmatic tendency, which in those days always hung about me. For six
15 weeks the cold deepened daily, in consequence of being in a very raw
cold climate,[1] without the possibility of fire day or night. Soon I
had developed a most fearful form of bronchial asthma with heart
failure, and for weeks was unable to lie down or recline in a chair,
the pulsation was so great in the whole body from the action of the
20 heart. Spiritually, I was much blest and quickened in faith for my
body just before I was taken ill, and was holding in God for full
deliverance for two forms of chronic suffering, namely, growths in
the head, inducing a very acute catarrh, which in turn caused an
asthmatic condition with extreme sensitiveness to every atmospheric
25 change.[2] Rom. 16:20 "God ... shall bruise Satan under your feet

[1] This testimony was written down by Miss SISSON for public
consumption in the United States of America (originally published in
Triumphs of Faith, Oakland, California); a British subject would not
have needed this explanation.

[2] One may wonder if this abundant diagnosis had the purpose of
catching the attention of the audience or readership because many

shortly," had been made very precious to me. On this word I was
holding for the complete healing when this new illness struck me.
With it came marvelous buffetings of the enemy. It was very difficult
to pray or get light from God. Occasionally He would burst through
30 the intense darkness with a great illumination[3] as after I had given
up thought of response to a call to Bombay for Pentecostal service,
and said, "Thy will be done" to sickness instead. He gave me the
whole of Ps. 18, with its promised answer to prayer, mighty power of
God in deliverance, use of His delivered one, among the heathen.[4] But
35 as soon as His immediate presence was withdrawn, the host of the
enemy closed in darker than ever upon me. The light of the Word
seemed literally swallowed up in the torture of the sleepless nights
and days. "This is your hour, and the power of darkness" was much of
the time my one text. Later, God came again with Isa. 54:11-17. Oh!
40 the wealth of love, with which he said: "Oh thou afflicted,
tempest-tossed, and not comforted" and the power with which He said,
"Behold, I will lay thy stones with fair colours," etc. down to the
end of the chapter. I thought then I was to be immediately healed. As
the days became weeks I could not understand the dealings of the Lord
45 with me.[5]

Villainy

The awful spiritual darkness increased. I seemed the tramping
ground for demon hosts. The enemy hissed into my soul, how I had
failed God and got off his ground, else I would be healed, or taking

---

could have identified with one or the other aspect of that medical
history. On the other hand, multiple diagnosis may have been common
in those days.

[3] The reference to the darkness/light theme is an archetypical
symbol universally understood.

[4] This language is not automatically understandable to non-religious
people. The question is if the plot of this testimony will clarify it
for them.

[5] The theodicy problem is brought into play, and met with an
analogous case of testing, cf. lines 63-90.

50 another tack, how God had failed me, and broken all His promises. How
he only mocked me, etc. I felt the malice of Satan would like to
foreclose on my body, because God had by me proclaimed our privilege
of "tarrying till Jesus comes" in a little tract of that name.

Testing of the hero

55   One of those darkest mornings I had fallen into a little doze.
I had no regular sleep, but when sheer exhausted caught five or eight
minutes by dropping my head upon a table in front of me, and was
wakened with Ps. 105:19, powerfully impressed upon me. "The word of
the Lord tried him." (This had been the peculiar thrust of the devil
60 that God's word had promised so much, but nothing materialized.)
"Until the time of His word came," I saw as never before that there
might be a time quantity in the promises of God. I waited for morning
light and my Bible that I might review the story of Joseph to which
the Ps. referred.[6] How truly it was "the word of the Lord" that tried
65 him, as he was standing on the promises! It was this that got him
into trouble when his brother sold him. It was this that thrust him
into prison from Potiphar's house, which prison was a university
course in the school of God. We learn of "two full years" that he
meditated there upon the fulfilment of "all the sheaves bowing down"
70 to his sheaf, sun, moon, and stars bowing to the star of Joseph, and
the outcome of all was months lengthening into years (there may have
been four or five of them for aught we know) - as a criminal in an
Egyptian dungeon! Yes, the word of the Lord tried him, and it seemed
to be the full intention of the Lord that His word should try Joseph.
75 Could the lesson have been otherwise learned? Could the fine
soul-qualities have been otherwise wrought? Could the faith and the
patience over which God triumphantly declares "His bow abode in
strength" (Gen 49:24) have else developed? But the word of the Lord
only tried him till the time of His word came, then how everything

---

[6] The test is resolved through a personalist reading of the Bible
providing disclosures à la I.T. RAMSEY; in this case it is the model
of Joseph's "testimony" (cf. also lines 198ff. and 275ff.). Typical
for a written testimony are interpretative inclusions of considerable
length (lines 64-80).

80 changed! "The king sent and loosened him," and with me it was much
the same. The King of kings sent and loosed me. But the time was not
yet; I had lessons to learn, and though there was a glorious
illumination that morning, I continued in my prison-house of pain and
sank even lower.

85   Helpers

One morning while suffering from frightful heart action the room
filled with brethren and sisters; some came to see me die, but most
to pray me through to health. Finally they sang the victory, and I
was able gaspingly to join the chorus, and after hours of distress
90 suddenly the heart became normal; we all praised the Lord, I was
well. They left rejoicing. A few hours after other forms of illness
set in; my head was again under water. Acute gastritis.

       Journey / difficult task

       Through force of circumstances I had been carried more dead
95 than alive from St. Andrews to Dunfermline and thence to Edinburgh,
and here the Lord began to talk to me of crossing the Atlantic.[7] At
first I could not make sure of His voice, and the journey looked
appalling. I could not walk across my bedchamber, nor dress, nor
recline in a chair, nor lie in bed. The journey from Edinburgh to
100 Liverpool alone was too formidable; from thence the steamer, the wide
stretch of ocean, the fatigue of the New York landing, then the rail
to Connecticut alone. My whole nerve force was now exhausted. I could
not contemplate it. But my Heavenly Father seemed to fairly coax me
to it. In answer to prayer He gave courage and wonderfully helped me
105 to pack, write, etc., and make all necessary arrangements.

---

[7] The passage from one way of life to another is often referred to as
a voyage or journey; it can again be called an archetypical symbol of
existence.

Provision

In fact from the time that, leaning on His arm, I consented to go, there was continued marked improvement in health.

I sailed October 1st, having been unable for many days to take
110 solid food. The increased suffering from nutriment was such that on the 6th of October I resolved to swallow no more until I reached home, where I arrived October 10th. Among other things said to me by the Lord before leaving Edinburgh was, "You shall have a nice room to yourself on the steamer." I thought "Yes, when they see how I am they
115 will take me into the ship's hospital." But no! when about half over the voyage the captain had an interview with me, offering me, a second class passenger in a room with three others, a first class left over state room all to myself! We had a smooth passage and many mercies.

120   ## 2nd Move

As soon as I reached home came the reaction from all the strain of the voyage. I fell into a bed from which I never rose till healed by the Lord the morning of November 16th. I only attempted liquid food, but nothing would stay on the stomach, and while various
125 parties were recommending what they thought I could retain, a physician who had made a specialty of sick-diet was asked simply to give advice on food. The doctor consented to come for that purpose only. In a few days I had failed so rapidly - taking nothing but granulated ice - and often for days together could not bear that,
130 living on air forced down my throat with two fans. Then to ease the awful sufferings a little medicine was given. I was too ill to know or care. Thus the doctor was soon in, two or three times a day.

Renewed Test / Riddle

Terrible hemorrhages[8] caused by the gathering and breaking of ulcers

---

[8] Here begins the "tissue" of a disclosure relating to a deeply personal application of the redemption (blood) of Christ.

135 in the stomach would be preceded by most frightful sufferings all
through the body. "Nerve storms I called them. The hemorrhages were
so violent the blood almost choked me as it poured from my throat,
and so great was my exhaustion that sometimes they would have to pick
the great clots from my mouth and throat. After every hemmorrhage I
140 would sink so low that they looked for me to pass away. With joy I
hailed these times of exhaustion, thinking that I was about to be
admitted to the open presence of my Lord. The joy of the thought was
great, for though I felt I was such a disappointment to God and to
myself in that I had failed[9] to rise above illness into His divine
145 Life, and failed to give Him in myself one for translation, yet He
made me constantly know how full my acceptance with Him through that
blood. I longed to meet His love and see His smile.

Transference

One night after profuse hemorrhages, from both the throat and
150 the bowels (and as I afterwards learned while they were watching for
the end), I seemed to slip the body and be borne away into space. Oh,
how much it meant to leave the tortured frame behind, and like a bird
on glad wing to be floating in the upper air! We rose high up above
the earth, for I realized that "underneath were the everlasting
155 arms." On these I rested as a bird upon wing. As we sped on we passed
far above a great city, in the full swing of a civic celebration.
Grand illuminations, bands of music, phalanx of soldiers; as we
passed by I thought: "How feeble all this to the light of the glory
of God, the heavenly music, the angelic hosts I shall soon be among!
160 Then on and on we went, far and in outer darkness. We seemed to be
passing with incredible speed through a night of limitless space,
inpenetrable gloom, but like a babe nestling in the dark in the warm
arms of mother-love, I only revelled in the Spirit-comfort of the God
arms that bore me on. Whether this was vision, dream, or the fancies
165 of a sick brain I know not, but toward morning I found myself again

---

[9] As with fairy tales the hero believes he is failing, whereas in
fact victory is imminent. In God-talk the parallel is, "He made me
small, that the exceeding greatness of God may be revealed."

in the sick chamber, the bed, the tortured body - but this I do know, that there was a spiritual joy in God from that hour on of which the enemy was never able to rob me.

Return

170 As I woke to consciousness I whispered to my sister what had transpired, and mournfully added, "I never expected to come back here." It was a terrible disappointment, and for this new phase of God's will I had to cry for fresh grace to bear. Thus again and again I sank so low only to measurably revive till it seemed to me I could
175 not die (and no wonder! so many holding on by faith for my healing as I afterwards learned). I felt like old King Saul (2 Sam. 1:9), though I dared not pray his prayer, "Stand upon me and slay me," but against every inclination was helped to cry "Thy will be done."

Negative Reaction

180 Shall I ever forget the 15th of November 1908? That was the darkest day my life had ever seen. "Life was too strong in me, it must take a long pining sickness to exhaust this remaining strength." "How could we afford this length of dying?" so my brain ran on.[10] My sisters were already exhausted with the care of me. As I said to the doctor,
185 we were working in a rule of subtraction - "kill four to save one." I was sure there would be some terrible breakdown if they had to care for me much longer. Then there was the expense, physician, trained nurse, etc. How could all this go on? It came to me, the free ward of a hospital would reduce expenses and relieve the family. I might be
190 till spring wasting into death, but I found there was no courage to leave the little home nest.[11] So all that blue day I was crying to

---

[10] The negative reaction is not to be confused with the heroine's concern for the others, which from a moral point of view is quite compatible with her faith.

[11] The third archetypical symbol, the home (womb), cf. also lines 162f. In a sense the nucleus of a standard narrative could be sketched as the movement: home, journey, light, journey, home.

God for courage, but it was a struggle! I would think God had helped
me all over to the point, then all at once eveything in me would
recoil, and the battle would have to be fought all over and the
195 victory regained.

2nd Riddle

All this went on till after midnight, when the Lord approached
me with the suggestion, "You are like Hagar crying and dying by the
side of the well." I had been contemplating all winter to die on. He
200 showed it was only a moment to be healed! How clear he made it, that
"Christ, the deep, sweet well of love," as a Fountain of Healing was
right by the side of every sick one. As with her it was only to turn
and live (Gen. 21:15-19).

Struggle with the Villain

205 Then the accuser of the brethren came in big, with all his showing of
what I was not; that at this juncture healing was never for me etc.,
etc. God applied with mighty power "By grace are ye saved, through
faith, and that not of yourselves, it is the gift of God." Eph. 2:8.
Grace - "free full unmerited favour," a provision all outside of me,
210 coming to me as the Christmas gifts to the children, because of the
love of the giver. "Through faith, through faith," says the enemy.
"You have got to take it and you have no faith." Within I could see
nothing, without I could see everything, such richness of provision
in Jesus. Then came the word with God-power "Through faith and that
215 not of yourselves, it is the gift of God." I ceased to resist[12] the
thought of healing and cried, "Oh, God, give me that faith which is
the gift of God." The spiritual atmosphere was moment by moment
warming. No wonder.

---

[12] Interesting is here the surrender to the good.

Helpers

220 One of my sisters was in another room on her face before God, crying
for Him to break through and bring deliverance. In many towns, aye,
in many countries, Faith in God's children was holding on for His
victory in my healing, and as near as we could figure it, at the very
hour when the power of darkness was broken in my bed-chamber, a
225 precious brother in the Lord, a cook in a hotel,[13] there in the early
morning making out his rolls for breakfast, and who had all along had
an assurance of my healing, was energized to cry with agony, "Lord
help, Lord help." He said that was all the prayer he offered, as the
vision of me came before him; but oh, the power that resisted his
230 believing! The conflict for a time was terrible, but thank God, he
got the victory.

New Provision

My dear sister got the victory ere she rose from her knees, and the
spiritual atmosphere was so clearing that this poor weakling, in the
235 jaws of death, was getting the victory. "Hallelujah, what a Saviour!"
As my sister came into my room I felt her quickened spirit, and she
felt mine, though neither knew of the spiritual exercises of the
other. I asked her to sing some hymns, and we spoke of the mercy and
might of God.

240   3rd Testing[14]

Then Acts 3:6 came into my mind with great force, "In the name of

---

[13] Indications of social standing seem important in many testimonies.
I presume that the witnesses were keen in pointing out that people
from all strata of society had found a similar experience of faith.
On the one hand, it meant that the Gospel was truly for all, on the
other hand there was the desire to show that the early Pentecostal
movement was not only a movement of the working class; cf. also
testimony (H).

[14] It is almost needless to point to the frequent trebling of tests
in folklore.

Jesus rise up and walk." Again the enemy came tremendously. "That is
Satan quoting Scripture to you. Don't follow that wild impulse. You
may succeed in pulling yourself up by your will-power, but the
245 consequences of further and more terrible illness, and far more
trouble to the family, will ensue," etc. etc. Spiritually everything
grew black around me, as I cried to God to protect me from Satan, to
take away the voice if it was his, or to intensify it if it were
God's. He made me know without a doubt that God was speaking.

250   Positive Reaction of the Hero

My heart cried, "Lord, I will, I will," if it costs me my life to do
it," for my whole nature gathered now into a spirit of obedience, and
what cared I for the consequences. The Devil said, "If you stir it
will kill you." (This was true enough in the natural; the doctor did
255 not allow them to raise me for fear of causing vomiting and then
hemmorrhage.) I thought, "What do I care if it kills me. I will obey
God." Then it occured to me how impossible it would be for all the
family to let me obey and all my prayer was "Lord prepare them."

Helper / Donor

260   Just then another sister came in bringing my morning mail,
which they daily opened and read me as much as they thought best,
when I was not too ill to hear. Now she read from a sister in
Winnipeg - Mrs. Lockhart, 629, Bannantyne Avenue[15] - to whom they had
written to pray for me. She replied she was not surprised with their
265 letter, though she knew nothing of my return to this country; but
while I was yet in Scotland God had revealed to her in the spirit
that I was very ill, and put upon her a great burden for me.

---

[15] The testimony rests on the reliability of other parties, the
witness is made public.

Magical Agent

Now she sent a handkerchief that had been prayed over, and asked us
270 to lay it on the diseased part, and wrote what assurance God had
given her of my healing. Oh, that letter! I knew God was breaking my
way to speak and act by that letter. It was but finished, when my
sister, who had been assured of deliverance before God that morning,
took the handkerchief and laid it on me, and bowed in prayer. I was
275 only waiting for the amen of her prayer till I should obey Acts 3:6
"Yes," I burst out, "God says," in the name of Jesus of Nazareth,
rise up and walk, bring my underclothes, stockings, slippers,
wrapper." The one sister turned white as death and fled the room. I
called again for my clothes. They had been laid aside all the long
280 weeks of my illness, and the sister who had since been sent for to
see me die did not know were to find them, so she followed the other
saying, "Bring her clothes." "Belle, I dare not," was the trembling
reply. Who would in the natural? (And God had intimated nothing of
His will to this one.) However, my clothes were found, and as my
285 sister began to put them on, I sat in the bed and drew on one
stocking; then as I put out my foot to walk my whole being gathered
in the word, "In the NAME of the Lord Jesus." I never seemed to put
my foot on the floor, but right in the Name, and in the Name each
foot fell till I had walked to a chair. Mentally I saw Peter walking
290 the waves on the word of Jesus ("Come"), and like Peter I was safe,
while I did not look round, but walked in the Name. (Oh, had not my
prayer for "that faith which was the gift of God" been answered?) The
joy of obedience - and faith comes in obedience - filled my soul. I
cried, "Sing the chorus:
295   "Come, come, and His bidding obey;
            Come, come, and believing you'll say
        Jesus hath healed me, praise Him to-day!
        Jesus hath taken my misery away."
As my sister sang I joined in with a full clear voice, and over and
300 over again we made it ring.

Reaction of the Others

The other members of the family came in, half happy, half frightened,
but how the colour was coming to my face and the appearance of
healing. Oh, the joy of that hour, as I believed, and then felt, I
305 was the healed of the Lord. And grace had been given me, even poor
me, to obey Him! Then came the whisper, "Walk in the other room." Two
of them took hold of me as I started. But they said, "How strong she
walked!" emaciated skeleton though I was.

Branding

310 When I took the chair in the second room I began to feel warm
currents of life from the soles of my feet to the top of my head and
finger-tips. (In bed I had three water-bags to keep me warm!) Oh, it
was delicious, the God-life flowing in! Wave after wave coursed
through my being. Next suggestion to "call for solid food." The devil
315 withstood here and tried to put a great care upon me, but it came.
"Well people can eat solid food, and I am well, 'the healed of the
Lord.'" So I called for the solid food and ate it, and have gone on
eating everything ever since. Nothing hurts me. It seems as if my
stomach was bomb-proof.

320   Wedding[16]

We went round the house that resurrection day and many times after,
crying "God is great in Zion." Hallelujah, what a Saviour! Oh, the
enrichment that has come through this illness and healing! Oh, the
lesson learnt! They cannot all be put on paper.

---

[16] The Proppian function referred to as "wedding" is in a religious
testimony an acutely doxological affair.

325   Liquidation of Initial Lack

Previous to my illness I was distressed before God for the
shallowness of my compassions for the sick, and had prayed for
deepening at that point, also that I might know the fellowship of His
sufferings and conformity to His death, as I had never experienced.

330 And[17] a blessed measure of answer has come to these prayers - though
I need much more. Then the reality of the Satanic battle against
God's life in the holiness of His people has been opened to me. Also
the beautiful truth of the unity of Christ's body, the members
prevailing for, and holding on with one another... But more than all
335 I was taught the all of God and nothingness of the creature,
especially this creature, during the long discipline of those painful
months. "I was brought low and the Lord helped me" (Ps. 116:6), and
He will help and heal any "low one" who will let his whole case go
into God's hands, and in simplicity rest in Him, to do all...

---

[17] At this point the testimony as such is over. What follows is a
self-examination, a trial brought to oneself, and words of encouragement, i.e. a pastoral commentary.

(E)

"A Wonderful Case of Cancer Healing by the Lord"

Confidence 5,3 (March 1912), pp. 65f.

All glory to His blessed Name - Jesus, Saviour.[1] Our sister,
5 who lives in Sunderland, gives the account in her own words. Her
first public testimony was given on Sunday last, February 25th, 1912,
at a Bible Class in a Church Vestry, where there was a large
attendance.[2] A timid, retiring woman about 50 years of age, at first
it was quite an effort to her, but the knowledge that it was for the
10 Lord's glory soon gave her confidence and all our hearts were moved
by her simple, earnest story.

Initial Situation

"Quite two years ago I began to notice a swelling on my breast
and under my left arm, which rapidly began to increase, the pain at
15 times being very bad to bear. I went to my Vicar's wife, and she
prayed with me, but, although I got a certain amount of relief and
comfort, I knew in my heart I did not **believe**, and at last I went to
the Infirmary and was examined by three of the best doctors there.

Worsening of the Situation

20   They had a long talk together and then told me I was to be good
to myself, and take all the care I could of myself, but they could do
nothing for me. No operation could be performed - it was too firmly
rooted in me, and I was not young enough to bear it. Well, I was very

---

[1] The introductory remark of the editor shows that the intention of
this testimony is doxological, although at the end he will add a
comment of apologetic nature. For the woman testifying there was,
however, only a doxological intent.

[2] The place and circumstance of "trial" seems important.

downcast at this. A lady visitor came to see me, and pointed out to
25 me that man could do nothing for me. Would I not trust the Lord
wholly? I had got my mind fixed on a visit to a good Christian
doctor, and thought if I could only go to him he might help me. So
the lady, seeing I would not be satisfied with anything else, agreed
that I should go. Well, he examined me and said it was a bad case of
30 Cancer, but he thought if I went into the Infirmary at once and had
an operation, it might cure me. I left him more discouraged than
ever, and as the pain was now awful to bear, and a great hole had
appeared in the lump, and my neck was drawn down, and altogether I
was a pitiable object to look at, I thought I could not bear it any
35 longer, but would go and drown myself.

Journey

On a Sunday evening, at last I made my mind up to do it. My
daughter asked me where I was going on such a wet night, and as I had
no good reason to give for going out, said she would go with me,
40 thinking I was not safe to be left. I was so wretched, and miserable,
and racked with pain, I did not know where I was going, when I found
myself at All Saints' open-air gathering near by,

Helper

and a man's voice rang out: 'Is there anyone who feels miserable and
45 despairing, and at an end of all things, hear the voice of Jesus
saying, 'Come unto Me all ye that are weary and heavy laden, and I
will give you rest.''[3]

---

[3] Here one may notice an example where the existential nature of
preaching conditions an existential response.

Donor

and my poor heart just cried out with hungry yearning, 'Oh, Lord
50 Jesus, I come, I do come, I come now to Thee.' It seemed as if all my
being went out to Him, and I felt I'd like to go face downwards on
the wet stones, but, as I looked up and the tears ran down my face, a
wonderful thing happened.

Branding

55 All my awful pain went away, right away, and a glorious peace and
rest came into my soul, and I turned to my daughter and said: 'Come
away hinney, come home. I'm healed. The Lord has healed me and
blessed me.

Return

60 Let us get home and I'll have some supper, for I'm hungry.' Before
this I could not eat anything, but now I felt I could.

Struggle

Well, through the night the devil came and tempted me, and said I was
not healed, and sure enough the pain came back, and for a moment or
65 two I went down in spirits, then I said: 'directly it is morning I'll
go to my Christian friend, she'll help me.'

Helper

Sure enough, I did go early in the morning, and she said: 'Won't you
now trust the Lord, and give Him the glory.' I said I would, so she
70 laid hands on me, and as she did, faith, the faith of God, came into
my heart, and I knew the Lord had come.

Back to the Situation Previous to the Misfortune

From that moment the lumps began to go down, and I had no more
pain. I got stronger, and last week I washed a three weeks' large
75 washing, and felt no worse.

Trial[4]

But I must tell you, I went to take one of my daughters to the
Christian doctor for herself, and when he saw me, he said: 'Oh,
Mrs.---, I've often wondered about you. Did you go through the
80 operation, and how are you?' 'No,' I said, 'No operation for me. The
Lord Himself healed me, and I am well.' So he said, 'I would like to
examine you, if you don't mind.' I let him, and he said, 'Well, this
is a miracle. There is no trace of cancer, all disease is gone. There
is only a small, drawn-in place, and if that fills up, there is no
85 sign of anything.' And now that is filled up, and I am every whit
whole. I'm just His 'bairn' now,[5] and if I make a slip, why I just
look up to Him and say, 'Lord Jesus, I'm your bairn now, you must
keep me,' - and He does. Glory to Jesus!"

So ended her simple story. You won't be surprised to hear that
90 we sang the Hallelujah Hymn Chorus **twice over**,[6] with all our hearts
saying, "Praise Him! Praise Him!" Many unbelievers have often said,
"Nerves, colds, and fanciful complaints may be healed, but can you
give a case of Cancer or any deadly disease being healed?"[7] And now -

---

[4] In Proppian analysis the function of trial is reserved for the
hero. But here the title indicates the hermeneutic trial of
testimony.

[5] The witness portrays herself as a child. This is a regressive
reading of the experience, but does not necessarily imply a negative
value judgment, rather it raises the question if perhaps every
christian testimony of grace is by its nature regressive.

[6] The congregation consented to the reliability of the testimony, and
perhaps more importantly to its doxological implications.

[7] Such a comment could not procede from the mouth of a witness,
because it would be self-defeating. If a testimony has any apologetic

95   although not the first - it is a most wonderful case of healing, and
      regeneration as well. Hallelujah! The Lord God Omnipotent reigneth!

---

value, it would have to be indirect and thus be conform to the
testimony of the Christ-Event.

(F)

"A Girl's Miracle-Cure"

Quoted from the Christian Herald (London) March 7th, 1912, reprinted
in Confidence 5,3 (March 1912), pp. 70f.

5 One will notice with what fervour testimonies of healing were spread,
as Dorothy KERIN's healing was also cause for the Swiss paper Die
Verheissung des Vaters to publish her visions (cf. vision (C) below).
The following excerpts reflect the sense of trial and the ambivalent
attitude towards medical science. It is a journalistic piece of
10 writing and cannot be considered as a testimony in the strict sense,
although excerpts in Dorothy KERIN's own words are included in the
original.

"Considerable public interest has been aroused during the past
fortnight by the sudden miraculous recovery of a young London girl
15 who was lying almost at the point of death, and we sent our special
representative to the house to verify the facts. Dorothy Kerin, who
resides with her parents at Herne Hill, in the southeast of London,
is a pretty, bright girl of twenty-two. She is one of a family of
five, and when fourteen years of age her parents saw with alarm that
20 she was losing health. Two years later she became altogether
bedridden, and has remained so for the past five years, Soon after
she first became ill she was sent to a Consumption Sanatorium outside
Reading, but, after nine month there, was sent home no better. Then
she went into St. Bartholomew's Hospital, and was there for two
25 months. Next a Nursing Home at St. Leonard's was tried, with like
result. Finally she was sent to the St. Peter's Home for Incurables
at Kilburn, from which she was sent home in an ambulance, with only a
week to live. More than twenty doctors altogether had seen her, and
from first to last seemed able to do little for her... The story of
30 her remarkable recovery is best given in her own words... When our

representative called at the house next day, Mrs. Kerin said, 'Yes, every word is authentic. Dorothy is well and strong and running about. In fact, her doctor is just taking her for a drive.'...

Subsequent inquiries tell us that this remarkable recovery is
35 maintained. The doctor who has been attending Miss Kerin, a well-known local practitioner, said, 'I have no explanation. I can only say that I cannot claim any of the credit for this extraordinary occurence. Under my direction the patient had lived for weeks, until Sunday, on brandy, opium and starch. Her muscles had no strength.
40 Where it comes from now baffles me. I can say absolutely nothing in explanation.'... Needless to say, the publicity given to the case caused a great stir in the district, and newspaper men, doctors, and enquires of all sorts flocked to the house. So much exitement was not considered good for Dorothy, so the Rev. A.J. Waldron and her doctor
45 made arrangements to have her moved at once to a nursing home, where she could have privacy and quiet, with country air."

(G)

Der alle deine Krankheiten heilt.

Die Verheissung des Vaters 9, 11+12 (Nov. Dec. 1916), pp. 6-8.

This testimony in interesting in terms of the formulation of
5 the will and action of God.

"Schon als Kind wurde ich wegen schwacher Lungen behandelt, war
sehr zart und nervös bis zum Alter von etwa zwölf Jahren... Einige
Jahre nach meiner Verheiratung jedoch kam ich wieder in ärztliche
Behandlung... Im Jahre 1911 verzogen wir nach Oakland und nun fing es
10 an rasch mit mir abwärts zu gehen... Da ich mich eines Tages
schlimmer denn je fühlte, beschloss ich um meines Mannes und Kindes
willen, einen Arzt zu befragen. Ueber die ganze Zeit hatte ich
versucht, den Namen "Schwindsucht" zurückzudrängen...
        Mein Mann ging mit zum Arzt und ich hatte das Gefühl, dass ich
15 mich auf den Weg gemacht habe, um mein Todesurteil in Empfang zu
nehmen; es kam auch so ziemlich darauf heraus. Dieser Arzt war sehr
ehrlich mit uns und sagte meinem Mann, er habe es nicht nötig, seinen
Verdienst an Aerzte zu wenden; er solle nur dafür besorgt sein, dass
mir das Leben so leicht als möglich gestaltet werde. Er riet mir,
20 Fischthran zu nehmen und gab mir einige Verordnungen für die Schwäche
meiner Lunge, sagte auch ich sollte viel an der frischen Luft sein.
Wir waren sehr entmutigt auf dem Heimweg, besonders mein Mann und
mein Knabe; ich für meinen Teil hatte in meinem Herzen gesprochen:
"Dein Wille geschehe."
25   Gerade am nächsten Tag erhielt ich einen Brief einer Freundin,
die mich auf Dr. Joakum in Los Angeles aufmerksam machte, der für die
Kranken bete und durch dessen Gebet schon viele Kranke geheilt worden
waren; sie erwähnte auch, dass er in zwei Wochen in San Franzisko
sein werde und wünschte, dass ich für mich beten lasse. Mein Mann und
30 ich fingen nun an, um Glauben zu bitten und die Bibel nach
Schriftstellen über göttliche Heilung zu durchsuchen. Gott fing

daraufhin an, in wunderbarer Weise an uns zu wirken; es war eine Zeit
des Erforschens. Ich kann hier nicht auf Einzelheiten eingehen, will
aber sagen, dass ich Gott versprach, wenn Er mich heile, so würde ich
35 im Dienst für Ihn ausgehen und jede, auch die geringste Arbeit tun,
die Er mich tun heisse. Ich fühlte es war ein Bund zwischen Ihm und
mir, zu dem der Heilige Geist zeugte. Da hatte ich Ruhe in meiner
Seele, und als die Zeit kam, gingen wir zu der Versammlung. Als mir
die Hände aufgelegt wurden zum Gebet, hatte ich eine plötzliche
40 Belebung in meinem Leib, und meine Seele wurde sozusagen in die
Gegenwart oder den inneren Hof meines Herrn versetzt, und während ich
nie ein lauter Anbeter gewesen war, fing ich sogleich an, des Herrn
Lob zu singen. Der Heilige Geist schien von mir Besitz genommen zu
haben und lobte Gott durch mich. Ich beteiligte mich nun auch am
45 Gesang, was ich seit Monaten nicht mehr hatte tun können. In der
Kraft des Herrn fühlte ich, wie wenn ich auf Luft gehe, als ich
unterwegs war vom Lokal zur Fähre. Wie ein Kind schlief ich die
kommende Nacht bis vier Uhr früh; da weckte mich der Heilige Geist
und fing wie folgt zu mir zu reden an: "Glaubst du, dass du geheilt
50 bist?" Ich antwortete: "Ja, Herr." "Gut denn," kam die Antwort,
"steh' auf diesen Morgen und mache deine Wäsche selbst." Ich fing an
zu zweifeln, dass dies die Stimme Gottes sei und bewegte die Frage
hin und her, dass ich noch nicht stark genug sei usw. Aber nach dem
ich ausgeredet, zeigte mir der Herr so sanft und zart, wie Er mir
55 übernatürliche Kraft gegeben habe, am Tag zuvor zur Fähre zu gehen,
wie die Freude am Herrn meine Stärke sei und wie Er wollte, das ich
Ihn prüfe. Ich lag eine Weile still, dann sprach der Geist etwas
schärfer wie vorher: "Glaubst du wirklich, dass du geheilt bist?" "Ja
ja, Herr, ich weiss, dass ich geheilt bin," und die Antwort kam
60 zurück: Leute, die nicht krank sind, können ihre eigene Wäsche
haben." Da sagte ich: "Ja, Herr, Amen. Ich habe Dir Gehorsam
versprochen; ich will jetzt aufstehen und gehorchen." Nun muss ich zu
meiner Schande gestehen, dass ich nie eine Wäsche mit solcher
Leichtigkeit erledigte wie diese, und als ich rieb und mich freute,
65 sagte ich immer wieder: "Die Freude am Herrn ist meine Stärke.
Hallelujah! **Ich bin** stark."

Der Herr goss Kraft in meinen schwachen Leib, und als ich eine
so köstliche Zeit über meiner Wäsche hatte, kam eine Nachbarin herein
und rief: "Was geht mit Ihrem Gesicht vor?" Ich wusste es nicht; als
70 ich aber in den Spiegel sah, gewahrte ich, dass die alte gelbe Haut
sich völlig schälte; in einigen Tagen hatte ich eine neue Haut und
war wirklich ganz neu. Aller Ruhm und Lobpreis sei Ihm, der die
Person nicht ansieht. Ich hatte es wagen dürfen, auf den
Erlösungsboden zu kommen. Ich werde nie aufhören, Ihn zu preisen. In
75 drei Monaten wog ich hundertdreissig Pfund, während ich vor meiner
Heilung nur ein Gewicht von 97 Pfund hatte."

(H)

"A Visit to Kilsyth"

Report by A. BODDY on the pentecostal beginnings in Scotland in
Confidence 1,1 (April 1908), pp. 8-10.

5 The following excerpts are valuable in terms of the public nature and
intentionality reflected.

"... As to Kilsyth, it is a small Scottish town twelve miles or
so from Glasgow.
Resounding detonations shake the windows as they blast stone in
10 the hillside quarries. Many of the men are miners. (We praise God for
the Spirit-filled miners)
Some critical investigators arrived one day by train. They
agreed to test this thing by putting questions to the first Kilsyth
man they met. It was the porter who opened the carriage door.
15   "Any Meetings being held here?"
"Aye, sir, there are."
"Have you been to any of them?"
"Yes, I've been."
"Is it true that some folks are speaking in Tongues?"
20   "It's true enough."
"Do you know anyone?"
"Yes, I'm one myself."
Yes, all ranks are represented in this movement, and we have a
Policeman, an Engine-driver on the North British Railway (John
25 McNicol, of Kirkintilloch; God bless him), and Miners who have
received their "Pentecost" at their work.
A fireman at the Colliery, as he was leaning on his shovel at
work, began to speak in Tongues.
A pitman at Motherwell (John McPhee, a Reservist), broke out in
30 the face of the coal - that is, while at work filling his wagon or
tub. He was singing,

"How I love that sweet story of old."
He said he felt something go down and then come up. Then, for two
hours, he sat on his pile of coal, speaking in Tongues as the Holy
35 Spirit gave him utterance.

The men in the adjoining working soon heard him, and one cried,
"There's Jock through in Tongues, and me not saved yet."

A number have been converted just through hearing others speak
in Tongues. It was so with young H. He loved cycle-racing, etc., and
40 kept away from the meetings, but when he heard his sister in the
house "speaking mysteries," praising God in an unknown tongue, he was
broken down. In the Mission Hall, from 3 one afternoon until 2 the
next morning, he dealt with God and was saved, sanctified, and
Baptized with the Holy Ghost with the Scriptural evidences. He and
45 his dear young brother are now longing for an opening for missionary
work, if the Lord makes the way clear.

A POLICEMAN

In a village in this part of Scotland the little Chapel got on
Fire, and about 20 received their "Pentecost" with Signs following,
50 and 13 have been soundly converted. They were holding a "Fellowship
Meeting" for those who had been fully anointed. Outsiders, hearing
the vehement cries of praise and the speaking in Tongues, gathered
round. A sympathetic policeman kept the door (his wife and daughter,
who had received the blessing, were inside).
55   At last he cried, "Lads, I can stand it no longer, here goes,"
and he flung open the door, and, putting down his helmet, was soon
pleading God for the Full Baptism of the Holy Ghost, and he received
it then and there and came through speaking in Tongues...

RESTITUTION

60   A Tobacconist, in a town not very far away from Kilsyth, said
to a Christian Worker, "I've been much touched to-day. A young man
from your Mission came in and said that he had owned me 2 1/2 d. for
years, for he got more tobacco than he had paid for. He said, 'Mr. --
I've come to apologize I mean to be true to God. I'm a changed man
65 now and I want to go on with Christ, and I could not rest till I had
asked your forgiveness and given you back the twopence-halfpenny,'"
He was so overcome that he had to look round his shop and handed him
a bottle of Brilliantine as his way of recognising real honesty of
purpose.

70   A boy on a Sunday School Trip noticed his teacher drop a
shilling. He slyly took it, but he could not get his "Pentecost"
until he had been to that teacher and given him the shilling and the
explanation.

        A man took a pair of tongs home from the Colliery years ago. He
75 had to take them back and confess to the manager before he could get
his "Pentecost."

        A Draper was retired from business. A woman seeking her
"Pentecost" was reminded of a debt of 18/, twenty-five years old. She
sent 10/-, and promised to pay the 8/- as soon as possible, and the
80 Lord then gave her her heart's desire.

        A "Flesher" (Butcher) said, "Westport Hall is doing a good
work. I got 7/- to-day which has been standing 15 years."

        A woman got a pound of steak and paid for half-a-pound. She
went and put this right and then she got through.

85   A young woman rose from her knees at an after-meeting and went
out. She soon returned, looking happy, and received her "Blessing"
quickly. She had remembered someone to whom she had not spoken for
long, and had been to her and put things right again.

THE MEETINGS

90   ... The meetings might appear quite disorderly to some minds,
and to others who are in sympathy full of the Power of God. Bro. A
Murdoch says, "We are not yet in I Cor. 14, only in Acts 2." He means
that too much must not be expected in the early days of this
wonderful work, that later it will be time enough at Kilsyth to
95 insist on perfect order...
        But many have come through in Bro. Murdoch's house (26, Eden
Grove). His bright kitchen is a holy place for many (see Brother
Martin's Testimony). Bro. Rennick, Evangelist of the Christian
Alliance, came through here one morning..."

(I)

Hermann RUETSCHI was the subject of much controversy because of
the healing ministry to which he saw himself called. In 1911 he was
accused of quackery and illicit medical practice, and subsequently
5 arraigned in court. After a medical doctor had spoken in his defense
and witnesses appeared, testifying of the healing they had experienced following Mr. RUETSCHI's prayers he was acquitted. Details were
published in the Schweizer National Zeitung and republished in the
German pentecostal journal Pfingstgrüsse 4, 19 (February 4, 1912), p.
10 151. The following, somewhat aggressive, account is revealing in
terms of the public nature of the report.

"Weitere Heilungen"

Die Verheissung des Vaters 6, 36 Juni (1913), p. 8.

Vater M. reiste extra in ein Evangelisationswerk nach T.
15 (Bernerjura), um dort öffentlich Zeugnis abzulegen von der 4fachen
Heilung in seiner Familie von Bern aus.

Solche Heilungen gehen doch über die Gescheitheit der
Weltmenschen, denn Suggestion, Hypnose, Gedankenübertragung,
Elektrizität, Röntgenstrahlen usw., der ganze wissenschaftliche Kram
20 heilt nicht solche Uebel, weder in der Nähe noch auf Distanzen. Gegen
diese dämonischen Kräfte hilft nur eine Macht: der Name "Jesus", vor
dem sie fliehen müssen.

Da wollen wir lieber **seine** kleine Brüderlein sein, und durch
ihn Sieger werden, als so ohnmächtige hochmütige Weltweise, deren die
25 Dämonen spotten!

Nach Bern kam im Monat März Monsieur R. von S. damit ich mit
ihm bete für seine 26jährige Tochter E. seit langem irrsinnig in der
Irrenanstalt von P. bei N. Darauf hin wurde sie bald entlassen als
geheilt. Die Leute in S. sind erstaunt, dass E. alle Sonntage in die
30 Kirche kommt, als normales, liebliches Kind; der Vater geheilt von

seinen schweren Kopf- und Kreuzschmerzen, der Bruder von seien epileptischen Anfällen, und die Schwester (20 jährig) von dem Wasser, das ihr von einer schlecht behandelten Brustfellentzündung zwischen Brustfell und Lunge geblieben war und Schmerzen und Atemnot
35 verursachte. Also vier Heilungen in der gleichen Familie.

Herr RUETSCHI wohnt vom 7.-15. jeden Monats in Zürich 3, Birmensdorferstrasse 206. Vom 18.-20. jeden Monats in Bern, bei Herrn BAEHNI, Cäcilienstrasse 15. Den Rest des Monats verbringt er in Ronco bei Locarno (Tessin). Er besucht im ganzen Schweizerlande herum die
40 Kranken, die nicht selber reisen können.

(K)

"Abenmahl"

<u>Königs Quartett</u>, Evangeliums Klänge, Bremen, n.d. (early sixties?)

The text of this spiritual song (originally by Ira STANPHILL)
5 is an example of a trivial setting for a disclosure in testimony
style. Evocative, archetypical, and/or intentionally trivial
expressions are emphasized in boldface.[1]

"**Vor vielen Jahren**, einst in meiner **Kindheit**,
Ich spielte bis der **Abendschatten** fiel;
10   Am **altbekannten Weg** ging ich nach Hause,
Und **hörte meine Mutter**, als sie rief:
        Komm Heim, komm Heim zum Abendmahl
        Es sieht gar **dunkel** aus,
        Komm Heim, komm Heim zum Abendmahl
15   Bald gehen wir **nach Haus**.
Doch eines Tag's stand ich an ihrem Bette,
Und **Engel sangen wunderbar und süss**;
Sie hört den Ruf für's Abendmahl im Himmel,
Und jetzt weiss ich, ist sie im **Paradies**.
20   **Komm Heim**, komm Heim zum Abendmahl
        Es sieht gar **dunkel** aus,
        Komm Heim, komm Heim zum Abendmahl
        Bald gehen wir **nach Haus**.
(Spoken intermezzo) Einige der liebsten **Erinnerungen meiner Kindheit**
25 spieten sich wärend der Abendstunden ab. **Wenn die Abendschatten
grösser wurden** und die **Sonne** langsam am **fernen Horizont** unterging

---

[1] It is possible that this record was produced to help finance the
construction of a Bible school building. The German Pentecostal
Alliance (Bund Freier Pfingstgemeinden, formerly: Arbeits-
gemeinschaft der Christengemeinden in Deutschland) has ties with the
German communities in Canada. Is it possible that the record was
promoted there on fund raising campaigns, evoking nostalgic memories
of the emigrants' youth?

wusste ich, dass es nicht mehr lange dauern würde bis meine Mutter
von der Hintertreppe unseres alten Hauses rufen wird: "Kinder kommt
Heim zum Abendmahl."

30 Nun es brauchte nicht viel Ueberredung um unsere Spielsachen beseite
zu legen[2] und eilend nach Hause zu gehen.

Jene Tage sind nun vorüber, doch die Erinnerung an sie erweckten eine
Wahrheit in mir, **die noch ergreifender ist**[3] **als die Erinnerung** jener
Kindertage. Denn ich bin gewiss es wird nicht mehr lange dauern, bis

35 der Abendmahlsruf von den Toren der Herrlichkeit ertönen wird, und
dann werden wir wie einst als Kinder, die Dinge unsere Lebens
beiseite legen, und dem Rufe folgeleisten zum grössten aller
Abendmahle mit allen Gotteskindern und mit Jesus.

> **Komm Heim,** komm Heim zum Abendmahl
40 > Es sieht gar **dunkel** aus,
> Komm Heim, komm Heim zum Abendmahl
> Bald gehen wir **nach Haus.**

---

[2] It is immaterial whether in reality a child is willing to lay down
his toys immediately. Important is that the poetic picture reflects a
harmony, which can later be transposed to a union in God.

[3] It is apparently the intention of the author and the interpreters
of this song to evoke feelings.

APPENDIX III

VISIONS

(A)

A Map of Bellicose Events

5   A vision of a pastor, ministering to the oppressed German-
speaking minority in Poland in the fall of 1938. Gerhard KRUEGER,
Erlebte Gottesgnade, Erzhausen, p. 86. An available translation has
been used.

      I rarely read newspapers. First, they were expensive, and
10 second, I had little time for that. In those days, Fall 1938, as the
"Sudetenland" was being occupied by Germany I had the following
vision (Gesicht). I saw Poland and Russia as on a map. A house was
being built in the West, which bordered on the river Bug in East-
Poland. In the sky was written in large letters "Five years." A deep
15 trench - like a tank trench - stretched from the Gulf of Finland to
the Sea of Azov. Behind it stood Russian soldiers. As the house was
completed, a large rock flew from the Minsk area onto the house. It
collapsed and I heard the sentence, "Five years." I knew what it had
to signify.[1] Germany would invade Poland and establish a "Small-
20 Poland" up to the river. However, the front line would pass from the
Gulf of Finland in the North to the Sea of Azov (Rostov) in the
South. The whole war in the East would last for five years. And so it
did indeed happen. In the fall 1939 Hitler marched into Poland,
erected the so-called "Polish General-Government," and the Russian

_____
[1] Frequently in visions the repetition of the message is a necessary
element for confirmation that the prophet has heard or seen well.

25 army stood before the Vistula in the fall 1944... We were on our
guard, having been called to attention by the Word[2] and the Spirit[3]
as to future events... We waited confidently for the things which
were to come.

---

[2] Meant are sermons and Bible reading.

[3] That is, the auxiliary charismatic communications.

(B)

The Division of the Waters

A prophetic presentation by pastor SCHOBER, at the General
Assembly of the brethren of the Mülheim Association in Berlin October
5 17, 1933. Christian H. KRUST, 50 Jahre Deutsche Pfingstbewegung. Mülheimer Richtung, Altdorf, 1958(?), pp. 177-179. The rather repetitive
and sometimes awkward style is typical of these oral narratives. It
also shows that the stenographer of the vision intended to remain as
faithful to the original delivery as possible. This vision was
10 printed for "public consumption" in the official organ of the Mülheim
Association, Heilszeunisse, February 1934, Nr. 3, (available
translation used).

I saw in the Spirit a great water. Something like a boat sailed
through this water from the side, a strange, unexplainable, boat-like
15 structure.

In the front at the bow there was a razor sharp cleaver. And
there was something else: a ram- or assault-prow. The task of this
boat was to separate the water; to cut and divide it. The purpose of
the ram was to destroy all possible obstacles and also to divide
20 them, so that everything was cut apart and divided. There was no
possibility for anything to avoid this operation. Everything that
hadn't previously yielded to the separation, was being destroyed, cut
apart and divided by the assault-block of the boat.

I saw how the waters were divided to the left and to the right.
25   The strange thing was, that the water to the left signified a
totally different world, as opposed to the water to the right. I saw
that the difference between the separated waters to the left and to
the right did not consist in the difference of the water in itself,
but in a different movement which could be recognized in this water.

30   It was as if the water to the left of the boat was being moved
by a totally different power and a totally different law than the
water to the right of the boat.

The water to the left of the boat was moved in a movement
similar to that of a large river. It began to move as whole in a
35 definite direction.

To the right I also noticed a movement in the water. At first
it seemed to me like a large ocean, but after close inspection it was
only a large self-contained pool. The movement of the water to the
right was not unified. It had no specific direction. These movements
40 originated from underground whirlpools in the middle of the water.
The unity consisted in the fact that all movement was due to the
underground whirlpools.

I realized, understood, had the presentiment and felt that
these waters would gradually begin to stink and to rot and eventually
45 become the source for innumerable germs and odors of death. In the
end they would be nothing but a swamp.

I noticed, though, also to the right of the boat a certain tendency to withdraw from the law that came from below.[1] But it was in
vain. The boat had brought about the separation with its sharp bow,
50 and the fate of the water to the right was sealed with that. It was a
water of death.

I saw above the boat-like structure a hand from above, the hand
of God.[2] And the question occured to me: Is this boat the thought of

---

[1] The theme of pan-determinism in visions is subjective. It not only
reflects God's sovereign presence, but also existential impressions
in view of the same; thus lending depth, tragedy (in the case of
discordant visions) and credibility to visions. A pure communication
of God's will could not be grasped by the human mind; it would be
unrelated meaning.

[2] The question who could be the author of judgment is here separated
from the question who is the means of judgment, as the next comment
indicates. The theodicy problem is approached in the classic way. But
the question why there is a separation taking place is up to the
recipient to answer. What seems to be a simple vision dividing
between good and evil (for the benefit of the saved remnant) turns to
be a moral challenge in view of the fact that at the end of the
vision a) the instrument of separation vanishes (thus leaving mankind
with the task to continue the "story") and b) the separated waters
remain on the same horizon (that is, within lived experience). As

God? Then it came clearly to me: "No! God uses this tool only for a
55 certain task. And this task is: separation! separation! separation!"
      And then it came to me that someone called to us: "It all
depends upon the right understanding of the thought of God in what is
happening in the water. It all depends to which side you are brought
by the bow of the boat; whether to the left or to the right!"
60   It depends under which law of movement we fall.[3]

      Again and again I see this very sharp bow working. One milli-
meter to the left or to the right brought the decision for the one or
the other side.

      Eventually, I saw the boat, after it had done its service, as
65 in a mist, as if it got into the fog, and then it dissolved in the
mist and was no more. It had fulfilled its task. To the left there
was the large river, to the right there was the sea-like pool, the
water which was moved from below.

---

with fairy tales and testimonies there is a "return."

[3] Pan-determinism in this sentence need not be understood as a
fatalistic expression. Rather, it is a reminder of responsibility.

(C)

Three Visions of Dorothy KERIN Related to her Healing
in Spring 1913

Taken from: Die Verheissung des Vaters, 6,36 (June 1913), pp.
5 4f.; which is probably a translation from the Christian Herald,
London (March 7?, 1913).

"Mit dieser wunderbaren Heilung standen drei Visionen im Zusam-
menhang. Die erste Vision hatte Dorothea am 14. Februar und erfuhr
durch dieselbe, dass sie nicht sterben sondern leben solle, trotz
10 alles (sic) Augenscheins.
Die zweite Vision am 18. Ferbruar vollzog gleichzeitig die Heilung, während die dritte am 10. März ihr den Zweck derselben offen-
barte. Dorothea hat selber folgendes darüber niedergeschrieben.

"Ich hörte das Geräusch einer herbeiströmenden Menge (am 14.
15 Februar), dann wurde es hell, es war ein unbeschreiblich schönes
Licht. Ich sah endlose Scharen in weisser Kleidung, einige hatten
Lilien in den Händen und viele hatten Flügel und Heiligenschein um
den Kopf. Sie flogen nicht und gingen nicht, aber sie strömten von
allen Richtungen einher. Einer unter ihnen trat aus der Menge zu mir,
20 er war so leuchtend und herrlich; ich dachte er sei Jesus und
streckte meine Hände ihm entgegen. Dann sagte er: "Nein Dorothea,[1] du
sollst noch nicht kommen." Hierauf verschwand die Vision.
Am 18. Februar hörte ich in meinem Schlaf jemanden ganz deut-
lich dreimal meinen Namen rufen. Ich sagte: "Ja, ich höre, wer ist
25 da?" "Merke auf", war die Antwort. Zwei warme Hände ergriffen die
meinigen,[2] berührten damit meine Augen und legten sie nieder. Ein

---

[1] Typical is the dialogue between what the visioneer thinks and the
subject of the vision answers. (Cf. also visions (B) and (D))

[2] This vision has a strong physical character, possibly because
Dorothy KERIN's illness had diminished her sensations.

herrliches Licht beleuchtete das Bett und den Schirm und ich sah
einen wundervollen Engel, der meine Hände in seinen Händen hielt und
sagte, "Dorothea deine Leiden haben ein Ende gefunden, stehe auf und
30 wandle." - Ich öffnete die Augen, sah meine Verwandten um mich und
sagte: "Gebt mir meine Kleider, ich soll aufstehen." Meine Mutter
wollte mich hindern, aber die Stimme sagte wieder: "Stehe auf und
wandle!"[3]

Meine Mutter sagte: "Du musst nicht aufstehen"; ich sagte zu
35 ihr: "Hörst du denn nichts?", aber sie konnte nichts hören. Endlich
gab man mir meine Kleider, das Licht strömte rund um mich, ich
stützte meine Hand darauf und so verliess ich das Bett und das
Zimmer, indem ich dem Licht folgte, welches mich führte. Ich suchte
meinen Stiefvater, bis ich ihn fand, ging dann in das Zimmer zurück
40 und setzte mich auf einen Stuhl. Meine Verwandten zitterten vor
Schreck und mein Stiefvater kniete auf der Erde und weinte. Ich
sagte: "Warum seid ihr so erschreckt, ich bin völlig gesund und
stark." Am 10. März rief mich eine Stimme plötzlich beim Namen. Ich
erwachte, setzte mich in meinem Bett auf und sah wieder das herrliche
45 Licht, welches sich mir näherte, bis es mich völlig umgab. Mitten
darin sah ich ein wunderschönes Frauengesicht mit einem
Heiligenschein. Die Schultern und Arme reckten sich ebenfalls aus dem
Licht hervor, sie erhob die Hände und ich sah in ihrer rechten Hand
eine grosse, weisse Lilie. Dann sagte sie: "Dorothea, du bist völlig
50 gesund, der Herr hat dich ins Leben zurück geschickt, um dich in
einem grossen privilegierten Werk zu gebrauchen, du wirst viele
Kranke in deinem Glauben und Gebet heilen." Der Engel sagte nicht
durch sondern in deinem Gebet und Glauben.[4] "Tröste die Traurigen,
gib Glauben den Glaubenslosen; du wirst viele Abweisungen erleben,
55 aber gedenke, dass du nun dreimal gesegnet worden bist. Seine Gnade
genügt dir, und er wird dich niemals verlassen."[5] Hierauf machte der

---

[3] Again there is repetition for the confirmation to the prophet.
Notice also the threefold calling above.

[4] An interpretative comment clearly originating from a situation of
trial.

[5] These therapeutic visions of Dorothy KERIN culminate in a comission
and promise.

Engel mit seiner Lilie das Kreuzeszeichen auf mir, **die Lilie kam
gerade auf mein Gesicht, so dass ich den herrlichen Duft riechen
konnte.** Dann legt er meinen Kopf auf das Kissen zurück und sagte:
60 "Schlafe jetzt, Kind." Ich schlief sofort ein und sah den Engel nicht
fortgehen, aber als ich am Morgen erwachte, war das Zimmer noch von
dem Duft der Lilie erfüllt."

(D)

Vision aux yeux ouverts du 1 Mai 1984 de Louise GRANDJEAN[1]

So the title, given by the 90 year old recipient of the vision.
The transcription is from a casette recording taken on occasion of an
5 annual business meeting of a christian hotel,[2] where this vision was
shared for the sake of edification. Slight syntactical corrections
have been made for the sake of fluency since the teller of the vision
thought in French but spoke in German. Instructive is the consistent
dialogue of the recipient with her pre-reflective impression and her
10 reflective knowledge.

Introduction

Es ist das erste mal, dass Gott so gesprochen hat. Er hat mir
eine Vision gegeben, mit offenen Augen. Und Gott - ist uns näher
gekommen,[3] weil er möchte - euch - uns, die Gemeinde, das Volk
15 Gottes, er möchte ihm näher kommen. Weil die Endzeit kommt. Gott hat
uns alles gegeben bis heute. Er hat uns sein heiliges Wort gegeben,
das uns alles sagt was wir wissen müssen. Er hat uns das grosse
wunderbare Heil gegeben in seinem Sohne. **Vergesset nie, nie das
grosse Heil meines Sohnes.**[4] Und jetzt möchte er uns näher kommen und

---

[1] The French title points to the francophone background of this
Christian from Switzerland, but the vision was told in German and
translated into Italian. This explains the concise style, and the
sometimes akward grammar, of this account.

[2] One notices the convergence between secular affairs (business
meeting) and religious encouragement.

[3] The incarnation of the divine, in a certain sense continued in
visionary pracice, is paralleled with the incarnation of the sacred
in the secular as the context in which this vision was communicated
shows.

[4] The salvific Christ-Event and its related blessings is the main
thrust of this vision, see context and line 137f. below.

20 mit uns sprechen wie er früher gesprochen hat mit seinem Volke.
Wahrscheinlich ist es wegen der - eben wegen der Endzeit, weil es
gefährlich wird.[5] Und er möchte ganz nahe bei uns sein und uns
leiten.

   Und jetzt zum ersten gibt er uns grossen, grossen Segen. Jetzt
25 muss ich halt anfangen und sagen wie diese Vision gekommen ist. Sie
war für mich selber eine grosse Ueberraschung.[6]

   ## The Vision

   Es war im Spätfrühling. Wir hatten viel Nebel. Jeden Morgen
hatten wir einen Vorhang Nebel vor unserem Hause, vor dem "Beltra-
30 monto." Und an einem Morgen war der Nebel wieder da, aber ich sah,
dass der Vorhang ganz hell wurde, und ich habe gedacht: "Die Sonne
kommt heute. Ich muss schnell hinaus, und vor dem Mittagessen noch
schnell in den Garten gehen, bevor wir an den Tisch gehen." Es war
viertel vor Zwölf. Aber Gott hatte ein anderes Programm für mich. Ich
35 ging zum Fenster und tat das Fenster auf, damit die Sonne in das
Zimmer kommen kann. Und was sehe ich in dem grossen hellen Vorhang?
Ich sehe einen grossen Strom der kommt, und ich bin verschrocken,
habe geschaut und habe gesehen, dass der Strom vorwärts kommt. Und
ich habe gedacht, dass ist doch etwas das nicht besteht in diesem
40 Vorhang und doch muss ich es sehen. Gott ist wunderbar gross, er kann
uns in unserem Gehirne, in unseren Augen etwas zeigen, was nicht
besteht.[7] Da habe ich einen noch grösseren Gott kennengelernt. Aber
ich hatte doch ein wenig Angst und habe gerufen: "Oh grosser Gott

---

[5] Explanations are not given as to why the purpose of God's presence
is related to the idea of the eschatological end times. It is
possible, therefore, that the reason given functions as a
legitimation for communicating the vision. A legitimation is,
however, not necessarily identical with the key to the interpretation
of the message (cf. footnote 4).

[6] The element of awe is conducive to the recognition of God as **auctor**
of the vision.

[7] The imaginary character of the vision is acknowledged, a sign that
visions in a secular age might well be understood, if they are do
create an **a priori** division of two hermeneutic worlds.

bewahre mich von der List Satans."[8] Und dann habe ich gezittert, aber
45 ich habe gedacht: "Nein! Du musst im Stande sein anzuhören, in voller
Ruhe." Und dann habe ich gefragt... nein,[9] der Strom ist gekommen und
ist in einem ganz grossen, breiten Wasserfall ins Land hinunter
gefallen. Und dann ist es mir in den Sinn gekommen, dass ich etwas
gelesen habe im Alten Testament von einem solchen grossen Strom. Aber
50 ich habe Gott gesagt: "Gott, erkläre mir bitte, damit ich verstehe
was Du mir sagen willst." Dann hat er mir gesagt: "Was weisst du von
diesem grossen Strom?"[10] Und ich habe gesagt: "Ja, ich weiss, ich
habe in der Bibel von diesem grossen Strom gelesen, der grossen Segen
gebracht hat. Willst Du uns so grossartig segnen? Willst Du uns
55 segnen? Willst Du mich segnen? Willst Du unsere Gemeinde segnen? Und
er hat geantwortet, - ich habe seine Stimme gehört: "Ich will euch
segnen. Ich will eure Familien segnen. Euch segnen. Dich segnen. Eure
Gemeinde segnen und alle die Christus annehmen." Und ich habe
gewartet und habe nachgedacht, was er gesagt hat, ganz früh schon, zu
60 seinem Volke: "Wenn ihr an mich **glaubet,** wenn ihr mich **liebet,** wenn
ihr mir **dienet** so will ich euch **segnen.** Ich will euch segnen und eure
Kindes Kinder segnen, und es wird meine Lust sein euch Gutes zu
tun."[11]
        Und auf einmal sehe ich das Bild noch einmal. Ganz genau gleich
65 zum zweiten mal. Der Strom der kommt, und der grosse Wasserfall, der
ins Land fällt. Ich habe gedacht: "Oh Du siehst in mein Herz, Du
siehsts, dass ich[12] - ich kann es nicht fassen - das ich das sehe.

---

[8] The awareness of the necessity for trial is expressed.

[9] A lapse in narrative memory.

[10] The divine answer is indirectly formulated in a new question. This
question and answer game exemplifies the didactic value of visions,
especially if they are appropriately shared with others.

[11] This conditional promise of blessing is a paraphrase of Penta-
teuchal blessings. But beyond that, could an unconditional blessing
be appreciated at all? Do visions without ethical surplus make sense?

[12] Admission of doubt! A sign in favour of the non-deceptive nature
of this vision.

Und dann war ich schon wieder voll von meinem Programm. Es war
fünf vor Zwölf. Ich musste hinuntergehen zum Tisch. Wir sind geboren
70 in der Welt und haben einfach das Programm unserer Welt in uns. Und
ich wollte gehen und hatte - bei der Türe, und ich konnte nicht
hinaus, und habe gewartet und habe gedacht: "Warum kann ich nicht
hinaus. Ich kann nicht hinaus! Gott hat gesprochen! Du läufst Ihm
wieder fort. Du bist nicht einmal sicher ob er fertig gesprochen hat.
75 Nein, ich kann nicht gehen." Und ich bin wieder zurück, und bin
wieder an das Fenster, und habe wieder an die Stelle geschaut wo ich
das Bild sah. Und Gott hat in mein Herz gesehen, dass ich es immer
noch nicht fassen konnte.

Und dann, auf einmal sehe ich zum dritten mal das gleiche Bild.
80 Dann habe ich aber geweint, dann habe ich - habe ich gespürt das Gott
in mein Herz sieht und das er mir noch einmal sagen muss bis ich es
begreife, dass es wahr ist. Und ich habe ihm gesagt: "Oh Gott,
grosser guter Gott. Du bist so gut, hast so grosse Geduld mit mir,
drei mal musstest du mir zeigen.[13] Und ich habe wirklich seine grosse
85 Güte und Gnade verspürt. Und da setzte ich mich, ans Fenster, und
habe immer noch nachgedacht: "Ja das kann wahr sein." Und es ist mir
in den Sinn gekommen, dass ich in der Bibel gelesen habe, dass Gott
zu Jeremia gesagt hat: "Jeremia was siehst du?" Und Jeremia hat
gesagt: "Ich sehe einen blütenden Zweig." "Du hast richtig gesehen
90 Jeremia."[14] Und dann habe ich gedacht vielleicht habe ich doch
richtig gesehen; **drei mal hat er mir's gezeigt, ich darf nicht mehr
zweifeln.**[15] Er will uns grossen Segen geben. Wunderbar, er will es
uns sagen, damit wir es wissen. Es kommt ein grosser Segen ins Land.
Und dann habe ich so auf den Boden geschaut. - Ich habe noch nach-
95 gedacht, immer noch nachgedacht.

Auf einmal sehe ich am Boden; auf dem Teppich sehe ich, dass
eine Quelle sprudelt. Wasser kommt heraus ganz schnell, aber sanft.
Wasser, Wasser, zehn Zentimeter, zwanzig, dreissig Zentimeter, und

---

[13] Again a case of trebled confirmation.

[14] Jeremiah 1:11-12.

[15] The extraordianry nature of the vision is accepted, but the
message is not yet known, because the "qualifier" is still lacking.

auf einmal sitze ich im Wasser,[16] und dann habe ich das Wasser so
100 angeschaut. Es war so schön klar, und ich habe gedacht dieses Wasser
ist nicht tot, es ist lebendig, lebendiges Wasser. Das kreiste immer
so um mich umher. Und ich habe geschaut und habe auf dem Boden den
Teppich gesehen, und habe gedacht: "Es scheint der Teppich sei nicht
nass." Und dann habe ich gedacht jetzt will ich schauen mit meiner
105 Hand und habe meine Hand in das Wasser getaucht und meine Hand blieb
trocken. Aber das Wasser war so klar. Ich sah das Wasser war einfach
so schön. Auf einmal ist es verschwunden. Und am Platze vom Wasser,
am Boden war alles voll Blumen. Ich war auf einmal in einem schönen
Garten und ich habe gedacht (es ist mir fast Angst geworden) - ich
110 habe gedacht es ist noch nicht fertig.[17] "Sage mir oh Gott, was
wollen diese Blumen sagen zu dieser Vision?" Er hat mir nie Antwort
gegeben. Er hat mir immer gesagt: "Was denkst dann du über diese
Blumen?"[18] Und ich habe gedacht, ja, das sind ja ganz kleine, alles
kleine Blumen, "Margeritli" und Wiesenblumen. Diese Blumen sprechen
115 mir doch von Demut, zeigst du mir Demut? Ja ich habe Demut nötig. Ich
bitte dich gibt mir, nimm mir allen Hochmut weg, gibt mir Demut.[19]
Und dann sah ich noch andere schöne Blumen. Diese Blumen erinnern
mich auch an den Schöpfer. Er war dabei und nichts wurde gemacht ohne
ihn. Alles was gemacht wurde, wurde durch ihn gemacht. Und das war
120 Jesus, das ist Jesus.[20] Und dann habe ich die grossen schönen Blumen

---

[16] The interpreter translating Mrs. GRANDJEAN into Italian is surprised by the turn of events and cannot avoid laughing, the congregation is also amused.

[17] The "qualifier" begins to announce itself. Awe and fear inspire the recipient because the "story" is not finished yet.

[18] The lack of an answer is not understood as empty silence.

[19] A diagnostic aspect is part of this vision.

[20] This interpretative comment reveals a typically pentecostal Christology. One could think of it as a mild form of modalism, the Trinity incarnated in Jesus through the presence of the Holy Spirit, spanning the past previous to memory, the present with its various aspects of awareness, and the expected future as a grand image of hope.
The tendency to a form of modalism can be detected in Pentecostalism in general (cf. Walter J. HOLLENWEGER, Pentecostals, pp. 311f.) and is not just a phenomenon in "Jesus Only" churches,

angeschaut. Grosse Ballen wie Pfingstrosen und sie wurden immer mehr
rot, rot, und ganz rot. Und dann habe ich gedacht: "Das ist ja blut-
rot." Und wirklich ich sah an den Blättern Bluttropfen. Und ich habe
gedacht: "Diese Bluttropfen erinnern mich an Gezemane. Dort hat Jesus
125 angefangen zu **leiden**. Und dann habe ich gedacht: "Diese Blumen, das
ist die stumme Natur, sie kann nicht sprechen, aber sie kann weinen."
Und diese Blumen hatten roten Tau. Und dann sah ich daneben eine
andere Pflanze, eine wunderbare Orchideensorte. Und das kam immer
näher, und ich sah ganz genau diese Blume. Sie hatte an dem Kelch,
130 hatte sie einen Sporn, einen Zacken, ganz unheimlich. Ich habe
gedacht diese Blume kann man nicht berühren sonst verletzt man sich.
Und habe ganz genau gesehen, die Sporren am Kelch. Auf einmal sehe
ich vor meinen Augen ein Mannsrücken der sich kehrt. Und ich bin
erschrocken; habe einen Schrei gemacht. Es war der Rücken Jesus. Der
135 Rücken war voll Blut und die Haut war zerrissen. Ich habe gesagt:
"Jesus, da sind auch meine Sünden dabei; und unsere Sünden. Und dann
habe ich eine starke Stimme gehört. Sie hat gesagt: **"Vergesset nie,
nie, nie!** Dreimal. Das aller Segen, den ihr bekommt - Jesus hat ihn
bezahlt mit Schmerzen, **Leiden**. Seid Jesus treu, seid ihm treu.[21] Und
140 dann auf einmal kommen alle die kleinen Blumen auf und werden alle
ganz weiss, weiss. Und der Himmel geht auf, und alles flieht in den
Himmel. Und ich habe gedacht: "Alles was demütig ist kommt in den
Himmel. Und dann habe ich noch eine Stimme gehört. Eine starke
Stimme; sie hat gesagt: "Aber, nach allen Schmerzen und **Leiden** hat
145 Gott Christus von den Toten auferstanden. Man hat ihn aufgenommen in
den Himmel. Man hat ihm den Ehrenplatz gegeben an seiner rechten
Seite. Und alle Macht im Himmel und auf Erden. Amen."[22] Und diesen

---

although most First World pentecostal denominations would consider
such a view as unorthodox. It has the advantage of relating the model
of Jesus Christ to all aspects of religiosity.

[21] The redemptive suffering of Jesus Christ is a pivotal point; it
can be understood empathetically through practical experience. Hence
also the emphasis on healing in pentecostal visions, testimonies and
preaching. As element of tragedy, suffering makes the representation
of life in narrative (**mimesis** and **mythos**) meaningful. But the surplus
value brings about a turn of events, and a reason for hope and
commitment.

Gott dürfen wir anbeten. Und dieser Gott ist so gut mit uns. Und er
will uns für die schwere Zeit vorbereiten. Er will uns näher kommen.
150 Er will uns segnen. Wir wollen dankbar sein, und ihm unsere Treue er-
neuern. Amen.[23]

Das muss ich euch sagen. Nachher habe ich die Stelle gesucht.
Die Stelle von dem Strom. Und habe sie gefunden in Hezekiel 47:
1-9.[24] Da steht, dass der Strom aus dem Tempelberg Gottes kommt. Und
155 im neunten Vers steht, dass alles was dieses Wasser berührt, das wird
gesund und wird leben. Und ich war im Wasser, das Wasser hat mich
berührt. Aber ich glaube Gott hat das nicht nur wegen mir gezeigt,
ich glaube daran, dass mein Bein geheilt wird.[25] Gott hat das nicht
nur wegen mir gezeigt, sondern wegen seinem ganzen Volke weil er mit
160 so grossem Segen kommt. Der Strom ist der Strom der Liebe Gottes. Und
er ist für alle, für euch alle, für uns, für alle die glauben an Gott
und an Jesus Christus und an den Heiligen Geist.[26]

---

[22] The "Amen" is a legitimation of the message by the divine
communicator, which is typical for biblical prophetic activity and
probably borrowed from it. Cf. David E. AUNE, Prophecy, pp. 332f.

[23] This "Amen" is not only a sign of closure, for at the same time it
is an overture, a response for the willingness to apply the promise
and its conditions as far as the recipient is concerned. It is also
an overture in terms of the communal process of interpretation that
may start.

[24] The whole vision of Louise GRANDJEAN can be understood as a
transformation of the Ezekiel vision of the holy waters in the light
of the Chirst-Event. Structural elements are to some extent
identical, e.g. the different stages of the water level, the dialogue
between the prophet and the divine voice.

[25] In spite of a personal significance of the visions to its first
receiver (she had hoped that an inconvenient ailment in one of her
legs would eventually be healed as a public sign of God's loving
care), she is aware that the vision has a larger significance which,
of course, promoted her to share it with others.

[26] The congregation sang a spiritual song, entitled "How great is our
God" as communal response to this vision and two prayers by members
of the community followed (the pastor had made a call for open
prayer, so that the congregation could respond to what had been
said).

(E)

Three Visions by a Participant of a Charismatic Conference

From A. BITTLINGER (ed.), The Church is Charismatic, Geneva, 1981,
pp. 19-20.

5   The following visions and their interpretations, besides being
noticable for their secular character,[1] reveal the relative value of
the same in view of the context in which they are told. They also
illustrate the need of didactic sensibility that the hermeneutic
process following the telling of visions makes necessary, even if it
10 is the simple suspension of an interpretation as in the case of the
third vision. A suspension may be more meaningful than an imposed
interpretation.

"First vision:

"I am cycling through B on a bicycle. Just near the School I
15 see a big house being built, higher than all the others. I dismount
and think to myself, "This is it!" The sun is shining on its steep
gables and the tower next to it. The workmen are hard at work. It
won't be long until the roof is put on. There is something wrong with
the gear transmission on my bicycle.[2] It's not a big job to replace
20 the broken screw."

---

[1] Not only is there an absence of God-talk, there are also no
stylistic devices of legitimation from "above" (cf. vision (D) lines
21f., 151).

[2] The theme of pan-determinism (there is no warning for the sudden
failure on the bicycle) besides being a real representation of life's
contingencies, allows for the introduction of a "qualifier."

One of the participants interpreted this vision:

"Perhaps the world-wide charismatic movement is the big,   ecumenical house that is being built and we can say,   "This is it!"
Beneath its roof Christians who in the past have avoided one another,
25 whether out of ignorance or fear, can perhaps learn to work together
in mutual respect and fellowship. At any rate, that's what the
reports from all over the world seem to suggest. The trouble is, that
in me and many other observers there is obviously something wrong
with the transmission. We are lagging behind with our "transmitting"
30 and "understanding".[3] There's a screw which needs replacing."

Second vision:

"I am in a high,   church-like barn, with a beautifully shaped
roof. High in the roof gable stands an earthenware pot holding a rose
bush in full bloom. The pot is standing on a long staff fixed to the
35 wall at the side by four wires. A psychologist says, "I like that.
The pot is safe."
I realize that the roses are artificial. The psychologist's
wife shakes the rose bush and says, "Some of the blossoms are real."
The real petals of crimson roses come falling down. You can
40 distinguish the real roses from the artificial ones: all the real
ones have several roses growing from one stem - the imitation ones
each have only one."

One participant interpreted this second vision:

"The discussions are much too 'elevated'. Some of what is said
45 is artificial and unnatural, but some people seem to like this
artificial 'elevation'.

---

[3]   As in the tales of the fantastic, the pan-deterministic element is
applied to the self, thus allowing for a pragmatic application, i.e.
diagnosis, of the vision's semantic content.

Yet there are some real blossoms there too. Some real things
also fall to the 'bottom' so that even simple people can understand.[4]
It is important to distinguish what is real what is artifi-
50 cial."[5]

Third vision:

"I am in a sheltered garden protected by high, old walls on two
sides. On the other two sides there is a view over a wide stretch of
beautiful coutry side. The garden is full of luxuriant fresh green
55 plants. I ask the old woman working there whether the plants are sown
or planted. She explains that some of the bushes are many years old,
some sown, some planted. A lot could also be transplanted. Now I see
MALLOW in bloom. The new mallow shoots are growing from an ancient
thick root, and young shoots are also growing all around the trunk.
60 The old woman says the root comes from SINAI."

There was no interpretation of this third vision."[6]

---

[4] This comment can be understood as a prophetic protest in favour of
a practice of communication understandable by all.

[5] What is artificial and what is real is left open, open to discussion. The pragmatic aim is a call for responsible discernment.

[6] May be there was no interpretation because the vision was too
"religious" for the audience, presupposing (?) knowledge of the Old
Testament (e.g. why a root from Sinai? why mallow?). Another reason
might be that not sufficient time was allowed for an interpretation
to emerge. In any case the image of the old woman is rich and
stimulating. I am tempted to imagine the following interpretation:
      The ecumenical charismatic movement is like a sheltered garden
in which healthy plants (i.e. people) can grow. The open view over
the country side means that the movement is in contact with the
reality of the world. The old women (the Spirit of God?) working in
this garden tells us that some members of the charismatic movement
are involved in this renewal for many years, while others are the
direct result of the movement's activities (evangelistic seed),
others have come to it through the invitation and lived example of
friends and relatives (planted), and others again are Christians who
formerly belonged to other communities (transplanted).
      The mallow in bloom (a medicinal herb) is the universal church
that brings salvation. New shoots (e.g. the charismatic movement)
are growing from the ancient trunk that has lived ever since God
began to speak with mankind.

Two Visions of Jesus

The Apostolic Faith 1,3 (November 1906), Los Angeles, p. 4.

The following two testimonies include visions of Jesus. The
context, however, is so telling that no attempt has been made to
5 shorten the accounts.

(F)

"Sister Lucy M. Leatherman writes from 231 Second Avenue, N.Y.,
of her work there witnessing to Pentecost. We have not space for a
full report, but her testimony will be of interest to all.
10   'While seeking for the Baptism with the Holy Ghost in Los
Angeles, after Sister Ferrell laid hands on me, I praised God and saw
my Saviour in the heavens. And as I praised, I came closer and closer
and I was so small. By and by I swept into the wound in His side, and
He was not only in me but I in Him, and there I found that rest that
15 passeth all understanding, and He said to me, you are in the bosom of
the Father.[1] He said I was clothed upon and in the secret place of
the Most High. But I said, Father, I want the gift of the Holy Ghost,
and the heavens opened and I was overshadowed, and such power came
upon me and went through me. He said, Praise Me,[2] and when I did,
20 angels came and ministered unto me. I was passive in His hands, and
by the eye of faith I saw angel hands working on my vocal cords, and
I realized they were loosing me.[3] I began to praise Him in an unknown
language.

---

[1] Here is a good illustration of "metamorphosis." The spirit/ matter
distinction is suspended. Similarly the trinitarian distinction fall
together into the all-embracing God.

[2] The request for a particular blessing is coupled with a command.
The request to praise brings about a self-transcending
intentionality, which is responded to in the rest of the story.

[3] The therapeutic function is the natural consequence.

In a few days, while on my way to church, I met a lady and two
25 little children. She was talking to her children in a language that
sounded like the words God had given me. I spoke a sentence to her,
and she said, 'What you say means God has given Himself to you.' She
is from Beyroute, Syria, and speaks Arabic. Eight years ago, in A.B.
Simpson's missionary school at Nyack, New York, I heard the Mace-
30 donian cry to go to Jerusalem, but it is to the Arabs.[4] I am told
there are more Arabs than Jews there, and God has been speaking to me
if I would be willing to go with Him to the wild Arab of the desert.
Anywhere with Jesus I will gladly go.

On land or sea, what matter where,
35   Where Jesus is 'tis heaven there.

Pray that God will send a revival to this city and pray for
Arabia."

---

[4] The "branding" of the experience is understood as a commission.

(G)

This vision does not include any pronouncement or dialogue and is interesting for its socio-religious conditioning.

"While Brother G.W. Evans was with us in Oakland, exhorting the
5 people to come to Christ, we observed he was speaking in verse with great earnestness, in which the great blessing of salvation and happiness and eternal life were held out to all who would come to Christ and obey Him. After speaking in this manner for probably five minutes he fell backward to the floor, and remained in an unconscious
10 state for probably ten minutes; and then arose.[1]

After the meeting a woman in the congregation went to him and requested a copy of the poetry he had spoken, and found he was oblivious to the fact that he had repeated a number of verses.

Later I talked to him about this experience, and he stated that
15 he had never committed any such verses to memory and knew nothing of having repeated them in the meeting.

He told me that while he was speaking the whole rear of the Hall became filled with faces of angelic beings from floor to ceiling and from wall to wall. A literal bank of beautiful faces, with Jesus
20 in the center, and all faces turned towards him.

He says he racognized (sic) Peter and James and John, also John Wesley.[2]

During his gaze at this Heavenly host he spoke unconsciously the invitations and exhortations[3] to all to come and receive the rich

[1] In the early days of the Pentecostal movement spells of unconsciousness and even trance were common. No attempts were made to tend to a person who was "resting in the Spirit." This explains the matter-of-factness of this account.

[2] Here is an indication how much depends on a vision's **Sitz im Leben.** In this vision a methodist influence is evident. In Dorothy KERIN's case (C) it is probably an anglican high church setting that has contributed to the background of the visions.

[3] The quasi-involuntary aspect (one is compelled to communicate) is typical of genuine prophetic speech. Just as true testimony is incompatible with a pre-meditated address, so is prophecy ideally the

25 blessings offered. He knew nothing of his fall, but returned to consciousness to find himself on the floor.

　　　The same thing occurred again, about ten days later in the meeting, with this difference he did not recognize any of the faces, except Jesus standing in the center.

30　　　At both times, he says, there were waves of spiritual power and glory coming from Jesus all over him.[4]

　　　I believe every one in the house felt the Divine power present, and the altar was instantly crowded with penitents."

---

communication of a pre-reflective impression (mimesis I) and not a piece of calculated rhetoric.

[4] The "branding" is a pragmatic result, especially in view of the audience's response.

Zwei Gesichte

Die Verheissung des Vaters 38, 3 (March 1945), pp. 8-10.

(H)

This is a typical example of a diagnostic vision of the "I know
5 you... but I have against you that" style. The emphasis is added.
Interesting is the interlacing of biblical quotations and imagery and
the word plays.

"Vor meinem geistigen Auge steht ein Bild: Eine grosse Schar
von Gläubigen, die vor ihrem Herrn versammelt sind. Ein jeder trägt
10 eine Harfe bei sich, und sie sind zusammen gekommen, um ihren Erlöser
zu preisen. Ein jeder ist beschäftigt, seine Harfe zu stimmen und in
Einklang zu bringen mit einem Ton, der noch nicht gegeben worden
ist.[1] **Jeder tut sein Möglichstes,** sein Instrument in Ordnung zu
bringen. **Beim näheren Hinzusehen aber sehe ich bei verschiedenen**
15 **Spielern so manches, das nicht stimmt.** Da sind solche, die auf ihrer
Harfe nur noch die Hälfte der Saiten haben. Das will sagen:[2] es sind
unter diesen Versammelten solche, die es mit ihrer Hingabe an den
Herrn noch nicht ganz ernst genommen haben, obwohl sie gekommen sind,
um anzubeten. Ihr Herz ist noch geteilt, mit den Worten der Schrift
20 gesagt: sie hinken auf beiden Seiten. Die Hälfte der Saiten ihres
Herzens ist noch bei der Welt, sie preisen die Dinge dieser Welt auf
der einen Seite, und doch wollen sie auch dabei sein, wenn es gilt,

---

[1] This paradox can be understood as a sign of pre-reflective thought,
but it is also the paradox of faith.

[2] In this case the interpretative comments are given by the
recipient; the vision would have gained public character if the
interpretation had been given by another participant of the group as
was the case in the visions recorded under (E).

des Herrn Lob zu singen (...)[3] Wieder andere Seelen sind unter dieser
Schar, deren Harfensaiten zum Teil von der Harfe losgelöst sind, aber
25 nur auf der oberen Seite, sie waren einst straff gespannt, aber nun
sind sie locker geworden und stehen in Gefahr, ganz losgelöst zu
werden. (Lieber Bruder und liebe Schwester oder treuer Freund[4] wie
steht es in dir drin? **Du warst einst eifrig für den Herrn,**
eingespannt in Seinen Dienst, du hattest ein Zeugnis oder eine
30 Botschaft von deinem Herrn an die Welt, deine ganze Liebe galt deinem
Erlöser, deines Herzens Saiten klangen harmonisch mit dem Willen des
Herrn. **Und nun wie steht es heute?...** Vor dieser Schar steht etwas
erhöht ein Altar, und auf dem Altar, ein Lamm, wie geschlachtet.
Hinter diesem Altar steht das Kreuz, und es erklingen die Worte:
35 'Siehe, das ist das Lamm Gottes, welches der Welt Sünde trägt.'
Hinter diesem Kreuz ersteht ein grosser Thron inmitten der
Herrlichkeit Gottes, und es ertönen die Worte aus der Offenbarung des
Johannes: 'Wer überwindet, dem will Ich geben, mit Mir auf dem Thron
zu sitzen, wie auch Ich überwunden habe.' Und auf einmal schwingen
40 die holdseligen Worte durch den Raum und erfüllen denselben, hörbar
für alle Versammelten vor dem Herrn: 'Jesus, Jesus, Jesus.'
Und nun lieber Bruder, ich möchte dich fragen, und auch an
dich, liebe Schwester, ergeht in der Gegenwart des Kreuzes die Frage:
Ist dein Leben im Einklang mit Gottes Willen, sind auch die
45 verborgensten Saiten deines Innenlebens gestimmt auf Jesum? Liebst du
das Kreuz, oder ist es dir gar ein Aergernis, wie es bei vielen der
Fall ist? Vor dem Thron seiner Herrlichkeit steht das Kreuz. Es gibt
keine Throngemeinschaft mit Jesus, wenn du nicht zuvor Kreuzesgemein-
schaft mit dem Herrn gehabt hast! Möge es doch von dir, wie von mir,[5]

---

[3] Another interpretative comment is added which apparently came from
an later interpretation of the vision and not from the vision itself,
otherwise it would not have been put in brackets.

[4] Visitors were also addressed! Although they needed to be acquainted
with apocalyptic imagery and the related notion of the redemptive
blood of Jesus, cf. below.

[5] The inclusion of the narrator is necessary in order not to give the
impression that he (?) is sanctified above all reproach.

50 dermaleinst heissen: 'Sie haben... überwunden durch des Lammes Blut
und durch das Wort ihres Zeugnisses und haben ihr Leben nicht geliebt
bis in den Tod!"[6]

---

[6] The final quotation illustrates the pentecostal understanding of
soteriology: the redemptive cross-event and the testimonial response.
Such a statement (rather esoteric to many ears) makes sense as long
as the believers recognize in it a prophetic and/or missionary
mandate in Jesus Christ (at the end of World War II), but it becomes
meaningless in terms of the gospel message when the aim is to justify
a middle class **status quo** (for instance in a situation of relative
affluence and social security). In other words, when Christianity is
considered in cultural and aesthetic terms alone, then the prophetic
element vanishes and the adepts lose moral acuity.

(I)

Die Verheissung des Vaters 38,3 (March 1945), pp. 9-10.

This is an example of a parabolic vision with a typical "disclosure logic".

5   "Vor meinem geistigen Auge steht ein Bild: Eine öder Gegend, die von den sengenden Strahlen der heiss niederbrennenden Sonne rotgebrannt ist. Einsam reitet ein Wanderer durch diese Gegend. Auf seinem Gesicht ist der Ausdruck innerer Not geschrieben. Er möchte im tiefsten Innersten befriedigt werden, doch ist ihm ein gewisser
10 Hochmut und eine eingebildete Grösse noch eigen. Einsam und verlassen reitet er auf seinem Tier dahin. Zu seiner Linken erblicke ich Brunnen, die zerfallen sind. Sie geben kein Wasser mehr. Es sind löchrichte (sic) Brunnen der Welt, die versiegt und nichts mehr zu geben imstande sind (Jer. 2:13). Zur Rechten dieses Wanderers ist
15 noch ein Brunnen. **Beim näheren Zusehen** fliesst tief unten das Wasser in raschem Fluss durch. Ich sehe, wie Steine, die im Schacht des Brunnens liegen, mit grünlichem Moos bedeckt sind, das noch feucht ist. (Diese bedeuten vergangene Segnungen des Herrn, die einmal erfreuten und erquickten, die aber nicht mehr imstande sind, die
20 Seele zu beleben. Wir müssen immer wieder neu den Herrn erleben und täglich neu vom lebendigen Wasser getränkt werden.) Der einsame Wanderer reitet seinem einsamen Weg weiter, bis er auf einmal eines wunderbaren Anblicks gewahr wird. Vor seinem Auge sieht er einen wunderbaren Brunnen. Eine kristallklare Quelle sprudelt aus dem
25 Erdreich hervor, und hinter dieser Quelle steht das Kreuz. Die sonnenverbrannte Wüste ist rings um die Quelle herum grün geworden, ein herzbelebender Anblick! Ueber das Ganze ist ein wunderbares Licht ausgegossen. Wie der Wanderer diese Quelle gewahr wird, lenkt er sein Tier darauf hin. Und wie er näher reitet und sich dieser Quelle
30 nähern will, weigert sich plötzlich das Tier, weiter zu gehen.[1] Wie

---

[1] The animal is the means of the pan-deterministic disclosure to the horseman, who presents those "selves" addressed through the vision.

vom Lichte gezwungen, fällt es auf die Knie, und dem Reiter bleibt
nichts anderes übrig, als herunterzu (sic) steigen. Er merkt, dass es
da um eines geht: sich zu demütigen. - Er reisst sich die Kleider vom
Leib und begibt sich in das Wasser dieser Quelle, und wie er sich
35 darin befindet, wird er auch sogleich mit dem Kleid der Gerechtigkeit
angezogen.[2]

Liebe Geschwister und Freunde: wollen wir den Herrn erleben,
gilt es, herabzusteigen von jeglicher Höhe, sich zu demütigen unter
die gewaltige Hand Gottes, uns ausziehen zu lassen, damit wir
40 bekleidet werden können. Gott widerstehet dem Hoffärtigen, dem
Demütigen gibt er Gnade.[3] Segnungen vergangener Tage genügen nicht,
du musst deinen Herrn heute, jetzt neu erleben!"[4]

---

[2] Wholeness follows divestment of the "self."

[3] James 4:6.

[4] This kind of argumentation is typical for reforming and charismatic
movements throughout history. What **can** be affirmed is that a static
representation of God and of the Church's task would not be in
accordance with the Scriptures and a christian theology developing
from them. What **cannot** be affirmed is a manmade postulation of an
experience of the Sacred. Visions and testimonies though, especially
within an open community of interpretation, can invite participants
to be receptive to spiritual disclosures.

(K)

Gesicht

Die Verheissung des Vaters 39,9 (September 1946), pp. 10f.

This is another example of a parabolic vision. Notice the
5 introductory comment.

"... Anschliessend an dieses Zeugnis muss ich noch ein Gesicht
abgeben,[1] das ich in jener Woche hatte. Ich hatte leider den Mut
nicht, es dort mitzuteilen.

In einem Gesicht sah ich eine Strasse, die bergauf ging. Am
10 Rande der Strasse waren Marksteine hingesetzt, und eine Kette verband
sie unten miteinander. Dann plötzlich war die Strasse ein Stück weit
eben, und da sah ich wie Menschen an diesen Ketten gebunden waren.
Sie stunden ganz hilflos da; über ihnen war der Himmel bewölkt, und
die Wolken neigten sich tief über die geketteten Menschen hinunter.
15 Plötzlich zerteilten sich die Wolken, und zwei grosse Hände kamen
hervor, die ein geöffnetes Buch hielten. Auf den Seiten dieses Buches
stand mit grossen goldenen Buchstaben geschrieben: 'Tut Busse!'[2] Dies
ging den gebundenen Menschen zu Herzen; sie spürten, wie eine Kraft
aus diesen Worten strömte. Sie beugten sich, und während sie ihre
20 Häupter gegen die Erde neigen wollten verspürten sie, wie ihre Hände
und Füsse befreit werden.[3] Sie knien nieder, tun Busse, wahre

---

[1] Does the word choice indicate an inner drive to communicate this
vision, to rid oneself of it?

[2] One is reminded of pietistic posters with caligraphed Bible verses,
in those days still frequently hanging in religious meeting halls and
private homes. Today, the golden letters have lost most of their
evocative appeal. In a secular version the call to repentance might
not come from "above," but in the face of a dejected woman, an
unwanted refugee, or a starving child, and a disclosure of
Christ-like grace.

[3] Here the grammatical tense changes.

aufrichtige Busse. In dem Augenblick gehen die Hände mit dem Buch
zurück, die Wolken schliessen sich zusammen und ergiessen sich in
Regen des Segens.[4] Die Kraft des Heiligen Geistes kommt über diese
25 bussfertigen Sünder, sie loben und preisen laut den Herrn. Dann
stehen sie auf als Befreite, mit strahlenden Angesichtern ihre
Strasse fröhlich weiter ziehend..."[5]

---

[4] The blessing follows responsive human action, but originates fron
another source. In other words, it is another way of illustrating
self-transcending pan-determinism.

[5] The account ends with an exhortation to do likewise and with the
promise of blessings.

(L)

Prophecy based on the Parable of the Ten Virgins

From: Walter J. HOLLENWEGER, Handbuch zur Pfingstbewegung, II.

Haupteil, 05.28.025, p. 2182. quoting: R. SCHWARZ, Kirchenblatt 25

5   (1910), p. 19

This prophetic "interpretation" of the parable of the ten virgins
seems at first sight estranged from the world and spiritualized. In
fact it is a condemnation of material wealth in view of the believers
own lower workingclass circumstances. This is understandable because
10 they could only express stylisticly that with which they were
acquainted (spiritual values), and condemned that of which they could
not be part (material possessions).[1]

"Die klugen Jungfrauen machen keine Schulden,
Die klugen Jungfrauen kaufen keine Vorräte[2]
15 Die klugen Jungfrauen haben keine Ersparnisse
Die klugen Jungfrauen haben keine Schränke,[3]

---

[1] Cf. Walter J. HOLLENWEGER, Handbuch, p. 2189.

[2] Matthew 25:4 indicates the very opposite! The prophet possibly had
a spiritual understanding of oil as the last comment seems to
confirm. The prophetic potential seems more important than the
hermeneutic one. It is a pity that nothing is known about the
reception of this message among those present in church.

[3] The chest was an essential component of a bride's dowry. Since many
early Pentecostals belonged to the poorest strata of society, they
could not have afforded a dowry, and would have identified with this
statement. Today, this interpretation could not be understood
anymore. Not only have the customs changed, which makes an
interpretation of such a prophecy necessary, but more significantly
Swiss Pentecostalism is no longer a movement of the "proud poor." It
has become an institutionalized "Free Church" with a middle to upper
middle class membership, which might still avoid getting into debts,
but certainly has well invested savings and material possessions such
as conference centers and television studios.

Die klugen Jungfrauen kümmern sich nicht um Nahrung

Die klugen Jungfrauen kümmern sich nicht um Speise, es wird ihnen
alles um sonst zufallen,[4]

20 Die klugen Jungfrauen sie lieben nur Jesum, sie lieben nur die
Schmach Jesu,[5]

Die klugen Jungfrauen sind nah bei Jesus,

Die klugen Jungfrauen sind immer fröhlich, sie haben ihren Mittler,
sie haben ihren Bräutigam,

25 Die klugen Jungfrauen sind in allem ihm gleich,

Die klugen Jungfrauen sind nicht unglücklich, wenn eine Nacht nicht
für ihren Leib Erquickung bringt.

Die klugen Jungfrauen haben Leiber, die von ihrem Bräutigam
inspiriert sind."[6]

---

[4] The prophetic condemnations result as a blending of the parable
with material from the Sermon on the Mount; cf. Matthew 6:19-21,
31ff. The spiritual application below is the logical result as it
also is at the end of Matthew 6.

[5] The poor believers do identify with the disgraced Jesus on the
cross. He sublimates their aggressions and impotence.

[6] This pneumatological statement indicates rudimentarily that the
indwelling of the Holy Spirit (which is understood as the Spirit of
Jesus) is appreciated in concrete terms, not just as a notion from a
catalogue of faith.

BIBLIOGRAPHY

A

ALLMEN, Jean Jacques, VON. Worship and the Holy Spirit, in Studia
Liturgica 2,2 (1963), pp. 124-135.

ANDERSON, Robert Mapes. Vision of the Disinherited. The Making of
American Pentecostalism, New York, Oxford
University Press, 1979.

The Apostolic Faith, 1,3 (1906), Los Angeles, p. 4.

AUGUSTINE, Saint.   Confessions, in A Selected Library of the Nicene
and Post-Nicene Fathers of the Christian Church
Vol. I, Grand Rapids, Wm. B. Eerdmans Publishing
Company, 1979.

AUNE, David E.   Prophecy in Early Christianity and the Ancient
Mediterranean World, Grand Rapids, Wm. B.
Eerdmans Publishing Company, 1983.

AUSTIN, J.L.   How to do Things with Words, Oxford, Oxford
University Press, 1962, 2nd ed.

B

BARR, James.   The Scope and Authority of the Bible, in Explorations in Theology, Vol. VII, London, SCM
Press, 1980.

BARTELMAN, Frank.   Another Wave Rolls In (formerly: What Really
Happened at "Azusa Street"), Monroeville,
Whitaker Books, 1970.

BEAUJOUR, Michel.   Autobiographie et autoportrait, in Poétique 32
(1977), pp. 442-458.

BELLAH, Robert et al. Habits of the Heart. Individualism and Commitment in American Life, Berkeley, University of
California Press, 1985.

BEN-CHORIN, Schalom.   Narrative Theologie des Judentums anhand der
Pessach-Haggada, Tübingen, J.C.B. Mohr, 1985.

BENVENISTE, Emile.   Problèmes de linguistique générale, Tome I,
Paris, Editions Gallimard, 1966.

BERGER, Peter L.   The Heretical Imperative. Contemporary Possibilities of Religious Affirmation, London,
Collins, 1980.

_____ .   The Social Reality of Religion, Harmondsworth,
                       Penguin Books, 1967.

BERRYMAN, Jerome W.   Becoming Fundamentally Scriptural Without Being
                       Fundamentalistic, Houston, Institute of Religion
                       Texas Medical Center, 1984.

BIEHL, Peter.   Erfahrung als hermeneutische, theologische und
                       religionspädagogische Kategorie. Ueberlegungen
                       zum Verhältnis von Alltagserfahrungen und reli-
                       giöser Sprache, in Günther HEIMBROCK (ed.),
                       Erfahrungen in religiösen Lernprozessen,
                       Göttingen, Vandenhoek & Ruprecht, 1983.

BIGSBY, C.W.E.   The Public Self. The Black Autobiography, in
                       Zeitschrift für Literaturwissenschaft und Lin-
                       guistik 9, 35 (1979), pp. 27-42.

BITTLINGER, Arnold.   Die charismatische Erneuerung der Kirchen.
                       Aufbruch urchristlicher Geisterfahrung, in
                       HEITMANN, Claus & MUEHLEN, Heribert (eds.)
                       Erfahrung und Theologie des Heiligen Geistes,
                       München, Kösel Verlag, 1974.

_____ . (ed.)   The Church is Charismatic, Genève, World Council
                       of Churches, 1981.

BLOCH-HOELL, Niels.   The Pentecostal Movement, Oslo, Universitets-
                       forlaget, 1964.

BLUMENBERG, Hans.   Säkularisierung und Selbstbehauptung, Frankfurt
                       am Main, Suhrkamp, 1966/1974.

BLUMHARDT, Johann Christoph. Seelsorge, Zürich, Gotthelf Verlag, 1949.

BOCOCK, Robert.   Ritual in Industrial Society. A Sociological
                       Analysis in Modern England, London, George Allen
                       & Unwin, 1974.

BOFF, Leonardo.   Kirche: Charisma und Macht. Studien zu einer
                       streitbaren Ekklesiologie, Düsseldorf, Patmos
                       Verlag, 1985.

BONHOEFFER, Dietrich. Ethics, London. SCM Press, 1955.

_____ .   Widerstand und Ergebung, München, Gütersloher
                       Verlagshaus, 1962. English edition: Letters and
                       Papers from Prison, London, SCM Press, 1953.

BRANDT-BESSIRE, Daniel. Aux sources de la spiritualité pentecôtiste,
                       Genève, Labor et Fides, 1986.

BROWN, Robert McAFEE. My Story and "The Story", in Theology Today 32
                       (1975), pp. 166-173.

BRAUN, Rolf Dieter.   Charisma und Liturgie. Die liturgische Praxis in
                      laikalen Gemeinden mit charismatischer Prägung
                      dargestellt am Beispiel der "Freien Christen-
                      gemeinde" in Altensteig, Tübingen, Hausarbeit
                      für die Abschlussprüfung, 1983.

BREMOND, Claude.   The Narrative Message, in Semeia 10 (1978), pp.
                      5-55.

BROCKELMAN, Paul.   Time and Self. Phenomenological Explorations,
                      Decatur, Scholars Press, 1985.

C

CAMPBELL, Ted A.   Charismata in the Christian Communities of the
                      Second Century, in Wesleyan Theological Journal
                      17,2 (1982), pp. 7-25.

CASTELLI, Enrico.   Le problème du témoignage, in Le témoignage,
                      Enrico CASTELLI (ed.), Paris, Aubier, 1972, pp.
                      13-21.

_____.   Les significations du témoignage, in Le
                      témoignage, Enrico CASTELLI (ed.), Paris,
                      Aubier, 1972, pp. 23-33.

CHAUVET, Louis-Marie. Du symbolique au symbole, Paris, Editions du
                      Cerf, 1979.

The Church of Cherubim and Seraphim (U.K.), Holy Hymn Book,
                      Birmingham, n.p., n.d.

Concilium General Secretariat / Nijmegen, Toward a Renewal of
                      Religious Language, in Concilium 42 (1969), pp.
                      174-180.

CONE, James H.   The Story Concept of Black Theology, in Theology
                      Today 32 (1975), pp. 144-150.

Confidence,   1,1 (1908), Sunderland, pp. 8-10; 2,3 (1909),
                      pp. 55-58; 5,3 (1912), pp. 65f., 70f.

CONGAR, Yves.   Der Heilige Geist, Freiburg, Herder Verlag,
                      1979, 1982.

_____.   Jalons pour une théologie du laïcat, Paris,
                      Editions du Cerf, 2nd edition, 1954.

COUSINS, Ewert H.   La métamorphose de la Sécularisation. Une
                      Perspective américaine, in Herméneutique de la
                      Sécularisation, Enrico CASTELLI (ed.), Paris,
                      Aubier, 1976, pp. 449-461.

CRICHTON, J.D.   A Theology of Worship, in Cheslyn JONES, Geoffrey WAINWRIGHT and Edward YARNOLD, The Study of Liturgy, London, SPCK, 1978, pp. 3-29.

CRITES, Stephen.   The Narrative Quality of Experience, in Journal of the American Academy of Religion 39 (1971), pp. 291-311.

CULLEY, Robert C. and OVERHOLT, Thomas W. (eds.) Anthropological Perspectives on Old Testament Prophecy, Semeia 21, (1982).

CULLMANN, Oscar.   Early Christian Worship, London, SCM Press, 1953.

D

DAHN, Karl.   oraō, in The New International Dictionary of New Testament Theology, Vol. III, Colin BROWN (ed.), Exeter, Paternoster Press, 1978 (English edition), pp. 511-518.

DA MARETO, Felice.   Visione, in Encyclopedia Cattolica Vol. XII, Vatican City, EECLC, 1954, p. 1485.

DAVIES, William R.   Rocking the Boat. The Challenge of the House Church, Basingstoke, Marshall Pickering,1986.

DAYTON, Donald W.   Theological Roots of Pentecostalism, Grand Rapids, Francis Asbury Press, 1987.

DERRIDA, Jacques.   White mythology, in Margins of Philosophy, Chicago, The University of Chicago Press, 1982, pp. 207-271.

DETWEILER, Robert.   Story, Sign, Self. Philadelphia, Fortress Press, 1978.

DINZELBACHER, Peter.   Vision und Visionsliteratur im Mittelalter, Stuttgart, A. Hiersemann, 1981.

DUBIED, Pierre Luigi.   Le rôle du récit de soi dans l'entretien pastoral. Une hypothèse-cadre pour sa prise en compte et son analyse, in Etudes théologiques et religieuses 60,1 (1985), pp. 45-53

DUQUOC, Christian.   An Active Role for the People of God in Defining the Church's Faith, in Concilium 180 (4, 1985), pp. 73-81.

DURKHEIM, Emile.   Les formes élémentaires de la vie religieuse. Le système totémique en Australie, Paris, Presses Universitaires de France, 1968, 5ème ed.

E

EAGLETON, Terry.   Literary Theory. An Introduction, Oxford, Basil
                    Blackwell, 1983.

ELBAZ, Robert.   Autobiography, Ideology, and Genre Theory, in
                    Orbis Litterarum 38 (1983), pp. 187-204.

ELIADE, Mircea.   Cosmogonic Myth and "Sacred History", in Sacred
                    Narrative. Readings in the Theory of Myth, Alan
                    Dundes (ed.), Berkeley, University of California
                    Press, 1984, pp. 137-151.

_____.   The Sacred and the Profane. The Nature of
                    Religion, New York, Harcourt Brace Jovanovich,
                    1959.

ELLUL, Jacques.   Essai sur l'Herméneutique de la Sécularisation
                    fictive, in Herméneutique de la Sécularisation,
                    Enrico CASTELLI (ed.), Paris, Aubier, 1976, pp.
                    153-170.

_____.   Témoignage et société technicienne, in Le
                    témoignage, Enrico CASTELLI (ed.), Paris,
                    Aubier, 1972, pp. 441-455.

ERMARTH, Michael.   The Transformation of Hermeneutics. 19th Century
                    Ancients and 20th Century Moderns, in The Monist
                    64 (April 1981), pp. 175-194.

EVERETT, William W. Liturgy and Ethics. A Response to Saliers and
                    Ramsey, in The Journal of Religious Ethics 7,2
                    (1979), pp. 203-214.

F

FENN, Richard K.   Liturgies and Trials. The Secularization of
                    Religious Language, Oxford, Basil Blackwell,
                    1982.

_____.   Secular Constraints on Religious Language, in
                    The Annual Review of the Social Sciences of
                    Religion 4 (1980), pp. 61-83.

FEYERABEND, Paul.   Agaist Method, London, Verso, 1975, 1978.

FOWLER, James W.   Life Maps. Conversations on the Journey of
                    Faith, Waco, Word Books, 1978, 1985.

FREI, Hans W.   The Eclipse of Biblical Narrative. A Study in
                    Eighteenth and Nineteenth Century Hermeneutics,
                    New Haven, Yale University Press, 1974.

FRIES, Heinrich.   Mythos, Mythologie, in Sacramentum Mundi, Bd.
                        III, Freiburg, Herder Verlag, 1969, pp. 661-670.

G

GADAMER, Hans-Georg.   Philosophical Hermeneutics. David E. LINGE
                        (ed.), Berkeley, University of California Press,
                        1976.

_____.   Témoignage et affirmation, in Le Témoignage,
                        Enrico CASTELLI (ed.), Paris, Aubier, 1972,
                        pp. 161-165.

_____.   Wahrheit und Methode. Grundzüge einer philoso-
                        phischen Hermeneutik, 4 ed. Tübingen, J.C.B.
                        Mohr, 1962, 1963, 1972.

GEE, Donald.   "Trophimus liess ich krank zurück...",
                        Schorndorf, Karl Fix Verlag, n.d.

GELDBACH, Erich. et al. Evangelisches Gemeindelexikon, Wuppertal, R.
                        Brockhaus Verlag, 1978.

GENNEP, Arnold VAN.   The Rites of Passage, London, Routledge & Keagan
                        Paul, (1909), 1960.

GILKEY, Langdon.   The Spirit and the Discovery of Truth through
                        Dialogue, in Concilium 10 (1974), pp. 58-68.

_____.   Addressing God in Faith, in Concilium 9 (1973),
                        pp. 652-76.

GILL, Jerry H.   Ian Ramsey. To Speak Responsibly of God,
                        London, George Allen & Unwin, 1976.

GILL, Sam D.   Beyond "The Primitive." The Religions of
                        Nonliterate People, Englewood Cliffs, Prentice
                        Hall, 1982.

GOGARTEN, Friedrich.   Verhängnis und Hoffnung der Neuzeit. Die Säkula-
                        risierung als theologisches Problem, München,
                        Siebenstern, 1958.

GOLDBERG, Michael.   Theology and Narrative. A Critical Introduction,
                        Nashville, Abingdon, 1982.

GOMEZ-MORIANA, Antonio. Autobiographie et discours rituel. La con-
                        fession autobiographique au tribunal de l'
                        Inquisition, in Poétique 56 (1983), pp. 444-460.

GOUTIER, Henri.   Témoignage et expérience religieuse, in Le
                        témoignage, Enrico CASTELLI (ed.), Paris,
                        Aubier, 1972, pp. 63-73.

GRABNER-HAIDER, Anton. Glaubenssprache. Ihre Struktur und Anwendbarkeit in Verkündigung und Theologie, Wien,
Herder Verlag, 1975.

_____.   Semiotik und Theologie. Religiöse Rede zwischen
analytischer und hermeneutischer Philosophie,
München, Kösel Verlag, 1973.

GRANDJEAN, Louise.   Vision aux yeux ouverts du 1 Mai 1984. Private
tape recording.

GREELEY, Andrew M.   Unsecular Man. The Persistence of Religion, New
York, Schocken Books, 1972.

GUSTAFSON, James M.   The Church as Moral Decision-Maker, Philadelphia, Pilgrim Press, 1970.

_____.   Treasure in Earthen Vessels. The Church as a
Human Community, New York, Harper & Row, 1961.

H

HABACHI, René.   Témoignage et faux-témoignage, in Le témoignage,
Enrico CASTELLI (ed.), Paris, Aubier, 1972, pp.
457-465.

HABERMAS, Jürgen.   Zur Logik der Sozialwissenschaften. 5 ed.
Frankfurt a.M., Suhrkamp Verlag, 1982.

HALL, Harrison.   The Rule of Metaphor, in The Philosophical
Review 89 (1980), pp. 117-121.

HASENHUETTL, Gotthold. Charisma. Ordnungsprinzip der Kirche, Freiburg,
Herder Verlag, 1969.

HAUERWAS, Stanley.   The Church in a Divided World. The Interpretative Power of the Chistian Story, in Journal of
Religious Ethics 8,1 (1980), pp. 55-82.

_____, ed.   Truthfulness and Tragedy. Further Investiga-
tions in Christian Ethics, Notre Dame,
University of Notre Dame Press, 1977.

HENDERSON, Edward H.   Austin Farrer and D.Z. Phillips on lived Faith,
Prayer and Divine Reality, in Modern Theology
1,3 (1985), pp. 223-243.

HOLLENBACH, David.   A Prophetic Church and the Catholic Sacramental
Imagination, pp. 234-263, in The Faith that Does
Justice. Examining the Christian Sources for
Social Change, John C. HAUGHEY (ed.), New York,
Paulist Press, 1977.

HOLLENWEGER, Walter J. After Twenty Years' Research on Pentecostalism,
                      in Theology 87 (Nov. 1984), pp. 403-412.

_____.   Erfahrungen der Leibhaftigkeit. Interkulturelle
                      Theologie, Bd. I, München, Chr. Kaiser Verlag,
                      1979.

_____.   Handbuch zur Pfingstbewegung, doctoral disser-
                      tation in theology, 10 volumes, Universität
                      Zürich, (1965/67).

_____.   Le livre oral. Portées sociale, politique et
                      théologique des religions orales, in G. POUJOL
                      and R. LABOURIE (ed.) Les cultures populaires.
                      Permanence et émergences des cultures minori-
                      taires locales, ethniques, sociales et reli-
                      gieuses (INEP, Sciences de l'homme), Toulouse,
                      Privat, 1979, pp. 123-134.

_____.   The Pentecostals, London, SCM Press, 1972.

_____.   Prophetische Verkündigung, in Das missionarische
                      Wort 31,2 (1978), pp. 54-57.

_____.   Umgang mit Mythen. Interkulturelle Theologie,
                      Bd. II, München, Chr. Kaiser Verlag, 1982.

HOLLERWEGER, Hans.   Die Liturgie als Antwort auf die Grundsitua-
                      tionen des Menschen, in Zeitschrift für katho-
                      lische Theologie 107, 1+2 (1985), pp. 64-75.

HONKO, Lauri.   The Problem of Defining Myth, in Sacred
                      Narrative. Readings in the Theory of Myth, Alan
                      Dundes (ed.), Berkeley, University of California
                      Press, 1984, pp. 41-52.

HUYSSEN, Chet & Lucile. Visions of Jesus, Plainfield, Logos
                      International, 1977.

J

JAMES, Edwin Oliver. Priesthood, in Encyclopedia Britannica. Macro-
                      paedia Vol. XIV, pp. 1007-1012.

JASPERS, Karl & BULTMANN, Rudolf. Die Frage der Entmythologisierung,
                      München, Piper & Co., 1954.

JONES, Gwen, (ed.)   Conference on the Holy Spirit Digest, Vol. II.
                      Springfield, Gospel Publishing House, 1983.

JONES, Hugh.   The Concept of Story and Theological Discourse,
                      in Scottish Journal of Theology 29 (1976), pp.
                      415-433.

JONES, Lawrence Neale. The Black Pentecostals, in The Charismatic
Movement, Michael P. HAMILTON (ed.), Grand
Rapids, Wm. B. Eerdmans Publishing Company,
1975, pp. 145-158.

JOSSUA, Jean Pierre. Un christianesimo senza christianità, in
Christianesimo nella storia 5, 1 (1984), pp.
151-166.

JUENGEL, Eberhard. Entsprechungen, Gott - Wahrheit - Mensch. Beiträge zur Evangelischen Theologie Bd. LXXXVIII,
München, Chr. Kaiser Verlag, 1980.

_____. Gott als Geheimnis der Welt. Zur Begründung der
Theologie des Gekreuzigten im Streit zwischen
Theismus und Atheismus, Tübingen, J.C.B. Mohr,
1977.

JUNGMANN, Josef Andreas. Liturgie als Schule des Glaubens, in
Liturgisches Erbe und pastorale Gegenwart,
Innsbruck, 1960, pp. 437-450.

K

KASPAR, Walter. Wort und Symbol im sakramentalen Leben. Eine
anthropologische Begründung, in Bild - Wort -
Symbol in der Theologie, Wilhelm HEINEN (ed.),
Würzburg, Echter Verlag, 1963, pp. 157-175.

KELLER, Albert. Säkularisierung, in Sacramentum Mundi Bd. IV,
Karl RAHNER et al. (eds.), Freiburg, Herder,
1969, pp. 360-372.

KELLER, Carl A. Verlangen nach Offenbarung in der heutigen Zeit,
in Neue Zürcher Zeitung, (October 4/5 1986), p.
37.

KELSEY, Morton T. Myth, History and Faith. The Remythologizing of
Christianity, New York, Paulist Press, 1974.

KERMODE, Frank. The Sense of an Ending. Studies in the Theory of
Fiction, London, Oxford University Press, 1966.

Königsquartett, Bremen, Evangeliumsklänge, n.d.

KRAEMER, Hendrik. Theologie des Laientums. Die Laien in der
Kirche, Zürich, Zwingli Verlag, 1959.

KRIEG, Robert A. Narrative as a Linguistic Rule. Fydor Dostoyevski and Karl Barth, in International Journal
for Philosophy of Religion 9 (1977), pp.
190-205.

KRUEGER, Gerhard.   Erlebte Gottesgnade. Erzhausen, Leuchter
                         Verlag, 1970.

KRUST, Christian H.   50 Jahre Deutsche Pfingstbewegung. Mülheimer
                         Richtung. Altdorf, Missionsbuchhandlung und
                         Verlag Altdorf (1958 ?).

KUENG, Hans.   On Being a Christian, New York, Wallaby Pocket
                         Books, 1976.

KWAN, Carlo Wing Chung. The Dimension of Time in Mythology, 2
                         volumes, Ph.D. dissertation, University of
                         Leuven, 1985.

L

LADRIERE, Jean.   The Performativity of Liturgical Language, in
                         Concilium 9 (1973), pp. 50-62.

LAEYENDECKER, Léo and THUNG, Mady A. Liturgy in a Politically Engaged
                         Church, in Actes de la 14ème conférence inter-
                         nationale de sociologie des religions Strass-
                         bourg 1977, Lille, 1977.

LAURENTIN, René.   Catholic Pentecostalism, New York, Doubleday &
                         Company, 1978.

LAUSTER, Herman.   Vom Pflug zur Kanzel, Krehwinkel, Verlags-
                         gemeinschaft W. Greiner & W. Schmid, 1964.

LAWLOR, Leonard.   Event and Repeatability. Ricoeur and Derrida in
                         Debate, in Pre/text 4, 3-4 (Fall Winter 1983),
                         pp. 317-334.

LEJEUNE, Philippe.   Le pacte autobiographique, in Poétique 14
                         (1973), pp. 137-162.

LESCRAUWAET, Josephus.   Confessing the Faith in the Liturgy, in
                         Concilium 6 (1970), pp. 126-133.

LISCHER, Richard.   "Story" in Luthers Predigten, in Evangelische
                         Theologie, 43,6 (1983), pp. 526-547.

LOEN, Arnold E.   Secularization. Science without God? London, SCM
                         Press, 1967.

LOEFFLER, Paul.   Das Zeugnis der Laien in der säkularen Welt, in
                         Fantasie für die Welt. Gemeinden in neuer
                         Gestalt, Gerhard SCHNATH (ed.), Stuttgart, Kreuz
                         Verlag, 1967, pp. 120-124.

LOHFINK, Gerhard.   Erzählung als Theologie. Zur sprachlichen Grund-
                         struktur der Evangelien, in Stimmen der Zeit 192
                         (1974), pp. 521-532.

LUCKMANN, Benita.   The Small Life-Worlds of Modern Man, in Thomas
                       LUCKMANN (ed.), Phenomenology and Sociology,
                       Harmondsworth, Penguin Books, 1978, pp. 275-290.

LUCKMANN, Thomas.   The Invisible Religion. The Problem of Religion
                       in Modern Society, London, The Macmillan
                       Company, 1967.

LUKKEN, Gerhard.   The Unique Expression of Faith in the Liturgy,
                       in Concilium 9 (1973), pp. 11-21.

M

McCLENDON, James W. Jr. Biography as Theology. How Life Stories Can
                       Remake Today's Theology, Nashville, 1974.

McDONNELL, Kilian.   The Function of Tongues in Pentecostalism.
                       Roman Catholic / Pentecostal Dialogue. Papers of
                       the Rome meeting Oct. 1977, in One In Christ 19,
                       4 (1983), pp. 332-348 + 348-354.

McLUHAN, Marshall.   The Gutenberg Galaxy, Toronto, University of
                       Toronto Press, 1962.

MacQUARRIE, John.   God and Secularity. New Directions in Theology,
                       William HORDERN (ed.), Vol. III, Philadelphia,
                       The Westminster Press, 1967.

MARTIN, Ralph P.   Carmen Christi. Philippians 2:5-11 in Recent
                       Interpretation and in the Setting of Early
                       Christian Worship, Grand Rapids, Wm. B. Eerdmans
                       Publishing Company, 1983.

MASLOW, Abraham H.   Religions, Values, and Peak-Experiences, New
                       York, The Viking Press, 1964, Preface 1970.

MECKING, Burkhart.   Christliche Biographien. Beobachtungen zur
                       Trivialisierung in der Erbauungsliteratur.
                       Europäische Hochschulschriften 197, Frankfurt,
                       Peter Lang, 1983.

METZ, Johann B.   Glaube in Geschichte und Gesellschaft, Mainz,
                       Matthias Grünewald Verlag, 1977.

_____.   A Short Apology of Narrative, in Concilium 9
                       (1973), pp. 84-96.

MEYERHOFF, Barbara G. Secular Ritual. Forms and Meanings, in Secular
                       Ritual, Sally F. MOORE and Barbara G. MEYERHOFF
                       (eds.), Assen, Van Gorcum, 1977, pp. 3-24.

MEYER ZU SCHLOCHTERN, Joseph. Erzählung als Paradigma einer alter-
                       nativen theologischen Denkform, in Theologische
                       Berichte 8 (1979), pp. 35-70.

MICHAELIS, Wilhelm.   oraô, in Theological Dictionary of the New
                       Testament, Vol. V, Gerhard FRIEDRICH (ed.),
                       English translation: Geoffrey BROMILEY, Grand
                       Rapids, Wm. B. Eerdmans Publishing Company,
                       1964, pp. 315-382.

MIETH, Dietmar.   What is Experience? in Concilium 113 (1979), pp.
                       40-53.

MOLARI, Carlo.   The Hermeneutical Rôle of the Christian
                       Community on the Basis of Judaeo-Christian
                       Experience, in Concilium 113 (1979) pp. 93-105.

MOORE, Sally F.   Secular Ritual. Forms and Meanings, in Secular
                       Ritual, Sally F. MOORE and Barbara G. MEYERHOFF
                       (eds.), Assen, Van Gorcum, 1977, pp. 3-24.

MUELLER, Karl Ferdinand. Living Worship, in Studia Liturgica, 7, 2-3
                       (1970), pp. 86-95.

MUELLER-BOHN, Jost.   Entscheidende Jahrhundertwende 1895-1905,
                       Reutlingen, Evangelistische Film-, Buch- und
                       Traktatmission, 1972.

N

NEUSNER, Jacob.   Invitation to the Talmud, New York, Harper &
                       Row, 1973.

NICHOL, John Thomas.   The Pentecostals, Plainfield, Logos Inter-
                       national, 1966.

NIEBUHR, H. Richard.   The Meaning of Revelation, New York, Macmillan,
                       1941.

O

OATES, Wayne E.   Conversion. Sacred and Secular, in Conversion.
                       Perspectives on Personal and Social Trans-
                       formation, Walter E. CONN (ed.), New York, Alba
                       House, 1978, pp. 149-168.

ONG, Walter J.   Orality and Literacy. The Technologizing of the
                       Word, London, Methuen & Co., 1982.

_____.   The Presence of the Word. Some Prolegomena for
                       Cultural and Religious History, New Haven, Yale
                       University Press, 1967.

OVERHOLT, Thomas W.   Prophecy. The Problem of Cross-Cultural
                       Comparison, in Semeia 21 (1982), pp. 55-78.

Oxford Advanced Learner's Dictionary of Current English, A.S. HORNBY
     et al. London, Oxford University Press, 1974.

P

PANNIKAR, Raimundo.   Myth, Faith and Hermeneutics, New York, Paulist
                       Press, 1979.

_____.   La sécularisation de l'herméneutique. Le cas du
                       Christ: fils de l'homme et Fils de Dieu, in
                       Herméneutique de la Sécularisation, Enrico
                       CASTELLI (ed.), Paris, Aubier, 1976, pp.
                       213-248.

_____.   Secularization and Worship, in Worship and
                       Secularization, Wiebe VOIS (ed.), Studia
                       Liturgica 7 (1970), pp. 28-71.

_____.   Worship and Secular Man, London, Darton, Longman
                       & Todd, 1973.

PASCAL, Roy.   The Autobiographical Novel and the Autobio-
                       graphy, in Essays in Criticism 9 (1959), pp.
                       134-150.

PATER, Wim DE.   Sense and Nonsense in Talking about God, in
                       Saint Louis Quarterly 6 (1968), Baguio,
                       Philippines, pp. 7-48.

_____.   Theologische Sprachlogik, München, Kösel Verlag,
                       1971.

PERRIN, Norman.   Jesus and the Language of the Kingdom. Symbol
                       and Metaphor in New Testament Interpretation,
                       Philadelphia, Fortress Press, 1976.

PESCH, Rudolf.   Form Criticism, in Encyclopedia of Theology. A
                       Concise Saramentum Mundi. Karl RAHNER ed.,
                       London, Burns & Oates, 1975, pp. 525-528.

Pfingstgrüsse,   6,23 (1914), Mülheim, p. 179.

PIOLANTI, Antonio.   Visione Beatifica, in Encyclopedia Cattolica
                       Vol. XII, Vatican City, EECLC, 1954, pp.
                       1485-1593.

PLUESS, Jean-Daniel.   European Reactions to Totalitarianism. A Study
                       of Ethical Commitment in the 1930's, in EPTA
                       Bulletin 4,2 (1985), pp. 40-55; 4,3 (1985), pp.
                       88-100.

POL, W.H. VAN DE.   The End of Conventional Christianity, New York,
                     Newman Press, 1968. Originally: Het einde van
                     het conventionele christendom, Roermond, J.J.
                     Romen & Zonen, 1967.

PRINCE, Gerald.   Narratology. The Form and Function of Narrative,
                     Berlin, Mouton Publishers, 1982.

PROPP, Vladimir.   Morphology of the Folktale, Austin, University
                     of Texas Press, 1968, 2nd ed.

_____.   Les racines historiques du conte merveilleux.
                     Paris, Editions Gallimard, 1983.

_____.   Structure and History in the Study of the Fairy
                     Tale, in Semeia 10 (1978), pp. 57-83.

R

RAD, Gerhard VON.   Theologie des Alten Testaments. Bd. I, Die
                     Theologie der geschichtlichen Ueberlieferung
                     Israels, München, Chr. Kaiser Verlag, 1957.
                     English edition: Old Testament Theology. Vol. I,
                     The Theology of Israel's Historical Tradition,
                     London, SCM Press, 1975.

RAHNER, Karl.   Beatific Vision, in Encyclopedia of Theology. A
                     Concise Sacramentum Mundi, Karl RAHNER (ed.),
                     London, Burns & Oates, 1975, pp. 78-80.

_____.   Experience of the Spirit and Existential
                     Decision, in Concilium 10 (1974), pp. 38-46.

_____.   Schriften zur Theologie, Bd. III, IV, VI,
                     Einsiedeln, Benziger Verlag, 1956, 1960, 1965.
                     English edition: Theological Investigations,
                     Vol. III, IV, VI, London, Darton, Longman &
                     Todd, 1967.

_____.   Visionen und Prophezeiungen, 2nd ed., Freiburg,
                     Herder Verlag, 1958.

RAMSEY, Ian T.   Religious Language. An Empirical Placing of
                     Theological Phrases, London, SCM Press, 1957.

_____.   Freedom and Immortality, London, SCM Press,
                     1957.

REMY, Jean, SERVAIS, Emile and HIERNAUX, J. Pierre. Formes litur-
                     giques et symboliques sociales, in Social
                     Compass 22,2 (1975), pp.175-192.

RENDTORFF, Trutz.   Gesellschaft ohne Religion? München, Piper & Co.
                     Verlag, 1975.

_____.   Theorie des Christentums. Historisch-theolo-
               gische Studien zu seiner neuzeitlichen Ver-
               fassung, Gütersloh, Gütersloher Verlagshaus Gerd
               Mohn, 1972.

RICOEUR, Paul. Le conflit des interprétations. Essais d'hermé-
               neutique, Paris, Editions du Seuil, 1969.

_____.   The Hermeneutics of Testimony, in Essays on
               Biblical Interpretation, Lewis S. MUDGE (ed.),
               Philadelphia, Fortress Press, 1974-1980, pp.
               119-154.

_____.   L'herméneutique de la sécularisation. Foi,
               Idéologie, Utopie, in Herméneutique de la
               Sécularisation, Enrico CASTELLI (ed.), Paris,
               Aubier, 1976, pp. 49-68.

_____.   De moeielijke weg naar een narratieve theologie.
               Noodzak, bronnen, problemen, in Meedenken met
               Edward Schillebeeckx, (Festschrift), Herbert
               HAERING et al., Baarn, Uitgeverij H. Nelissen,
               1983, pp. 80-92.

_____.   The Narrative Function, in Hermeneutics and the
               Human Sciences, John B. THOMPSON (ed.), Cam-
               bridge, Cambridge University Press, 1981, pp.
               274- 296.

_____.   Poetische Fiktion und religiöse Rede, in
               Christlicher Glaube in Moderner Gesellschaft, F.
               BOECKLE et al., Bd. II, Freiburg, Herder Verlag,
               pp. 96-105.

_____.   The Rule of Metaphor. Multi-Disciplinary Studies
               of the Creation of Meaning in Language, London,
               Routledge & Kegan Paul, 1977.

_____.   Structure, Word, Event, in The Conflict of
               Interpretations. Essays in Hermeneutics, Don
               IHDE (ed.), Evanston, Northwestern University
               Press, 1974, pp. 79-96.

_____.   The Symbolism of Evil, Boston, Beacon Press,
               1967.

_____.   Temps et récit, Tome I, Paris, Editions Seuil,
               1983.

_____.   Temps et récit, Tome II, La configuration dans
               le récit de fiction, Paris, Editions Seuil,
               1984.

_____.   Temps et récit, Tome III, Le temps raconté,
               Paris, Editions Seuil, 1985.

_____.   Toward a Hermeneutic of the Idea of Revelation, in Essays on Biblical Interpretation, Lewis S. MUDGE (ed.), Philadelphia, Fortress Press, 1974-1980, pp. 73-154.

RIMBACH, James A.   Prophets in Conflict - Who Speaks for God? in Currents in Theology and Mission 9,3 (1982), pp. 174-177.

RITSCHL, Dietrich.   Zur Logik der Theologie. Kurze Darstellung der Zusammenhänge theologischer Grundgedanken. München, Chr. Kaiser Verlag, 1984.

ROGERSON, J.W.   Slippery Words. Myth, in Sacred Narrative. Readings in the Theory of Myth, Alan DUNDES (ed.), Berkeley, University of California Press, 1984, pp. 62-71.

ROTHERT, Hans-Joachim. Einleitung, in Friedrich SCHLEIERMACHER, Ueber die Religion. Reden an die Gebildeten unter ihren Verächtern, Hamburg, Felix Meiner Verlag, 1799, 1958, pp. VI-XII.

RUH, Ulrich.   Säkularisierung, in Christlicher Glaube in moderner Gesellschaft, Bd. XVIII, Franz BOEKLE et al., Freiburg, Herder Verlag, 1982, pp. 62-100.

S

SASSE, Hermann.   aiōn, in Theological Dictionary of the New Testament, Vol. I, Gerhard KITTEL (ed.), English translation: Geoffrey BROMILEY, Grand Rapids, Wm. B. Eerdmans Publishing Company, 1964, pp. 197-209.

SAUSSURE, Ferdinand DE. Grundfragen der Allgemeinen Sprachwissenschaft, Berlin, Walter De Gruyer & Co. 1931.

SAUTER, Gerhard.   Wie kann Theologie aus Erfahrung entstehen? in Theologie im Entstehen, Lukas VISCHER (ed.), Theologische Bücherei 59, München, Chr. Kaiser Verlag, 1976, pp. 99-118.

SCHILLEBEECKX, Edward. Jesus. An Experiment in Christology, London, Collins, 1979.

_____.   The Teaching Authority of All - A Reflection about the Structure of the New Testament, in Concilium 180 (4, 1985), pp. 12-22.

_____.   The Understanding of Faith. Interpretation and Criticism, London, Sheed and Ward, 1974.

SCHLENDER, Rudolf.   Lernen im Erfahrungsraum Gemeinde, in
                      Erfahrungen in religiösen Lernprozessen, Hans
                      Günter HEIMBROCK (ed.), Göttingen, Vandenhoeck &
                      Ruprecht, 1983, 191-200.

SCHMIDTCHEN, Gerhard. Gottesdienst in einer rationalen Welt.
                      Religionssoziologische Untersuchungen im Bereich
                      der VELKD, Stuttgart, Calwer Verlag, 1973.

SCHOLES, Robert & KELLOGG, Robert. The Nature of Narrative. New York,
                      Oxford University Press, 1966.

SCHOONENBERG, Piet.   Baptism with the Holy Spirit, in Concilium 10
                      (1974), pp. 20-37.

SCHREITER, Robert.   The Specification of Experience and the
                      Language of Revelation, in Concilium 113 (1979),
                      pp. 57-65.

SCHRIJVER, Georges DE. Initiatie in het heilige in een post-theïst-
                      ische religiositeit, Katholieke Universiteit
                      Leuven, 1984.

SCHWEIZER, Eduard.   Gemeinde und Gemeindeordnung im Neuen Testament,
                      Zürich, Zwingli Verlag, 1959.

_____.   pneuma, in Theological Dictionary of the New
                      Testament, Vol. VI, Gerhard FRIEDRICH (ed.), pp.
                      389-455.

SEARLE, John R.   Speech Acts. An Essay in the Philosophy of
                      Language, Cambridge, Mass., Cambridge
                      University Press, 1969.

SHOPSHIRE, James M.   A Socio-Historical Characterization of the Black
                      Pentecostal Movement in America, Ph.D.
                      dissertation, Northwestern University, 1975.

SINGER, Aaron.   Introduction to Talmudic Thought and Teaching,
                      126/71, Jerusalem, The Hebrew University of
                      Jerusalem.

SMITH, Ray E.   Visions and Dreams, in Conference on the Holy
                      Spirit Digest, Vol. II, Gwen JONES (ed.),
                      Springfield, Gospel Publishing House, 1983.

SOELLE, Dorothee.   Die Hinreise. Zur religiösen Erfahrung Texte und
                      Ueberlegungen, Stuttgart, Kreuz Verlag, 1975.

STAEHLIN, G.   mythos, in Theological Dictionary of the New
                      Testament, Vol. IV, G. KITTEL (ed.), pp.
                      762-795.

STAROBINSKI, Jean.   Der Autor und die Autorität. Notizen über Dauer
                      und Wandel einer Beziehung, in Neue Zürcher
                      Zeitung (October 13/14, 1984), pp. 67f.

_____.   Le style de l'autobiographie, in Poétique 3
                      (1970), pp. 257-265.

STEENDAM, Guido VAN. De nacht van duizend-en-één verhalen. Orientatie
                      bij de narratieve theologie, in Tijdschrift voor
                      Theologie 19 (1979), pp. 3-27.

STIRNIMANN, Heinrich. Language, Experience and Revelation, in Conci-
                      lium 113 (1979), pp. 117-130.

STROUP, George W. III. A Bibliographical Critique, in Theology Today
                      32 (1975), pp. 133-143.

SYNAN, Vinson.   The Holiness Pentecostal Movement, Grand Rapids,
                      Wm. B. Eerdmans Publishing Company, 1971.

T

THEISSEN, Gerd.   Soziale Schichtung in der korinthischen
                      Gemeinde. Beitrag zur Soziologie des helle-
                      nistischen Urchristentums, in Zeitschrift für
                      neutestamentliche Wissenschaft 65 (1974), pp.
                      232-272.

THURMAN, Joyce V.   New Wineskins. A Study of the House Church
                      Movement, in Studien zur interkulturellen
                      Geschichte des Christentums, No. 30, Frankfurt
                      a.M., Peter Lang, 1982.

TINSLEY, E.J. (ed.)   Rudolf Bultmann, Modern Theology, Vol. II,
                      London, Epworth Press, 1973.

TODOROV, Tzvetan.   Introduction à la littérature fantastique,
                      Paris, Edition Seuil, 1970.

TRACK, Joachim.   Sprachkritische Untersuchung zum christlichen
                      Reden von Gott, Göttingen, Vandenhoek &
                      Ruprecht, 1977.

TRAUTWEIN, Dieter.   Mut zum Fest, München, Chr. Kaiser Verlag, 1975.

TRAVIS, Stephen H.   Form Criticism, in New Testament Interpretation,
                      I. Howard MARSHALL (ed.), Grand Rapids, Wm. B.
                      Eerdmans Publishing Company, 1977, pp. 153-164.

TURNER, Victor W.   The Ritual Process. Structure and Anti-
                      Structure, London, Routledge & Kegan Paul, 1966.

_____. Variations on a Theme of Liminality, in Secular Ritual, Sally F. MOORE and Barbara G. MEYERHOFF (eds.), Assen, Van Gorcum, 1977, pp. 36-52.

V

VANSINA, Frans.   Ancient Symbols and Modern Myths. Philosophy of Religion, Vol. I, Leuven, Acco, 1974.

Vatican Council II.   The Conciliar and Post-Conciliar Documents, Austin FLANNERY (ed.), Dublin, Dominican Publications, 1975.

VERGOTE, Antoine.   Interprétation du language religieux. Paris, Seuil, 1974.

_____. La Sécularisation. De l'héliocentrisme à la culture d'ellipse, in Herméneutique de la sécularisation, Enrico CASTELLI (ed.), Paris, Aubier, 1976, pp. 345-364.

Die Verheissung des Vaters, 6,36 (1913), Zürich, pp. 4, 8; 9,11+12 (1916), pp. 6-8; 38,3 (1945), pp. 8-10; 39,9 (1946), pp. 10f.

Volksmissionar,   Stuttgart, 33,11 (1981), p. 11; 35,4 (1983), p. 14

VOLPE, Rainer.   La liturgie en tant que comportement social, in Social Compass 22,2 (1975), pp. 157-174.

VORGRIMLER, Herbert.   From Sensus Fidei to Consensus Fidelium, in Concilium 180 (4,1985), pp. 3-11.

W

WACKER, Bernd.   Narrative Theologie? München, Kösel Verlag, 1977.

WAELHENS, Alphonse DE. Ambiguïté de la notion de témoignage, in Le témoignage, Enrico CASTELLI (ed.), Paris, Aubier, 1972, pp. 467-476.

WAINRIGHT, Geoffrey.   Doxology. The Praise of God in Worship, Doctrine and Life, London, Epworth Press, 1980.

WALLISCH-PRINZ, Bärbel. Religionssoziologie. Eine Einführung, Stuttgart, W. Kohlhammer, 1977.

WEINRICH, Harald.   Der Autor des Lesers. Ueber eine Beziehung im Geiste, in Neue Zürcher Zeitung (October 13/14, 1984), pp. 65f.

_____.   Narrative Theology, in Concilium 9 (1975), pp.
                       46-56.

WILDER, Amos N.   Myth and Dream in Christian Scripture, in Joseph
                       CAMPBELL (ed.), Myths, Dreams, and Religion. New
                       York, E.P. Dutton, 1970, pp. 68-90.

_____.   Story and Story-World, in Interpretation 37
                       (1983), pp. 353-364.

WILLIAMS, Michael E.   Story as Oral Experience, in Explor 5 (1979),
                       pp. 2-11.

WITTIG, Susan.   A Theory of Multiple Meanings, in Semeia 9
                       (1977), pp. 75-103.

WORGUL, George S.   From Magic to Metaphor. A Validation of
                       Christian Sacraments, New York, Paulist Press,
                       1980.

WRIGHT, George E.   God who Acts. Biblical Theology as Recital,
                       London, SCM Press, 1952.

Y

YOCUM, Bruce.   Prophecy. Exercising the Prophetic Gifts of the
                       Spirit in the Church Today, Ann Arbor, Word of
                       Life, 1976.

Z

ZUCK, John E.   Tales of Wonder. Biblical Narrative, Myth, and
                       Fairy Tale, in The Journal of the American
                       Academy of Religion, 44,2 (1976), pp. 299-308.

STUDIEN ZUR INTERKULTURELLEN GESCHICHTE DES CHRISTENTUMS
ETUDES D'HISTOIRE INTERCULTURELLE DU CHRISTIANISME
STUDIES IN THE INTERCULTURAL HISTORY OF CHRISTIANITY

Begründet von/fondé par/founded by
Hans Jochen Margull †, Hamburg

Herausgegeben von/edité par/edited by

Richard Friedli   Walter J. Hollenweger   Theo Sundemeier
Université de Fribourg   University of Birmingham   Universität Heidelberg

Jan A.B. Jongeneel
Rijksuniversiteit Utrecht